King Alpha's Song
in a Strange Land

JASON WILSON

King Alpha's Song in a Strange Land

THE ROOTS AND ROUTES OF CANADIAN REGGAE

UBCPress · Vancouver · Toronto

© UBC Press 2020

All rights reserved. No part of this publication may be reproduced, stored in a retrieval system, or transmitted, in any form or by any means, without prior written permission of the publisher, or, in Canada, in the case of photocopying or other reprographic copying, a licence from Access Copyright, www.accesscopyright.ca.

29 28 27 26 25 24 23 22 21 20   5 4 3 2 1

Printed in Canada on FSC-certified ancient-forest-free paper (100% post-consumer recycled) that is processed chlorine- and acid-free.

Library and Archives Canada Cataloguing in Publication

Title: King Alpha's song in a strange land : the roots and routes of Canadian reggae / Jason Wilson

Names: Wilson, Jason

Description: Includes bibliographical references and index.

Identifiers: Canadiana (print) 20190240342 | Canadiana (ebook) 20190236426 | ISBN 9780774862271 (hardcover) | ISBN 9780774862301 (EPUB) | ISBN 9780774862295 (PDF) | ISBN 9780774862318 (mobi)

Subjects: LCSH: Reggae music – Ontario – Toronto. | LCSH: Reggae music – Canada. | LCSH: Jamaicans – Canada.

Classification: LCC ML3532 W749 2020 | DDC 782.4216460971354—dc23

Canadä

UBC Press gratefully acknowledges the financial support for our publishing program of the Government of Canada (through the Canada Book Fund), the Canada Council for the Arts, and the British Columbia Arts Council.

This book has been published with the help of a grant from the Canadian Federation for the Humanities and Social Sciences, through the Awards to Scholarly Publications Program, using funds provided by the Social Sciences and Humanities Research Council of Canada.

A reasonable attempt has been made to secure permission to reproduce all material used. If there are errors or omissions they are wholly unintentional and the publisher would be grateful to learn of them.

Printed and bound in Canada
Set in Caslon and Minion by Artegraphica Design Co. Ltd.
Copy editor: Lesley Erickson
Proofreader: Sarah Wight
Cover designer: Martyn Schmoll

UBC Press
The University of British Columbia
2029 West Mall
Vancouver, BC V6T 1Z2
www.ubcpress.ca

FOR MA FAITHER

Contents

List of Illustrations / ix

Preface and Acknowledgments / xi

Introduction: King Alpha's Song / 3

1 Hybridity and Jamaican Music / 18

2 Music of the Black Atlantic / 43

3 Jamaica to Toronto / 60

4 Place and Meaning in Toronto's Reggae Text / 96

5 The Bridge Builders / 140

6 Blackness and Whiteness / 189

7 In Search of the Canadian Sound / 208

8 A Strange Land / 238

Notes / 249

Bibliography / 312

Index / 335

Illustrations

Photographs follow page 172.

The Mighty Pope, Lucea, Jamaica, 1960s

JuLion King with his sister and mom before coming to Canada

Mike Smith and his family, reunited in Toronto

The Harvey boys' first winter in Canada, 1966

Jackie Mittoo, reggae's keyboard king, 1969

Leroy Sibbles, live in Toronto

Keyboardist Jackie Mittoo, artist manager Karl Mullings, and guitarist Lynn Taitt

Carl Harvey

Ernie Smith and Roots Revival, 1979

Truths and Rights

Chalawa with Stranger Cole, 1979

Carlene Davis, 1980

Fergus Hambleton and Jo Jo Bennett

The Sattalites, promo shot

Rupert "Ojiji" Harvey

Messenjah, promo shot

Earth, Roots and Water and 20th Century Rebels' frontman, Adrian "Sheriff" Miller

Sunforce frontman Michael Garrick

x *Illustrations*

Bamboo Club calendar

Bonconganistas live at the Waterfall Stage, 1991

Wayne Hanson and Natasha Emery

Mike Smith's graduation photo

Fujahtive, promo shot

DJ Friendlyness

Andru Branch, promo shot

Songstress Tanya Mullings

Saxophonist Isax InJah

Bruce Robinson (a.k.a. "Preacher") and the Sattalites

Preface and Acknowledgments

In 1966, Rupert and Victorine Harvey left Clarendon, in rural Jamaica, and ended up in Toronto. They brought with them their two sons, Carl and Rupert Jr., or "Ojiji." Both sons, as you'll soon discover, continue to enjoy successful careers in music. A few months before they arrived, in March 1966, my dad, John Wilson, had convinced my mother, Jessie, to leave rural Ayrshire, Scotland, for Downsview, in Toronto's northwest end. In tow were my gran Mary, my great-aunt Susan, and my sister, Juli. Each family produced a Canadian son. The Wilsons had me; the Harveys had my best friend, Richard. While we lost Richard far too soon, the time I had with him changed my life forever. In a "hoose fou o'" Ayrshire folk, there was little doubt that I would grow up seriously Scottish. But thanks to Richard, the Harveys, and so many of my other dearest friends, I grew up a little Jamaican too.

With that in mind, I now submit my reggae curriculum vitae. As a solo artist, I am a two-time Juno Award nominee (for Best Reggae Recording, 2001 and 2009), a Canadian Reggae Music Award Winner (2009), and a four-time Reggae Music Achievements Award nominee. I was also the first recipient of the Karl Mullings Memorial Award (2007) for commitment to reggae in Canada. On March 2, 2019, I was honoured to be asked to participate as one of the Titans of Toronto Reggae alongside Leroy Sibbles, Stranger Cole, and many of the city's other surviving reggae pioneers. Toronto Mayor John Tory marked the event by calling March 2 "Titans of Reggae Day."[1]

In the last twenty-some years, I have – as a solo artist and with my bands, Tabarruk, Wilson and Swarbrick, and Sumach Roots – performed over twenty-five hundred shows in Canada, the United States, the United Kingdom, and, of course, Jamaica. I have several times served as the Canadian bandleader for ska pioneer and jazz guitar virtuoso Ernest Ranglin. I am likewise the Canadian bandleader for the two-time Grammy nominee Brinsley Forde, founder of UK reggae great, Aswad. I was the onstage musical director for the popular Jamaica to Toronto project, which toured the Canadian festival circuit in 2007 and 2008. I am also, alongside Sattalites' lead singer Fergus Hambleton, a founder of the Two Bobs, a project that unites the musics of Bob Marley and Bob Dylan.

I have had the good fortune to perform and record with some of Jamaica's musical legends, including reggae's most famous rhythm section, Sly and Robbie; composer of the Clash's "Armagideon Time," Willi Williams; ska giants Prince Buster, Eric "Monty" Morris, Derrick Morgan, and Ken Lazarus; Jamaican jazz legend Sonny Bradshaw; rocksteady trailblazers Hopeton Lewis and Lynn Taitt; Jamaican folk and reggae icon Ernie Smith; early reggae stars Big Youth, Dawn Penn, Dennis Alcapone, Bob Andy, Boris Gardiner, and Larry Marshall; and one of the island's most integral backing bands, the Fab Five. I have also had the pleasure of performing with UK reggae artists such as the English Beat's Dave Wakeling, Tippa Irie, and UB40. My cousin Michael Virtue was UB40's keyboard player for nearly forty years. My black Jamaican uncle, Sid Virtue, Michael's dad, was pivotal in importing Jamaican music into the United Kingdom in the 1960s. His 45s and LPs supplied the backdrop to many of the blues dances that UB40 members attended when they were youths and which they later paid tribute to on their multiplatinum-selling *Labour of Love* series. Uncle Sid's collection has likewise had a considerable influence on me.

In terms of Canadian reggae, I played my first nightclub date with Messenjah a month after my fourteenth birthday. At fifteen, I joined Rannie "Bop" Williams's band Yahwedeh. Williams appeared on several cuts with Bob Marley and Jimmy Cliff. I had the fortune of performing live with Toronto's "Big 3" Canadian reggae acts of the 1980s: Messenjah, the Sattalites, and 20th Century Rebels. I have also performed and recorded with various other Canadian reggae acts, including Jay Douglas, Errol Blackwood, Lazo, Mohjah, R. Zee Jackson, King UJah, Andru Branch, Adrian "Sheriff" Miller, Rupert "Ojiji" Harvey, Jackie James,

Michael St. George, Bob and Wisdom, the Mighty Pope, Tanya Mullings, and Noel Ellis. I have been dubbed by the local scene and Toronto media the protégé of Studio One keyboardist the late Jackie Mittoo (I am, of course, flattered to be mentioned in the same sentence as the man who helped to invent the genre). This moniker likely stems from the close relationship I enjoyed with Jackie in my teens, which coincided with the last years of his short life. One of Jackie's last recordings was made with me. Knowing that he was near the end, Jackie suggested that I might play him in a made-for-television movie about his life, a joke he made from his deathbed at Wellesley Hospital in Toronto. I, of course, reminded Jackie that I was much taller than he was.

Outside of the music, I have been surrounded by Jamaicans and their culture all my life. I was born at Branson Hospital in North York in 1970 and grew up at Keele and Finch, where I attended Stilecroft Public School, Elia Junior High, and C.W. Jefferys. This area of north Toronto was the most densely populated square mile in Canada and boasted an incredibly high number of Jamaican expats. The nurse that helped Dr. Rubenzahl bring me into the world was Jamaican (she insisted that my mom call me Willie and not Jason). Roan, my first school chum in kindergarten, was Jamaican. My first kiss was given to me by Sonia, a young Jamaican girl who lived a few doors down from my townhouse. My best friend, as I mentioned above, was Jamaican Canadian Richard Harvey. I usually spent Saturday nights up at the Harvey house, where I experienced Jamaican culture, cuisine, and spirituality (both Seventh-Day Adventist and Rastafarian) for the first time. It was with Richard that I started my first band when I was twelve. I am now, at the time of writing, nearing the half-century mark and have lived happily within this Scottish Canadian Jamaican kaleidoscope.[2]

While my life's own unique kaleidoscope may have presented the raw materials for this book, it took a great number of people to help me to realize the end result. First, I need to thank Catharine Wilson for her supreme guidance and kindness throughout my graduate studies. She provided me with the necessary clues to make sense of what I had found, not to mention the direction I so needed to articulate it here. She often knew what I was trying to say before I did. I will also be eternally indebted to Richard Reid and Henriette Donner for long ago recognizing a scholar lurking in the soul of a high-school dropout, perhaps even before I saw it myself.

I am extremely grateful to James MacNevin, Darcy Cullen, copy editor Lesley Erickson, Ann Macklem, Carmen Tiampo, and all at UBC Press for their commitment and thoughtful encouragement throughout the publication process. I would not have been able to finish this book on time without the careful indexing done by my good friend and author, Jessica Dee Humphreys. She rather saved the day! I am likewise grateful to Alan Gordon, Jessica Humphries, Barbara Lorenzkowski, Bruce Muirhead, James St. G. Walker, Rob Bowman, David Monod, and the late Rex M. Nettleford, without whom this project would not have been possible. I would also like to thank Vivian Crawford and everyone at the Jamaican Institute in Kingston and – for their efforts on my behalf – Michael Tooley, Peter Kiernan, Janet Morgan, Juli and Dave Genoa, and Sebastian Cook.

I am especially fortunate to have had the assistance of reggae guru and historian Klive Walker, whose *Dubwise: Reasoning from the Reggae Underground* (2005) remains the high-water mark in Canadian reggae literature. Klive is a kindred spirit, and I only ask that he forgive the many errors and shortcomings he'll discover here. To that end, I look forward to the marathon phone calls that will no doubt follow.

I could not bring such an undertaking to completion without the loving support of my wife, Alana. She is the best human person I know and is far cleverer than I (too clever, if you ask me).

Ultimately, this project is about the people and their music. I would like to thank the dozens of folks who were willing to open up their hearts to me. It was an honour and a privilege to hear your stories.

King Alpha's Song *in a Strange Land*

INTRODUCTION

King Alpha's Song

In the summer of 1937, Marcus Garvey returned to Toronto to attend the annual conference of his own United Negro Improvement Association (UNIA). The UNIA had purchased a building for its use in Toronto at 355 College Street a year earlier.[1] Garvey had arguably been, at least for a time, the most important black man in the world. Now, the Jamaican-born, Pan-Africanist leader was beleaguered after having served five years in prison on charges that had been trumped up by the US government. In failing health and with the zenith of his career (his part in the Harlem Renaissance) well behind him, Garvey valiantly tried to push his UNIA initiative forward in the Great White North and elsewhere.[2] After three intensive weeks in Toronto, Garvey travelled east. His last Canadian stop was at Menelik Hall in Whitney Pier, Nova Scotia. There, Garvey delivered a speech that would have wide-reaching ramifications: "We are going to emancipate ourselves from mental slavery because whilst others might free the body, none but ourselves can free the mind."[3]

Four decades later, another Jamaican, born only thirty-five kilometres south of where Garvey had come into the world, took inspiration from these words – delivered in Canada – and worked them into something of his own: "Emancipate yourself from mental slavery, / None but ourselves can free our minds."[4] "Redemption Song" remains perhaps the most sacrosanct number in Bob Marley's formidable canon. This connection, tangential as it may appear, anticipates the important role that Canada would play in reggae's global story. It also illustrates how a single text can be reimagined and made into something new, for a different time and place.

Three years after his Canadian speech and just one month before the Battle of Britain began, Garvey died in London, England, on July 10, 1940. "Redemption Song" – the final song of Marley's last studio album – was the last song he ever performed live: the King of Reggae died in a Miami hospital on May 11, 1981. The building that Garvey's UNIA bought has long since disappeared, but for nearly twenty years, Thymeless Reggae Bar was the occupant at 355 College Street.

During the period between Garvey and Marley's death, Canadian immigration laws experienced a transformation. By 1972, Canada's doors had been pushed open to accept black Jamaicans. Migrants, including popular artists such as Jackie Mittoo and Leroy Sibbles, brought their rich Jamaican music with them to Toronto, and reggae helped facilitate a cultural dialogue between Jamaican migrants and their Canadian host society during the 1970s and 1980s. The discourses and musical exchanges taking place along the city's ethnic frontier reveal a variety of social issues that were crucial to both sides at this time, including racism, the immigration and acculturation process, notions of both whiteness and blackness, and the host's patent curiosity about Jamaican music and culture. All these matters informed the evolution of an indigenous and multiracial Toronto reggae scene. Through reggae, migrants were at once able to enact their Jamaican ethnicity and access, at least in some measure, the dominant society. Music, for some Jamaican migrants, was part of a successful acculturation strategy. At the same time, a significant number of Toronto's non-Jamaican and mostly white youth were, for a variety of reasons, drawn to the Jamaican music of their migrant friends. Reggae soon became an expected part of the city's musical vernacular.

Reggae is a hybrid. It is also a transnational popular music form. For over forty years, reggae's transoceanic sound has relayed back and forth across the black Atlantic with Jamaican migrants, labourers, domestics and, of course, musicians. It has articulated a Caribbean diasporic consciousness while transcending it, emerging as something new in urban outposts such as London, Birmingham, and Toronto. It has, like ska before it, united sometimes seemingly strange bedfellows: punk rockers, new wavers, rude boys, and Rastafarians have all been brought together by this Jamaican music that has echoed down urban streetscapes, boomed across multiracial neighbourhoods, cut through working-class spaces of labour, enveloped the schoolyard, and claimed many nightclubs. Crucially, reggae brought black and white youth together in Toronto in a sometimes highly politicized, oppositional movement that rebelled against the status quo of the late 1970s and 1980s.[5] Since then, Jamaican reggae has leaped from the status of folk music or underground music to an international billion-dollar industry with a global infrastructure, millions of fans, and thousands of artists of various ethnicities throughout the world. In terms of international popularity – and when compared to countries of similar size and population – Jamaica's musical output is matchless.

Reggae was not constrained to one place. Scholars have used the conceptual and interconnected frameworks of motion, encounter, and identity to assess how cultural expressions (for our purposes, music) have been advanced and altered through communication routes that transcend national borders.[6] Indeed, some scholars have proven how the local is inextricably linked to the transnational or the global through systems of production and consumption and also through systems of thought and meaning.[7]

More recently, though, other scholars have demonstrated how an emphasis on globalization has perhaps overshadowed the uniqueness of the local.[8] The local remains, as various academics argue, crucial to studying memory making, remembering, and commemoration through the course of historical inquiry.[9] The local, however, gets complicated when its collective property is transported from one place to another. While retaining an essence, the old is, necessarily, rerooted in the new and, once there, experiences a transnational transformation. This was certainly the case for Jamaican migrants and their music. Reggae transformed space to place in many parts of Toronto. The city – as place – was crucial to the cultural and musical blending that ensued between migrant and host, and it gave meaning to the resultant reggae music made there.[10]

Meaning, then, conjoined as it may be to broader patterns linking people and processes across nation-states, remains grounded in and constantly modified by the local. In other words, the roots of a riddim delivered in Kingston 12 may very well bubble through the black diaspora, yet when it was broadcast to, consumed by, and reinterpreted through the "other" on the ethnic frontlines of a city such as Toronto, it imbibed new connotations and therefore varied – sometimes slightly, sometimes vastly – from the initial intention of the original musical and lyrical text.[11] And that is, of course, how music has always behaved.

The popular music that developed in Jamaica in the late 1950s and 1960s evolved in concert with various processes in that country, not least of which was the significant increase in labour migration, chiefly to the United Kingdom and, later, Canada.[12] Mento, ska, rocksteady, and reggae came to Canada through the transnational flow of labour migration and musical ideas.[13] Toronto in particular served as an urban flashpoint for these processes.[14] There, Jamaican music would provide a much-needed soundtrack for those migrants who had left their island in the sun.

The migrants broadcast reggae on to the streets of Toronto. While there were separate immigrant enclaves, their borders were porous enough to allow the drum and bass line to penetrate Toronto's mainstream youth culture. There were a few pockets of Jamaican migrants in the city's east end and Scarborough. Jamaicans also boasted significant numbers in Malton, near Lester B. Pearson International Airport. Perhaps most famous, though, were the main Jamaican enclaves of the Jane-Finch Corridor (which more broadly extended east to Keele Street and south to Sheppard Avenue), the "Black Bottom" (running south from Eglinton on Bathurst) and, by extension, Eglinton Avenue West, which is now known to most as Little Jamaica.

Few of the musical migrants who moved into these communities laboured under the assumption that they would make their living exclusively through music. Most didn't. Yet the names of those reggae musicians who at one time or another possessed a Toronto address reads like a who's who of reggae. Indeed, some of the genre's true pioneers at one time or another called Toronto home. Additionally, indigenously produced reggae music grew to a formidable quality that was recognized both in Canada and in the country of reggae's birth. As a reggae outpost, Toronto had the West Indian Federation Club, Club Jamaica, and, later, the city's central nerve for reggae – the Bamboo Club on Queen Street West. These clubs roughly paralleled London's Flamingo, the Sunset Club, the 59, and A-Train.[15] And just as it had done in Britain, Jamaican music in downtown Toronto brought young people from all walks of life together.

King Alpha's Song in a Strange Land is not a study of migrants. It is a study of the process of migration of one group (Jamaicans) and the migration of music (reggae) as seen from both the migrant and the host's perspective. It is, therefore, as much about black Jamaicans as it is about white Torontonians.

There is a danger in only following the migrant's path from origin to destination (and, if it applies, back again). A strict teleological reading of the migration process can produce inelastic, essentialized notions about groupness and, in our case, blackness and whiteness. It can also obscure exceptions in the various groups in question, including both the migrants and the host. Certainly, there were exceptions – abolitionists, internationalists, antimodernists, activists, artists, authors, and, yes, musicians, too – who provide untidy realities that trouble some critical race theories.

Jamaicans were not a homogeneous group. No migrant community is. In Barbara Lorenzkowski's *Sounds of Ethnicity: Listening to German North America, 1850–1914,* the author cleverly chooses to view German ethnicity as something that is practised, something that happens, instead of viewing it as a strict set of inflexible norms and monolithic ideals.[16] In this way, ethnicity as practice allows room for a multiplicity of lived experiences.[17] Reggae in Toronto gave the Jamaican a way to enact her or his Jamaicanness that was not only culturally satisfying for the migrant but also attractive to some non-Jamaicans.

In the interest of being transparent, I am not Jamaican. I have, however, been a Canadian reggae artist for over thirty-five years. As such, and by virtue of growing up where I did, in North York, Ontario, I have lived among Jamaicans all my life. I have also enjoyed some successes in the reggae world and have had the privilege of playing and recording with some of the genre's true greats. I have had as much fun playing with the not-so-famous too. Still, I will leave the question of whether I possess an insider's perspective up to the reader (but please read the preface).[18]

Whatever you decide, reggae is part of my culture and has been a fixture of my personal day-to-day environment since I was a child. Perhaps the impetus for this book came from being asked many times, by the media and others, "What's a white guy like you doing playing reggae?" The most remarkable aspect about this question is that I have rarely been asked it by Jamaicans and never, at least in my memory, by Jamaican musicians, whether in Canada, Britain, or in Jamaica itself. My stock answer is this: though I may be a Scottish Canadian, reggae chose me, and I have sincerely dedicated much of my life to the promotion, proliferation, and performance of Canadian reggae. It has been immensely satisfying.

The CBC's Peter Mansbridge once said I wore multiculturalism "like a comfortable sweater."[19] I believe that mine is more a case of interculturalism, for, in truth, the government brochure version of multiculturalism is a misleading representation that cannot be effectively legislated. It is also incongruous with the realities of many of the people I consulted to write this book. Real cultural interaction, or interculturalism, occurs in a place where cultures in fact collide before meaningful dialogue commences.[20] Rumours, good and bad, lie in the shadows cast by official multiculturalism. Superficial rumours suggest that all Jamaicans would have great rhythm, love ackee and salt fish, hate winter, be quick to anger, and play threatening, bass-booming reggae. It was therefore surprising for me to find Eli, who could not possibly hope to find "beat one" if his life depended on it; Lincoln, who was allergic to ackee; Robbie, who tired quickly of summer and couldn't wait for hockey season; Charles, a gentle giant who possessed the patience of a Buddha; and Mr. and Mrs. Harvey, who for years hoped that I would grow out of this "reggae thing" and concentrate on classical piano. These realities demonstrated the variance in what was supposedly a homogeneous group. Happily, the "narrowness of ethnicity," as cultural critic Neil Bissoondath has called it, is often trumped by the wildly different tastes of the various individuals who happen to be born in a particular place.

When a popular Toronto radio show asked me to put a band together for one of their live broadcasts, the producer asked me what the makeup of the band was. I began to explain that I was going to bring a bassist, a tenor saxophonist, a drummer, and so forth. I was interrupted, and she explained that she really wanted to know what the band members' cultural background was: what was the ethnic makeup of the band? This barometer of ethnicity is, sadly, the true test for prescribed Canadian multiculturalism, and it will always undermine musical or artistic considerations. It didn't matter what my band might sound like; it was more important that they suited the prescription of what a reggae band should look like (the irony of it being a radio show notwithstanding). Needless to say, the producer was delighted to hear that I had a Sri Lankan, a Trinidadian, a Jamaican, and a St. Lucian in my mix, which I presume, for her at least, nicely offset my Scottishness. With all CRTC requirements apparently satisfied, and on the strength of our multiple hues, we had the gig.

The zenith in Jamaican migration to Canada came in the 1970s, and while some work has been done on this diaspora in various countries, few scholars have concentrated on the Jamaican experience in Canada, and fewer still (if any) have appraised the host society's response in depth. Furthermore, most historians of immigration have focused on the immigrants' adaptation to the host society in both economic and material terms and have not specifically viewed this process through a musical lens.

The transnational and organic nature of reggae music served as a conduit between migrant and host, a fact that bears some consideration. Through traditional sources such as mainstream and community newspapers, music trade magazines, government documents, Canadian-produced reggae music, and oral evidence I explore the cultural dialogue and diffusion that occurred between Jamaicans and non-Jamaicans in Toronto. I use the music of Canada's golden age of reggae (1979–90) as a prism through which various inquiries of a more theoretical kind can shine. Through this prism, one can witness how the reggae text, its performers, and audiences have changed over time and adjusted to fit the Canadian context.

Though this book at times harkens back to various periods (early twentieth-century Jamaica, post–Second World War Canada, and Thatcher's Britain, to name a few), it opens in 1973, the year that saw the arrival of Jamaican reggae legend Leroy Sibbles in Toronto's northwest neighbourhood, the Jane-Finch Corridor. This was also the year that reggae exploded on the international scene with the unexpected cult

10 *Introduction*

success of the Jamaican film *The Harder They Come*. The story closes in 1990, when the multiracial Toronto reggae act the Sattalites won the Juno Award for Best Reggae Recording at the tail end of Canada's golden age of reggae.

To tell this story, I interviewed over twenty Jamaicans and over twenty non-Jamaicans who were willing to share their experiences.[21] Each group had the possibility of providing both *emic* and *etic* accounts.[22] Through them, we get the opportunity, as the poet Burns wrote, "to see oursels as others see us!"[23] We get the immediate benefit of hearing the actual lived experience of the migrant, according to him or her, while viewing the same experience from the perspective of the host who witnessed the process.

These perspectives, however, can only ever be imperfect. Recollections are important not only for what is remembered but also for what is not. The workings of memory are not infallible. People's stories change over time, certain aspects of a particular experience can be misremembered, and many folks often fall back on clumsy, weather-beaten tropes to simplify their thinking of a previous time.

The perspectives included here, however, are perhaps among the sharpest available. Everyone I interviewed had some reasonable link to the Canadian reggae scene. Over twenty-five of them were musicians, and the others were involved directly with the music industry and include reggae concert and festival promoters, radio DJs, authors, journalists, publicists, a photographer, and one record-company employee. All the Jamaican interviewees immigrated to Canada between 1964 and 1989 (seventeen before 1980), and all the respondents, Jamaican and non-Jamaican, were at least in their teenage years during Canada's golden age of reggae and were in some way active in it.[24]

In addition to these interviews, I conducted a few with first-generation Canadians of Jamaican heritage to craft a more nuanced account of how the acculturation process differed among Jamaicans over time. For further musical context, I also undertook a few interviews with legendary reggae artists, including Jamaican guitar virtuoso Ernest Ranglin; British reggae icons UB40's Ali Campbell, Astro, and Michael Virtue; and former Aswad frontman Brinsley Forde.[25] Because the folk traditions of the British Isles are linked with Jamaican folk musics, I also interviewed the late English fiddle legend and folk historian David Swarbrick.[26]

The title for this book, *King Alpha's Song in a Strange Land,* was inspired by the Melodians' classic 1970 reggae cut "By the Rivers of Babylon," which articulates the cyclical nature of Jamaica's people in motion.[27] Its structure is loosely chronological and focuses on three geographical centres: Toronto, Jamaica, and the United Kingdom. Migration has been an inescapable element of Jamaican history, and Jamaican music reveals the transoceanic musical dialogue that was occurring between Britain and Jamaica, Jamaica and Canada, and Canada and Britain. From the late seventeenth century onward, African folk traditions intersected with European ones in Jamaica's cultural economy. The resultant creolized Jamaican folk musical tradition was continuously updated by outside influences (especially British and later American popular and folk musics) and ultimately played, by the second half of the twentieth century, a significant role in the emerging Jamaican exports of mento, ska, rocksteady, and reggae.

These exports were brought to Toronto by Jamaican migrants and had a profound effect on the non-Jamaican youth subculture of that city in the 1970s and 1980s. Yet by the time it reached Toronto, the non-Jamaican host was already familiar, if subconsciously, with some of reggae's catholic musical signifiers. By putting Jamaican reggae under the microscope, it's possible to find DNA that can in some measure explain why nondiasporic musicians and enthusiasts embraced Jamaican reggae music to the extent they did within the urban centres of Britain and, of course, Toronto.

Immigration to Canada was not an easy process for most Jamaicans. The official policies of the Canadian government were often calibrated to popular and pervasive attitudes about race and culture in the country, and only when economic or labour needs called for it did Canada open up its doors to Jamaican workers, including the many migrant musicians of Toronto's Jamaican music scene. Still, these migrant musicians or musical enthusiasts believe that they had an advantage over other migrants in the acculturation process because of their association with music. Many feel that they were able to draw strength from the sense of community that music and musicians could provide and were able to use music to build bridges into the city's mainstream culture.

After the migrants arrived, a robust cultural dialogue occurred between Jamaican migrants and non-Jamaicans along Toronto's ethnic frontlines. In time, Canadian reggae texts were crafted in those places that bridged migrant with host. These texts concurrently reinforced and resisted metanarratives of Canadian multiculturalism and, indeed, the Jamaican musical art form itself. Ultimately, Toronto's reggae protagonists, fans, and critics cast their own varied meanings on reggae.

Toronto's Jamaicans personally introduced reggae to non-Jamaicans through various means, including lending albums and singles to classmates in school, attending reggae concerts or dances with them, or simply sharing marijuana. At the same time, many non-Jamaicans were highly influenced by British musical trends that were often responding to the United Kingdom's own Jamaican population. Punk music, the second wave of ska (or the two-tone movement), and the popularity of English reggae bands such as Aswad, Steel Pulse, and UB40 were trends that had great currency in Toronto's youth culture in the late 1970s and into the 1980s. Indeed, given the strong bonds between the three countries, reggae as a genre in Canada was constantly being updated by musical trade winds that blew north from Jamaica and west from Britain.

Some non-Jamaicans were also profoundly affected by the international rise of Bob Marley and his music. Through him, a few non-Jamaicans turned Rasta. Others were attracted to his endorsement (and other reggae musicians' endorsement) of marijuana, a fact that blended with the recreational drug culture found in other popular musics of the day. For some, these various bridge-building activities in leisure and private spaces along the frontline opened up the possibility of more meaningful and long-lasting relationships between migrant and host.

There were also, of course, the gatekeepers who instead chose to draw their bridges skyward when they felt that their notion of reggae had been compromised. Indeed, some gatekeepers viewed participation in musical bridge-building operations as an act of disloyalty to the Jamaican group and any resultant sound as an offence to an imagined "authentic" Jamaican text. Interestingly, many of the gatekeepers were from the dominant host society: journalists and ethnomusicologists who had a limited idea of what Canadian reggae should sound and look like.

And what of the Canadian sound? More often than not, Canadian reggae artists felt compelled to chase an authentic Jamaican sound. These acts continued to look south to the island for inspiration and validation. Nevertheless, some brave migrant acts such as Messenjah, Lillian Allen, and Truths and Rights and some multiracial acts such as 20th Century Rebels and the Sattalites sought to articulate a Canadian-centric experience within their songs and found some success, at least artistically, in doing so. The Sattalites in particular were successful in conveying a multiracial expression that simultaneously reflected the experiences of those on stage and those in the audience.

While the Jamaican migrant may have brought the main ingredients for the reggae music made in Toronto, the non-Jamaican host certainly added to the broth, creating something uniquely Canadian. Who then owns the Canadian reggae text? Part of the trouble with quests for ownership of the authentic reggae text is evinced in its audience. Bob Marley's live audiences were largely white. Burning Spear – many people's idea of the defender of Rasta reggae's truest text – has made most of his money in Europe and North America, playing to audiences that boast sizeable white contingents.[28] Today, as was the case by the mid-1970s, reggae artists, especially Jamaican ones, make most of their living on fees and royalties emanating from outside of Jamaica. As Leroy Sibbles observed as early as 1982: "Nothing's happening in Jamaica. They've even stopped selling the cheaper disco 45s in Jamaica because nobody's buying them. Most people who do recording down in Jamaica don't bother to release the songs down there. They export them. All the reggae records are being sold abroad."[29] In terms of a music industry, then, Jamaican artists have relied on a global audience, particularly in Europe and North America, to fuel the reggae machine.

A significant number of reggae texts have been crafted by non-Rasta Jamaicans, but dreadlocks; the smoking of marijuana; the sartorial requisites of *ites* (red), gold, and green; and devotion to Haile Selassie (at least publicly) have cumulatively assembled the normative iconography of reggae. It hardly needs stating that fleshing out the important linkages between Rasta, the drum, poverty, slavery, oppression, and its oppositional responses found in the texts of ska, rocksteady, and reggae is a valid and worthwhile endeavour.[30] But it's not what I'm doing here. This book is, at least in part, a response to the standard austere and teleological narrative of Jamaican music that jettisons its hybridity and folk roots. The irresistible image of Bob Marley may have given reggae its face and put the genre on the world stage, but that face limited what reggae could and certainly did mean to a great many of its faithful practitioners, including those in Canada.[31]

Jamaican musicians are diverse. Rastafarians make up less than 1 percent of Jamaica's population, and while they are disproportionately represented in reggae music, many non-Rasta Jamaicans have been pivotal to the development of the genre.[32] Carlene Davis, an Afro-Jamaican reggae and gospel artist who spent a few years in Canada, provides one apt example of such diversity. As a Christian woman, Davis troubles some people's perception of what a reggae artist should look or sound like.[33] Yet no one in Jamaica would deny that she is a bona fide reggae star who has always been comfortable expressing and stretching her elastic reading of the Jamaican musical art form: "I can't help where I've been. I started out singing folk music in England and I've done pop and country and a whole bunch of things since. Whatever I've heard is going to come out, it just flows naturally."[34] Interestingly, Davis believes she enjoyed more artistic freedom when she returned to Jamaica after her time in Toronto: "In Canada, it seemed as if I would have to project myself totally as a reggae artist if I wanted to make it. I couldn't sidetrack, I'd have to be pure. Here [in Jamaica] there's room to spread out – the Jamaican audiences will listen to anything. I love reggae, but here I don't have to stick exclusively to it."[35] Though existing ideas about what reggae should look and sound like outside of Jamaica pervaded Canada's music intelligentsia, Jamaicans in Jamaica were far less exclusionary. Feeling artistically pigeon-holed, Davis returned to live in Jamaica in 1981 and missed the better part of Reggae Canadiana's golden age.[36]

There are other important examples that complicate the reggae stereotype. Hopeton Lewis, whose 1966 hit "Take It Easy" is considered by most to be the first rocksteady song ever, was a Christian.[37] Jimmy Cliff, whose soundtrack to *The Harder They Come* introduced reggae to the world, is Muslim. So, too, was Prince Buster, the man who delivered ska to England. Bob Marley was, indeed, a Rasta, but his father was a white Englishman. And UB40, though continuously maligned by journalists in official reggae histories (if included at all), is the world's most commercially successful reggae band, after Marley and his Wailers. In addition to being multiracial, the band is an assemblage of Rastas, agnostics, and atheists. In many of these authenticities, one's skin colour and faith system (or lack thereof) is irrelevant.

When compared to blues and jazz, however, reggae scholarship has some catching up to do.[38] Unlike UB40's lot in the body of reggae literature, Bill Evans – one of the most influential post–Second World War jazz pianists – does not merit an asterisk beside his name in jazz histories to denote "white pianist."[39] Moreover, few ethnomusicologists would question the various authenticities of jazz played by musicians who may not even be from the United States.[40] Indeed, Jamaicans such as Joe Harriott, Monty Alexander, and Ernest Ranglin have made significant contributions to the proliferation of "American" jazz. Yet the fruits of reggae roots (and routes) – when presented by many non-Rastas, non-Jamaicans, and even by nonblacks around the world – have been held, by some, under deep suspicion.

Compounding the problem for reggae is that its attendant scholarship is quite small and has not yet had the chance to mature like the bodies of literature associated with jazz, folk, blues, and even rock and roll. Unlike the literature on these genres, there have been no major pitched battles between competing academics on questions of authenticity, race, and commercial exploitation. And so the discourse on authenticity persists in the small, nascent body of reggae literature. In *Dangerous Crossroads,* for example, George Lipsitz, an American studies professor at the University of California, suggests that the British reggae band Musical Youth's representation of reggae was disconnected from the genre's organic roots. Lipsitz argues that this is indicative of the record industry's commercial remodelling of the reggae text. Lipsitz seems unwilling to consider that the idea for Musical Youth (who were the first black group to appear on

MTV) and their hit song "Pass the Dutchie" (which sold over 4 million copies) were the product of existing Jamaican texts and had been conceived entirely by Jamaicans.[41] Simply put, scholars need to accept the multiplicity of new traditions and authenticities in the reggae text.[42]

In 2008, a Global Reggae Conference was held at the University of the West Indies' Jamaican campus to consider scholarly contributions to the literature on reggae.[43] In her opening plenary, award-winning Jamaican cultural historian Erna Brodber observed that the reggae music of the 1970s had created a black space.[44] For Brodber, reggae was

> an incubator for a kind of knowledge that needed to work its way out of the ground and into the minds of the young descendants of Africans enslaved in Jamaica. Not just chatter among the platters; the early reggae allowed meditation while you danced and even if you did not want to be black, you could at least understand why others would want to be. Reggae made converts, but it also produced an environment that was sympathetic to those who wanted to be more than listeners to the works of the "singers and players," the only professionals mentioned by the Psalms as being there.[45]

This is so. Moreover, reggae is synonymous with the struggles and triumphs of black Jamaicans throughout the diaspora, including those in Toronto. Most reggae, and certainly most of the best reggae, has been written, recorded, and performed by black Jamaicans (while it need not be restated, I ask you to keep this declaration in mind as you read this book).

This book, however, explores plurality in the lived reality of the reggae experience. I'm interested in, as Brodber alluded to, the converts that reggae made. With its massive population of expatriate Jamaicans and its importance to the global reggae scene, Toronto offers not only a place to show how Jamaican music claimed a foothold on the streets of a non-Jamaican city, infiltrating its mainstream, but also a space to test the absolute that reggae should be the exclusive preserve of black Jamaicans and Rastafarians. In this respect, Canadian reggae is a success story. The

Canadian reggae experience serves as an example of how interculturalism brought migrant and host (and other migrants, for that matter) together in Canada. Interculturalism, however, is largely unrecognizable from the cliché governmental prescriptions and portrayals of multiculturalism, which do not resonate with migrants.

Alas, Canadian reggae is also a story of failure. The mainstream music industry's lack of commitment to reggae, residual public attitudes towards race and ethnic music in general, and a lack of cohesion in Canada's reggae community itself helped chase Leroy Sibbles (among others) back to Jamaica, preventing Canada from competing with other international reggae markets such as the United Kingdom. Despite being stacked with talent and a huge West Indian population, Canadian reggae stagnated after its golden age, and it never came close to approximating its far more successful British cousin.

1

Hybridity and Jamaican Music

Reggae is a hybrid. Reggae is not homogeneous. Jamaican music emerged out of a transnational and multigenerational collision between African and European traditions, musical and otherwise (outmoded as these terms may be, as we will soon see). Folk musics and customs from West and Central Africa nevertheless collided with European ones, especially those from the British Isles. Sea shanties, dances, and ballads, for example, traversed the Atlantic and were co-opted and reimagined by Jamaicans of various hues. Indeed, melodies from all over the world flowed through the hub of Jamaica's cultural economy and were picked up and adapted by the locals. The skilful Jamaican tunesmith could gut a song of its original context and use its rawness for a new and wholly Jamaican composition.[1] This process continues today within the reggae oeuvre, wherever it is crafted.

Over the course of two centuries, a hybridized version of these Afro-European traditions sprouted in Jamaica's cultural hothouse, flowering in the musics of mento and ska and then rocksteady and reggae. By the early 1970s, Jamaican reggae – informed as it had been by African and European musical, folk, pedagogical, and religious customs – was ready for export to the world. Like the sea shanties of an earlier time, reggae, too, would be recontextualized by many different peoples, including those of a certain age and disposition living in Toronto.

This chapter traces this process, but it does not include an exhaustive musicological overview of the trajectory of twentieth-century Jamaican music. It could be argued that I gloss over the variety of African and even

Latin influences found in Jamaican music. This is intentional. For the purposes of linking reggae's past with its present, Britain with Jamaica, Jamaica with Canada, and Canada with Britain, I am concerned here with the spheres of European, and particularly British, influences on Jamaica's popular and traditional musics. These influences, it must be stressed, are only a part of a much larger palette found in the musics that have given so many Jamaican artists worldwide recognition. Yet these ingredients have also played a significant role in the important creolization processes occurring within the musical culture of Jamaica and, indeed, Jamaican society at large.

Locating some of the British influences is a way to explain – in part – the degree to which non-Jamaican and even nondiasporic participants, music makers, audience members, and writers around the world, especially those in the urban centres of Britain and Toronto, embraced reggae music. Encrypted within the reggae that was ferried to Canada via the Jamaican migrant were signifiers not wholly unknown to the Canadian host. Despite its seeming exoticness, its oppositional qualities, and its articulation of the black struggle, reggae was for many non-Jamaicans – and perhaps only on a subconscious level – already familiar. Here, I flesh out some of the long-standing processes that directly affected various Jamaicans and non-Jamaicans, processes that were later repeated on Toronto's ethnic frontline.[2]

At the same time, considering the collision between African and European traditions in Jamaican society reveals the issues of race and racial dynamics. Unpacking how race behaved in Jamaica in the twentieth century is a daunting task. It is nevertheless essential to see how anthropologists, musicians, and folklorists trained in the British school, heard, collected, and disseminated the folk songs and stories of Jamaica.

It is true that whiteness, at least in the early twentieth century, was branded with characteristics such as privilege, prejudice, domination, and possession of an acute indifference to the other, a monolithic notion that still abides. Yet two individuals – Walter Jekyll and Astley Clerk – troubled this popular and prevailing construction of whiteness. Early twentieth-century folklorists such as Jekyll and Clerk – individuals who eschewed privilege, rejected empire, and valued the "African" in the Jamaican – have been too untidy for some scholars to unpack. Ignoring the uniqueness of Jekyll and Clerk's whiteness, however, is an endemic issue in reggae scholarship, a point I return to later. While a man such as Jekyll was certainly unique for his time, his empathy for and understanding of black Jamaica was less so. The Jekyll archetype stretches backward towards lighter-skinned Jamaicans such as George William Gordon (executed for his role in the Morant Bay Rebellion) and Zachary Macaulay (the Scottish-born plantation bookkeeper turned abolitionist) just as it springs forward to touch people such as future Island Records founder Chris Blackwell (instrumental in bringing reggae to the world) and multiracial reggae bands such as England's UB40 and Canada's Sattalites. All these characters have, to varying degrees, complicated the whiteness construct.

There is also the question of music. The music of the British Isles, more so than its people, figured early and often as an organic agent that shaped Jamaica's traditional and popular musics. It was an organic relationship because the music emanating from Britain informed Jamaican music from the eighteenth century right through to the twentieth, in much the same way that original Jamaican music would profoundly influence musical trends in Britain after the Second World War. Canada – caught somewhere in between – acted as both a tributary and a reservoir of Jamaican culture, providing a route and harbour for centuries-old musical ideas pushed along by the trade winds of the black Atlantic.

Melody and Rhythm

The late Jamaican scholar Rex Nettleford spoke of an oscillation between the "melody of Europe" and the "rhythm of Africa" and argued that this tension dominated not only the evolution of the island's musical culture but also Jamaican identity itself. As Nettleford explained in 1970:

> In the absence of a strongly preserved cultural memory and in the wake of the deliberate uprooting of ancestral institutions by the slave system among the African immigrants, the African slave was to become the nearest thing to a *tabula rasa* on which the new vocabulary of creole existence could be written. As a result, some of his descendants today boast the claim that of all comers to the Plantation

societies of the New World, the African has been the prime agent of creativity through which all the experiments in the new living have been carried out. He therefore becomes the richest expression of all the contradictions, the failures, successes, the fears and hopes of the new society. He is black man, white man, brown man and all the "in-betweens" rolled into one. He is Europe's melody and Africa's rhythm, at once the dissonance and the harmony of both.[3]

Certainly, many Jamaicans have celebrated the Afro-Euro blend and its attendant creolization processes, as quadrille dance expert Caroline Muraldo testified: "As the cultures of Africa and European contrast in so many ways and were the main influences on Caribbean culture, the creolization process resulted in Caribbean culture existing on a continuum, the influence of each continent residing at opposite ends. At the centre dwell the parts of Caribbean culture, which can be attributed to nowhere else but the Caribbean."[4]

There are, however, inherent problems in assigning origins to specific musical or folk traits, and despite their importance in documenting Jamaica's folk traditions, early twentieth-century folklorists such as Jekyll contributed, though perhaps indirectly, to a romanticized vision of Jamaican "folkness."[5] This dangerous vision would set the bar for what was and what was not deemed culturally authentic.[6]

More recently, scholars have argued that the very idea of African and European "survivals" – that is to say, specific cultural traits – in Jamaica's folk art and music are themselves constructions.[7] By extension, this black-white binary has been used at different times during the early twentieth century to serve a national or cultural narrative that privileged the European quotient in the Jamaican. At its worst, colonial social agents and proponents were able to use any European-ness that had been "found" in Jamaican folk as way of legitimizing ideas about colonial control and European hegemony.[8] This approach would, however, change in Jamaica's post-Garvey era. Though denigrated from the advent of slavery, all things African became crucial to Jamaica's nation building in the years leading up to and during its obtaining independence from Britain in 1962.[9] Come independence, the pendulum had swung so far in this direction that, despite vague allusions to the African-rhythm–European-melody model in various histories of Jamaican music, the European quotient was often referred to pejoratively or was, at the very least, soft-pedalled.[10] Henceforth, Jamaican music, and especially reggae, was viewed through a narrow lens. The African elements were lauded by scholars, musicologists, and journalists. And it was the "African" that, for many, carried that essential oppositional swing within Jamaican music. On balance, the African-rhythm–European-melody hypothesis is well worn and in need of further nuance.

Afro-Jamaican

European influences came to Jamaica hand in hand with colonial subjugation. Three centuries prior to independence, the British had banned the drum in Jamaica. Hans Sloane, whose drum collection helped to kick-start Britain's Natural History Museum and who was also the man who brought chocolate milk to Europe, visited Jamaica in 1688. While there, he and his French colleague, the musician Baptiste, bore witness to the music that African slaves were playing and singing in "the ring."[11] Sloane sketched drawings of the various African instruments used in the performance, which were foreign to the Europeans, while Baptiste notated, to the best of his abilities, the songs he heard.

These songs, according to the Irish overseer who acted as a go-between for Baptiste and the slaves, emanated from the Angola, Papa, and Koromanti traditions.[12] As Sloane explained, the slaves

> formerly on their Festivals were allowed the use of Trumpets after their Fashion, and Drums made of a piece of a hollow Tree, covered on one end with any green Skin, and stretched with Thouls or Pins. But making use of these in their Wars at home in *Africa*, it was thought too much inciting them to Rebellion, and so they were prohibited by the Customs of the Island.[13]

Still, the drum survived through the efforts of the faithful, who persevered with their covert African worship ceremonies, hidden from the watchful eye of the slave drivers. Indeed, Kumina drumming and the Pocomania Revival, with its *funde, kete,* and repeater drums, were alive and well in Jamaica and refused to perish with each new generation that became increasingly removed from their antecedents in Angola, from the Ibo and Yoruba peoples of Nigeria, from the Mandingos of Sierra Leone, and from the Coromantees (or Koromantis) of Ghana's Gold Coast, who founded the dreaded Maroon tribe.[14]

Twentieth-century academics, however, debated whether such African "survivals" had in fact survived. Jamaican sociologist Orlando Patterson and Barbadian-born historian Edward Kamau Brathwaite, for example, took contrary stances on whether true African survivals could be found in Jamaican culture.[15] In *The Sociology of Slavery* (1967), Patterson argued that every African institution that the slaves brought over with them to Jamaica – including family, marriage, and religion – had been virtually wiped out with slavery. Thus, true African culture had, according to Patterson, been unable to persist.[16] Brathwaite, on the other hand, contended in *The Development of Creole Society in Jamaica, 1770–1820* (1971) that Patterson's work missed those aspects of African-based cultures that were invisible to or ignored by the planter society.[17] These traits played a crucial role in Jamaica's resultant creole culture and afforded much of the defiant, oppositional quality so crucial to reggae music.[18]

It is useful to remember that Jamaica's slaves were not a homogeneous group. Intra-African creolization processes in music and language were occurring among the slaves themselves from the moment people from different regions of Africa were introduced to one another. Anthropologist Kenneth Bilby has observed that the historical literature relating to the earliest developments of creolization is, to be charitable, imprecise. Yet concrete evidence of creolization is apparent in the documented musics and dances of the past and in, as Bilby states, "the many continuities of context, style and form displayed by their present-day musical descendants."[19] The Western Kwa and "Angolan" cultures were coalescing in an acculturation process that saw the former's upper-register singing and eight-stringed harp matched by the latter's lower-register, two-stringed lute.[20] The result was a pidginized African sound produced wholly in the Americas.

While European traces of melody may have been captured by slaves, they had been adapted and subsequently reimagined into something wholly original. This salient point was missed by many of the earlier folklorists. Normally, slaves were coerced into playing music that was pleasing for their masters.[21] Therefore, the learning of European tunes could be, for many musicians, a strategy for their own survival.[22] While the slaves may have produced a faithful rendering of the quadrille that was pleasing to their masters, the musicians developed their own unique style that could at once be musical and, surreptitiously, oppositional.[23] In this way, music behaved in much the same manner as language: ridiculing the masters, exaggerating their pomposity, and rebelling against or opposing the circumstances that slavery brought with it. This rebellious quality in the music, like Jamaican Patois, was held in deep suspicion by many of the island's upper and middling classes. It was not until the latter part of the twentieth century that Patois, ska music, rocksteady, and reggae were embraced by most Jamaicans as the cultural and liberating parlance of independence.

An overarching African presence persisted in mento and was likewise manifest in ska, rocksteady, reggae, dub, and dancehall. The pulsing of the burru drum, for instance, replicates the thumping of a human heart. With emphasis on beat three, it is the one drop that recalls the ominous time kept by the plantation's human machinery. It is this heartbeat that has shaped the trajectory of popular Jamaican music from its inception.[24]

Over the course of the colonization period, however, many Jamaicans turned away from African traditions in favour of European Christian ones. As a result, many black Jamaicans often look with suspicion upon the raw elements of Pocomania. When I interviewed him, Earle Heedram, a Jamaican Canadian music legend, recalled an example of this from his childhood:

> When I was a kid living in the middle of the town, certain times in the evening ... all through the night you could hear the drums, the Pocomania drums. And I remember my mother always telling me "Don't listen to that." But you could never ignore it, and it went on all night. It was the Rastas up in the hills, but it would just waif through, and that stays in my mind. You never saw them, but you'd hear the music all night.[25]

Defiantly, the drum would remain the most pervasive element in the island's traditional and popular musics.

The European influence could not sterilize the African in the Jamaican. Moreover, the European influence cannot reasonably be considered the dominant feature of any of Jamaica's current musics. Importantly, though, it is a feature, a sometimes perceptible pattern, a sometimes hidden stitch in the hybridized fabric known as Jamaican reggae. This is significant when we consider what happened to reggae when it was carried from Jamaica by the migrant musician out to the rest of the world, including Canada, and when we assess the process by which non-Jamaicans embraced reggae through appreciating, performing or, indeed, writing about it. There are likely more white-skinned journalists making a career out of writing about reggae than there are white-skinned musicians making a living out of playing it. Though it was not always the intention of its black Jamaican proponents, the appeal of reggae – given its DNA – has always been cross-racial and cross-generational.

Dr. Jekyll and the Folklorists

In a modest cemetery in the small coastal village of Lucea, in the parish of Hanover, lie the remains of the eccentric gardener-folklorist and anti-modernist Walter Jekyll. The Englishman had a deep reverence for Jamaican folk traditions and left behind the most important collection of Jamaican folk music: *Jamaican Song and Story: Annancy Stories, Digging Sings, Ring Tunes, and Dancing Tunes* (1907). This work remains a vital ethnographic tool for anthropologists, ethnomusicologists, historians, musicians, and folklorists.[26]

Jekyll's contribution to Jamaican culture, however, transcended his ethnographic work. As the island's wise guru, Jekyll was often called upon to settle many important questions about music, literature, religion, botany, and science for the islanders.[27] It was difficult to best him intellectually, yet Jekyll earnestly shared his wealth of knowledge with his Hanoverian neighbours and with Jamaicans in general.[28] One admirer confirmed that Jekyll's day was "devoted to giving help to someone. Music lessons for this one, singing lessons for another ... Was there anything not understood, it was always 'Ask Mr. Jekyll.'"[29] It was the centrality of music in Jekyll's Jamaican life, though, that produced the most essential part of his legacy. Given his parents' musical pedigree, his direct association with Mendelssohn and Lamperti, his piano and vocal competence, and his renowned (and daily) open-window piano performances from his living room, Jekyll captured the imagination of many Jamaicans, who were able to directly or indirectly benefit from his rich musical mind.

Jekyll's folk music collection is important because it reveals the trans-oceanic nature of Jamaica's folk music traditions. But more importantly, a review of Jekyll's character, inclinations, and predispositions redresses various misrepresentations of the man, along with his protégé, the poet Claude McKay.[30] Indeed, scholarly works often frame Jekyll in an antagonistic colonist-to-colonial role. In actuality, the radical folklorist had a far more nuanced relationship with and attitude towards race.[31] A member of England's ruling class, Jekyll was an aristocratic rebel who rejected much of the cachet of empire and all that modernity promised.

Jekyll and his legacy also intersect with a future Jamaican Canadian music star. Buried in the very same cemetery with Jekyll are the parents of Earle Heedram. Born in Lucea only sixteen years after Jekyll's death, Heedram – the "Mighty Pope" – would become the first black solo artist to be signed to a major record label in Canada, with RCA Records in 1977.[32] Before coming to Canada in the 1960s, Heedram attended Rusea's High School in Lucea, where only a generation previous, promising students, urged by their teacher, had undertaken the eight-mile trip to Bower Hill on Saturday mornings to hear Jekyll discuss literature and music.[33] Miss Irene Dixon, the local piano teacher, had also started a tradition of sending Jekyll some of her more gifted students so that he might help them prepare in advance of their examinations.[34] Heedram, too, would walk to Miss Dixon's for his niece's biweekly lessons with Jekyll's musical colleague. It is obvious that Jekyll added to the local musical culture of Lucea and inspired people like Dixon to continue the work of administering formal musical instruction to Hanover hopefuls such as Heedram and his niece.

Still, it was Jekyll's work as a folklorist that served not only budding musicians but also the whole of the island and its culture. Jekyll's seminal collection demonstrated a vernacular Jamaicanness that fused African and European influences and folk traditions, and Jekyll was less invested in the amusical agendas that informed the works of so many of his contemporaries.[35] The purpose of his *Jamaican Song and Story* was not to evangelize nor to assist in building a national orthodoxy for England and empire.[36] Nor was Jekyll's collection a means of confirming a racial hierarchy with whites at the top. Challenging the Bible, questioning progress, and frowning upon colonial expansion as he did, Jekyll was more concerned with and ever on the hunt for the real thing. By riding along with Jekyll on his hunt for African survivals, we can see the countertrends that existed along the touchlines of Britain's dominant society.

As far as Jekyll was concerned, he had found the real thing in his friend and protégé, Claude McKay. McKay would become Jamaica's poet laureate of the twentieth century and, writing as he often did in Jamaican Patois, was considered by many to be the Robert Burns of Jamaica.[37] The following passage from McKay's literary classic *Banana Bottom* (1933) pays homage to Jekyll, who is couched here in the guise of Squire Gensir:

> How different his life had been from the life of the other whites. They had come to conquer and explore, govern, trade, preach and educate to their liking, exploit men and material. But this man was the first to enter into the simple life of the island Negroes and proclaim significance and beauty in their transplanted African folk tales and in the words and music of their native dialect songs. Before him it had been generally said the Negroes were inartistic. But he had found artistry where others saw nothing.[38]

Jekyll had been born into privilege on November 27, 1849, at Bramley House, Guildford, in Surrey. Despite being ordained a deacon, the Harrow- and Cambridge-educated man openly rebelled, questioned the Bible, turned his back on a life in the church, and took a keen interest in the new criticisms of Christianity that Darwin's findings had inspired.[39] In time, Jekyll would also turn his back on England.

A variety of reasons may have contributed to Jekyll's exodus to Jamaica. Initially, he may have been inspired by the paintings of Marianne North, one of the Jekyll family's many celebrity friends.[40] The Jamaican climate also suited Jekyll's struggle with respiratory issues, and a battle with asthma was given as the official reason for leaving England. Still, Jekyll may have been homosexual, and as this was the age of the Oscar Wilde–type witch hunt, the former reverend's "lifestyle" might have figured in his decision. In any case, Jekyll sailed from Southampton to Jamaica on October 24, 1894.[41]

Jekyll, like his famous gardening sister Gertrude, never married, and when the siblings were travelling together in Italy, Jekyll met the Parisian-born English painter Hercules Brabazon, who may have introduced "homosexual desire" to him.[42] If Jekyll was homosexual, however, he cannot be counted among other active and repressed homosexuals of his day who worked fervidly for the colonizing causes of the Empire.[43] For Jekyll, Jamaica was a retreat not an outpost, and the musical horticulturalist soon created a life that eschewed the obligations of Britain's dominant class. Once there, Jekyll became obsessed with the folk traditions of the Jamaican people and, but for one brief return visit to England in 1895, he never left Jamaica again.[44]

Jekyll chose to give up his life within Britain's elite social circle and opted to "live like a peasant except for his books."[45] This decision can be explained, at least in part, by his and his sister's cultural prerogative: the Jekylls were reacting to and rallying against modernity. In their search for the vernacular, the siblings were led back to the land where even the simple act of tilling a garden could be regarded as a form of protest against encroaching modernity.[46] It follows that Jekyll also lamented the presumed abandonment of folkways in not only England but also around the world. His collection of Jamaican songs and stories was his most poignant response.

Unlike the work of others of his era, Jekyll's work would not help to nurture an orthodox English culture. Jekyll was simply not in the nation-building game.[47] Instead, *Jamaican Song and Story* embraced another tradition and allowed for, in no small measure, the history of the other.

Jekyll was not, of course, alone. Attitudes towards national identity among the likes of Jekyll and McKay spoke to an early twentieth-century utopian internationalism. This internationalist philosophy linked the colonized and racially oppressed with others who were not bound to nation-building prerogatives.[48] Internationalists, perhaps as a strategy for healing the displacement caused by slavery, began to reimagine the Empire and gave value to otherness.[49] Internationalism was in many respects akin to the classless utopia of prehistoric times imagined by the English anthropologist Edward Tylor, and offered a suitable articulation for those like Jekyll who cared little for progress and rejected modernism. Importantly, internationalism also anticipated – by a century – new ideas about whiteness.

Many scientists and intellectuals of Jekyll's age, however, were interested in proving the racial superiority of whites and shared little interest in others. Skin spectrometry, craniology, linguistics, and eugenics became, as Colin C. Eldridge confirmed, "the tools of renewed racial prejudice."[50] Primitive anthropology, too, could be used as a tool, and though Claude McKay may have "devoured greedily" the sixpenny reprints of Herbert Spencer's work, that philosopher's theory of survival of the fittest was soon used in scientific racism to illustrate the superiority of whites.[51]

Folklorists and anthropologists could also, in their pursuit of English purity, be vaguely or sometimes certainly racist as they sought to render blacks as a separate, inferior species.[52] Jekyll was not interested in helping assemble a racial hierarchy. While some of his field notes conjure up images of a musical "noble savage," Jekyll did not see himself as a member of a superior Anglo-Saxon race.[53] Though Jekyll was privileged by virtue of his class, position, and skin colour, he was aware of the privilege afforded lighter-skinned people on the island.[54] Ergo, to view Jekyll as but a garden-variety colonist, as some have done, does a disservice to the man, whose ideology suggests a more complex character.[55] Jekyll never went back to England to share his findings with the social elite; he never yearned to leave his Jamaican "laboratory" for home. He was home.

Jekyll's work was assembled at a time when white nation building was occurring throughout the English-speaking, self-governing colonies of the Empire. This was the age of the Natal formula.[56] First employed in the British province of Natal at the end of the nineteenth century, the formula impressed colonial representatives, who believed that it would, by subjecting non-European or nonwhite immigrants to impossible literacy tests, greatly reduce, and in some cases eliminate, undesirable immigration without undermining the Empire's facade of egalitarianism, which promised freedom to all British subjects. Thus, while the language of immigration policy was not necessarily exclusionary (it did not specifically discriminate on grounds of race), a racialized outcome (keeping nonwhite immigrants out of the colonies, including Canada) was achieved.

The construction and consolidation of whiteness was occurring throughout the British colonies during the early twentieth century. This construction was an extension of the late-nineteenth-century move, as described above, to establish the racial superiority of whites. Yet it also addressed a vulnerability in the state of the white race that many influential social and political agents in the British colonies felt needed correcting.[57] This feeling was exacerbated when Japan defeated Russia in 1905 in the Straits of Tsushima. This was one of the few times in history that a white army had been defeated by a nonwhite force.[58] The consolidation of white identity was well under way when Jekyll was writing his book. Lord Milner's public address in 1903, for example, proclaimed: "The white man must rule, because he is elevated by many, many steps above the black man; steps which it will take the latter centuries to climb, and which it is quite possible that the vast bulk of the black population may never be able to climb at all."[59] At a time when white identity building left little room for cultural pluralism, Jekyll's collection, by its very nature, did.

Still, the presence of a white aristocrat in the mountains of Jamaica must have presented an unnatural set of conditions for Jekyll's source singers. The bulk of Jekyll's collection was culled at his Jamaican home, where he would sit his subjects "down to their recital and make them dictate slowly; so the stories and songs are in their *ipissima verba*."[60] For Jekyll, amendments, improvements, or changes of any sort were not tolerated except in the case of toning down the language or subject matter lest the volume found its way into a nursery.[61] Jekyll was interested in a strict reading of the ethnological data; it was always about the melody, the "very word," the "article," the "real" Jamaica.[62]

Mr. Clerk

Following closely in the footsteps of Walter Jekyll was Astley Clerk, who was born in Montego Bay in 1868 and was likewise on the hunt for the "real" Jamaica. Clerk's paternal grandmother was a "mistress of African descent." In Jamaica's incredibly nuanced parlance relating to racial hues, Clerk's father was, according to the *Jamaica Journal*, "the second son of a dark skin 'coloured,'" while his mother was of "Scottish ancestry."[63] Clerk's interest in Jamaican folklore and music was manifest in the establishment of the Cowen Music Rooms in Kingston. Here, Clerk organized concerts and musical competitions and began the long-standing annual Christmas show at Kingston's Ward Theatre.

Clerk provides another example of someone who complicates the construction of whiteness. In 1913, he gave a lecture on "The Music and Instruments of Jamaica" and took on the Institute of Jamaica for its British elitism and its decision to withhold certain texts from him throughout the course of his research.[64] Clerk was no doubt influenced by Jekyll and dedicated his published lecture to the Englishman.[65]

All told, Clerk collected some four hundred Jamaican folk songs, a number that far exceeded Jekyll's seminal collection. Moreover, Clerk notated the music and vocal stylings of some of Jamaica's street vendors of his time, which were then performed by Spanish Town's famous tenor Granville Campbell.[66]

Clerk also edited the Kingston-based *Winkler's Musical Monthly,* a periodical that published open debates on the subjects of race and music and, more specifically, estimations on the value of the African element within Jamaican music.[67] As the *Jamaican Journal* attested, Clerk "proclaimed his resolution to any ambivalence in favour of Jamaica. This was exceptional for his time and even more so given the privileged social and racial status which he enjoyed in society."[68] Like Jekyll, Clerk famously defended the use of Patois by the island's poets, including Claude McKay. As the *Daily Gleaner* reported:

> [Mr. Clerk] attaches importance to native dialect, and joins issue with those who would discourage its use as a means of poetic diction, for the reasons that it is the vernacular and, therefore, a true representation, it has its own peculiar charms, on investigation it can be made to disclose the history of our people: on certain important lines of development, it has its own individuality and genius and inimitably conjures up images too elusive for description in the words by the most erudite English. It is true to its function as a vehicle of thought.[69]

Clerk was awarded the Musgrave Medal in 1937 for his work in the development of Jamaican orchestral music and for his efforts to preserve the folklore of Jamaica.[70] Half a century after Clerk received his medal, and three thousand kilometres to the north, in Toronto, his grand-nephew Dr. Tomaz Jardim, one of the world's foremost collectors and authorities of Bob Marley's music, would take up reggae guitar.

Jekyll's and Clerk's collections remained the only works of their kind until Jamaica began to develop its native culture in the years leading up to the Second World War. This move inspired new interest in African heritage and its potential to buttress the country's cultural narrative, and it drew heavily on Jekyll's and Clerk's findings.[71] The evidence suggests that Jekyll and Clerk were hardly moved by the European heritage in Jamaican musical culture.[72] At the same time, these two quiet rebels complicated notions about whiteness and blackness decades before the first reggae song was sung.

The Collection

Musically, Jekyll was supremely qualified to undertake his study. A competent pianist, he possessed a fine voice and a broad knowledge of music.[73] He used a piano "to record the native airs he wrote down,"[74] and he used multiple singers to capture and correct any nuance of a given melody.[75] But these practices proved difficult for the collector, as the source singers "varied the tunes according to their whim."[76] The folklorists of Jekyll's and Clerk's time often cast the source singer as a "musical noble savage."[77] The English folklorist Lucy Broadwood, for example, was delighted that nearly all the Dunsfold singers she had engaged for her study were illiterate.[78]

Likewise, the so-called folk in the Port Royal Mountains, just beyond the reach of the island's bustling capitol of Kingston, may have satisfied Walter Jekyll's own pursuits. Jekyll let his readers know when he felt that he had lost the scent of the "African" during the hunt: "What I take to be certainly primitive about them is the little short refrains, like 'Carry him go'long' (Dry Bone) and 'Commando' (Annancy and Hog). These suggest tapping on a drum ... some of the tunes are evidently popular songs of the day ... but others are a puzzle, showing as they do a high order of melodic instinct."[79] Such observations hammer home the author's suppositions about what African survivals might or should resemble, but they also give Jekyll's work an elasticity that avoids an absolutist approach.

Jekyll declared that his was not a definitive collection but rather "a mere sample both of stories and song" and that those districts outside of the Port Royal Mountains would, necessarily, have their own sings that were reliant on their own local topics.[80] Jekyll collected his stories and songs at a time in Jamaica when those in their seventies could remember the days of sugar and slavery.[81] The ethnographer witnessed first-hand what Jamaican historian Philip Sherlock has dubbed "the living roots."[82]

Jekyll also became the first to document the Jamaican interpretation of Annancy (or, at least, his idea of it).[83] Annancy the spider served as the central figure of this collection of parables and songs of the animal-fantasy variety.[84] As Rex Nettleford explains in his preface, Annancy is the national folk hero who throughout Jekyll's collection embodies the Jamaican spirit "in his ostentatious professions of love, in his wrong-and-strong, brave-but-cowardly postures of bluff, in his love for leisure and corresponding dislike for work, in his lovable rascality."[85] Perhaps most importantly, though, Brer Annancy was a survivor, one who captured the imagination of his audience, helping them to survive racism, inequity, and even slavery.

The collection, then, illustrated the evolution of a real, indigenous Jamaican folk tradition through the hybridity of African and European influences. Jekyll broke down the collection into four separate parts: (1) "Annancy Stories," which often, but not always, included an accompanying piece of music; (2) "Digging Sings," which were sung during field labour and were distinctive given their call-and-response style; (3) "Ring Tunes," an extension of Annancy stories that referred to "playing in the ring," which had originated, in part, from English children's games; and, finally, (4) "Dancing Tunes," which reinterpreted popular melodies that had been disseminated in Jamaica by visiting sailors.[86]

Much to Jekyll's chagrin, hybridity was a dominant feature of the collection. Part of Jekyll's view on hybridity is revealed in McKay's *Banana Bottom* when Squire Gensir shows Bita Plant a native Jamaican tune from the "hill country" that had been fiddled and sung to a dance called the minto (probably "mento") but whose melody was originally Mozart's.[87]

Her imagination captured, Bita asks Squire Gensir whether there were other Jamaican tunes that had not been "original," to which he replies: "Some are; some aren't. I don't think it matters. Everybody borrows or steals and recreates in art. Next to enjoying it, the exciting thing is tracking down sources and resemblances and influences."[88] Yet Jekyll seems at times to mourn the European influence within his collection while otherwise taking obvious delight when something was "thoroughly Jamaican" or "typically Jamaican."[89] Likewise, Jekyll explained that the dancing tunes demonstrated a "marked departure from what may be called the Jamaican type of melody."[90] This was due chiefly to the fact that the bulk of the dancing tunes had come from popular tunes that had been spread by sailors visiting the seaports of Jamaica.[91] Still, Jekyll stressed the adoption of "local topics," pointing out that while melodies may have been retained, "the tunes are refitted with a complete set of new words, describing some incident which has lately happened in the district, or some detail of daily life."[92] In this case, hybridity serves as a golden thread, spanning the earlier folk traditions of Jamaica through to the modern genres of ska and reggae, including the Canadian variety. Jamaicans would continue to be experts in the reimagination of an existing text or song, as evidenced in the centrality of cover songs or do-overs in Jamaican music. Half a century earlier, source singers sang their own hybrid do-overs for the eccentric Englishman.

Not all English folklorists were so eccentric or open-minded. The constructions of Africa and Europe in the discourse of early twentieth-century folklorists reinforced contemporary notions about European and colonial racial superiority.[93] The language used by Broadwood (who also served as folklorist assistant to Ralph Vaughan Williams), for instance, reflected a dangerous consensus held at this time. Discussing Jekyll's collection of Jamaican songs and stories in 1907, Broadwood highlighted the mimetic quality of Jamaica's singers and musicians – in other words, their ability to mimic European melodies and song.[94] Though it is unlikely that Jekyll himself felt this way, these conclusions were later galvanized in the works of two Americans: the ethnomusicologist Helen H. Roberts and the folklorist and ethnographer Martha Beckwith. Writing in the 1920s, Roberts and Beckwith further articulated the perceived dialectic of African and

European survivals in Jamaican music and drew a distinction between the African rhythm and the European melody. Roberts and Beckwith contributed to a racially and ethnically defined body of research concerning Jamaica's musical traditions. Their work, as Daniel Neely explains, "equated organized melodic aptitude with modern European progress, and rhythm with a state of under-development and darkest Africa." Importantly, neither Roberts nor Beckwith consulted Jekyll over the course of her research.[95]

While Broadwood's interpretation of Jekyll's collection may have reinforced a colonial prerogative of European racial superiority similar to Roberts's and Beckwith's work, her contribution to Jekyll's work – an appendix titled "English Airs and Motifs in Jamaica" – demands further consideration.[96] Despite circumstance and tone, a dispassionate rereading of Broadwood's analysis does, indeed, suggest the possibility of linkages between European melodies and Jamaican songs.

According to all the folklorists involved in the publication of Jekyll's collection in England, at least eleven of the fifty-one stories were either directly or indirectly of European origin.[97] Yet even within these eleven, as Alice Werner cautioned, African prototypes may have existed.[98] As with European stories, African stories would also be modified to suit Jamaican sensibilities.[99] Charles Samuel Myers, who also wrote an appendix for the first edition titled "Traces of African Melody in Jamaica," confirmed Lucy Broadwood's assessment that Jamaicans had learned many of the songs via sailors' shanties but stressed that "a community does not adopt exotic music without at the same time exercising selection" and that "adoption always involves adaptation."[100] Though his assessment almost certainly satisfied an underlying colonial prerogative, Myers rightfully claimed that a song is "modified to suit the current canons of taste."[101]

Certainly, the Europeanness of Jamaican musics may not be terribly obvious or celebrated or much discussed, for a variety of reasons, but this does not alter the shared DNA of reggae, rocksteady, and mento with the quadrille, strathspey, and hornpipe.[102] When I spoke with him, the Jamaican-born bassist Peter Holung, who moved to Canada in 1975, spoke of the residue of the British influence on his homeland:

The English, out of all the European countries that occupied Jamaica, had the most influence because they were there the longest – number one – and they were the ones who started out the educational system in Jamaica [and] is still to this day what we know ... So, because of that, England was able to train that sovereign nation in the way how England's culture is ... and that translated down into the poor, because what the poor do in Jamaica ... they try to emulate people who "have" ... and that's the English influence that we still have. We still drive on the left-hand side of the road; we still have the Oxford-York educational standard ... and that just had a whole grasp on our culture. It's bittersweet. They [English] gave us quadrille in music [and] dance. Quadrille, mixed with Kumina, mixed with Pocomania, those three things evolved into what reggae music is today. Long before there was ska and R&B, there was the quadrille, there was Kumina, there was Pocomania on the streets all the time.[103]

Before slaves came to Jamaica, the island's first peoples, the Taino, had fashioned violins out of bamboo and reeds, which, of course, predated the arrival of fiddles, which came with Jamaica's Irish and Scottish overseers and bookkeepers.[104] Yet it was the English and Celtic melodies, dances, and storylines, as Holung suggests, that were absorbed into the canon of Jamaica's folk tradition. This was what the Scots, Irish, and English brought to the island's cultural tableau. And so the jigs, strathspeys, hornpipes, and quadrilles were, as Vivien Goldman correctly notes, "lurking in the soul of mento and other Jamaican musics."[105]

Originating in the royal courts of France in the middle of the eighteenth century, the quadrille had, by the early 1800s, travelled west to the British Isles before sailing on to Jamaica shortly thereafter. The dance calls for four couples in a square and is effectively square dancing (which still commands some currency in Jamaica).[106] The quadrille soon became part of the musical vocabulary of the Scottish and Irish indentured servants who, in turn, introduced it to Jamaica's slaves. Plantation owners used African slaves and indentured servants to perform the dance music for their amusement.[107] These quadrille bands were usually composed of a fiddle, fife, banjo, and, later, a rhumba box, effectively a bass sansa.[108]

Two styles of the quadrille dance developed in Jamaica following emancipation in 1838: the so-called camp and the more formal ballroom.[109] As in the tradition of Trinidad and Tobago's Carnival, enslaved servants used the quadrille to mimic and ridicule their European masters.[110] There were five sections to the quadrille: *le pantalon, l'été, la poule, la trénis,* and *finale* (or *gallop*). Emancipated Jamaican slaves appropriated this fifth and final figure of the camp style of the quadrille, and from it mento music was developed.[111]

Mento was frowned upon by Jamaica's civil and religious elites.[112] Mento was particularly popular and grew in fame with Jamaicans – and tourists – during and after the Second World War.[113] The genre, through singing stars such as Stanley Motta, Ivan Chin, Slim and Slam, Stanley Beckford, the Jolly Boys, Ken Khouri, and the Toronto-bound Lord Tanamo, would inform all the major musical developments on the island in the twentieth century.

In some instances, non-Jamaicans throughout the centuries have been able to discern the Britishness within Jamaican music. This was especially so in places such as Toronto, where non-Jamaicans could regularly hear musicians such as Lord Tanamo perform and discuss mento from the throne of his rhumba box. Over his long career in reggae, Sattalites' co-founder Fergus Hambleton observed that

> Jamaican music is very absorbent, so it's able to absorb a lot of other traditions, you know. I guess I've got an English-Scottish kind of background, and certainly there's a lot of influence there ... The Jamaican culture carries those kinds of elements; it just has those other different components that don't appear in the folk music of England and Scotland ... But a lot of the themes are the same and, of course, a lot of the folk songs came from England and went to Jamaica and were transformed there by adding in certain musical things.[114]

Bajan Canadian Jeffrey Holdip, Canada's premier reggae sound engineer and Nelly Furtado's front-of-house mixer, was likewise uniquely positioned to assess the deep connections between the Caribbean quadrille and Scottish musical antecedents. At one end of the spectrum, Holdip has professionally mixed Jamaican reggae legends such as Augustus Pablo and Gregory Isaacs; at the other, his uncle was a notable fiddle player who toured southwestern Ontario and imparted his knowledge to his young nephew. He observed:

> All these musics ... are dances: jigs, reels, hornpipes, and the strathspey. The strathspey, that's mento ... if you listen to the cadence of the tunes – and they're very complex, some of them can be very complex as a dance ... It's a very complex music and time signature – but if you listen to those traditional Scottish folk, those dance musics, you can pick out the rhythm and go, "Jeez, man, that's where those guys got that from."[115]

Holdip himself learned how to play fiddle, including the various Scottish dances he discussed, while simultaneously embarking on a love affair with reggae music.

Some seventy years before Holdip made the connection between old and new worlds, however, Lucy Broadwood had already revealed, in her appendix to the collector's work, several strains of the English, Scottish, and Irish folk traditions found within Jekyll's compilation. The interconnectedness of the newish Jamaican tradition with older and more current British folk traditions was something that was reinforced throughout the twentieth century in both popular Jamaican music and theatre. Annancy stories, for example, were featured in pantomimes produced by the Little Theatre Movement in Jamaica during the middle of the twentieth century. These presentations were themselves a hybrid of West African storytelling, loosely structured within a British music hall context where vaudevillian representations comingled with slapstick and pathos.[116]

Similarly, few scholars have followed the golden thread of Jamaica's folk tradition and its effect on present-day Jamaican music. A teleological reading of modern Jamaican popular music reveals that dancehall artists drew on its use of the absurd, reggae artists on its storytelling elements, ska artists on its use of the topical, and mento artists on traditional instrumentation as well as the songs and stories themselves.[117] Jekyll's collection strengthened the golden thread found throughout modern Jamaican cultural and artistic expression by supplying a companion text to the island's extant oral traditions.

Fortunately, Broadwood listed the most apparent adaptations of English, Scottish, and Irish motifs in Jekyll's collection. "King Daniel," both premise (a parrot revealing a murder) and melody, can be found in two of the ballads in Frances James Child's collection *The English and Scottish Popular Ballads:* "May Colvin" and "Young Hunting."[118] "The Three Sisters" covers several extant worldwide motifs found not only in the Child ballads but also in a variety of African prototypes.[119] "Pretty Poll," also off of the "May Colvin" or "The Outlandish Knight" storyline, has a melody that Broadwood suggested was "rather reminiscent of one traditional air to the ballad sung still in different parts of England."[120] The melody of "Man Crow" comes from a Worcestershire children's song "A Finger and Thumb Keep Moving," while "Saylan" counts no less than three English antecedents in "The Maid Freed from the Gallows," "The Golden Ball," and "The Prickly Bush."[121] Likewise, "Tacoma and the Old Witch Girl" was borrowed from the triumvirate of "The Keys of Heaven," "Blue Muslin," and "Madam I Will Gi'e You."[122] "War Down a Monkland," was, according to Broadwood, a traditional tune of either English or Irish descent.[123] And she observed that "You Worthless Becca Watson" was definitely a play on "We Won't Go Home Till Morning."[124] "Me Lover Gone a Colon Bay" originated from the children's game song "Here Come Three Dukes a-Riding," while "Crahss-Lookin' Dog Up'tairs" emanated from a northern English and Scottish children's game titled "Hullaballoo Ballie."[125] "Oh We Went to the River" was quite similar to the Scottish dance tune "There's Nae Luck aboot the Hoose," while "Bahs, Bahs, You Married You Wife" also originated from a Scottish or English dance tune.[126] One of the most obvious examples of Scottish hybridity among Jekyll's collection of digging sings can be found in "Gee Oh Mother Mac" (also known as "John Tom"):

> Gee oh Mother Mac, Gee oh John Tom;
> Gee oh Mother Mac, Gee oh John Tom;
> a me lassie gone, Gone oh John Tom.[127]

40   *Hybridity and Jamaican Music*

Such Scottishness abounds in Jamaican culture. Freed slaves, for example, were more apt to take on Scottish names than English ones, as there had been far fewer Scottish masters and a greater number of Scottish indentured servants.

There are several traces throughout the collection's texts that suggest lineages that are neither from a "pure" African nor a pure British Isles folk tradition. "Man-Crow," at least the story portion, was a variation on the theme of Rombas, a story that likely reached Africa via the Portuguese.[128] "Parson Puss and Parson Dog" was, at least in part, derived from the French air "Ah, vous dirai-je, Maman?" while "Complain, Complain, Complain" was a derivative of the Italian "La Mandolinata."[129] And although traces of African American traditions and revival songs were sparse within the collection, Broadwood confirmed that "Bungo Moolatta" was a variation of "O Dem Golden Slippers."[130]

Obvious as the European influences may have been, Jekyll privileged what he considered to be "pure African" in the songs and was acutely aware of the rhythmic differences between the African and European folk-song traditions. According to him, the former had gained "a peculiar and almost indescribable lilt from a peculiarity in the time-organization of the Negro. If you ask him to beat the time with his foot, he does it perfectly regularly, but just where the white man does not do it. We beat *with* the time; he beats *against* it."[131] Such sensitivity to syncopation and nuance in the organization of musical time was crucial to notating such a collection. Olive Lewin, who annotated six collections of Jamaican folk songs in the 1970s, explained that "it was by his considerable knowledge as a musician that [Jekyll] made the most valuable contribution to this all too neglected field of scholarship."[132] In this sense, Jekyll was uniquely positioned to conduct the study given his years of musical training, combined with his having lived on the island for, by 1907, over twelve years.

Among the purer African influences, according to Jekyll, were the digging sings. These were sung during field labour and were often accompanied by the partaking of rum. The most common labour associated with these songs was the digging of yam hills. Digging sings are distinctive for their call-and-response style in which the leader raises the tune, which is met with the bobbin, the short chorus refrain sung by the rest of the men.[133] The nature of the digging sing allows for some improvisation on the part of the leader, who can tailor his lines to topical and almost always humorous matters.[134]

Likewise, ring tunes, an extension of those Annancy songs and parables that refer to playing in the ring, originated, in part, from English children's games. Ring tunes differ from dancing tunes, which are grounded in the storytelling tradition. "Sally Water" is the most common ring tune; it begins with children playing in the ring and frantically culminates with a wheel, or a rapid turning dance. The child left in the ring becomes Sally Water.[135] Similarly, "Quaco Sam," as found in Jekyll's collection, was a central part of Jamaica's creole musical culture in the 1830s.[136] The melody was derived from the Scottish tune "White Cockade." The initial text of the song, relating to the Jacobite Rebellions of 1715 and 1745, had undergone various updates and was even used as a marching song by the British during the War of 1812. The Jamaican version, however, while invoking the Scottish melody, also incorporates an Ashanti tradition – Quaco being the name given to a boy born on the fourth day of the week.[137] This sort of adaptation was noted by Astley Clerk, who described it as Afro-Jamaican.[138]

These were the sorts of Afro-Jamaican qualities in the island's folk traditions that were privileged in Jamaica's cultural renaissance prior to the Second World War. This movement gained even greater traction after Jamaican independence in 1962 when popular poets and musical artists looked inward to the island's own creolized folk traditions. Still, the new musics that emerged out of the post-independence era continued to be informed by external forces from the British Isles and also from the United States.

The omnipresent British connection to the island remains apparent to anyone who visits Jamaica. As Jamaican reggae guitar legend Rannie "Bop" Williams explained:

> We were definitely focused, looking on England for most of our early interests ... We tried to speak like the English; we do like the English ... At school we have those English teachers ... Anyone will tell you that the English had a great influence on Jamaican people and our

music, because they were the ones we used to dance to first and listen to and everything ... We concentrated on English because we had our eyes on England.[139]

In 2012, Jamaica celebrated its fiftieth anniversary of independence from Britain. In a survey conducted the year before, 60 percent of Jamaicans held the view that their country would have been better off had it remained under British rule.[140] While it is well outside the boundary line of this book to fully assess popular opinion polls, this statistic speaks to the importance of the transoceanic cultural currents flowing back and forth between Britain and Jamaica. How important these currents would prove to be in the creation of indigenous Jamaican music and culture.

2

Music of the Black Atlantic

Walter Jekyll died in 1929. Yet musical and cultural conversations between the shores of Britain and Jamaica only intensified in the years after his death. Not ten years after Jekyll passed away, Jamaica began to experience a cultural awakening that privileged those African survivals Jekyll had collected. Mento and then ska, rocksteady, and reggae evolved in response to a growing sense of Jamaican national pride.[1]

The island nevertheless continued to engage in a dialogue with the cultural sensibilities of Great Britain. Following the Second World War, Jamaica in turn began to inform movements within British popular music. At the same time, American jazz, blues, country and western, and rock and roll figured in the maturation of Jamaica's indigenous popular musics. These vital American influences added yet another dimension to the Jamaican sound, and with its catholic blend, Jamaican music proved to be instantly recognizable to British and Canadian audiences.

The transnational nature of Jamaican music, however, transcended musical signifiers. From the colonial period, Britain's Protestant churches blended deeply with the island's African survivals. Linked as they were with the abolitionist movement, various Protestant faiths (Baptists in particular) and their music found favour among black Jamaicans.[2] Many Jamaicans therefore practised Christianity while retaining some elements of African faith traditions. This complicated religious duality endured and remained an important piece of the cultural baggage of Jamaicans, wherever they roamed.

The British educational system also informed the way some Jamaican music was institutionalized and disseminated. This was evidenced in the remarkable musical output of the graduates of Alpha Boys' School. Alpha graduates profoundly shaped Jamaican music both on the island and in Britain and Canada. The reggae text emerged in concert with these long-standing transnational and transoceanic conversations. Music, faith, and education served as familiar meeting places for Jamaican migrants and their non-Jamaican hosts.

Black Nation Building

Jamaica's cultural awakening occurred in the aftermath of the 1938 labour riots, a period of nation building that privileged, perhaps for the first time, Afro-Jamaican culture. Afro-Jamaican art, storytelling, and music began to find favour, at least superficially, among the island's lighter-skinned elite. "Blackness" was a stock on the rise, and it rose at a time when the country was moving towards independence from Great Britain. Yet to gain political traction for independence, Jamaica's ruling and lighter-skinned class, whether representing the Jamaica Labour Party or the People's National Party, now had to consider and vie for the nation's black voters.

Though Afro-Jamaican traditions were now being lauded in Jamaica by influential agents throughout the country, popular British and American currents continued to gush into the island's musical reservoir. Foreign music was played at Kingston dances and broadcast over the nation's radio wavelengths. The average person living in Jamaica after the Second World War, consequently, was exposed to many external musical influences.[3] Many black Jamaicans nevertheless began to consider their country's own folk traditions in the years leading up to independence in 1962.

One particular champion of native folk traditions rose to prominence in this period. Louise Bennett, a.k.a. Miss Lou, emerged as the godmother of Jamaican folklore.[4] A graduate of London's Royal Academy of Dramatic Art, the breadth of her knowledge of the island's folk traditions was unsurpassed. Bennett's poetry often mixed the joyful metre of mento with sobering content; it anticipated the critical black liberation poetry of reggae artists and dub poets of the 1970s. Bennett's "Bans O' Ooman" (which tackled gender discrimination), "Colour Bar" (which tackled Jamaica's preoccupations with race and racial bias), and "Pinnacle" (which addressed the poor treatment of the island's Rastas) poignantly articulated black Jamaican attitudes. "Bans A' Killing" in particular was a brilliant statement that defended Jamaican Patois by exposing the evolution of the English language itself:

> Yuh wi haffi kill de Lancashire,
> De Yorkshire, de Cockney,
> De broad Scotch and de Irish brogue
> Before yuh start kill me!
> Yuh wi haffi get de Oxford Book
> A English Verse, an tear
> Out Chaucer, Burns, Lady Grizelle
> An plenty a Shakespeare![5]

Written as they were in the 1940s, Bennett's serious poems were fairly revolutionary. And while her persona is so often associated with the merriness of mento and the reinterpretation of classic island folk songs such as "Linstead Market," her early critiques of colonialism should not be ignored as they demonstrate an oppositional thread that ties early island rebel songs such as "War Down a Monkland" (1865) to later songs such as Marley's "Blackman Redemption" (1981).[6]

While her body of work foreshadows a postcolonial paradigm, Bennett would later cast her gaze backwards to an earlier time to pay homage to a certain Englishman. From her unassailable position as the country's most important poet and folklorist of the twentieth century, Bennett suggested that "the present generation of Jamaicans and especially we in the theatre are deeply indebted to Walter Jekyll for so faithfully and painstakingly recording the Jamaican folk stories and songs."[7] Bennett is, after all, Jekyll's collection come alive. Moreover, hers were not simply a faithful rendering of Jamaican folk songs; rather, her songs bore witness to the organic nature of folk musics everywhere – adapting and adjusting in order to survive. Indeed, if one were to draw a line between Jamaica's folk song tradition and the later traditions of ska, rocksteady, and reggae, that line would intersect with Bennett's impressive catalogue of work. As reggae historian Klive Walker confirms, "Louise Bennett's poetry not only serves as sustenance for reggae but is also one of its integral building blocks providing the very language with which it communicates."[8] Bob Marley, who employed dozens of the island's folk sayings throughout his body of work, was intimately familiar with Bennett's treatments. "Concrete Jungle," "Them Belly Full (But We Hungry)," and "Simmer Down" are among the many Marley-penned tunes that harvested Bennett's lexicon.[9]

The folk traditions of Jekyll's age – thanks to Bennett – also helped inform future reggae artists and dub poets. Dub poetry, a subgenre of reggae, captured the essence of Bennett's oppositional poetry, which itself was influenced by the black consciousness work of Edward Kamau Brathwaite and Robin "Bongo Jerry" Small in the 1960s. The United Kingdom's Linton Kwesi Johnson, Jamaica's Mutabaruka, and Canada's Michael St. George, Clifton Joseph, and Lillian Allen are greatly indebted to Bennett's groundbreaking artistry. So, too, were Canadian reggae acts such as Ernie Smith and Messenjah. Rupert "Ojiji" Harvey of Canada's Messenjah recalled: "We used to all gather around the radio on a certain day when she came on. We never missed Louise Bennett."[10] Few did.

Reggae's link to its folksy past, to earlier creolized folk traditions, however, has been undervalued by journalists and ethnomusicologists (a theme I return to later). These traditions nevertheless made their way to Canada via the Jamaican migrant musician. Harvey explained that the incorporation of such traditions "was a natural progression for me, I didn't just go and *learn* folk songs. I grew up with that."[11] It was therefore natural for Messenjah to rework Bennett's version of "Emanuelle Road":

> Go down Emanuelle Road, gal and boy fi go bruk rock stone
> Go down Emanuelle Road, gal and boy fi go bruk rock stone
> Bruk dem one-by-one, bruk dem two-by-two
> Bruk dem three-by-three, finger mash no cry
> Remembah ah play wi a play.[12]

It was this folk song, as performed by a Canadian band of Jamaican expats, that won over a skeptical Jamaican crowd when Messenjah first played on the island in 1985.[13]

Faith Music

Nonsecular influences, especially of the Protestant faiths, also made a significant impression on the maturation of Jamaican musics.[14] Pentecostals, Methodists, Nazarenes, and Seventh-Day Adventists were among the Christian groups that took root in Jamaica, and they all figured in the island's musical culture. Jamaicans, however, were able to retain a special place for their African heritage and its attendant rituals while adopting Christianity. When I spoke with her, the Jamaican singer Carol Brown discussed the elasticity that existed within the island's Protestant denominations:

> You know when you're from Jamaica ... so many churches; you've got to visit one of them at some time. My mom had us in the Pentecostal, but I went to just about every church because my school friends would say, "My church is having a supper" or "My church is having a concert," and as a young child, you visit all the churches.[15]

Similarly, before he came to Canada, Mike Smith was introduced to the various Protestant faiths in Jamaica. Smith's dad was a Rastaman, his grandmother was a Baptist, and his uncle's family was Seventh-Day Adventist. Smith felt, however, that he got his "religion" from his dad. He therefore considered himself a "partial Rasta" and believed he learned biblical stories through the lens of his Rasta father.[16]

Contrary to popular perception, though, there are surprisingly few Rastafarians in Jamaica; as of 2011, there were only a little over thirty thousand Rastas, representing roughly 1 percent of the country's population.[17] Men such as Joseph Hibbert, Archibald Dunkley, and Leonard P. Howell helped to popularize the Rasta movement in Jamaica in the 1930s and 1940s. The Jamaican-born Hibbert grew up in Costa Rica, where he was a member of the occult Masonic group the Ancient Mystic Order of Ethiopia. Later, in 1938, Hibbert, alongside Dunkley, launched the Jamaican branch of Haile Selassie's Ethiopian World Federation, while Howell founded Pinnacle, the island's first Rasta commune. Rasta's principal text, the *Kebra Nagast,* is an ancient and sacred text that merges Christ with the Old Testament. Haile Selassie, regarded by Rastas as the 225th regal descendant, traces his lineage back to Menelik, son of Solomon and Sheba, and, thus, he is a direct descendant of Jesus Christ. For Rastas, when Selassie was crowned King of Ethiopia in 1930, biblical prophecy had been fulfilled.[18] The sociophilosophical quotient of Rasta is deeply connected to the Pan-Africanism so prevalent in the works of Marcus Garvey.[19] Elements of the hard-core Rasta movement also harkened back to Kenya's anticolonial rebels' battle cry: "Death to the white oppressor." This battle cry had, by the 1960s, been fine-tuned to call for "Death to black and white oppressors." There nevertheless remained a prevailing binary racialism in the embryonic movement's ideology.[20]

Representing, as they do, only 1 percent of Jamaica's population, Rastafarians have had a disproportionate impact on Jamaican music. This is important when considering the so-called authenticity of what scholars refer to as the cultural text of reggae, a music that was made – at least since its inception and through its glory years of the 1970s and 1980s – by a significant number of non-Rastas.

To be sure, post-Garvey themes such as Zion and its antithesis, Babylon, remain ubiquitous in Rasta imagery and reggae music. In them, Zion and Babylon are not simply metaphors (though they can be used as such) but truly represent heaven and hell, righteousness and idolatry, utopia and a worldly system of oppression enforced by the devil's henchmen, politicians, soldiers, and the police.[21] Willi Williams's "Armagideon Time," written by a resident of Pickering, Ontario, for example, remains a classic piece in the reggae canon, one that was later covered by punk rockers the Clash:

> A lotta people won't get no justice tonight
> So a lotta people going to have to stand up and fight now
> But remember to praise Jehovah
> And He will guide you in this Iration
> It's Armagideon.[22]

This statement on the gravity of the situation on earth became a veritable reggae anthem.

Obeah traditions – West Indian folk magic or sorcery – were likewise abundant in Jamaican folk music and the island's more popular musics.[23]

Duppies, for example, are the souls of the dead. There are good duppies and bad duppies. They roam the earth at night and can assume various forms, both human and animal.[24] For his part, Walter Jekyll observed that "everybody in Jamaica believes in Duppy, and many women and children will not go out at night for fear of meeting one."[25] Future Canadian Ernie Smith's "Duppy or a Gunman" was also a significant hit in Jamaica in 1974:

> It mus be a duppy or a gunman
> I man no fin' out yet
> I an I did so frighten
> All de daughter name I feget.[26]

Superstitions and faith systems of both the European and African variety contributed to the thematic mélange of Jamaican music that would one day be performed in Toronto.

Alpha Boys' School

Jamaica's various musics were given form through a British-style school system that had, together with the island's various Christian missions, cultivated a nationwide musical culture by the end of the nineteenth century.[27] The instruments that British soldiers brought to the island were, by the 1880s, finding use among members of Kingston's fledgling brass bands, who regularly took their sound to the capital's main streets.[28] It was there that the European wind tradition began to coalesce with extant Afro-Caribbean musical forms, furthering the creolization process. More formally, European band masters were imported to assemble and train military brass bands in Jamaica.

Kingston's Alpha Boys' School played an important part in this process. Alpha was founded in 1880 as a home for "wayward boys" by the Jamaican-born Justina Ripoll and her two close companions, Josephine Ximenes and Louise Dugiol.[29] Ten years later, the school was given a boon when the Sisters of Mercy in Bermondsey, London, decided to lend a hand.[30] In terms of approach, it was a classic case of tough love. The sisters provided a mixture of strictness and positive reinforcement.[31]

By 1892, the school boasted the Alpha Drum and Fife Corps. By the end of the first decade of the twentieth century, the famous Alpha Boys' Band was firmly in place and would prove to be a blossoming nursery not only for brass band music in Jamaica but also for the country's popular musical forms of ska, rocksteady, and reggae.[32] The band began operations after receiving a generous gift of brass instruments from the Roman Catholic bishop of Jamaica in 1908.[33] This gift helped to establish the most important musical institution in the island's history, the products of which would, in one way or another, inform most of the essential Jamaican-produced recordings of the twentieth century.[34]

It would not be an overstatement to say that a disproportionate number of foundational Jamaican musicians of the second half of the twentieth century were Alpha alumni. Four of the original Skatalites – Don Drummond, Tommy McCook, Lester Sterling, and Dizzy Moore – were Alpha students. So, too, was reggae drumming legend Leroy "Horsemouth" Wallace, who studied under the school's Lennie Hibbert. Wallace would provide the backing for essential Rasta anthems such as the Abyssinians' "Satta A Massagana" and Burning Spear's "Marcus Garvey."[35]

Certainly, the school's military drum regimen had a profound effect on Jamaica's popular musics. Canadian reggae radio DJ David Kingston observed that

> if you listen to all the reggae drummers from Jamaica from Sly [Dunbar] all the way back, they all go back to Lloyd [Knibb], and they go back to Alpha ... And what do you learn? It's military. They're military drummers; those snares are all military. It's the blood of the Scots rising. You get in your kilt, and you go over the hill ... if you listen to Lloyd and those Skatalites, it's from steady, steady, serious practise of military drumming, band marching, and where does that come from? You're hearing things that are hitting you on a sub-conscious and/or conscious level.[36]

To be sure, there were more elements than military-drumming techniques at play in the evolution of ska. Theophilus Beckford, for example, combined his Alpha schooling with American R&B influences such as

Rosco Gordon to become one of the chief architects of the piano off-beat in ska, but the Alpha quotient remained paramount.[37] As the great Jamaican bandleader Sonny Bradshaw observed: "We didn't have a School of Music ... Alpha was the School of Music."[38] While the country would have a long time to wait before Jamaican music was earnestly taught in the postcolonial period, Alpha Boys' School had met a need and, in so doing, created a sound.[39]

Alpha graduates had the added benefit of being musically literate, which gave them an advantage over other musicians who were perhaps not as theory-savvy.[40] Unsurprisingly perhaps, opportunities on the island were few, compelling some Alpha grads to leave the island and ply their trade in the United Kingdom. Tenor saxophonist Joe Harriott, for example, became a British jazz legend, pioneering an avant-garde form that even predated Ornette Coleman's more famous free jazz movement of the early 1960s.[41] Other Alpha musicians found success in Britain with Jamaican music too. Ska-era trombonist Rico Rodriguez enjoyed something of a renaissance during the two-tone wave in Britain, playing with the Specials in the late 1970s. Similarly, Vin Gordon was a central figure in the British reggae scene and appeared on several crucial Aswad cuts. Trumpeter Eddie "Tan Tan" Thornton, whose dizzying resume includes sessions with Jimi Hendrix, the Beatles ("Got to Get You into My Life"), the Rolling Stones, and Georgie Fame, still found time for reggae, playing with Bob Marley, Boney M., and Aswad.[42] Perhaps most notably, Desmond Dekker had what might be considered the first international Jamaican hit with the "Israelites" in 1968, which charted in the United Kingdom, United States, and Canada.[43]

A few Alpha grads headed north to Toronto. Sheiks' saxophonist Headley Bennett (a.k.a. Deadly Headley), for example, relocated for a time to the Great White North in the late 1960s, as did Karl "King Cannonball" Bryan and "Warrior" composer Johnny Osbourne, who led Ishan People (the first reggae band to be signed to a major label in Canada) before returning to Jamaica to embark on a highly successful solo career.[44]

One Alpha Boy stayed in Toronto and would, over time, become one of Canada's most influential reggae ambassadors. Jo Jo Bennett was born into West Kingston's notorious ghetto. When he was two, Bennett's mother took him to a children's home, hoping that he would have a better chance in life. When he was ten, he went to Alpha, where he learned bookbinding, gardening, shoemaking, carpentry and, of course, music. Under the tutelage of the classically trained Ruben Delgado, Bennett picked up the trumpet (though he would change to flugelhorn in Canada). When I spoke with him, he commented: "Well, in the military band, it was mostly the classical stuff, you know ... Beethoven and all them guys but in a different form, like a brass-band form. But it's the same classical type of music, Calypso and a little bit of classical, because that's what I learned, and that's what I grew up on."[45] Bennett successfully made first solo trumpet in the Alpha Military Band and lead trumpeter in the Jamaica Military Band.[46] This was no easy feat. As the celebrated Jamaican dancer and author Ivy Baxter concluded in 1970, the Jamaica Military Band "formed ... the nucleus of any musical ensemble."[47] Alpha gave Bennett the gumption to survive as a working musician in Jamaica. His horn brought him to Toronto but not before he served an important term blowing in Byron Lee's group, which happened to be one of the island's (and later the world's) most popular ska bands.[48]

The Making of Jamaican Pop Music: Ska

Technology changed the way music was carried and shared among the Jamaican public. Musical evolution and fusion were no longer reliant on what was carried by boat or by foot. The sale of broadsides, the advent of the gramophone and 78s, and, eventually, the introduction of radio accelerated the island's absorption of popular music from the British and American canon. From the late nineteenth century onward, vaudeville entertainments, "race records" from the early blues and swing era, and American R&B found currency among those Jamaicans who possessed the means to afford a piano, gramophone, or wireless.[49] The famous early twentieth-century Jamaican street-singing duo Slim and Slam drew as much from popular "outside" musical currents as they did from Jamaica's own folk heritage.[50]

By the late 1950s, American R&B was immensely popular in Jamaica, playing on popular shows on Radio Jamaica and Rediffusion (RJR).[51]

During the day, Jamaicans who could afford a radio might also tune into the Spanish-language station broadcasting American songs by artists such as Elvis Presley and Pat Boone. At night, many listened to WINZ out of Miami. As Jay Douglas recalled:

> That's when you get the real deal ... Professor Longhair, B.B. King, James Brown, Bobby "Blue" Bland. Thank God for all of that. You have to have your pencil and paper ready fi ketch dem lyrics yu know, Papa. You have to go to the jukebox with your sixpence and punch the song over and over fi get de lyrics fi learn it.[52]

Once again, Jamaicans were ready and able to artfully reimagine the songs washing onto their shores.

Before the ska craze took hold of the island, American R&B was king at the various sound system (or mobile disco) dances of the 1950s. It was at these dances that people from rural areas and members of the urban proletariat could be exposed to the fresh American sounds without having to buy records or a record player, or even own a radio.[53] Sound system DJs such as Tom the Great Sebastian and Duke Reid carefully selected from imported American records for their highly competitive (and often violent) dances. Rosco Gordon, Fats Domino, and Louis Jordan were particularly popular.[54] Radio re-created a process that had occurred a century previous among travelling sailors. Now, British pop, calypso from Trinidad, American soul, R&B, country and western, and jazz were all being broadcast across the island's wavelengths.[55]

At first blush, country and western may seem like a red herring, but it certainly belongs as a piece in the puzzle of Jamaican music. Country music fit in with Jamaicans' love of the western movie and frontier justice and later informed the aesthetics of the rude boy during the age of ska. Moreover, the storytelling component of the music – especially among artists such as Johnny Cash – had great currency with Jamaicans.[56] Cash's tunes about violence, murder, and prison were particularly popular in Jamaica. They were also really well-crafted songs. With them, Cash, alongside Hank Williams and Patsy Cline, managed to carve out a place within the island's popular culture.[57]

Country music's lyrical text also had a universality that resonated with people in Jamaica.[58] Reggae legend Toots Hibbert and future Jamaican Canadian artists such as Ernie Smith and Earle "Mighty Pope" Heedram were profoundly influenced by country and western, and in their own work they would give what Klive Walker describes as "a Jamaican flavour in a very creative way, because it was part of the building blocks, part of the tools that you use. Everybody's music is as a result of stuff that they've heard and that they've imbibed."[59] Indeed, when not imbibing Otis Redding, Heedram was devouring Charlie Pride, Hank Williams, and Johnny Cash: "We used to sit up as kids listening to this radio station that used to come on shortwave from Miami. Strangely enough, it was a lot of country music ... They're telling a story. God, I have periods where it's all I listen to, the pain in their voice."[60] When he played some of Canada's more remote places, before audiences who had not had a lot of contact with black people before, Heedram was often called Charlie Pride.[61] For seminal reggae guitarist and future Jamaican Canadian Rannie "Bop" Williams, country music provided a soundtrack to his youth. Cash's "Ring of Fire" is Rannie's song![62] Ernie Smith's country music experience is more quantifiable. In 1975, a couple of years before Smith moved to Toronto, he wrote "Tears on My Pillow," which was performed and produced by the American singer Johnny Nash. The single would be Nash's only number-one single in the United Kingdom.[63]

While the storytelling aspect of country music claimed many Jamaican admirers, American jazz also deeply affected the island's musical culture. For many, jazz offered a space that united people who may have previously been separated by economics, race, and other signifiers. Jazz also anticipated the more liberal political clime that reggae brought in the 1970s.[64] For Jamaican musicians, jazz opened up a new musical vocabulary. The improvisational sensibilities in jazz, for instance, can be found in Jamaican ska. Indeed, members of the Skatalites' horn section were all "jazzers" first and were likely encouraged by the successes of expat Joe Harriott in the United Kingdom.[65] Jamaican musicians, trained as they were in the military tradition, were ready to deliver a distinct, native sound. They were now able to bring together older Jamaican musical forms, such as mento, and supplement them with multifarious trends in British and American popular culture to produce a uniquely Yard sound.[66]

Music of the Black Atlantic   55

When it finally did arrive (unofficially in 1959), ska showed up with an attitude.[67] Born out of the music, ska's rude boy image – replete with high-cuff pants, suspenders, and boots – came to embody a vast segment of Jamaica's disenfranchised youth who had left the island's rural areas to find work in cities such as Montego Bay and Kingston.[68] These youth, including some women, were disillusioned by the lack of opportunity and became highly oppositional, defying authority, speaking in highly codified Jamaican Patois, drinking white rum and Red Stripe (often to excess) and, for some, engaging in petty crime. The Mighty Pope recalled his experience with the early rude boy era before he moved to Toronto, when many Jamaicans were particular about speaking "proper" English: "they did not like the way the [ska] records were and the things they were saying ... It wasn't as vulgar as what's out there now, with the rap, but it ... wasn't proper English; it wasn't Queen's English."[69] The rude boy image had been cobbled together by Jamaican youth via a variety of cultural commodities that had found their way to the island, including western films, television shows such as *Bonanza,* and the James Bond film series, the first of which was filmed in Kingston and surrounding area in 1962.[70]

Ska's rough edge was, of course, part of its appeal. The rude boy aesthetic had become the "look" of ska. And ska artists also had a publicly relaxed attitude towards and association with the Rasta movement. This association, however, didn't work for everyone. It would seem that some people could only engage in rude boy behaviour quietly.

The ownership of rude boy culture also depended on one's address. If the Skatalites were the gritty "downtown" Kingston ensemble, Byron Lee and the Dragonaires, from Jamaica's north coast, were the country's polished "uptown" act. In what was one of the more controversial developments in Jamaica's musical history, it was the Dragonaires – with guest singers Prince Buster, Eric "Monty" Morris, and Millie Small – who were chosen over the Skatalites to represent Jamaica at the 1964 World's Fair in New York. The selection upset those who believed the Dragonaires' rude boy cred was less believable than that of the Skatalites.[71]

While the Dragonaires may have been the first to bring ska to the world, it was the Skatalites – stacked with Alpha talent – who produced success after success, often remaking hits from the American and British pop music world. The same year the band was overlooked for the World's

56   *Music of the Black Atlantic*

Fair, it made good with an unlikely cover of Dimitri Tiomkin's "The Guns of Navarone."[72] The song was based on the theme music from the movie of the same name, which starred Gregory Peck, David Niven, and Anthony Quinn. Having a finger on the pulse of the musical trends of Britain and America was vital to Jamaica's musical rude boys.

Foreign music held sway in the early ska era. Bob Marley, for example, was employed by producer-magnate Coxsone Dodd to listen to 45s coming out of the United States to see which ones could be covered in a reggae style.[73] Indeed, Bob Marley and the Wailers at one point dressed in gold lamé jackets and did renditions of Burt Bacharach and Hal David's "What's New Pussycat" and the Beatles' "And I Love Her."[74] Yet these processes of adaptation simply continued a long-standing Jamaican musical tradition that had begun centuries earlier in the island's ports, places where sea shanties, strathspeys, and quadrilles were reimagined for a domestic audience. This tradition continued when reggae arrived in the early 1970s.

Reggae Routes: Kingston, London, Toronto, and Back Again

Rock and roll also penetrated the Jamaican airwaves. Somewhat bizarrely, it was the Canadian rock band Bachman Turner Overdrive's "You Ain't Seen Nothing Yet" that was the first song that Peter Holung, honing his craft as a musician in Kingston, Jamaica, learned to play in 1974 before coming to Toronto.[75] Perhaps more impactful was the fact that from the early 1970s onward, Bob Marley and the Wailers began to explore a rock-reggae fusion that incorporated elements of rock's heavy sound.[76] American rock guitarist Wayne Perkins, for example, added pedal steel while American rock organist John "Rabbit" Bundrick supplied additional keyboard vibes to Marley's *Catch a Fire* album.[77] (The former later confessed that reggae had been so foreign to him at the time that he had no idea where beat one was.)[78] Two American lead guitarists would later be added to the Wailers' fold as full-time touring members, Donald Kinsey and Al Anderson. Later still, the Jamaican-born British guitarist Junior Marvin would serve as the Wailers' resident rocker. For some scholars, the choice to include rock guitar ranks among the list of commercial compromises that Marley made to achieve his success.[79] Yet many of Marley's successes did not simply fuse rock with Jamaican reggae; they had also been recorded – sometimes in part and sometimes wholly – in England. The centuries-old cultural dialogue that stretched across the black Atlantic may never have been more stirring than it was in 1976, when Marley crafted his genre-defining *Exodus* album in both Kingston and London.

Britain's reggae scene predates the Canadian brand of the genre. In 2011, legendary Jamaican record producer Bunny Lee declared that England was "the gateway to reggae music."[80] The British Jamaican musical linkages actually grew stronger after Jamaica gained its independence from Britain in 1962, the year Lee began working for Duke Reid's Treasure Isle label in Kingston.[81] Certainly, some of the more important staples in the canon of popular Jamaican music were recorded in England. From Prince Buster's seminal ska overture "Madness" to Marley's *Exodus,* England remained a vital venue and launch pad for Jamaica's various art forms.[82] Just as the mother country had introduced the poetic works of Claude McKay to the world during the First World War, so too did England break ska, rocksteady, and reggae to the baby-boomer generation.

Millie Small's "My Boy Lollipop" (1964) was a watershed moment in Jamaican music and, by extension, Reggae Britannica. Produced by Chris Blackwell and arranged by Ernest Ranglin, who was then living in Britain, Small's single represented the first international hit for Jamaica's fledgling popular music. Some 6 million copies were sold, and the song hit number one on the UK charts and number two on the American hit parade.[83] On the heels of this success, several ska artists chose to try the British market out by relocating there. Wilfred "Jackie" Edwards, Owen Gray, and Bajan-born Jackie Opel moved to London and experienced varying degrees of success.

Adaptation was not, however, a one-way process. By the mid-1970s, reggae-esque arrangements had begun to appear in music made by the top British and American pop and rock groups of the day. The Eagles' "Hotel California," 10CC's "Dreadlock Holiday," Kate Bush's "Kite," Steely Dan's "Haitian Divorce," Paul Simon's "Mother and Child Reunion," and Led Zeppelin's "D'yer Mak'er" were among the many popular songs that used reggae.[84] There were direct translations too. Bizarrely, Eric Clapton's version of Marley's "I Shot the Sheriff" reached number one on both the US and UK charts in 1974.[85] American soul singer Johnny Nash also had some success with Marley's "Stir It Up" and his own reggae-fied "I Can See Clearly Now."[86] While these tributes demonstrated the significant inroads that reggae had made into pop's mainstream, the pop artists' treatment of the genre divorced its lighter aspects from its original rebellious Jamaican text.

Some record companies tried to make reggae, rocksteady, and ska more accessible to a wider British audience. One famous example was when the England-based Trojan Records added strings to Bob and Marcia's "Young Gifted and Black." While it could be argued that this was a classic case of co-option, Jamaican Bob Andy was pleased to be a part of the experiment: "I was very satisfied and very pleased with the strings. And, so, to hear a Jamaican recording – probably the first – to be so well endowed with such beautiful arrangements, it felt good to be a part of that."[87] Further, it is unlikely that even the more skeptical ethnomusicologists would draw into question Trojan's commitment to the proliferation of Jamaican music since 1968.

By the mid-1970s, British reggae was beginning to develop its own text. Initially performed by first- and second-generation West Indian musicians living in Britain, such as Matumbi, Aswad, and Steel Pulse, the British reggae text soon branched out to include non-West Indian musicians. Multiracial bands such as UB40, the Specials, and the Beat took Jamaican music into even more British households.[88]

Indeed, British reggae began to inform aspects of Jamaican reggae. London's Aswad, for example, were particularly influential. Aswad was Burning Spear's backing band for his classic *Live* album, which was recorded on tour in 1977.[89] That same year, members of Aswad and Third World joined Bob Marley in a London studio to record an updated version of Curtis Mayfield's "Keep on Moving."[90] Dennis Brown, Jamaica's "Crown Prince" of reggae, also used Aswad's "Love Fire" rhythm track for his own "Promised Land."[91] Spear, Marley, and Brown were not fringe players on reggae's periphery; they were leaders on the genre's international stage and, as such, tacitly issued Aswad a stamp of approval. Music that had fused African and European musical traditions in Jamaica had been ferried by the Jamaican migrant to Britain, only to come full circle back across the black Atlantic to Jamaica via a British reggae band.

These were transnational, cross-cultural, and organic sounds that had been centuries in the making. Reggae was, of course, grounded by the African drum, but it had also taken on the playfulness of a quadrille dance, mento's joyful off-beat strum, the discipline and instrumentation of a military brass band, the heartache of a country and western storyline, the improvisational potential opened up by jazz, and the catharsis of a distorted rock guitar solo. And this sound evolved outside of any one place and was constrained to neither Kingston nor London.

3

Jamaica to Toronto

Certainly, Toronto was another place where reggae happened. Music played a significant role in the acculturation process for Jamaicans who migrated to the city. Migrants who had a close association with music and the music industry believe they had an advantage over other migrants in the acculturation process. They felt that they were able to draw strength from the sense of community that music and musicians can provide, and they were able to build bridges through music into the city's mainstream culture. For many, this was a good strategy for success in their new adopted land. Moreover, some felt that they were able to articulate the struggle of their own acculturation process through their art, which engendered a much-needed dialogue with non-Jamaicans.

Before this dialogue could occur, however, Jamaicans had to get to Canada. The possibility for black Jamaicans to gain access to Canada was often calibrated to the official policies of the Canadian government. These policies were in tune with popular and pervasive attitudes about race and culture in Canada. And these attitudes were often trumped only by economic need or outside forces that compelled Canada to open its doors to Jamaican workers further.[1] In time, the doors would be cracked open. From the end of the 1960s right through to the 1980s, Jamaica provided nearly 40 percent of Canada's black immigration.[2]

At the same time, a variety of push factors were compelling migrants to leave Jamaica. Cyclical political violence in the country convinced many Jamaicans to embark on a new life in Canada. Most of those who did so believe that their exodus to Canada was a worthwhile endeavour and that the burden of the journey was assuaged by music.

Jamaicans and Canadian Immigration

It could be argued with some conviction that reggae's zenith was achieved with the release of Bob Marley and the Wailers' *Exodus* in 1977.[3] Recorded in England, this genre-defining album would later be called "Album of the Century" by *Time* magazine.[4] With *Exodus,* Marley retold a story that had long resonated with the Jamaican migrant. And Marley was certainly not the first Jamaican to tell it. In 1970, for instance, the Melodians recorded "By the Rivers of Babylon," a song that liberally borrowed from *Psalm* 137:1 and outlined the exodus narrative some seven years before Marley's reggae masterpiece: "'Cause the wicked carried us away, captivity, required from us a song. / How can we sing King Alpha's song in a strange land?"[5] Earlier still, in 1956, American singer Harry Belafonte, the son of a Jamaican housekeeper, introduced mento to the world with his staggeringly popular "Jamaica Farewell":

> But I'm sad to say, I'm on my way
> Won't be back for many a day
> My heart is down, my head is turning around
> I had to leave a little girl in Kingston Town.[6]

Migration for the Jamaican, then, was commonplace. Invariably, someone's uncle had "gon a Englan" to work in London's underground while someone else's sister had "gon a Cyanada" as a domestic or nurse. Yet entry to Canada was not always easily secured, as the official policy of the Canadian government was to ensure that the Jamaican Canadian population remained low.

The black population in Canada had always been modest. The number of blacks living in Canada in 1881, for example, was 21,400, less than half of 1 percent of the approximately 4,324,000 people living in Canada at the time.[7] This number was more or less in stasis for the next fifty years. There was even a small dip, down to 19,500, in 1931, the result of a particularly xenophobic era. From that point through to the end of the Second World War, black immigration to Canada was heavily curtailed.[8] The vast majority of Canadians remained white, and approximately half of the population claimed English, Irish, Scottish, or other British descent.[9]

Race commanded a significant role in the government's decision-making processes regarding who were or were not allowed into Canada. Black West Indians did not rate high on the "were" list. Canada may well have been a nation of immigrants, but only a selected few blacks managed to get in.[10] Officially, Canada may have trumpeted an "open door" policy that appeared to encourage immigration, but the fine print set terrific restrictions on just how far the door would be opened.

A variety of rationales – some transparent, others opaque – kept many black migrants out of Canada. First, there was a biological argument crafted within the antiquated An Act Respecting Immigration (1910), which prohibited, at least to 1962, "the landing in Canada of immigrants belonging to any race deemed unsuited to the climate or requirements of Canada."[11] Simply put, the government suggested that the Canadian climate was too cold for Caribbean blacks.

While Depression-era racism in Canada might have lacked the chilling consequences that its American counterpart produced, the sentiment was, nevertheless, just as pervasive and ugly. On July 11, 1936, for example, Fred Christie, a Jamaican-born black man living in Montreal, and a couple of friends were refused service at the York Tavern, which had been recently relocated to the Montreal Forum, home of the Canadiens hockey team, of which Christie was a fan. The tavern refused to serve Christie on the grounds that he was black. Christie implored the local police to persuade the tavern staff to reconsider. The police did nothing, and four years later Christie's case went to the Supreme Court of Canada. His claim, however, was rejected; the court ruled that the commercial interests of the tavern keepers trumped the rights of a "coloured" person in Canada. A decade later, on November 8, 1946, Viola Desmond refused to sit in the balcony designated exclusively for blacks in the Roseland Theatre in New Glasgow, Nova Scotia, and was subsequently fined twenty-five dollars for ignoring the theatre's unofficial racist policy.[12]

Some social theorists of the day were concerned about the future of British racial balance in Canada. In 1943, for instance, one *Saturday Night* journalist suggested that Canada would have to devise a postwar immigration policy in which "the cardinal consideration ... must be to keep the British content in the population dominant."[13] It seemed, at least in the immediate postwar period, that immigration policy would ensure the dominance of British content. Certainly, the country experienced a significant increase in immigration, the likes of which had not been seen since the early 1920s. Yet while the number of immigrants that came to Canada between the end of the Second World War and 1960 was considerable (over 2 million), the type of immigrant remained mostly British and nearly entirely white.[14] Though most Canadians had become painfully aware of human rights issues following the war's end, it took a long time for popular opinions – and policy – to catch up with the nation's official sentiment, as expressed in the signing of the United Nations' Universal Declaration of Human Rights in 1948.

Popular attitudes towards race had a symbiotic relationship with the country's immigration policy-making, a relationship that endured well after the Second World War. Caribbean blacks were being incorporated within a global labour market where they adapted to Western policies, racialized laws, and prevailing attitudes towards blackness. Some scholars have suggested that a conspiratorial world order (held primarily between the United States, the United Kingdom, Australia, and Canada) existed at this time, uniformly constructing the racial category of "black" and placing it at the bottom of the heap in terms of state policy-making.[15] These First World governments monitored one another's handling of black immigration policies. While the language of these policies became less overtly racist, a new, nonracial language emerged that enabled nation-states to achieve similar racialized ends.[16] A real paradox was created when immigration policies that were vague regarding blacks were tested by Canadian employers specifically interested in black Caribbean labour. This was the case for Jamaican domestic servants and nurses who came to Canada (and mostly Toronto) in the 1950s.[17]

The old argument of climatic unsuitability was increasingly viewed with suspicion by some Canadians in the 1950s. The government, as the *Canadian Unionist* explained in 1954, "has itself admitted that it has no statistics available to support" this theory.[18] And just to be clear, there never was any evidence in support of it.[19]

Toronto's black community actively tested and resisted these racist policies and attitudes. The Toronto-based Negro Citizenship Council, led by the Bajan-born Don Moore, applied force from the 1950s onward. The council was one of the first black delegations to be received in Ottawa, in 1954, when it lobbied for the admittance of West Indian nurses and domestic labourers. Their proposal found favour with some MPs, given the country's growing need for both types of labour. The brief the council presented to Walter Harris, then minister of citizenship and immigration, recommended several amendments to the Immigration Act. Specifically, the brief called on officials to review the definition of "British subject" and to amend the act "so as to include all those who are, for all other purposes, regarded as 'British subjects and citizens of the United Kingdom and commonwealth.'" It also asked that "provision be made in the Act for the entry of a British West Indian, without regard to racial origin, who has sufficient means to maintain himself until he has secured employment."[20] During his campaign, Moore identified the racial prejudices that informed policy-making in Canada, comparing, as he did, Canadian immigration policies with those of the apartheid regime in South Africa. The council – with Moore in the vanguard – helped to affect real and positive change.[21]

On the strength of Moore and company's efforts, in the late 1950s Canadian immigration officials began to seek out young, healthy, educated black women in the Caribbean who had no dependants to come to Canada for domestic work. This workers' program, however, contradicted attitudes towards blacks that were prevalent in the era before the points system, allowing, as it did, black immigrants into Canada to work who did not necessarily meet the sponsor requirements set out in official immigration policy. The demand for domestics – especially in Toronto's upper-scale neighbourhoods – prevailed over other considerations, including, most significantly, maintaining the "racial balance."[22]

While these initiatives satisfied a demand for domestics and nurses, they fell short of changing attitudes in Toronto, not to mention the rest of the country. The earliest wave of Jamaican nurses, for example, experienced a sense of isolation in Toronto, and racially based obstacles did much to restrict their access to mainstream society. Many of the nurses were demoted to aides and assistants upon their arrival. Jamaican-born singer Jay Douglas explained the limitations that his young mother faced when she arrived in Toronto as a domestic worker in the 1950s:

> It wasn't easy ... She worked in the homes. Most [domestic workers] got their day off on Thursday. Working in those English and Jewish homes – hard work too. They didn't really have anywhere to go. They had to meet each other on the streets, and they'd probably go to stores, and then they sat in restaurants until it was time to go back in.[23]

Some of the children of these often lonely domestics and nurses would nevertheless play a role in Toronto's nascent reggae scene.[24]

Strong-willed Jamaican women pushed back and successfully argued for equality on the grounds that they had been British-trained. They were, after all, nurses, not just "black nurses" of some lesser value. This particular wave of workers also took pride in mixing with other races and cultivating relationships with "others" on their own initiative and terms.[25] Moreover, as West Indian neighbourhoods began to flourish and take root on Eglinton Avenue and Bathurst Street by the late 1960s, the sense of isolation that Jamaican nurses and domestics felt began to give way to a greater sense of community.[26]

But long before this sense of community emerged, Canada's flagrant bigotry of the Second World War era shifted to the equally abhorrent if quiet racism that has defined so much of Canada's race relations. This systemic racism found expression in a variety of ways during the 1950s. *Saturday Night* journalist Gordon Donaldson, for example, confirmed that in the small community of Dresden, Ontario, blacks were refused "a shave in a barbershop, a game of pool or a meal in a restaurant because they were Negroes."[27] In another instance, Sault Ste. Marie's *Daily Star* came to the defence of a local resort owner who refused black guests so as not to offend American tourists.[28] Likewise, in a survey of Toronto landlords, 50 percent of respondents admitted that they would not rent apartments or houses to blacks.[29]

This survey is even more disconcerting when the black population of Canada at the time is considered. In 1958, the total number of "Negroes" in Canada was under 25,000.[30] And while Canada's problem with discrimination was relatively small when compared to the monstrous one percolating in the United States, it was not, as Donaldson affirmed, "because Canadians are noticeably more tolerant than anybody else but because the Department of Citizenship and Immigration has done its best to keep Negroes out."[31] Very few Jamaican blacks had managed to slip into Canada since the First World War, and the country's black population was in stasis. Nevertheless, one-third of the 4,400 blacks who managed to arrive in Canada prior to 1961 came from Jamaica.[32]

There were some reforms to the immigration guidelines in 1962 as official policy inched away from preserving the racial balance.[33] Ironically, real change in Canada's immigration policy, at least as far as Jamaicans were concerned, was accelerated, in part, by pressure from Britain. When official immigration policy, not to mention popular attitudes, in Canada remained stubbornly in favour of white Europeans, many West Indians chose instead to go to the mother country. In 1960 alone, some sixty thousand West Indians made the trek across the Atlantic to take up jobs that the British did not want.[34] With the rising standard of living in the postwar era, a plethora of new menial and manual labour jobs needed filling, and many West Indians filled the breach.[35] Jamaicans from the skilled and professional set were also making their mark in British society as lawyers, engineers, and doctors. Canadian politicians and officials were therefore forced to countenance more Jamaican immigration.

Jamaicans were seemingly not put off by warnings of growing racial prejudice in Britain and its outposts. British welfare workers were keen to report visible successes in London's "ghetto" of Brixton, which apparently boasted "the closest and most harmonious integration possible."[36] Perhaps unsurprisingly, Brixton commanded a central position in the United Kingdom's reggae story.

Harmonious or not, the British government could not refuse Jamaicans' entry into Britain in the years before Jamaican independence. Jamaicans, at least prior to 1962, were themselves British. As an alternative strategy, UK authorities implored Canada to open up its doors to Jamaicans, a move that was welcomed by many West Indians who wanted to come to Canada. West Indian Commission workers in London predicted that somewhere in the neighbourhood of 30 percent of West Indian immigrants to Britain in the early 1960s would actually favour

Canada if given the choice and that Canada was positioned to attract the top echelons of West Indian society.[37] As Patsy Pyne of the commission's London office explained in 1961:

> You should remember that most West Indians are hardworking and ambitious. The ones that would choose Canada would be mainly from that group attracted by the possibility of good salaries and education for their families. A lot of them would be the sort that wouldn't ordinarily go to Britain at all – the middle class of person earning around £1,000 a year in professional or skilled work. And you know, to be blunt about it, we West Indians really are rather a better bet for Canada than some of your present immigrants. We think far more in North American terms than Europeans do, we are well accustomed to North American customs and values. For us, there's little real change involved in moving from one English-speaking Commonwealth area to another in the same hemisphere. All we ask is the chance to prove this to you in practice.[38]

While the degree of real change involved in moving from Jamaica to Canada might have surprised Pyne, Jamaicans and West Indians at large would, indeed, get their chance to prove their worth in Canada. But apart from the nurses and domestics that came in the postwar era (and the other precious few who were highly skilled), many Jamaicans would still have to wait for Canada to crack its doors open further.

Established in 1963, the Royal Commission on Bilingualism and Biculturalism officially recognized those Canadians who counted neither English nor French heritage. The so-called deracialization of Canada's official immigration policies, however, did not yield meaningful change. In actuality, the recruitment of Jamaicans into Canada was still very much informed by racist attitudes. The seemingly random whims and discretionary powers of individual immigration officials, not to mention the racist residue surrounding the issue of sponsorship, could and often did determine which Jamaicans would access Canadian shores. This discretion was at odds with the Canadian government's advertisements of an idyllic, multiracial Canadian society.[39]

The crack widened in 1966 with the tabling of the White Paper on Immigration. Upon its delivery, Liberal MP Jean Marchand, the minister of manpower and immigration, diplomatically apologized for the delay:

> No one who understands the immigration problem will be surprised that this white paper could not be produced quickly and easily ... There are few issues, indeed, that bring into play so comprehensively all the delicate balances and tensions of our Canadian society. Our problem is to avoid the ill consequences of these inevitable complexities. Immigration policy and procedures have to adjust to changing circumstances.[40]

In reality, though, Canada had dragged its feet and could no longer ignore changing circumstances or postpone the inevitable and necessary revamping of its attitude towards immigration.

The White Paper promised an expansionist, nondiscriminatory immigration program. Yet the much-touted points system that Canada adopted in 1967 was not without issue, privileging as it did those who were educated. Some historians have argued that given the high cost of educational training, the points system was a modern-day head tax. Like Australia and South Africa, Canada also adopted protective measures within the law that allowed it to maintain a modicum of fairness within the language of the legislation while continuing to eliminate unwelcome immigrants. Still, the White Paper established, as Marchand declared, "a new balance between the claims of family relationship and the economic interest of Canadians as a whole."[41] A new immigrant could bring family members who were dependants prior to gaining citizenship, a step that anticipated Trudeau's equally expansionist family-reunification measures of the early 1970s.[42] The days of preserving a British racial balance were, at least for officials, over.

The new direction in immigration policy forever changed the complexion of some Canadian neighbourhoods. In 1971, some 34,400 blacks lived in Canada and accounted for roughly 0.2 percent of the population. Within ten years, that number would increase sevenfold to 239,500; blacks accounted for 1 percent of Canada's population in 1981.[43] By 1991, their number had more than doubled again, with 504,300 blacks accounting for roughly 1.9 percent of the population.[44]

Jamaican immigrants led the way during the boom period of black immigration to Canada. Between 1970 and 2000, over 130,000 Jamaicans migrated to Canada.[45] During the '70s and '80s, over 175,000 people, or 40 percent of Canada's total black immigration, was of Jamaican ethnicity. By 2001, Canada's 211,700 Jamaicans were the fourth-largest non-European ethnic community, behind the Chinese, East Indian, and Filipino communities, respectively.[46]

During the 1970s and 1980s, 96,715 Jamaicans relocated to Toronto, and they represented 83 percent of the total number of Jamaicans living in Canada.[47] Considering that only 34,400 blacks were living in the whole of Canada in 1971, the trebling of the number of blacks living in Toronto alone in the space of twenty years was quite remarkable.[48] In the twenty-first century, the Jamaican population in Toronto towers over other Caribbean groups. According to the 2016 Census, 200,330 of the people who lived in Toronto were of Jamaican ethnicity, and 99,660 of them had been born in Jamaica.[49] Of the 442,020 blacks who lived in the city, people of Jamaican origin accounted for approximately 45 percent.[50]

"Jamaica North" neighbourhoods began to flourish across the Greater Toronto Area in the 1970s. Lawrence Heights (roughly Lawrence Avenue and Bathurst Street) was nicknamed the "Jungle," a moniker that corresponded with the infamous neighbourhood of West Kingston. The "Village," which was part of what an older generation might refer to as the "Black Bottom," covered the St. Clair and Eglinton area.[51] It was into this neighbourhood that many of Canada's early ska and reggae pioneers such as Jo Jo Bennett relocated.[52]

The most famous Jamaican enclave in the city was the Jane-Finch Corridor.[53] Designed as a model suburb in the 1960s, the corridor's labyrinth of high-rise and low-rise apartments was Canada's answer to an American-style urban project. However, few of the city and social planners working with the Ontario Housing Corporation anticipated the impact that rapid urban growth would have on the area.[54] Though it was designed to accommodate new immigrants and, more generally, a higher-needs population with low income and public housing, the community was bereft of the social infrastructure required to sustain itself. Instead, it became a haven for criminal (mostly drug) activity. (Fortunately, several community-driven initiatives in the twenty-first century managed to reverse and repair the corridor's poor reputation.[55]) It was into this neighbourhood that so many Jamaican migrants moved, including Leroy Sibbles, perhaps the most important figure in Reggae Canadiana.

Moving Out of Babylon

Cyclical violence plagued Jamaica for centuries. From the Maroon-led victory over the British in the eighteenth century to the Morant Bay Rebellion of the nineteenth, from the union unrest of the 1930s to the high-water mark of political violence in the late twentieth century, Jamaicans have often had to adapt to or flee from highly treacherous and unpredictable circumstances. Political violence has at times ravaged the island, directly engaging Jamaica's poorest in gang warfare. This violence provided the single most important push factor behind the northbound exodus to Canada.

Violent eruptions in Jamaica were particularly acute and ubiquitous during the 1970s, and these eruptions were decades in the making. Colonial Jamaica was essentially a feudal banana republic run by twenty-one "brown-skinned" families. It was from within these families that the country's two major political parties or adversaries emerged. The Jamaica Labour Party (JLP) was founded in 1943 by William Alexander Clarke Bustamante. Though he had once been a trade unionist imprisoned for subversive activities and had helped to lead the anticolonial movement of the 1930s, Bustamante's party platform came to roughly represent the interests of the elite. On the other side of the political ring stood the People's National Party (PNP), founded by Norman Washington Manley (a cousin of Bustamante). The PNP appealed more to socially minded populists. By the early 1970s – only a decade after securing independence from Britain – the political temperature was particularly hot, and a tribal war between supporters of the PNP and the opposing JLP soon followed.[56]

The PNP leader during this era was Michael Manley, Norman Washington Manley's son.[57] Manley roared into power in 1972 with a convincing majority: thirty-seven seats, versus the sixteen held by the incumbent, JLP's Hugh Shearer (Manley's cousin).[58] Manley's opposition throughout the 1970s was the ethnomusicologist and Harvard-educated Edward Seaga. Seaga, who in 1955 had coproduced a field recording of Jamaican spiritual drums, proved to be a formidable opponent. Both men had hard-liners who were not afraid to use brute force and intimidation to make their point.[59]

If Seaga served an American master, Manley's idealistic views dovetailed better with Castro and the Soviet prerogative.[60] In terms of a Canadian connection, Manley's ties to the country were forged, somewhat bizarrely, in the Second World War, when he served with the Royal Canadian Air Force.[61] Two decades later, Manley cultivated a relationship with Pierre Trudeau, whose relaxed attitude towards the far left, including Castro and the charming Jamaican prime minister, allowed for the passage of a greater number of Jamaicans to Canada.[62]

The 1976 edition of the Manley-Seaga saga heralded a new age of violence for the island. During the buildup to the election, Kingston was a violent and lawless police state. The climate was unforgiving for musicians, including the island's folk hero Bob Marley, who survived an assassination attempt.[63] And the violence endured long after the 1976 election was decided. On January 4, 1978, for example, political violence once again shook Jamaica when the Green Bay Massacre resulted in five JLP members being killed in an ambush. It was in this fragile atmosphere that many Jamaicans chose to leave their country, or at the very least, send their children to England, the United States, or Canada.

After having written "Jah Kingdom Go to Waste," Ernie Smith knew his life was in danger. The song was considered incendiary by the Jamaican government and banned from radio under the Emergency Measures Act. As a result, Smith packed his bags for Toronto in 1978.[64] The political temperature, however, remained scorching hot and showed no sign of cooling. The 1980 election crippled the nation, leaving some 750 dead before the last ballot was counted.[65] Accordingly, many resigned themselves to joining the exodus.

Not everyone, however, was trying to get out. Manley's platform had given some young Jamaicans hope. Concert promoter Denise Jones, for instance, returned to Jamaica for a period in the mid-1970s: "It was a time of the nonaligned nation, the great Manley-Trudeau relationship, and at that time Jamaica was at the height of democratic socialism, where it was young people who were going to Cuba to be trained as doctors. And we were saying [to the United States] we're an independent nation, and we're not your guy in the Caribbean."[66] While some may have been charmed by Manley's dalliances with the hard left, the volume of northbound traffic between Kingston and Toronto grew heavy. Though Toronto promised cold, it at least promised peace from one bloody election after another.

Taking the Leap of Faith

In leaving the Caribbean, Jamaican migrants took a leap of faith with the hope of securing a better life in Canada. Employment for Jamaican migrants diversified during the 1970s. While positions for nurses and domestics declined a little, there was a small increase in professional and technical opportunities. There was also a significant jump in entrepreneurial and technical positions, and skilled work increased. Between 1970 and 1974, 17 percent of migrants were involved in assembly, fabricating, and manufacturing work.[67] Jamaicans wanted to work; according to the 1986 Census, over 79 percent of Jamaican women and 86 percent of Jamaican men held full-time positions in Toronto's labour force, which was above the Canadian norm.[68]

The processes involved in coming to Canada, however, demanded a certain mental resiliency. As demonstrated in a variety of academic studies, the acculturation strategy of Jamaican migrants evolved over time.[69] According to early acculturation studies, integration into the broader society was considered the best strategy for immigrants because it reduced acculturative stress. These studies also showed that Jamaicans' satisfaction with Canada and their integration into dominant society were tied to their occupation, length of residence in Canada, and skin colour.[70] Indeed, lower-class, darker-skinned Jamaican immigrants were found to be less satisfied with their experience in Canada and less likely to integrate into the dominant society. The more satisfying and successful strategy belonged to those immigrants who were able to penetrate the social and economic mainstream.[71] Musicians, in this respect, may have held an advantage by virtue of having a job that kept them constantly in the public eye and that demanded a degree of socialization with non-Jamaican Torontonians.

The success of such a strategy, however, has come under scrutiny by academics and later waves of migrants. Some scholars have begun, for instance, to consider the social-psychological processes associated with migration from one place to another within the West Indian diaspora.[72] Unsurprisingly, these studies show that migrants were restricted from fully integrating into the dominant societies of major North American urban centres for reasons of race and ethnicity.[73] In response, many West Indian immigrants within some of these studies listed "ethnic identity" and "intra-cultural socialization" at the top of their list for strategically reducing acculturative stress.[74] For some, enacting ethnicity within the group setting, eating at the local Caribbean restaurant, visiting the local Caribbean barber shop, attending the Caribbean church, and generally operating within the Caribbean North community made the most sense for social-psychological success.

Toronto's Jamaican Canadian Association (JCA) served as the unofficial hub of Jamaicanness for those migrants who sought comfort within their own community.[75] Launched in August 1962, the JCA sought to bring together the disparate collection of nurses, domestics, and university students who had relocated to Toronto. The association's original mandate was to provide opportunities for new arrivals, but it expanded to include helping migrants to focus on the educational needs of children. Ultimately, though, the JCA represented the Jamaican community as it participated in collective public activities in the city. By extension – and in an effort to reduce tension on the streets – the association began to liaise between the black community and the Metro Toronto Police Force. For example, the JCA advocated for a civilian review board for the police force, which was successfully established in Ontario in 1981.[76]

For some more recent migrants, however, identifying with their blackness took priority over identifying with their Jamaicanness as a strategy for surviving acculturative stress. Some studies suggest that Jamaican migrants may have actually fared better in American cities such as New York and Miami over Canadian centres such as Toronto because these large American cities had greater native-born black populations and more comprehensive and black-friendly infrastructures.[77]

Yet Canada remained the more attractive option for many Jamaicans. Marcia Vassell, for instance, related how a friend who had moved to New Jersey compared her experience there to what she had known in Toronto:

> You know my girlfriend ... she says, "Every day, I'm reminded of race. When I'm here, all my friends are multicultural, and we're so cool with each other. And I go [to New Jersey], and even the blacks are not accepting me because they're saying that I'm too 'white,' or I'm too 'proper,' or I'm too 'this' or I'm too 'that' ... They're not accepting me, and the whites don't accept me either." And I'm, like, "Oh my gosh, you poor baby. Come home."[78]

Others, too, believed the United States to be less friendly and more race obsessed than Canada.[79]

Still, as far as many Jamaicans were concerned, Canada's multiculturalism policy did not safeguard Jamaican migrants; it instead fuelled cultural intolerance against the Jamaican community.[80] Yet despite this sentiment, many Jamaicans also believed that their move to Canada was the right choice. Moreover, those dedicated to a life in music felt that they were better poised to negotiate the murky waters of the migration process than their fellow nonmusical Jamaicans.

And so they came, some on solo missions to chase work or escape the growing violence, and others with a sibling to be reunited with mom under the new family reunification policy of the Canadian government. They came to working-class neighbourhoods such as Eglinton Avenue West and Bathurst Street in the city's core, to Jane and Finch in the city's north end, and to the Danforth in the east. They came to the city's newer suburbs such as Malton by the airport. Here a sponsor and there a job – so many splintered Jamaican families reunited in the Great White North.

Twelve-year-old Mike Smith came to Canada on Air Jamaica in September 1974 with one of his sisters and planted roots in the College and Ossington area.[81] It was the same for Sunray Grennan, who, along with his younger brother, flew to Toronto to meet his mother, a domestic, and moved into the Jane and Sheppard area in 1976.[82] Eighteen-year-old bassist Peter Holung thought his parents were sending him to Toronto for a couple of weeks in 1975. He did not know that the master plan was for him to stay in Canada, which he did, spending the rest of his teenage years in Malton.[83] JuLion King's mother was looking out for her son's best interests when she brought him to Canada in July 1976. In her mind, it was a safer place for JuLion to grow up and somewhere that might settle her young boy down a little:

> With the violence and the change in the political climate, [my mom] had two young children. When you walk the streets of Kingston, Jamaica, you're either a lion or sheep. And I didn't choose the sheep route. And [my mom] started to see changes in me as well, by the time I'm fourteen, fifteen and sixteen, and she realize ... she didn't feel safe protecting us by herself. So she thought, "Well, Canada would be a good place to be." So she step off.[84]

As violence was ramping up in advance of the 1976 Jamaican election, the lion was plucked from the streets of Kingston to roam Toronto's Don Mills and Sheppard neighbourhood.

While a clear majority of Jamaicans came to Canada in a piecemeal fashion calibrated to mesh with Trudeau's family reunification policies, there were some cases where a whole family was able to emigrate together. Canada promised new financial opportunities for families such as the Vassells, who came in 1975. As Phil Vassell explained:

> I think it's the typical immigrant story: [our parents] saw this as a place where there were better economic opportunities for them and better education opportunities for their children ...The older I got, the more I realized how fortunate we were to have that. All they asked from us in exchange for that was that we got a good education, and once you took care of that, the rest would take care of itself.[85]

The Vassells chose Toronto's Oakwood and St. Clair area, near the Black Bottom.

Certainly, education was valued by most Jamaicans who were hoping to give their children a better life. Higher learning counted as a pull factor for migration to Canada. Mike Smith's mom, for example, wanted her children to have a good education, and the economic reality of rural Jamaica could not compete with the sophisticated metropolis of Toronto.[86] It was the same for the Harvey family. In 1966, Rupert "Ojiji" Harvey, future frontman of Messenjah, arrived in Toronto with his brother Carl, future musical director for Toots and the Maytals.[87] The Harveys were a distinguished Jamaican family and were concerned about their country's political uncertainty. Because Rupert's dad was a scientist and his mother a schoolteacher, they easily met the pre-points system criteria for immigration to Canada. Indeed, Rupert's grandmother was one of the first black women in Jamaica to attend college, quite a feat, given that her mother had been in bondage until she was ten years old.[88] Rupert, then eleven, was accustomed to raising donkeys and rabbits in the rural area of Clarendon. Naturally, he experienced a culture shock when the family moved into the Vaughan and Oakwood area of downtown Toronto. Yet, like so many others, Rupert's dad brought the family north to Canada to escape political uncertainty, for a decent job, and to give his boys a good education.[89]

Denise Jones, who is today the CEO of the entertainment group Jones and Jones, had a similar experience. As a child, Jones was interested in performance, and after graduating from high school in Jamaica, she won a scholarship to the Dance Theatre of Harlem in New York. But Jones was persuaded not to take the scholarship by her parents, who insisted that she choose another path, one that led her to Canada. That path brought her to the University of Windsor, where she studied broadcasting and communications.[90]

Not all the young immigrants stuck to their studies. For example, Earle "Mighty Pope" Heedram's parents didn't want him to stay in Lucea, Jamaica, where they felt he would just be hanging out and likely getting into trouble. The couple, encouraged by what they had heard about Canada from relatives who had already relocated, viewed the country as a possible corrective for their son. Heedram explained:

> I didn't really have any ambition as to "go do this" or "do that." My mother wanted me to further my studies and what have you. And I

did do some courses. [With] the lady I stayed with, it was important that you go to school. And it was some data-processing course that I was taking, but the minute I discovered Club Jamaica, all that stopped and, really, [I] just started hanging out there in the week, rehearsing and play[ing] on the weekend, which I'm not very proud of it, but I didn't want to do anything else.[91]

Becoming the first solo black artist to be signed to a major label in Canada did much to reverse any disappointment that mom, dad, and perhaps even Heedram himself may have harboured.

Jay Douglas, who came to Canada in 1964 and attended Central Tech, considered a career as an architect. But each year the high school had an open house that included entertainment. Backed by a classmate on guitar, Douglas sang Shep and the Limelites' "Daddy's Home." Douglas was then asked to sing it again for the school's morning ceremony, and the result was overwhelming. This was, according to Douglas, where his music career was launched:

That's where other [Canadian] guys with bands saw me, and they offered me to sing with their bands. That's where it really got started. So, I ended up singing in bands, and every Sunday evening we would be performing at Catholic church halls and different places ... I was thinking architectural drafting at Central Tech, but after a while the music started to take priority.[92]

Singing with white Canadians in Toronto helped Douglas establish a formidable North American repertoire that served him well in his new and successful, if unexpected, career.

Some Jamaicans, however, did come to Canada to secure a career in music. Before joining Byron Lee and the Dragonaires in the late 1950s, Jo Jo Bennett had honed his craft as the first solo trumpet player in the Alpha Boys' School Military Band. The future Sattalites cofounder started touring with Jamaican music legend Byron Lee, including throughout North America in 1965.[93] Bennett, however, was enamoured with Toronto and saw an opportunity. In 1967, the Sheiks, a Kingston-based ska band that featured lead singer Jackie Opel from Barbados, disbanded following their North American tour, and some of the players decided to permanently relocate to Toronto.[94] Bennett had the idea of putting together his own Toronto ensemble with a couple of the ex-Sheiks.[95] However, as Bennett recalled, escaping the clutches of Byron Lee proved to be even more difficult than getting into Canada:

> I'm thinking way out now in my head, "Oh, fuck, how can I get away and go back to Toronto?" [Byron] always hang on to all of the passports, so you can't make no move ... I said, "Byron, blah, blah, blah." The war started. It didn't lead to blows, but it was about to. It was about to, man, because I wanted my passport.[96]

Ken Parker from Ken and the Blues Busters, a singing group on tour with the Dragonaires, convinced Byron to give Bennett his passport:

> Here I go and get my freedom now ... [I] didn't even go to bed. I went down to the bus station, and I fall asleep on a chair there waiting to get a ticket to jump on the bus and come across the border. When I reach the border, though, the man say, "Mr. Bennett, where you going?" And I said, "I just finished a tour, and I kinda physically tired, so I want to go spend a few days with my cousin here in Toronto." And he said, "Okay, no problem, Mr. Bennett, you can go." And that was that.[97]

And that's how one of Reggae Canadiana's foundational members stepped forward to blow his horn in the Queen City.

Rannie "Bop" Williams was equally hopeful about the Jamaican music market in Toronto. One of the most important and wildly unheralded rhythm guitarists in Jamaican music history, Williams was the first to play up the mento rhythm style into reggae music and was a much-sought-after session player who recorded several critical sessions with Lee Perry, including some with Bob Marley.[98] As Williams mused: "We were wondering when the Canadians were really going to get involved with this music. Because if they do get involved, then we have a chance to earn some money. So I try to help black Canadian, white Canadian to understand reggae music."[99] Yet Bennett and Williams and, later, Jackie Mittoo and Leroy Sibbles were very much in the minority. Few Jamaican migrants laboured under the impression that migrating to Canada would produce or indeed sustain a career in music.

Willi Williams, composer of the Clash's hit "Armagideon Time," was perhaps more realistic about the relocation: "I decided to make it an adventure, to come and check it out and see what it was. And when I came here, I met some people here who ... were part of my upbringing, my influences in what I was doing, which was music and, namely, Jackie Mittoo."[100] Whether they were pursuing adventure, fleeing political violence, seeking education, looking for work, or hoping to make music, all the migrants were, as singer Adrian Miller observed, "basically looking for a better life."[101]

Welcome to Canada

For many Jamaicans, Canada was a complete mystery. Outside of some cursory understanding of snow, hockey, and "Eskimos," few who migrated in the 1960s and 1970s really knew what awaited them. Klive Walker believed that he possessed the same stereotypes that most Jamaicans had about Canada – that it was cold and cultureless.[102] For Walker, Canada was a blank slate. He thought Lorne Green, William Shatner, and Donald Sutherland were Americans. (Walker now finds himself defending or fighting against Canadian stereotypes back in Jamaica.)[103] Likewise, coming from rural St. Andrew, where he grew up with no television, Mike Smith could scarcely envisage what Toronto was like from his mother's letters home: "I couldn't imagine what snow was like."[104] The Mighty Pope's premigration appraisal of Toronto was similar:

> Quite frankly, I did not know what to expect ... In Jamaica, we studied a book called *North America*, and I remember reading for the first time about hockey. It didn't make sense to me – and another game, lacrosse, which the mind couldn't even picture what it was. And what stuck in my mind was Saskatchewan and wheat. The book, looking back, wasn't that informative ... And, of course, it's totally different now ... but really there was dearth of [information].[105]

Regardless of what they knew, Jamaican migrants soon became aware of Canada's winters.

Though governmental agencies had hoped to stem migration from Jamaica and the rest of the West Indies through the dubious "climatic unsuitability" argument, the truth of the matter was that Canada's bitter cold winters profoundly affected newly arrived immigrants from the sunny island. As the Mighty Pope pleaded: "Take my word for it, and I came in December. Now I've never seen snow, and just the darkness. I was totally depressed for months, you know. I wanted to go home."[106] It was similar for Leo Cripps, future curator of Calgary ReggaeFest: "I came in mid-January ... the middle of winter, so experiencing snow was quite fascinating. The novelty wore off fast, however, as the winter months dragged on: the longing for familiar faces, places, and food, the hardship of not having a job, therefore no money, and just the everyday grimness of the outside cold."[107] Paul Bennett simply stated: "Landing in Canada at wintertime, I really could not believe just how cold it was. That took a little bit to adjust to."[108] The shocking climate was not restricted to the heart of winter. When the two Harvey brothers went to the Canadian National Exhibition at the end of their first Canadian summer in 1966, they were the only ones wearing sweaters because they still thought Toronto's late "summer breeze" was freezing.[109] It is perhaps not surprising, then, that in 1988 Rupert Harvey and Messenjah faithfully rendered their shivering experiences into song when they recorded "Love is Summer in the Winter Time."[110]

While the weather might have been chilly, some Jamaicans found everyday interactions with strangers in Canada to be equally cool. Having grown up in the rural area of Cave Valley, singer-songwriter Wayne Hanson was surprised when people in Toronto didn't say hello when passing on the street. As Hanson observed, people in Canada were "a little bit more reserved. That was a little bit of a shock too."[111] Marcia Vassell also found Toronto to be "colder and not as friendly."[112]

Many black Jamaican migrants experienced equal measures of racism, ignorance, and general curiosity. Indeed, so few were the number of blacks in Toronto in the late 1960s that, as the Mighty Pope explained, "You'd see a black person across the street, you'd run over just to talk to them because they stuck out."[113] The culture shock, for both migrant and host, endured into the 1970s. Bassist Peter Holung remembers one particular day in 1975:

> We went to Mosport and got lost, and we stopped to ask for directions. And one of the guys [travelling with Holung] was Michael, a black Jamaican guy. We asked for directions, and the guy who owned the farm came out, and he touched him, he touched him like this [*touching arm*], 'cause he's never seen a black person before in his life.[114]

Coming from a country whose motto is "Out of many, one people," Holung admitted that he hadn't known prejudice in terms of skin colour until he came to Canada.[115]

Teenagers found it especially tough going. Klive Walker, who was actually born in London to Jamaican parents but moved to Jamaica at age eleven, came to Canada in 1972 against his will:

> I didn't want to come to Canada. I mean, remember I'm eighteen now ... I'd made close friends. I didn't want to leave. I think my mother had to pack my bags for me ... But once I got to Toronto and really settled in and recognized that there was a Jamaican community here that I could relate to, then all of that was washed away in a matter of a few months, and I grew to really appreciate and love Toronto.[116]

Like Walker, JuLion King was less than impressed with his mother's decision to relocate to Toronto's Don Mills and Sheppard neighbourhood:

> I was so vexed at my mother for bringing me here ... I think it lasted for at least, say, a year where there was just limited conversation between us. George S. Henry [Secondary School] was a tough lickle ting because there were so many white people. They were used to talk to people anyway them felt like it ... One time, my sister was in a class, and she come home every day crying and talking to my mom, but they never want [to] tell me, so me find out seh why she wasn't

in an English class ... Every time she would speak, this breddah at the back of the class would mimic her voice and make some lickle monkey sounds and ting ... So I skipped class one day and went to her class and listened by the window, and I ketch Mr. Man. So, when I see him after school, [suffice to say] him never mek no more monkey sounds when me sister talk, e? [117]

King was not the only migrant of teenage vintage whose transition into Toronto became intensely physical.[118] Upon his arrival in Malton, Adrian Miller recalled that he "had to fight and then assimilate. That helped shape the person I became."[119] Surviving racism was central to the Jamaican migrant's story.

Some incidents, however, could be far more serious than a simple playground scuffle. The Jamaican migrant community was shaken up by the 1979 shooting death of Albert Johnson, a thirty-five-year-old black man who was shot dead by two constables with the Toronto Police Service. The shooting and the subsequent acquittal of Constables William Inglis and Walter Cargnelli on manslaughter charges was a watershed moment in Toronto's black community. In 1988, Toronto Police made a discreet settlement with the Johnson family in a civil lawsuit.[120]

By the mid-1970s, various social agents determined that a crisis existed within Canada's race relations. Various studies were undertaken to appraise the situation and to advance recommendations that might soothe racial tensions.[121] Antiracist movements such as the Urban Alliance on Race Relations articulated a response by Toronto's black, Jewish, and South Asian communities to hate-motivated violence against them in the city's public spaces.[122] These real-life racial collisions were incongruous with what was presented in the governmental brochure of multiculturalism.

Racism – in any form – exacted a psychological toll on many migrants. Mike Smith, for example, described some of his negative encounters when he attended Kane Middle School in Toronto's Keelesdale neighbourhood:

Kids will pick on you for just about anything in school. Sometimes there were some negative things in terms of the way you spoke ...

Just saying the word "orange," for example ... We never said "orange." We said "horange." Or the number three – it's not "three" but "tree" ... So sometimes the kids made fun of you because of the way you spoke ... Sometimes they would tell you to "go back where you came from." That was always a thing whenever you got into an altercation with anyone: "Go back where you came from."[123]

These experiences were exacerbated by prevailing attitudes towards blackness in Canadian society and also by the lack of black representation in the media.

Jamaicans' own attitudes towards race and class, however, had also been packed up along with the family belongings and brought to the new country.[124] These attitudes were renegotiated in Canada, as Smith explained:

That was the thing that you kind of felt, like, they [white kids] were better. And it seemed like some point in my life, too, I thought that they were better. Because ... that's what I kept on hearing; that's what I kept on feeling ... All of the commercials on TV were all about white people. I didn't see a lot of blacks on TV at that particular time. So, hey, they built such a great society I thought that these guys were better. They know what they're talking about ... You know what, this is "their" country, so, yeah, I believed that for a while. I believed that they were better than I was at many things.[125]

Like so many other migrants from all walks of life, Smith was fortified by his religion and the strength of his family, and he ultimately came to believe that "all men were created equally."[126] In a study done in 2007, over half the Jamaican Canadian respondents believed that they had been treated unfairly or experienced discrimination in Canada based on their race, religion, ethnicity, and language, including their Jamaican accent.[127]

While racist incidents tested the resolve of some Jamaican migrants, other experiences made them feel special. Smith recalled that some of his non-Jamaican friends were naturally curious and interested in his Jamaicanness: "[They] liked the way [we] spoke. They wanted to hang

84 *Jamaica to Toronto*

around the Jamaicans. They wanted to learn certain words ... and they thought the Jamaicans were pretty cool in the way they dressed and the way they played sports and so on."[128]

Indeed, some migrants felt that enacting Jamaican ethnicity was a far better acculturation strategy than trying to curtail it. Rupert Harvey, for instance, found that

> a lot of black people when they come to these countries and they try to be who they're not, in a way, thinking that people will like them if they conform, I found it was the opposite. I found that when you were a rebel and stuck to your culture and your ideas, that's when people actually liked you. So, "to thine own self be true." Not that I didn't accept Canadian and actually cross-bred it into my life, but the fact that I still was Jamaican and proud of it is what made me have good white friends ... I think it's the boldness of Jamaicans, in that our attitude has always been "no apology: we are who we are." And I think that resonates with people, no matter whether black or white or brown. People want that; they want to be bold.[129]

It was precisely this "no apologies" attitude – commonly characterized as Jamaican feistiness – that attracted many young non-Jamaicans to Jamaican culture.[130]

The attraction was sometimes mutual. Many Jamaican migrants were happy to have been exposed to new cultural experiences. To its credit, Toronto's school system helped to facilitate some of this cross-cultural exchange when the city's complexion began to change drastically in the 1970s. Initiatives such as the United Nations Educational, Scientific and Cultural Organization (UNESCO) were specifically designed to foster understanding and encourage cross-cultural collaboration, as Marcia Vassell recalled: "[UNESCO] was something that the schools, Winona, McMurrich, Oakwood, they all did that just so the students can get to know other cultures and just be comfortable with who they are and what they are, and I thought it was great, and I participated in all of the UNESCO carnivals ... It was a great thing for the schools to do."[131] While Vassell was delighted with the more official initiatives of the multicultural era, other migrants forged friendships with Canadians through more informal means. As Sunray Grennan observed, simply by virtue of where he attended school, he was exposed to and had "the opportunity to meet so many different kinds of people and learn about their culture, and they're sharing my culture as well."[132] These initiatives – official and otherwise – built bridges between young migrant and host.

Jamaican music and culture were accepted by many non-Jamaican Canadians, and the extent of this acceptance surprised some migrants, as Grennan observed:

> Somehow reggae music is a thing that brings people together, and Canada is a place that I've seen this process [happen] ... I think they [non-Jamaicans] loved the idea of the music, that it was different, and they were psyched about learning about it. It was very new to them ... I didn't really expect that, but it was quite flattering to know that your culture has come so far and that other people would accept the culture and come and check it out and tell their friends.[133]

Others were less surprised, as Phil Vassell explained: "Being in Jamaica, you're amazed at people that would come to Jamaica and record with Jamaican musicians. Living outside of Jamaica, you then start to appreciate the seductiveness of the music and how it pulls people in. I think I was always struck by the magic of that, music taking hold of people."[134] Reggae music itself could beckon the non-Jamaican to cross the metaphorical bridge.

Certainly, Jamaica's prereggae culture was rich. From Claude McKay's poetry to Louise Bennett's folk art to Rex Nettleford's national dance program of the early 1960s, Jamaican artists had built formidable inroads into the international art scene long before the first reggae one drop had been recorded. Yet once it had been recorded, the success of reggae music dwarfed the rest of Jamaica's significant artistic output. Reggae greatly accelerated cultural bridge building between Jamaicans and non-Jamaicans.

That the rise of reggae music around the globe coincided with the adjustment period in Canada was a positive boon for many. This was a time when Toronto's youth were becoming politically aware and began to participate in various international and domestic movements such as anti-apartheid and civil rights. For good or bad, teenagers of the 1970s inherited a position carved out for them by a previous generation. It was, after all, during the 1960s that the category of "youth" arrived on the political scene. Teens of the hippie era were influenced by New Left ideologies that encouraged them to ask questions and resist – at least for a time – the expectations of their parents.[135] Politicized binaries were constructed that pitted the young (under thirty, a force for good, oppositional, and peaceful) against the old (over thirty, corrupt, conformist, racist, and violent).[136]

These binaries and the rebellious spirit of the hippie generation were holdovers for many of Toronto's young people growing up in the 1970s and 1980s. Central to this spirit was Bob Marley, who had quite literally became the poster boy for many of the city's young rebels. The biracial reggae rebel disseminated Jamaicanness to the non-Jamaican.[137] Toronto's non-Jamaican school children began to draw links between their new Jamaican friends and the "Tuff Gong" (Marley), the gun-toting "Rhyging" (Jimmy Cliff), and Jamaica's rebel music in general. Reggae's rise was also the migrant's gain.

Many migrants believe that having a strong association with Jamaica's popular music afforded them an advantage in their own acculturation process. For Denise Jones, music was "a place to go back to. It's a place to find the centre of yourself, your security ... You know when you go over to somebody's house on a Saturday evening ... we sort of sought out everywhere there was something cultural happening just to refurbish ourselves."[138] Marcia Vassell echoed Jones's observation:

> What music provided was this amazing outlet for when things get tough. And music in itself created its own community of people that you could draw on for support. In that sense I do believe we had an edge. And because my father was so heavily into the music, people came to us for their dose of reggae music. On the weekends, there was always something happening at our house.[139]

Music could communicate the various strains of acculturation, as Marcia's brother Phil Vassell reflected:

You know the expression "a fi we music"? There's always that kind of ownership and pride of the music that I think a lot of people took with them. Because it [music] was able to express things that perhaps they themselves couldn't express; either they could go back in time, or it could articulate things for them in a way that they might not be able to do.[140]

Played loudly and proudly at various family events, Jamaican 45s and LPs could, for so many Jamaicans, articulate Jamaicanness within a new Toronto context.

While music could help some Jamaicans enact ethnicity and offered them strength in the communal setting, others used it for more solitary purposes, as Rupert Harvey explained: "I had a song inside of myself ... I think the culture that I brought with me in the music made us very proud of our heritage and made us very strong. I had a song in my head – always singing – and that's not stopped, by the way."[141] Music from home helped migrants adjust, heal, and recharge on their own.

More than a place of comfort, music could also be a formidable tool. In short, being associated with Jamaican popular music could build bridges into the dominant society for new migrants, as Sunray Grennan observed:

I think music was that bridge – in terms of culture – for me to merge with other cultures. Because being so young, and being that I could play this magical music from somewhere that everyone goes to on a vacation, and suddenly they see this little guy, and he's playing reggae, and he's playing ska, and, yes, that helped me to feel comfortable in Canada.[142]

Moreover, some migrant musicians believed that their musical calling gave them a direct advantage over other Jamaican migrants. Drummer Paul Bennett, for example, believed that music saved him from the same racially charged scrapes and travails that his older brothers were continually involved in when they lived on Blake Street, near Jones Avenue in Toronto's Greek Town.[143] The Mighty Pope felt that he had an advantage as a singer simply because of the nature of the job: "There was sort of a carefree *joie de vivre*. Everything was fun ... I integrated quite easily. It was a party atmosphere. [People] were brought together by music."[144] Wayne Hanson agreed that as a musician "you are on the vanguard. You're in the limelight, and many people are likely more inclined to approach a performer than they are another person who is not quite in the forefront."[145] Indeed, many non-Jamaicans' first interaction with Jamaican migrants often occurred in a musical, sometimes party, environment.

A few migrant musicians also saw the benefit of being able to broadcast their feelings and opinions outwards to a sometimes diverse audience who were willing to listen, as Adrian Miller confirmed: "I'm quite sure you have people who are nonmusicians who might have the same kind of outlook like me. It's just that they probably won't be acknowledged because they're not a part of the arts scene that gives you a platform to stand on."[146] As Miller noted, migrant musicians also had the means to draw attention to themselves, and Rannie "Bop" Williams observed, "I think [music] gave me an advantage, because some people who would see me, and they don't pay me no mind, but as soon as I pick up my instrument, a lot of respect."[147] Success on the stage, then, could sometimes help facilitate a better standing both within and outside of the Jamaican Canadian community.

In terms of a career move, however, some musicians felt that coming to Toronto put them at an economic disadvantage, as Willi Williams observed:

> Number one, if it was this country alone, I couldn't keep my family together. I couldn't eat food. I wouldn't be able to pay my rent or anything. I had to go outside of here to do the thing that I love so as to make some money from it ... It wasn't economically viable right here in Canada because ... the system didn't allow that. Because even when we took our music to the radio stations, they didn't play it, and they still don't play, even until today.[148]

While the infrastructure would not allow for the same successes enjoyed in other Jamaican outposts in the United Kingdom, a great many migrants believe that an association with Jamaican music afforded, if not an economic advantage, then at the very least a psychological one over other migrants. As a "place to go back to" or an "outlet for when things get tough," reggae music was the sound of ethnicity, so crucial to feeling home in a strange land.

Northern Reflection

A joint survey conducted by Statistics Canada and Canadian Heritage in 2002 found that 81 percent of Canadians of Jamaican origin felt a strong sense of belonging to Canada; 71 percent of them also felt a strong sense of belonging to their ethnic or cultural group.[149] These statistics speak to the prevalence, comfort, and usefulness of multiple identities among Jamaican migrants.[150]

Not all migrants, however, agree. Working on his fourth decade in Canada, Adrian Miller stated that he did not yet feel Canadian:

> I'm still what you'd consider an immigrant because you still need to make allegiance to the Queen, right, to get your papers and be looked upon as a so-called Canadian. And even when you get that, people still look at you as an outsider because living in this country everything is about image ... even wearing this leather jacket, it's political.[151]

At the opposite side of the spectrum stands the Mighty Pope: "I can't remember not being Canadian. I've lived here more of my life ... That's probably sacrilegious. Some people hear me say would think, you know. But I know my culture and everything, but the formative years, it seemed like everything happened here for me."[152]

Still, identifying with Jamaican culture was, for some, easier than trying to nail down an often elusive Canadian identity. Identity for migrants often operated within a binary set of circumstances, as Leo Cripps explained:

> If I am in Jamaica, I am referred to as Canadian and in Canada as Jamaican. I do feel and probably will always feel more Jamaican than Canadian, I believe just because of the attachment I have to the culture. Canada has many "cultures," and identifying with any one

is impossible. On the other hand, it is easy to identify with the "Jamaican" culture.[153]

Cripps is not alone on this point; while Sunray Grennan said he loved Canada because it provided him with a hands-on education with other cultures, he still felt that he was "always a Jamaican." Paraphrasing a famous Sting tune, Sunray sang: "I'm an alien, I'm a legal alien, I'm a Jamaican living in Canada."[154]

Many migrants expressed the belief that they were "in between."[155] Yet there were subtle gradations of just how "in between" they really were. JuLion King, for example, said he felt that he was a Jamaican, but he also stated: "I'm exceedingly proud of Canada. My children are Canadian, but where you're born is where you're born."[156] It was the same for Peter Holung: "I'm kinda, like, in-between there. I didn't want to lose something that means a lot to me. That made me who I was."[157] These migrants maintained multiple identities, adopting transnational strategies to live, as they did, in and between two worlds.[158] Klive Walker further explained: "I'm a true child of the diaspora. I'm not like the 1940s, 1950s immigrant that was leaving [Jamaica] to seek a better life in those kind of airy-fairy terms."[159] Though today, with three Canadian children, Walker also said that he identifies with Canada but that there is still something special about his Jamaican connection: it's where he went to high school, and this at the time when rocksteady and reggae were evolving into Jamaica's cultural vernacular. Jamaica was, after all, the homeland of his parents.[160] Consequently, Walker, in his life and work, was uniquely poised to provide both a voice of the diaspora and a voice for anyone outside of the diaspora who happened to love reggae music.[161]

A few in-betweeners, however, came to identify more with the black diaspora and less with specific nationalistic identities. Phil Vassell, for example, said his feelings were well represented in his magazine: "I think I've always identified with [the black diaspora]. *Word* magazine consciously reflected the larger diaspora – not just Jamaica or reggae – but instead black music at large, jazz, reggae, gospel, blues."[162] The black population was large enough in Toronto that Vassell saw the need for a publication like *Word*, which catered to those whose sense of identity transcended geopolitical borders.

Identity became even more elastic in the lives of the migrants' children. Certainly, a disconnect existed for some second-generation Jamaican Canadians who, unable to identify with hegemonic Canadian culture, were equally removed from their parents' West Indian culture. For these children, cultural identity was sometimes developed along transnational or racial lines because the cornerstones of Canadiana were far less enticing than African American youth culture.[163]

Others, however, were not so willing to yield their Canadian identity. Denise Jones, for example, related a story about how Jamaicans' enacting ethnicity had caused confusion for her son Jesse, who was born in Sudbury. At school one day, Jesse explained that he had been born in Sudbury, but the other children didn't believe him. The others, as Denise explained, had been "telling him, 'You *mus* come from Jamaica not Sudbury!'" It was important for Jones to let her sons know that they were Canadian and, as such, that there were no limitations for what they could achieve in Canada. Both of Jones's children today regard themselves as Canadian and will – when pushed – freely say to their mother: "Mom, I'm not Jamaican."[164]

Some Jamaican migrant musicians learned to positively exploit local possibilities. Willi Williams, for instance, maintained his presence in the international reggae scene from his Pickering, Ontario, home by making frequent trips back to Jamaica. In fact, Williams felt more connected to the music scene in Jamaica than he did to the one in Canada.[165] A true transnational, Williams lived equally in Canada and Jamaica.

As touring remains a hallmark of the professional musician, Jamaican musicians in Canada led a transnational lifestyle long before that term became popular. Those Jamaican Canadian musicians who toured, jumping back and forth between Canada and Jamaica, soon mastered their dual identities. As Rannie "Bop" Williams confirmed: "I'm Canadian. I'm in Canada and a citizen. If war breaks out here, I've got to fight for Canada! When I'm in Jamaica, I'm Jamaican because I was born there."[166] Perhaps musicians were trained to slip in and out of the multiple realities that a transnational life demands.

While there may be subtle differences between the regular Jamaican migrant and the Jamaican migrant musician, there is a far more discernible difference across the generations. The majority of Jamaican migrants of the 1960s and 1970s felt that theirs was an entirely different set of circumstances when compared to more recent waves of immigration. With a Jamaican community already established, those who arrived in the post-White Paper era entered a more familiar cultural landscape than did their predecessors. That is not to say that newer waves of Jamaican migrants did not have to contend with their own set of issues, only that Toronto's highly integrated Jamaican community provided newer arrivals with a home-style comfort that those who came before did not enjoy. Mike Smith, for instance, recalled that his family had to journey clear across the city to get West Indian food when they arrived in the mid-1970s. Newer migrants scarcely have to walk a city block or two to find good Yard (Jamaican) food. According to Smith, they've "got it much easier it seems ... And the people that have come before us have paved the way."[167] The Mighty Pope concurred: "Given the size of the community and the number of Caribbean outlets, mediums, community radio shows, et cetera ... there's no incentive for them to try."[168] Every Toronto neighbourhood provides migrants with their requisite ackee, saltfish, rice, and peas.

Some migrants of an earlier time also believed that there was a difference in the makeup of the migrants themselves. Marcia Vassell, for example, said that she believes that the new wave of Jamaican migrants in Canada "appear to be more rough around the edges."[169] Drummer Sunray Grennan likewise stated that new migrants are completely unlike those of the Trudeau years: "A lot of them are not into music ... There were a lot of older Jamaican men [in Canada] who had sound systems, and they are the ones who urged us younger ones to want to play the music."[170] Rupert Harvey was perhaps the most unforgiving. For him, there could be no excuses:

> We paved the road for these people to come through, and all the hassles and all the tribulations that we faced, they don't anymore. Really, they ain't got no excuses to mess up, because, like, it's already been done for them. They should be up here just achieving, not going on with badness, and all that stuff. There's no reason. They're not walking down the street with people calling them "nigger" ... We

shouldered those burdens so that they could come after us ... and they would just come and focus on their education and make a better life for themselves. Unfortunately, you see what's going on. A lot of them choose a different path.[171]

For Harvey, the opportunity for a migrant to better one's self and get an education in Canada was a path less faithfully observed by newer waves of Jamaican migrants.

Not everyone agreed. Adrian Miller, for example, did not recognize a material difference between the waves: "It doesn't matter what time period you live in, you still have to go through the same shit."[172] Similarly, Denise Jones opined that newer Jamaican migrants were "the same people in a different decade."[173]

It cannot, however, be argued with confidence that Jamaicans' awareness and knowledge of Canada has remained in stasis. Technology has, in some measure, taken the sense of adventure away for newer waves of Jamaican migrants, and with so many friends and family members already here, Jamaicans considering a move today know far more about Canada and Canadians than their predecessors did. For Leo Cripps, who came in January 1983, Canada "was still a mystery. With modern communication, all that mysterious aura is now gone."[174] Wayne Hanson, who quickly left a politically hot and violent Jamaica in July 1976, said he felt that newer migrants have more information and, because of this, they "probably plan more."[175]

Canada is no longer a snowy northern enigma that holds the promise a of better life. Yet what of the so-called better life? Despite the various challenges and obstacles that they encountered, a majority of migrants said that they believed that coming to Canada was the right choice. However, times have changed in Jamaica, and it now boasts a much larger middle class than it did in the 1960s and 1970s. Some migrants said that they felt that they might have done just as well or better by staying in Jamaica. Denise Jones needed no convincing on this point:

I can tell you that my colleagues working in Jamaican are way better off than I am. I think they have a lot of debt, like everybody else, but their houses are bigger, their cars are nicer, their clothes are more fabulous, they've got somebody who cooks, somebody who cleans. They don't seem to be pressured like we are here.[176]

Musicians, too, believed that they may have left some money on the table back in Jamaica. In terms of an actual music career, Canada fell short in providing the necessary infrastructure for financial success, as Carol Brown confessed:

In Canada, it's been a struggle with the music. There was a time when it seemed like, yes, it's going to find its place. The music [found] its place, but we, as artistes that migrate, that come into the country, it became very difficult at times, even until today. So I still tell myself, wow, being back home would have maybe made a lot of difference to my career; [it's] where the music's from.[177]

Despite these shortcomings, Canada paid dividends for many Jamaican migrants. Jay Douglas, for example, arrived on Thanksgiving weekend, 1964, and felt that his move to Canada was providence-guided. Thanksgiving remains a sacred time of reflection and giving thanks for Douglas, each and every year.[178] For Marcia Vassell, Toronto "opened up our eyes to other opportunities."[179] Likewise, Mike Smith recognized the opportunities:

I don't know what my life would have been otherwise. Maybe it would have been successful because I know of other people that have become very successful in Jamaica ... But I know that, for myself, the ability to go to school was one of the greatest things here ... In terms of just having the ability to finish school and get a job and do all the things that I want to do, I think it's been pretty good for me.[180]

An association with Jamaican music – either directly or as a music enthusiast – uniformly gave migrants a psychological advantage in their own acculturation process, strengthening their sense of self and helping them to build successful lives in this new strange land. As Rannie "Bop" offered: "I see a great light shining my way because most of my colleagues, a lot of them died. And the same thing could have happened to me. But something keep me going here and make me feel young and strong. So, a great light shine on me here."[181]

4

Place and Meaning in Toronto's Reggae Text

Reggae "happened" in various places across the city. Naturally, it was first broadcast within those neighbourhoods that boasted a strong Jamaican community such as Bathurst's Black Bottom, Little Jamaica (Eglinton west of Bathurst), Kensington Market, Malvern in Scarborough, Mississauga's Malton community, and North York's Jane-Finch Corridor. As its popularity rose throughout the 1970s and 1980s, however, reggae graduated from the confines of Jamaican-centric events and gatherings and became accessible to the city's non-Jamaicans, especially those who frequented the central nerve of Toronto's musical culture: the nightclubs of Queen Street West. The popularity of the clubs was, of course, in part due to the rise of reggae on the international stage from 1973 onward and the popularity of artists such as Jimmy Cliff, Toots and the Maytals, and, Bob Marley and the Wailers. Reggae, as a "peace and harmony-loving" music, was touted in various forums as something that could bridge the divides of age and race. Yet the Toronto reggae experience was not a homogeneous affair, and one person's idea of reggae could and often did appear to be quite different from someone else's.

There was a dynamic relationship between place, meaning, and text during the golden age of Toronto's reggae scene, a place where migrant and host collided, where differences were negotiated and sometimes, over time, even celebrated. All the while, reggae provided a backing score and libretto for these cross-cultural transactions. As scholars have shown, spatial analysis can be very compelling. Spatial analysis that involves music is perhaps even more so., When applied to a musical movement, place can be viewed not only as a category of historical analysis but also as a historical agent, as something that informed historical events and affected the way they are remembered.[1] Place informed the music heard along Toronto's ethnic frontlines, and the music meant different things to different people.[2]

Place can alter existing texts, producing new meanings for older works of art, songs, and poetry and producing meanings that may even be at odds with the original intentions of the artist. Spatial readings can expose the disparate meanings that a group or audience who witnessed an identical performance attached to the music. Separate as they might have been for author, performer, audience member, and critic, these meanings are, nevertheless, valid experiences for all individuals involved.

Place, as a historical agent, influenced the new texts that Jamaican migrant and host were authoring in Toronto at this time. The physical structures, the surrounding environment, the sounds, the sights, and even the smells of these places all figured in the way reggae and Jamaican ethnicity occurred in Toronto.[3] Indeed, place and the act of placing are central to the way we remember events; they are full of meaning and ripe for historical inquiry.[4] If every memory is a "memory of a place," then the nightclubs, school rooms, dance halls, church basements, shebeens, and even lonely streetscapes were organic actors in the Canadian reggae scene.[5]

It was within these various places that Toronto's reggae subculture problematized notions of political authority, social order, and societal norms in Canada's dominant society.[6] Places such as the Bamboo Club were flashpoints for defying the dominant culture.[7] At the same time, Toronto's reggae subculture was itself diverse. It was not the exclusive preserve of a migrant Jamaican experience. Indeed, the imagined community of Toronto's nascent reggae scene in the 1970s and 1980s is sometimes at odds with the material reality and actual lived experience of the players involved. Through a backwards-gazing lens that is mindful of place, it's possible to deconstruct a monolithic text that champions official multiculturalism and reggae clichés to reveal alternatives that are far more convincing.

The Ethnic Frontline

Jamaican migrants transmitted sound waves across the frontline, and reggae spilled into places where non-Jamaicans could listen in.[8] These transmissions, however, were regulated by cultural gatekeepers (on both sides) who wanted to preserve a sort of musical purity. All the while, bridge builders (on both sides) fought to break down the artifices that inhibited the free transmission of music from migrant to host and back again.[9]

By the 1970s, Jamaicans living in Toronto had plenty of outlets in which to "enact" their ethnicity in both the public and private realms.[10] Individual expressions of Jamaican ethnicity, however, differed – sometimes slightly, sometimes vastly – within the same "group." These diverse expressions resist a cumbersome metanarrative for the Jamaican Canadian migrant.

The very fact that frontlines or boundaries exist is, of course, important.[11] However, the bridges that connect host to migrant – those places where boundaries, both physical and emotional, are sometimes relaxed – can be far more intriguing, for it is here that old texts can be reimagined. In the Jamaican Canadian case, many of the bridges erected along Toronto's ethnic frontline were engineered through and articulated in sound. In reviewing how Germanic "snatches of song" transformed Buffalo during the 1860 singers' festival, historian Barbara Lorenzkowski explains that "sound demarcated space, but also transformed it. While marking difference, it allowed for a wide range of cultural exchanges. And despite its fleeting nature, it helped create an ethnic consciousness – forged in the acts of speaking and music-making – that would alter the soundtrack of public culture itself."[12]

Ska, rocksteady, and reggae, too, demarcated Toronto's urban streetscapes. Billowy bass, Nyabinghi rhythms that had been seasoned with "other" musical influences in the Caribbean for four hundred years, and plaintive vocal harmonies escaped from residential blues dances, wedding receptions, school gymnasiums, and even car stereos to probe Toronto's avenues and boulevards from as early as the late 1960s. These unusual sounds exacerbated the fear some Canadians already harboured regarding the black Jamaican migrant. Some white Canadians, for instance, feared growing Jamaican enclaves such as those in the Jane-Finch Corridor.[13] Also, public fear of Rastafarianism grew with Bob Marley's rising stock on the international scene. For some, Rastas were violent, drug-using anarchists who were essentially walking time bombs.[14] Others were drawn to the music precisely because it was, at least for them, a little dangerous. Others still found themselves inexplicably charmed and intoxicated by Jamaica's musical export, and reggae came to be the sound of summer and, for some, the sound of holidays. But up and down Toronto's main drags and backstreets, ethnicity was occurring, cultural exchanges were taking place, and meaning was being ascribed to "Jamaican Canadian" for both migrant and host.

Reggae 'Pon the Street

Full-on ska or reggae nights were usually restricted to Jamaican Canadian wedding receptions at the community hall, parties in the church basement or, sometimes, the all-night blues dance in someone's home or apartment. It was here, in a sparsely furnished basement or the unused backroom of a main street storefront, that Jamaicans set up their sound systems and claimed a space for themselves in the city. While reggae music would eventually penetrate Toronto's club scene and find a non-Jamaican audience, the social dynamic in the nightclubs differed somewhat from these more exclusively Jamaican gatherings.

The church hall gathering, for instance, had a cross-generational, family atmosphere. As Rupert "Ojiji" Harvey recalled:

> There was a cultural thing going on at the church. And that's when, you know, the parents started seeing old friends from Jamaica that'd started migrating to Canada. And they made their little churches, and then you could start getting Jamaican food. They'd get together and talk about the old country and the old days ... The church was a big part of the initial experience.[15]

During these experiences, the congregation might heartily belt out Jamaican folk songs, share Annancy stories, or watch youngsters display a talent at singing or dancing while trying to ignore the mouth-watering aromas emanating from the kitchen, usually vats of curried goat with rice and peas.[16]

Similarly, music played a central role at family get-togethers at someone's home. Phil Vassell's dad, for example, owned a sound system. As Vassell remembered: "We all took turns, starting with me [spinning records] at his parties in his basement or occasionally at a hall or occasionally at a wedding reception ... Music was always at home."[17] Likewise, Mike Smith, trombonist and schoolteacher, remembered that his uncle had a bunch of old records and a little sound system in the basement of his home, where he played some ska, mento, and reggae music for his guests in the mid-1970s. For Mike, the sound system at his uncle's was pivotal in providing a much-needed outlet for Jamaican musical culture in Canada:

> That's what would pull us together ... in the basement, everybody dancing. We were kind of losing part our culture because we're not in Jamaica any more, but here we are, and there were different groups of people. His friends would come over, and we'd all sit and cook ... And after the eating was done, then it was all about sitting around listening to music, or the guys playing dominoes, or they would have a little dance competition: Can you dance like when you were in Jamaica? I think that was a big thing for us.[18]

These sorts of affairs, however, stood in stark contrast to the all-night party, where there was little care for dominoes. The blues dance was a staple for migrant Jamaicans wherever they travelled. Vivien Goldman, who experienced these parties first-hand in London, England, during the 1970s, remembered:

> Two decades after large-scale Caribbean immigration began from the newly independent islands, yesterday's colonies, the first generation of black British youth claimed their right to an all-night life. Their parents had come to the so-called motherland to do the hard slog work of keeping the country running that the homecoming World War II heroes hoped to avoid. But a good portion of their restless children, not content to fit in and slide unnoticed through

the status quo, started to make their own music and invent a self-determined world within a sometimes hostile community.[19]

There was sex too. The sweaty rub-a-dub dancing, oiled by plenty of Red Stripe, Guinness, Dragon Stout, and Jamaican rum, coupled with the sweet, pervasive aroma of Jamaican sinsemilla, sometimes allowed for a suspension of reality from the struggle of migrant life. Young lovers could transcend the spare room of a barber's shop, and with reggae's swelling bass, the "vertical orgasm," at least according to Goldman, was not uncommon.[20]

And so it was in Toronto. These rub-a-dub dances were usually the preserve of the younger set. The parties were commonplace in West Indian homes, as Wayne Hanson recalled: "Every weekend there's a Jamaican party. And you'd be invited, or you can just show up and meet other Jamaicans."[21] Replicating the carnival spirit of the all-night parties in Jamaica, blues dances provided a crucial meeting point for Jamaican migrants in their late teens and early twenties.

While the blues dance was a haven for Jamaicans, some non-Jamaican youths managed to penetrate the inner sanctum of the all-night party.[22] The sheer volume of the music might have alarmed many non-Jamaicans, but some were attracted to it. Being privy to these cultural experiences could often engender tales of exotica. Witness, for instance, *Globe and Mail* journalist James Hill's account from 1978:

> We enter a bare cement basement lit only by the orange glow of two vacuum tubes in a stereo amplifier. A disc jockey sits at a turntable spinning reggae singles, and the music dominated by the bottomless groan of the winding bass line, booms through a pair of PA speakers ... I am told that there are dozens of basements like this around Toronto, each one an incubator for subterranean homesick roots, an oasis of darkness and dreams ... Slowly we learn to dance. And we dance late into the night.[23]

While some of Toronto's non-Jamaicans came to reggae in this dimly-lit environment, where sinsemilla smoke squalls got even the nonsmokers high, others were exposed to Jamaican music in less shadowy ways.

This exposure came at a number of different access points around the city. If the blues dance filtered the number of non-Jamaicans entering the fray by virtue of requiring people to descend into sometimes dark and dank basements, the reggae experience at school was far more inclusive and less threatening. Non-Jamaicans were introduced to Jamaican music through their friends who were either children of Jamaican migrants or migrants themselves. Non-Jamaicans who, for example, attended schools along Eglinton or in the Jane-Finch Corridor could be exposed to some reggae at their school dances. As Mike Smith remembered:

> I know that the people liked Jamaican music because whenever we were at dance, a school dance ... whenever reggae music came on, it was a very big thing ... They would play ten or fifteen quote-unquote Canadian songs ... and then they'd play maybe two or three Jamaican songs, and everyone danced for those songs, so I realized that at that time that this music is very powerful.[24]

Similarly, Jamaican drummer Sunray Grennan, who attended Oakdale Junior High, recalled that the reggae bug afflicted more than just his fellow students:

> I became the drummer, and I started to express this reggae or ska [beat], and my bandmates found it interesting, and I would teach them how to play little things ... So I think there was a merging there ... Even the music teacher actually started to ask me to play a reggae beat because he had never heard reggae before.[25]

Non-Jamaican David Kingston, who attended W.A. Porter, heard Jamaican toasters through the boom boxes in the school grounds: "It was a time everyone had boom boxes, so if it wasn't *Saturday Night Fever,* you'd hear Dillinger and Big Youth, and so you'd get to know people, and it was just fascinating because it was a whole parallel world of music."[26] These cultural exchanges and the sharing of parallel musical worlds helped to establish friendships between migrant kids and their new Canadian friends.

When Jamaicans began broadcasting reggae into Toronto's social spaces, the music transformed portions of the city. When played boldly, Jamaican music can claim a space by moving the air around it with thundering bass. This can be intimidating to the uninitiated. Yet the different ways by which non-Jamaicans responded and contested these spatial claims is worth exploring.[27] With reggae wafting out of a car stereo or a boom box, the migrant, in such fleeting moments, could claim spaces such as Bathurst Street or Finch Avenue or Goreway Drive or Keele Street as places that one might hear reggae. Jamaican music transformed space into a place full of cultural meaning.[28]

Loud reggae did not always please non-Jamaicans. Indeed, listening to reggae was not always an elective practice for non-Jamaicans living or within earshot of Jamaican music. In his exposé *Selling Illusions: The Cult of Multiculturalism in Canada,* Neil Bissoondath suggests that the policy of official multiculturalism could scare outsiders away from making complaints about noise or demanding that the volume be lowered. Those who did complain might be accused of cultural aggression.[29] As Jamaican Canadian Phil Vassell confirmed, one could usually tell where a Jamaican's house was, "because they like to play their music loud."[30] In 1979, *Globe and Mail* journalist Dick Beddoes (better known for his take on hockey games than reggae) had his own, albeit playful, concerns about reggae: "Physical frenzy is a part of the reggae din ... Chances are you'd have to be a musicologist on the distinguished order of John Kraglund to interpret the difference between reggae, the mindless clatter of disco, the sock of rock and the soothing song of the hermit thrush."[31] Whether welcome or not, Jamaican music, with its imposing, bottom-heavy sound and hypnotic (or, depending on the ears, annoying) polyrhythms, cut a wide swath through Toronto's streetscapes.

Central to Toronto's reggae map was the Black Bottom of Bathurst Street.[32] There, one could find the Home Service and the Negro Library, the hub of black political consciousness. There was also Joyce's, one of the first restaurants to offer Caribbean food, and Third World Books and Crafts, which offered the city's only repository of books on black themes by black authors. In terms of its importance to Toronto's black community, journalist Norman Otis Richmond declared that Bathurst

104 *Place and Meaning in Toronto's Reggae Text*

Street "is what Central Avenue is to Los Angeles or Lennox Avenue is to New York City."[33] Many Jamaicans who came to Canada in the late 1960s or early 1970s chose to live on or near Bathurst Street, from Eglinton southward. It was there that black merchants provided food, hair care, fashion, and, of course, music for the city's black populace.

Jamaican migrants could also find ska, rocksteady, and reggae records at a variety of West Indian stores that imported their musical wares from Yard or England. One could buy black music at Theo's Record Shop on Bathurst, and a string of record shops sprouted up on Eglinton, which boasted, at various times, Joe Gibbs, Solar Sounds, and Monica's Hairdressing, Cosmetics and Records. Even Jackie Mittoo and Lord Tanamo had a shop at Vaughan and Bathurst for a spell.[34] All these shops sold the sounds of home in the form of LPs and disco 45s.[35]

Many young Torontonians growing up in the 1970s proved to be Jamaican-curious. This generation did not harbour the same inhibitions towards reggae – and, by extension, black or immigrant music – that an older generation might have done. The city's primary, middle, and high schools fostered an atmosphere of musical exploration between non-Jamaican youths and their migrant counterparts. Without this freedom, the golden age of Canadian reggae in the 1980s – with its heavy reliance on a young punk and even younger postpunk demographic – might not have occurred.

Still, there were plenty of nightclubs for an older generation to discover ska, rocksteady, and calypso in Toronto. The Caribbean Club (a.k.a. the Carib), Club Tropics, the Bermuda Tavern, the Latin Quarter Club, the Calypso Club, Club Trinidad, Soul Palace, and Le Coq d'Or all emerged in the city in the late 1960s and early 1970s.[36] All these venues, as journalist and reggae historian Kevin Howes explains in the liner notes to Jackie Mitoo's *Wishbone*, "catered to mixed-race crowds looking for island hospitality and warmth."[37] Scarborough, too, had its Carib Restaurant and Tavern on Eglinton East, where the steel drum sounds of Jerry Jerome and the Cardells were often featured.[38]

There were, however, a couple of clubs that were of particular importance to Jamaican migrants. The West Indies Federation Club (or WIF Club) at Brunswick and College opened in 1961. It was founded by Harry Gairey (a former CP Rail porter and, later, a founding member of the

Negro Citizenship Committee), Kermit and Kingsley Lyn (both of whom would become correctional officers at Mimico Correctional Centre), Jim Moxley, and Clarence Lucey (who also worked on the railroads). Beyond a music venue and restaurant, the WIF Club operated as something of a welcome centre for Jamaican and West Indian migrants. Migrants could dance the night away but also make important contacts for housing and employment.[39] It was a public space for an ever-growing Jamaican community.[40] It would also be the spot where singing hopeful Jay Douglas made his mark with the Cougars.

Formed in 1966, the Cougars were a unit of West Indian musicians that played a variety of genres, including the Beatles, Matt Monro, and James Brown, to Toronto crowds mixed in with some of their ska, calypso, and rocksteady repertoire. The classic, mostly Jamaican lineup included Lloyd Spence on bass, Newton "Dizzy" Barker on keyboards, Bobby Gaynair on saxophone, Everton "Pablo" Paul on drums, Jo Jo Bennett on flugelhorn, Clive Barry (a.k.a. Jay Douglas) on lead vocals, Bobby Roseau as the MC-singer, and Roland Prince from Antigua on lead guitar.[41]

Jamaican migrants also listened to music at Yonge Street's Club Jamaica. Jamaican singer the Mighty Pope recalled his days singing with bands such as the Sheiks and the Hitch-Hikers at the club and described how it satisfied not only the needs of the rising number of Jamaicans in the city, but also the public's interest in all things Jamaican:

> As more Jamaicans came [Club Jamaica] got really, really established, and that's where they went and congregated every weekend ... [The Club] was right on Yonge Street, and it was like a novelty, so it was three-quarters white ... It was all positive, because they [whites] could hear the music from downstairs, and it was a novelty ... it was a bit of Jamaica, I guess.[42]

And a "bit of Jamaica" was exactly what Canadians who had been to Montego Bay or Ocho Rios were hoping for. After all, a thirty-something non-Jamaican could easily muster up the gumption to take his date to a Yonge Street nightclub to hear the Cougars or the Sheiks perform popular West Indian tunes and perhaps the odd sample off the American

Hit Parade. On the other hand, a blues dance in an apartment on Driftwood Avenue in the Jane-Finch Corridor might as well have been three thousand kilometres to the south away.

James Hill, a journalist with the *Globe and Mail*, was privy to the city's reggae underground. He witnessed the arrival of new Jamaican music to Monica's shop in 1978:

> A new shipment of singles has just arrived from Jamaica, and there's a large crowd pressed around the counter. The atmosphere resembles an auction: as the sales clerk spins each new release, customers raise their hands to indicate if they want to buy it. Toronto's West Indian record stores are more than simple sales outlets; they provide a direct pipeline to the shifting tides of culture in the homeland.[43]

Vassell and his father were usually in that crowd pressed around the counter:

> I remember as a kid growing up going on Eglinton Avenue and standing around with [my dad] and a bunch of other guys who'd go there on Saturday morning when the new batch comes in, and the guy behind the counter would play thirty seconds of a record. They'd all listen in and either they wanted it after hearing thirty seconds or they'd say, "Ha, leave that one alone."[44]

Similar shops such as Peabody's Clef Records and Music were, by the mid-1970s, also doing a brisk trade in the heart of the Black Bottom on Bathurst, just south of Dupont. Sid Lovejoy set up his Lovejoy Records and Productions, which included a recording studio for Jamaican migrants. Noel Walker owned the Tropical Gift and Record Store on the east side of Bathurst. Walker's sizeable inventory was diverse and included jazz, American soul, and the occasional white artists that seemed to resonate – sometimes inexplicably – with black Torontonians. Sports journalist Jack Batten, for example, was simply amazed to find Engelbert Humperdinck at the Tropical Gift and Record Store.[45] Still, Walker's clientele was, according to the owner, 95 percent black, and most were Jamaican: "They're the ones, Jamaicans, who are most crazy about music.

I import records from Jamaica and England that people can't get anywhere else. I brought in maybe $20,000 to $30,000 worth of imports last year from overseas."[46] The demographic, however, would change over time as more and more non-Jamaicans became interested in hearing and buying Jamaican music.[47]

By the early 1980s, reggae had floated downtown and into Kensington Market, which had been cultivating a reggae culture for years. Tiger's Coconut Grove, for instance, opened in 1976 and was owned by Eric Vernon "Tiger" Armstrong Jr., a Jamaican-born musician who often performed under the pseudonym Lord Power.[48] When two established reggae acts opened rival record shops in 1980s, Kensington became a place where reggae and Jamaican culture could be enacted and heard on a daily basis. Stranger Cole was a significant Jamaican singer of the ska era while his rival and friend guitarist Ranford Williams (or Rannie Bop) was a top-notch session player who had recorded with Lee Perry, Paul Simon, and Bob Marley.[49] Cole and Williams were constantly vying for trade by blasting reggae at each other out of massive speakers in what locals called the wobble zone.[50] In Toronto, Williams, a Canadian Reggae Music Awards winner (1985) ran the band Yahwedeh as well as the record store.[51] The difference between this location and the Eglinton strip was that it attracted non-Jamaicans shopping for reggae, including tourists who may not have possessed the gumption to shop on Eglinton or in the Black Bottom. By 1985, there were between twenty-five and fifty reggae and West Indian record stores operating in the city of Toronto, all keeping local reggae alive.[52] By selling Canadian reggae, Williams's store in Kensington Market was crucial to the local scene.[53]

While there were many outposts for reggae records, the music itself only sporadically found space on Canadian airwaves. In the 1970s, Toronto's CHIN Radio had its *Island Music Hour,* as did Mississauga's CHWO and CJMR. Both of these stations featured West Indian programming on the weekend.[54] Many black Torontonians also listened to WUFO out of Buffalo, though this station catered to a black American crowd and less so to fans of West Indian music. By the mid-1970s, CHIN boasted Bill Payne, a white DJ who was popular among black Torontonians for spinning soul, gospel, and blues.[55] By the early 1980s, CFNY's Deadly Hedley had a popular Sunday night show, and campus radio stations such as

CKLN (Ryerson College) featured Canadian David Kingston's hugely popular *Reggae Showcase,* which aired on Sunday nights from 1982 to 1987 and on Fridays from 1987 to 1992. Though most of these shows were hardly featured during prime-time hours, fans hungry for rocksteady and lovers of rock and roots reggae would seek them out and soon became devoted followers of the city's reggae radio.[56]

Reggae legitimately contested for the hearts (and dollars) of a soon-to-be club-hopping, vinyl-buying critical mass.[57] It became an accepted part of a swelling musical underground fuelled by campus FM radio. Some Canadian reggae acts such as Messenjah and the Sattalites later enjoyed television exposure on CBC and MuchMusic, particularly when the latter was in need of CanCon videos.[58]

But long before Messenjah and the Sattalites commanded national exposure, champions of Jamaican music had to fight for space in the city's print media. *Contrast,* one of Toronto's first West Indian newspapers, founded in 1969 by Olivia Grange-Walker, kept its readership attuned to political and cultural movements in Jamaica. Grange-Walker's weekly column was titled "Olivia's Pepperpot" and was, according to *Globe and Mail* journalist Adele Freedman, "a disarming synthesis of the ingenuous and the sophisticated with the power to draw you in like a vacuum cleaner."[59] The column also helped raise the profile of local reggae artists, including those that Grange-Walker herself managed: Ernie Smith, O. Travis, Chalawa, and Leroy Sibbles.[60]

There were enough Jamaican musicians working in the Toronto by the 1960s to warrant managers. Karl Mullings, for example, co-owned Club Jamaica on Yonge Street and was pivotal in managing early Jamaican Canadian acts such as the Sheiks and the Cougars. He helped parlay the success of the West Indian exhibit at Expo 67 and annual events such as Caribana into regular performances in Toronto and around Ontario and Quebec for his roster.[61] That generation of Jamaican Canadian musicians, however, had to present a diversified set list to entertain their mixed audiences. Sets might be seasoned with some of the island's flavour, but only the odd ska or rocksteady number would be surreptitiously slipped in between the standard fare of Top 40 and American R&B classics. Still, bands such as the Sheiks, Jo-Jo and the Fugitives, and the Hitch-Hikers, featuring the Mighty Pope, worked constantly in the city's nightclubs.[62]

The style of show they put on was attractive to non-Jamaicans who may have heard some ska, courtesy of Byron Lee and the Dragonaires, while holidaying on the island's north coast.[63]

Some events even featured reggae in mainstream spaces, allowing the genre to transcend the city's youth subculture and cut across generational lines. The famous annual West Indian festival, Caribana, for instance, began in 1967 and took place on the streets of Toronto, inside homes and nightclubs, and even in Maple Leaf Gardens. Although the festival was based mostly on Trinidad's Carnival, Caribana did feature some reggae acts. In 1971, for example, the Blues Busters, the Cougars, and Jackie Mittoo were thrown into the mix with a host of calypso artists.[64]

Reggae's growing popularity meant that it was no longer restricted to the confines of West Indian homes and establishments. Reggae had entered the mainstream spaces of the city's nightclubs and movie theatres. This access was won by the international success of reggae acts such as Toots and the Maytals and Jimmy Cliff, who had, by the mid-1970s, performed in Toronto.[65] Also, the popularity of the Jamaican-made movie *The Harder They Come* had a huge, positive effect on the proliferation of reggae around the world. Ivan, the film's main character, was styled after Jamaica's lawless and gun-toting folk hero Ivanhoe "Rhyging" Martin. Rhyging resembled a cynical Robin Hood but couched in the western genre so popular in Jamaica. The movie popularized several reggae artists all at once, most notably Jimmy Cliff, who not only wrote much of the soundtrack but also starred in the lead role. The film's soundtrack contributed several classics to reggae's canon, including Cliff's "You Can Get It If You Really Want," "Many Rivers to Cross," and "Sitting in Limbo"; Toots and the Maytals' "Pressure Drop"; Desmond Dekker's "(007) Shanty Town"; the Slickers' "Johnny Too Bad"; and the Melodians' "Rivers of Babylon."[66]

Upon the film's release, entertainment writer Robert Martin spoke to its importance (and success) in Toronto:

> As might be expected, [the film] has a fanatic following among Toronto's West Indian community and there's a lot of repeat business at Cinema Lumiere where it is in its ninth week. But the number

of whites in the audience has been steadily increasing as the word spreads that this film has much to say to anyone who loves pop music and living close to the edge where death doesn't matter as long as it's done in style.[67]

Later, in 1975, *Globe and Mail* theatre critic Lawrence O'Toole confirmed that "*The Harder They Come* has become a cult and reggae music a growing, popular taste."[68]

The Birth of Canadian Reggae

As reggae was being introduced to the world via the silver screen and also through popular crossover hits by acts such as Eric Clapton and Johnny Nash, Toronto was fast becoming a place where reggae was not only heard but also made. In fact, many of Jamaica's key players were relocating to Toronto. Two musicians in particular stand out. Bassist-vocalist Leroy Sibbles and keyboardist Jackie Mittoo were genre-defining house musicians à la Motown's Funk Brothers in the assembly-style confines of Coxsone Dodd's Studio One. Sibbles had scored several hits – including "Fatty, Fatty" (which he cowrote with Mittoo) and "Book of Rules" – in Jamaica and even a few in England with his Heptones trio.[69] Mittoo was a master arranger and organist who, at the age of only fourteen, had been a founding member of the famous Skatalites. He later went on to work with the Sheiks, Soul Vendors, and Sound Dimension and was the musical director and producer at Studio One. Mittoo came to Toronto in 1969; Sibbles followed in 1973.[70] Added to this powerful duo was a mix of other high-calibre Jamaican musicians who, having grown tired of political violence at home and encouraged by the positive reviews of those who had "gone a' Cyanada" before them, chose to relocate to Toronto: Lord Tanamo, Stranger Cole, Wayne McGhie, Eddie Spencer, Joe Isaacs, Leroy Brown, Bob Williams, Jimmy Wisdom, Pluggy Satchmo, Lloyd Delpratt, Johnny Osbourne, Ernie Smith, and Willi Williams. Jamaican music had enough qualified local ambassadors that it could begin to infiltrate Toronto's music scene.

Jamaicans started recording reggae in Toronto. Dave and Ansell Collins (of Double Barrel fame), for instance, recorded a full album in

Toronto in 1974.[71] But before that, a triumvirate of early Canadian reggae recordings by Jackie Mittoo managed to convert some local radio disc jockeys to the Jamaican sound.[72] *Wishbone* (1971), *Reggae Magic* (1972), and *Let's Put It All Together* (1975) are especially noteworthy because Mittoo used white Canadian musicians, including members of the Toronto Symphony Orchestra, jazzers Rob McConnell, Guido Basso, and Moe Koffman, and classically trained composer Howard Cable.[73] Cable recalled the dynamic that emerged between the migrant musicians and Toronto's first-call session players during the recording of *Wishbone* at the high-end Eastern Sound Studio:

> Carl [DeHaney] introduced me to Jackie, and we got together on the things he wanted ... He brought his own gang in. We had already decided long before that the white boys that I had wouldn't quite make it. He gave me the tracks, and I scored the instrumentation. It was pretty simple, with a lot of tones and things like that. It went very well, actually.[74]

The original liner notes for the album invited listeners to "Meet Jackie and his Reggae Beat!," and *Wishbone* certainly provided a striking hybrid of Mittoo's vision and Cable's orchestration in what was likely the first real sample of Canadian reggae – that is to say, reggae recorded in Canada, on local studio gear, and with at least some input from non-Jamaican Canadian musicians and producers.[75]

The collaboration boded well for Mittoo. The keyboardist told *Reggae Report*'s I. Jabulani Tafari in 1988 that working with the Canadian Talent Library

> gave me a lot of recognition on all the Canadian stations ... At the time I had qualified for Canadian content because I'd already lived there for about four years. So I did one album for them called *Reggae Magic* ... They didn't have to put up with no lyrics and all that, but them was still getting reggae. And so that became the favourite reggae album in Canada. This is in 1972. Financially, it was a non-profit thing, but I could have never financed the amount of advertisement that I got from these people.[76]

As both Mittoo's and reggae's profile were on the rise, other Jamaican Canadians looked to documenting the growing pool of talent in the Toronto region.

In the mid-1970s, for instance, Jerry Brown set up Summer Records in the Malton community, where another block of Jamaican migrants had begun making their home. While Summer Records enjoyed only modest financial success, the company recorded a bevy of transplanted Jamaicans, including Willi Williams; Earth, Roots and Water; Noel Ellis; and popular Jamaican singer Johnny Osbourne, who, like so many of his counterparts, decided to embark on a life in Canada.[77]

Two years after Mittoo released the third and final instalment of his large-scale Canadian albums, reggae found another Canadian patron. In 1977, David Clayton-Thomas, the British-born Canadian singer-producer of Blood, Sweat and Tears fame, lent his significant musical credibility to the debut album of Canada's first self-styled reggae band, Ishan People, featuring Johnny Osbourne. Their self-titled album was released on the GRT label, and though the chosen themes of Ishan People's two albums did not necessarily speak to the Caribbean Canadian experience, the mere fact that they had secured a record deal and had gotten Clayton-Thomas to produce it inspired other would-be Canadian reggae artists to do the same.[78]

In fact, enough locally produced reggae was being made that some aspiring entrepreneurs even considered the possibility of exporting records to Jamaica. Olivia Grange-Walker put forth the ambitious idea of selling Canadian reggae to the West Indies.[79] This audacious move prompted journalist Peter Goddard to claim that while Toronto was "still a colony, compared with what's happening back in Kingston and, to some, it's still a remote outpost compared with New York and London. Yet, unlikely as it sounds, there's not only reggae music here, but a reggae music industry."[80] While the export business may have been a little too ambitious, there was, at least by the end of the 1970s, something approaching a full-fledged reggae scene in Toronto, replete with Jamaican entrepreneurs such as Grange-Walker, bona fide reggae stars such as Mittoo and Sibbles, and a growing number of would-be reggae musicians and fans of both Jamaican and non-Jamaican heritage. Toronto began to feel the birth pangs of Reggae Canadiana.

Place and Meaning in Toronto's Reggae Text 113

But reggae's exposure to the mainstream continued to be stifled by poor radio presence. To be fair, the music was hardly played on Jamaican radio in the early 1970s, let alone on Canada's airwaves. As Rap Rose, manager of Joe Gibbs Record Store, lamented in 1978: "The major radio stations refuse to play it ... Even the records that are produced locally and can be considered Canadian content are not played ... And I was under the impression that we were supposed to be fighting for multiculturalism ... The way our music is accepted in Britain shows that it is capable of entertaining people."[81] But Canada was not Britain. And Rose, and others like him who were acutely aware of the successes of Jamaican music in London and Birmingham, struggled to reconcile the Canadian government's multicultural policy with the reality of what was actually being played on Canadian airwaves. Mike Smith was similarly frustrated: "I had a hard time getting and finding Jamaican music at that particular time on the radio. So there was a program on, on Sunday nights ... and I remember staying up ... to record some of the music."[82] Despite the introduction of new regulations that forced Canadian radio to play more Canadian music, reggae still had to fight for precious radio time in Canada throughout the 1980s, and even when it did come (mostly on FM or campus radio), the music would never experience the level of success or acceptance that the British brand of reggae did.[83]

In 1982, the white Vancouver band the Payolas scored a massive hit with the reggae-tinged "Eyes of a Stranger." Cofrontman Paul Hyde later remarked on its success: "I never thought it would get as much airplay as it did because I thought it was too reggae for the airwaves at the time."[84] The lack of reggae's presence on mainstream radio was apparent to more than those in the reggae community. Though more and more Jamaican artists were calling Toronto home and adding to the richness of the city's artistic community, mainstream mediums remained impenetrable, and the inclusiveness promised in the multicultural policies was at odds with the material reality of the migrant musician.

Yet the music was making its mark in the city. In 1978, James Hill declared that "there is a Trench Town in Toronto, as there is in Jamaica. It's everywhere."[85] Yet Hill also observed that the local reggae scene "remains largely invisible outside the West Indian community. Ignored by the mainstream of the music industry, it's confined to the fringes, to

Harbourfront, and suburban outposts such as the Club Carib, to rented dance halls and disco basements, to record stores and homemade studios."[86] But Hill had to update this view in less than year because 1979 was, as author Klive Walker rightly noted, perhaps the most pivotal year in the development of reggae in Canada.

That year, Bob Marley played the last of his Canadian shows at Maple Leaf Gardens (he had played the Gardens the year before). It was an eye-opener for Jamaican Phil Vassell, who attended the show:

> Going to Maple Leaf Gardens ... and watching Bob Marley fill that place and seeing how people responded to Bob Marley and the Wailers at Maple Leaf Gardens! That's when you realize that it isn't just your immediate friends around you that were digging the music, but a whole slew of people that didn't look like you, didn't sound like you, came from different walks of life, but they had that in common.[87]

Jamaican music had already been demarcating Toronto's streets and nightclubs. Now it had taken the city's biggest venue by storm.

That same year, Bruce Cockburn, living in the city and enamoured with the energetic reggae scene, chose Ishan People's Larry Silvera and Benbow to back him on "Wondering Where the Lions Are," which appeared on the *Dancing in the Dragon's Jaws* album.[88] The song was Cockburn's biggest American hit and managed to climb to number twenty-one on the Billboard charts. It broke Cockburn outside of Canada and won him an appearance on *Saturday Night Live* in 1980.[89] The reggae that was being broadcast on Toronto's streets, then, was crucial to Cockburn's career, as Canadian music mogul Bernie Finkelstein remembered: "If Bruce doesn't live in Toronto, he doesn't know about Leroy Sibbles' band, he doesn't go into clubs such as the Bamboo where reggae is being played, [then] I don't think he gets the inspiration for 'Wondering Where the Lions Are.'"[90] Cockburn was able to parlay the extensive airplay of "Wondering" into larger tours and bigger venues.[91]

The singer-songwriter's integrity in terms of doing reggae "right" was extremely important to Cockburn: "I didn't want to fake it in the studio.

I thought if I was going to use this music I want the real guys to play on it and invite them in and have it be real."[92] Cockburn's chasing of the "real thing," the real Jamaican sound, presented a paradox for the local reggae scene. By virtue of the song's success, reggae had fully arrived in the nation's musical mainstream. Yet the language used by Cockburn also delineated, although perhaps not intentionally, an "us and them" line of thinking that lingered in the consciousness of the Toronto media. Such language made permissible the idea that henceforth only Jamaican musicians could or, indeed, should play reggae in Canada.

Still, for many young white Torontonians who might have had only a vague interest in reggae, Cockburn's stamp of approval helped to accelerate the genre's popularity among the cool set along Queen Street West, where the city's musos, profoundly affected by the do-it-yourself aesthetic of British punk and new wave, regarded reggae as an equally underground and subversive art form that struck sympathetic political chords with their own rebellious musics. Reggae was no longer the insipid island music that their parents might have heard at Sandals on holiday. It was a fiery, oppressor-naming, and dangerous tool that both distressed and confounded mom and dad.

Reggae's stock rose further in the Toronto scene when clubs such as the Horseshoe and the El Mocambo began featuring local reggae acts.[93] The El Mocambo even managed to bring in some big-name acts. In 1980, the *Toronto Star* exclaimed that the city's reggae fans "still talk about [Burning Spear's] sensational shows at the El Mocambo" and that while Marley's postponement of another Maple Leaf Gardens show was a letdown (though few would have known at this point that the singer had been diagnosed with an advanced form of cancer), fans could look forward to highly attractive packages including Third World and Black Uhuru.[94]

There was also a swell in the formation of local reggae bands. The Chelsea International Show Lounge and Disco on Isabella Street, for instance, boasted Limbo Springs, which was a combination of new wave and reggae.[95] The band featured former academics, including Kim Cameron, a white, Canadian sociology professor from Trent University and the University of Quebec who, at least for a time, had turned his back on academia. Cameron hadn't the mildest regret:

After all, thousands of PhDs are lined up to occupy the positions I once held. They have the joy of setting the exams for future note-takers. Meanwhile, I have learned to respect the thoughts and accomplishments of many rock and reggae singers and musicians who, through their experience in intangible and subjective worlds, have been able to assimilate innumerable things they need to know, in ways which often surpass the insights of science as a means of dealing practically with the world.[96]

Reggae as a profession was attracting more than just the Jamaican migrant musician.[97]

The fact that a career in reggae attracted non-Jamaicans in Canada while the genre was still in its infancy bears witness to how irresistible the music could be for some. Still, Canadian reggae was, in the main, performed by recently arrived Jamaican migrants. From the early 1970s onward, Jackie Mittoo had been able to breach, with his "vibrant reggae music on the electric organ," the better rooms around Toronto, such as the chic Dr. Livingstone's at the Bristol Place Hotel on Dixon Road.[98] Even verifiable "A" rooms such as Harbourfront began putting on reggae showcases that included local talent, as did the Forum at Ontario Place, where thousands of reggae fans showed up annually to support home team sides such as Sibbles, Messenjah, and the Sattalites.[99] With the coming of a new decade, several Jamaican expatriate musicians were regularly playing reggae in Toronto.[100]

In October 1980, Harbourfront's one-day all-Canadian reggae festival featured Truths and Rights, Chalawa, Ernie Smith, and Carlene Davis, who collectively sold out the centre's Brigantine Room. The *Globe and Mail*'s Adele Freedman reported that she had walked into a Toronto-style "reggae Woodstock":

> Truths and Rights, a group which has acquired a substantial following in the city in a short time, was in the middle of a scorching finale and there wasn't a pelvis in the room that wasn't rocking to the reggae backbeat. Little children stood on chairs for an unobstructed view of the stage; and anyone with a fedora to wave was waving it.[101]

The crowd's demographic caught the attention of the journalist, who seemed flabbergasted that there were "even a few balding quinquagenarians" in the mix.[102] The night's climax arrived when the group featuring Smith and Davis slowed the tempo down, as Freedman explained, "to a reverent adagio with a stirring performance of 'By the River of Babylon.'"[103] Indeed, Toronto's Jamaican expats were now – with ardor and avidity – singing King Alpha's song in a strange land.

Reggae Takes Root

Non-Jamaicans, as it happens, were also humming along. Monica Lewis, the proprietor of Monica's Hairdressing, Cosmetics and Records saw a rise in the number of white people interested in reggae music in the early 1980s:

> When I opened up in 1971, I was the only one ... When I started, I was importing records from Jamaica and England for my black customers. Now I get all kinds of customers; more and more of them are mature, older white people who have travelled to the Islands. When they're there, the music they hear is reggae and it becomes natural to them. When they come back, they want to remember what it was like, so they come searching for reggae records.[104]

Although this was true, the jet-setters were less likely to be found checking out Queen Street West for local reggae acts. This practice belonged to the younger generation of whites who hastened reggae's deliverance in Toronto.

Andru Branch, a white Canadian born in Nova Scotia who grew up in North Toronto, articulated his reggae baptism, which occurred at a Truths and Rights performance:

> Somebody took me to see a Truths and Rights concert at the Palais Royale, and I was, like, "Oh my God, this is my life." And then the very next night we went back to the Palais Royale to see the 20th Century Rebels, and from I saw those two groups play live, that was just completely it for me, I knew my calling and what I wanted to do.[105]

While Branch may have been immediately captivated by the city's local reggae stars, his introduction to the music was directed, at least in part, via a trend in British popular music.[106]

The British two-tone phenomenon had hit Canada in a big way. Bands such as the Beat, the Selecter, Madness, Bad Manners, the Specials, and the Bodysnatchers were all part of the second generation of ska that emerged in England in the late 1970s. These bands – mostly biracial – made a significant impact in Toronto, where they had a cross-genre appeal and where they also enjoyed decent airplay on radio stations such as CFNY and CKLN. The *Globe and Mail*'s Paul McGrath was amazed by the demographic at the Selecter's first Toronto show at the Palais Royale in 1980: "The multitude congregated inside to watch Leroy Sibbles and an English ska band called the Selecter was forced into a mass sandwich on the dance floor, leathered punks found themselves back to back with two-tone-suited mods, who were cheek by jowl with standard hippies."[107] Though perhaps not by design, ska and reggae crowds were considerably more varied in terms of race and age than other genres of the day; and second-generation ska encouraged harmony by virtue of the bands' two-tone racial makeup.[108]

Journalist William Littler confirmed the success of the two-tone movement and its impact on the city's music scene during the 1980s. For Littler, the rise in popularity of reggae in Toronto stemmed from "the fact that the New Wave of rock has brought a new wave of young, white reggae fans. British bands such as the Clash and the Police began exploring reggae rhythms in their music a few years ago, and recently several British groups, some of them racially and sexually integrated, have revived ska, an uptempo predecessor of reggae."[109] White Canadian youth, looking to Britain for guidance in musical trends, discovered that quality reggae existed in their own backyard.

The city's music-savvy youth culture began exploring the various reggae experiences the city had to offer. Dill Pickles, a Jamaican-born DJ spinning records in Toronto in 1982, exclaimed:

> The white kids like this music ... because it's different from any other music they've heard but it's still like their own. They've been hearing all sorts of things that don't have what they want. Maybe with reggae

it's the heavy bass-and-drum they like. They need something to get their head together tight. Reggae does that, and they like it. And I love them for that.[110]

Likewise, for Brian Robertson, former royalties manager for EMI Music Canada and white teenager during the 1980s, discovering the parallel universe of reggae, replete with its own subgenres and star system, was transformative: "It started to come in bunches, because you'd go to one, you'd think, 'Oh, man, this is great,' and as you'd discover some legendary band such as Toots and the Maytals, 'Holy crap, they're coming to town!'"[111] Just as it had in various centres in Britain, reggae had transcended Toronto's youth subculture and had even become accepted (though perhaps only conditionally) by some middle-class Torontonians.[112] It was, nevertheless, within the critical mass of the city's youth subculture that Canadian reggae was appreciated, consumed, and eventually produced.

While most commercial radio stations continued to give reggae a miss (with the exception of CFNY), campus radio, courtesy of Ryerson College's CKLN and, later, the University of Toronto's CIUT, gave Canadian reggae much-needed space on the airwaves. Truths and Rights had a college radio hit in 1981 with "Metro's No. 1 Problem."[113] Similarly, 20th Century Rebels scored a campus and CFNY hit with "Running from the F.B.I." in 1983.[114] Yet reggae's biggest breakthrough in Canadian radio came in late August 1983, and once again it was courtesy of a British band that would make reggae history.

UB40's version of Neil Diamond's "Red Red Wine" hit number one in the United Kingdom and all over Europe.[115] Crucially, the song hit number one on the Canadian charts and made the multiracial band from Birmingham the world's biggest reggae story since the death of Bob Marley. The song would eventually hit number one in the United States, and it remains one of the only reggae songs ever to do so. "Red Red Wine" was featured on the first *Labour of Love* album.[116] *Labour of Love I* was on the UK charts for one hundred weeks and has since sold 10 million copies worldwide, while the band's catalogue has collectively sold over 75 million albums.[117]

The group is held in suspicion by some music critics and ethnomusicologists as being inauthentic. Still, UB40 is a reggae band and regarded as such by the very Jamaican reggae artists who helped build the genre. When the Masonic Temple and Massey Hall proved too small for the band, UB40 was able to play (and sell out several times) Toronto's fifteen-thousand-seat outdoor venue Kingswood Music Theatre. Bob Marley remains the only other reggae artist to have been able to consistently draw as many people into Toronto's biggest live music spaces.[118]

But even the mid-size rooms and smaller nightclubs had started opening their doors to the reggae groove. As Adele Freedman observed following a show by the Jamaican band the Gladiators at Toronto's infamous Brunswick House in 1983:

> A few years ago, reggae festivals in Toronto were likely to be haphazardly organized and attended, but now that reggae has become a fact on the charts, continuing to express the kind of unpasteurized excitement that once characterized all forms of black American music, all that has changed. The crowd at the Brunswick, probably 90 per cent white, knew exactly what was in store and they weren't disappointed.[119]

By the mid-1980s reggae was no longer a mysterious "island music" that mom and dad raved about, nor was it circumscribed within the backstreets, delineating Toronto's Jamaican enclaves. Canadian reggae was dubbing in and around the city's streetscapes, regenerating itself like a space echo loop.

Despite the small size of the island from which the music had emanated, reggae had become a household name in Toronto. It was on solid footing in the city's counterculture and had even surfaced into the mainstream. The genre's trademarks had been absorbed into the aural vocabulary of Toronto's working musicians regardless of whether they were of Jamaican descent.

Some of Canada's other ethnic musics – from places such as Italy, India, or the Ukraine, countries that, it must be said, had far bigger population bases in Toronto and Canada at large – could not compete with the national profile that reggae had amassed.[120] Few non-Italian Canadians could have told you who Lucio Battisti was, but Bob Marley's dreadlocked image was instantly recognizable to many. There were no separate categories for bhangra or bilyj holos singing at Canada's Juno Awards, but reggae, on the other hand, was singled out.[121] Winning such distinctions on the national stage, given that reggae hailed from a migrant group that in 2001 represented only 0.7 percent of Canada's population, was nothing short of remarkable.

Metro's Grand Old Man of Reggae

Leroy Sibbles was a star long before he made landfall in Canada. His voice already occupied spaces around the city where Jamaicanness was being enacted. Nearly a decade into his Toronto stay, Sibbles, the young Heptones singer, was hailed by *Toronto Star* music critic Peter Goddard as "Metro's grand old man of reggae."[122] Entertainment journalist William Burrill likewise saw Sibbles as the "patriarch of Canada's reggae scene."[123] Sibbles' centrality to the Canadian reggae experience is undeniable. As Goddard confessed, "if anyone in reggae has succeeded in this city, he has. No reggae club is complete without his appearance, no concert, no party, no benefit is complete without Leroy Sibbles."[124] At the fourth annual Canadian Black Music Awards, held in 1983, for instance, Sibbles walked away with no less than five awards.[125] Sibbles himself knew that he was something of a father figure to younger reggae musicians in the city, claiming that "they look up to me and I'm thankful for that."[126] The migrant had made good.

Sibbles had come to Toronto in January 1973, when he moved to the Jane-Finch Corridor to be with his girlfriend and near other Jamaican expats (namely, Jackie Mittoo) who had come before him.[127] The singer was well aware of his poor timing. Sibbles left Jamaica when its music was on the ascent: "The big break came in Europe about a year after I left ... and a lot of small fries cashed in." Sibbles was convinced that he would have been "doing bigger things than he is now if he hadn't left Jamaica."[128]

While his opinion of the Canadian experiment would change over time, Sibbles – at least in 1982 – seemed far more positive about his time in the north:

> I think it was the right move. I made myself a household name for one thing. I got to know the top entertainment people, so that it

would be easier to get support for reggae from all these people. And I think it's gone to the point where you can make a living out of reggae. That's no small thing, you know. Now you can live from your music. I've survived.[129]

Few others – for a variety of reasons, not least of which was the financial unpredictability involved with being a musician – have made a living from reggae music in Canada, and almost none over such an extended period of time.

Toronto's mainstream rock critics began to recognize the talent in the former Heptones frontman. As early as 1981, the *Globe and Mail's* Alan Niester likened Sibbles to, of all people, Bing Crosby: "His voice is such a smooth tenor (in a field usually dominated by histrionic shouters) and he is a veteran in a field of usually younger men. But his sweet voice and wealth of experience help give a form to a performance that, in the hands of lesser performer, becomes little more than background for dancing."[130] Yet Toronto's reggae crooner was, despite his new address, constantly in demand in Jamaica. The singer was invited back to perform at Reggae Sunsplash (Jamaica's biggest annual reggae event) for five consecutive years in the late 1970s and 1980s.[131] At the same time, Sibbles enjoyed great currency in England, where the Heptones had made their mark a decade earlier.[132] Sibbles was a legitimate star in the city's nascent reggae scene.

More importantly, Sibbles infiltrated the arteries of Toronto's and, arguably, Canada's mainstream artistic community. While it is true that certain provincial and federal government initiatives alluded to multi-cultural participation and collaboration in the arts, these often insincere schemes (at least as far as reggae was concerned) hardly explain the extent to which the genre infiltrated Toronto.[133] Simply put, reggae was cool. Leroy Sibbles was cool. Jamaicans were cool.[134] The feisty, "no apologies" attitude of the Jamaican migrant musician appealed to other non-Jamaican musicians in the punk and early postpunk era.[135] Reggae musicians did not cower from club owners, journalists, skeptics or, indeed, one another. They were tough survivors and rebels, and the city's non-Jamaican musicians were empowered by their new friends' self-assurance.[136]

In 1984, Sibbles continued his foray into the Canadian arts scene by providing the soundtrack for Jennifer Hodge's National Film Board production *Home Feeling: Struggle for a Community*. It was a film about the Jane-Finch Corridor.[137] The movie addressed the palpable racial tension, crime, and despair in the six square blocks that constituted the Corridor.[138] Directed by Hodge and Roger McTair, *Home Feeling* was hopeful; despite the enduring poor reputation of the neighbourhood, the people of the community (including many Jamaicans, people of other ethnicities, the police, and social workers) were committed to improving both the Corridor and its image. Importantly, the movie, with Sibbles' soundtrack, linked music to space. Through this representation and others like it in the popular media, Jamaican reggae claimed the sonic space of the Jane-Finch Corridor.[139]

Apart from Jamaican-centric projects, Sibbles also began to pay explicit homage to the musical traditions of his newly adopted country. On his 1982 album, *Evidence*, for instance, Sibbles employed mainstream Canadian musical heavyweights, including Bruce Cockburn, Murray McLauchlan, and Colleen Peterson, as well as some top-flight session players such as violinist Hugh Marsh, pianist Jon Goldsmith, and flautist Kathryn Moses. The album, recorded on the major label A&M, was a decided departure from a "purer" Jamaican-reggae feel, as was part of a strategy. Sibbles and his management were attempting to position the singer away from a strictly reggae setting and audience.[140]

After all, despite making international inroads, reggae still suffered from underexposure on the city's radio waves; outside of the odd Bob Marley or UB40 track, space on Toronto's mainstream radio stations was limited. If Sibbles could somehow breach the city's radio stations, then perhaps his success could open the door for more straight-ahead, locally produced reggae tracks. The album's single, "I'm Thankful," helped take Sibbles down that road by charting on Toronto's CFTR. Top-40 station CHUM, however, gave it a miss as it continued to demonstrate a general apathy to reggae and contemporary black music in general.[141] Nevertheless, the cultural dynamic that had compelled Bruce Cockburn to use a Jamaican backing band for his biggest North American hit had now compelled a black Jamaican migrant to do the same, but in reverse.

Sibbles' new approach may have cost him a portion of his dedicated fan base, but he was well aware of this potentiality. Sibbles confessed that the city's reggae faithful "will be surprised. They might even get mad. But hard-core reggae fans are limited too. I want to be heard by everyone. And I'm opening the way for more reggae."[142] Somewhat ironically, given the absence of actual reggae, the new album succeeded in raising the genre's national profile, in part because of Sibbles' shrewd casting of Queen Street West musicians. As journalist Liam Lacey confirmed, the talented ensemble that Sibbles put together "underscores the notion that *Evidence* is as much a community project as a musical one."[143] The communal project won many new converts to Jamaican Canadian reggae: a hybrid of a hybrid.

The exchange between migrant musician and Canadian pop star culminated, in 1985, in a special show at the twenty-five-thousand-seat National Stadium in Kingston Jamaica. Jamfest '85 was held to commemorate the United Nations' International Youth Year. The weekend festival included Jamaican reggae stars such as Sly and Robbie, Rita Marley, Ziggy Marley, Yellowman, and Marcia Griffiths, as well as the Toronto-based Sibbles and Kitchener-based Messenjah. But, surprisingly, intermingled among these reggae artists were Toronto acts such as the avant-garde songstress Jane Siberry, Queen Street West new wavers the Parachute Club, classical guitarist Liona Boyd and, of course, Bruce Cockburn.[144] And when Cockburn launched into "Wondering Where the Lions Are" on the final night of the festival, the Jamaican crowd leapt to their feet.[145] The white Canadian's crossover reggae hit touched the Jamaican audience. He won them over. The transnational musical circle was complete: the Jamaican migrant (Sibbles) had taken the music to the Canadian host (Cockburn), who, having fashioned the most important song of his career from the reggae sounds he had heard Sibbles and others perform in the city's downtown spaces, had taken it back to Jamaica.

The Nature of the Performance

Musical performances such as Cockburn's in Jamaica are fleeting, and if any meaning can be ascribed to them, then surely the audience must play a role in contributing to that meaning.[146] Music making, and even the more passive practice of music listening, can be viewed as a cultural activity, a process that, when enacted, can shape and define the characteristics of a given group.[147] Notoriously fickle reggae audiences – even in Canada – expect a certain presentation, codified with cultural nuances that signify a shared experience between performer and audience.[148] People choose certain performers to act as a mirror so they can reflect a certain political or cultural aesthetic and representation with which individuals and the collective might identify. Any given reggae song contains ritualistic messages that demand complicity from the audience. An unwritten contract between those on and off the stage requires the audience to be present and to participate for the meaning of a performance to be realized. Cockburn's Jamaican performance met with approval from the audience. It passed the great litmus test of authenticity; his song resonated with the audience, and they responded favourably.

In his crucial work on the British music hall, historian Peter Bailey highlights the discourse that emerged between stage performers and the audience in Victorian London: "The Music Hall performer could count on the active engagement of an audience well practised not only in being hailed but in hailing back, for the language of the street and market-place that informed the exchanges with the audience was very much one of give as well as take."[149] And so it was in Toronto's own reggae scene. Concealed within the entertainers' performances were important rituals and coded messages that demanded the crowd to be compicit. One needed to be in the "ken" to fully access the meaning of the reggae experience in Canada.

The nature of the performances, of course, changed over time. In the late 1960s, Jamaican performers in Toronto generally relied on popular, if sometimes racy, innuendo-laden songs of the "Big Bamboo" variety to build bridges between migrant West Indians (both on and off stage) and audience members from the dominant culture who were brave or curious enough to attend. Yet by virtue of where they occurred, these performances developed and made audible the Jamaican Canadian experience. Considering the growing number of non-Jamaicans at such shows, *where* often determined who would, or could, attend. Depending on where a given event took place, audiences could coproduce an experience that was not exclusively that of Jamaican migrants. This was even more the case in the mid-1970s, when non-Jamaican musicians from Toronto's music scene were put into the mix. Place helped create an indigenous Canadian reggae sound.

By the 1980s, many non-Jamaicans had been adequately indoctrinated by ska and reggae's rituals and repetition, and they had decoded well enough the cultural mysteries and seemingly impenetrable patois that hitherto would have kept the faint-of-heart at bay. In other words, Jamaican and Jamaican Canadian reggae artists in Toronto were not obliged to present a "reggae light" demonstration for the uninitiated. By then, Toronto reggae fans were among the most reggae-savvy fans in the world. Reggae had carved out a place for itself among Torontonians of various hues. Moreover, Canadian reggae artists and DJs were not only broadcasting to the people – they were broadcasting of the people. The entertainers were able to hold up a mirror to the audience that reflected a shared commonalty that transcended the performer-audience divide.

Audiences, their expectations, and their codes differ throughout the reggae world. Most performers will, in order to find favour with their audience, try to meet these expectations. In essence: they want to be validated. The authenticity or validity of a given performance relies on the artists' ability to create music that resonates with an approving audience in a particular place and at a particular moment in time. Given this, is the experience of a racially mixed reggae band performing in North York, Ontario, any less valid than a performance by the Fab Five in a Kingston nightclub?

As soon as Jamaican migrants began broadcasting their music up and down Toronto's streetscapes, the original or intended Jamaican meaning of the ska or reggae text was automatically transformed. To be sure, this was not through any grand design by those non-Jamaicans who happened to be in proximity to Jamaican culture. Nor did Jamaican migrants intend to indoctrinate other Canadians with the music of their homeland. But the process occurred, nevertheless, just as it had in Britain a few years earlier.

And the results were far-reaching. Reggae took on a new Canadian meaning, and that process was informed by the audience, Jamaican and otherwise. Audiences that voluntarily packed the Bamboo Club in Toronto in the 1980s, for example, authenticated the performers' role, including biracial and multicultural bands such as the Sattalites, Culture Shock, Fujahtive, and Sunforce. "Original" reggae texts aside, the success and longevity of the club afforded its black and white patrons (and musicians) an authentic, if hybrid, reggae experience.

Book of Rules: The Meaning of a Text

In 1967, the oft-maligned French philosopher Jacques Derrida, the pioneer of the deconstruction movement, challenged the academic world when he claimed that there was "nothing outside of the text."[150] Everything, in Derrida's dramaturgical model, could be read (people, philosophies, art, and so on). Texts, at least for Derrida, could resist both authorial intent and context.[151] Importantly, Derrida contended that the meaning of texts would proliferate infinitely over time.[152]

In the case of reggae music, as discussed, the actual text of Jamaican popular music problematizes some ethnomusicologists' perceptions of it. Ethnomusicologists need to accept the multiplicity of reggae texts, just as they have done in other genres such as jazz and blues. Hybridity, as evidenced in Canadian-produced reggae, has, in part, laid claim to *an* experience. This experience was as unique to the Jamaicans living in Canada as it was to those Canadians that either lived alongside or chose to make music with Jamaican Canadians. If a Canadian reggae text exists, then, it surely speaks to both the transnational existence of the Jamaican migrant and the plurality of cultures that have added to it.

When reggae was made on Canadian soil, even its most mindful replicators could not keep the Yard sound free of contamination from Canadian elements. While reggae artists in Canada retained a generous portion of the "old," they also scraped their palette knifes over "new" northern mixtures. While the imagined ideal of a pure, diasporic reggae text may have been the goal for some, such a result was impossible because the music makers were exposed to other influences on Canadian radio and television and through exchanges with their non-Jamaican school friends, neighbours, and musicians.

Non-Jamaican influences were everywhere, directly and indirectly shaping the end result. Jamaican migrant musicians who endeavoured to produce reggae in Canada therefore had to adjust their expectations. They were also at the mercy of new and different equipment and engineers and producers who might have been brand new to the genre and struggling to faithfully replicate an "authentic" Jamaican sound. This was not necessarily a bad thing, and Reggae Canadiana could look to the more sonically recognizable and commercially successful British reggae scene to provide a precedent.

Some journalists and ethnomusicologists from both within and outside of the Jamaican Canadian community, however, were quick to denounce the authenticity of the new non-Jamaican reggae text. Here were the gatekeepers. This was especially so for those bands that achieved any commercial success.[153] The cynical language of the gatekeepers plagued, at least for a time, reggae music makers outside of Jamaica, including those living in Canada. Few have considered the different traditions and multiplicity of texts associated with reggae, including those that transcend the Caribbean diaspora.[154] Indeed, reggae "authenticities" exist apart from those that are exclusively black Jamaican, or Rasta, or even British Jamaican. As *Toronto Star* journalist Peter Goddard observed in 1980: "To Peter Tosh, roots reggae, and radical social change are one and the same. To Ken Boothe and others, it can be a dance music, background music for love-making or just about anything."[155] To deny these multiple authenticities is to deny the multitude of influences and people that helped to create reggae in the first instance. Gatekeepers struggle to reconcile the fact that authenticity largely depends on who is listening.

It also matters where the music is being listened to. Place, as we have seen, greatly affects the way a musical expression is transmitted and can dictate the behaviour of a performance and modify its meaning. Although the performance of a popular Jamaican song in Canada – even if performed by the original Jamaican artist – may evoke the essence of a uniquely Jamaican experience, it can only ever be an essence. A mixed audience of Jamaicans, Jamaican Canadians, and non-Jamaican Canadians in a Canadian setting will ultimately have different takeaways.

To illustrate this point, consider the trajectory of "A Bag of Tools," a text that has, for many, become a bona fide reggae anthem in Canada and wherever there are reggae fans. This reggae anthem was first crafted by Robert Lee Sharpe, the son of a white Confederate soldier.[156] Sharpe worked with his father in the family's newspaper business and printing shop in Carrollton, Georgia, before becoming a freelance writer for various magazines in the 1920s and 1930s. He later tried his hand at poetry, and "A Bag of Tools" eventually became part of the canon of American poetry:

> Isn't it strange how princes and kings,
> and clowns that caper in sawdust rings,
> and common people, like you and me,
> are builders for eternity?
> Each is given a bag of tools;
> a shapeless mass; a book of rules.
> And each must make, ere life is flown,
> A stumbling block, or a stepping-stone.[157]

The poem was included in Hazel Felleman's *Best Loved Poems of the American People* (1936), A.L. Alexander's *Poems That Touch the Heart* (1941), and James Dalton Morrison's *Masterpieces of Religious Verse* (1948).[158]

What is interesting is the multiplicity of meanings that have been ascribed to "Bag of Tools" and how they compare to the author's intention. This plaintive text, written by the son of a Confederate soldier living in the Deep South in the early part of the twentieth century, continued to resonate with many different people long after the poet died in Georgia on April 19, 1951.[159] Principally, the poem was used in religious teachings, and with its cross-denominational appeal, "Bag of Tools" still enjoys currency among church leaders.[160] But the builder allegory in the poem also served the Masonic cause, and even though Sharpe may not have ever been initiated as a Mason, the poem has been cited often in the works of the Secret Brotherhood.[161] Sharpe's verse has also struck sympathetic chords with bankers and entrepreneurs who have used it to illustrate the building of financial security.[162] And it has been reinterpreted in a musical form many times.[163]

It was, however, as a religious parable that "Bag of Tools" endured for over ninety years. Somehow, the poem found its way to Jamaica, where Christianity had planted its roots deeply. Today, Jamaica's Christians account for approximately 70 percent of the population, and something closer to 80 percent have declared a religious affiliation.[164] As Eric Doumerc has observed, Sharpe's spiritual lyrics would have resonated with Jamaicans and the very idea of the poem

> must have appealed to the Heptones, who grew up in a deeply religious society where the emphasis on moral choice must have been equally strong. What must have appealed to the group too must have been the opposition between the haves and the have-nots, the "clowns" and "princes" and the "builders," in other words the opposition between the lower classes and the well-heeled.[165]

While Leroy Sibbles claimed that none of the Heptones had learned Sharpe's poem in church or school and that his bandmate Barry Llewellyn had simply come across the verse and thought that it might make for a good song, the poem nevertheless had a life in Jamaica.[166]

That life was affirmed with the release of the film *Rockers* in 1978. Written and directed by Theodoros Bafaloukos, *Rockers* was a documentary-style feature that captured Jamaica during what some music journalists might call Jamaican reggae's golden age.[167] *Rockers* featured a who's who of Jamaican popular music, including Jacob Miller, Gregory Issacs, and Big Youth. While it may not have enjoyed the high profile that *The Harder They Come* won, the film became a cult classic, and its soundtrack is a must-have for reggae devotees.[168] The album helped win a place in reggae's popular canon for a number of songs, including Junior Murvin's "Police and Thieves," Jacob Miller's "Tenement Yard" and, of course, the Heptones' "Book of Rules," a song truly at the heart of the soundtrack.[169] The success of *Rockers* forever immortalized the Heptones' song for reggae fans around the world. Moreover, "Book of Rules" became a non-negotiable mainstay in the Heptones set and later in Sibbles' own solo career repertoire.

The Heptones' "Book of Rules" began to take on added importance; it was a cultural touchstone that cracked open a window into a particular moment in Jamaican pop culture. In his review of the soundtrack, *Globe and Mail* music journalist Jerry Johnson identified the "historical overtones" that connected "Book of Rules" with Toronto's own Leroy Sibbles.[170]

Sibbles was, in Johnson's eyes, one of the hometown guys that had "made good" abroad. Many such as Johnson believed that on the strength of "Book of Rules," the country's reggae stars could and should claim a stake on reggae's international stage.

For some reggae aficionados, the importance of "Book of Rules" can hardly be overstated, as Citizen K. exalted: "'Book of Rules' is not only an essential Heptones track, it is one the essential songs of the reggae canon. If your reggae collection does not include 'Book of Rules,' it is incomplete."[171] Fergus Hambleton, frontman of the Sattalites and the man who cut his reggae teeth performing with Leroy Sibbles, was particularly struck with "Book of Rules": "The song was an anomaly. The lyric is odd, not a cry against oppression, as in many early reggae songs, not a humorous piece of Jamaican culture or a romantic love song ... Although musically rooted in Jamaican culture, the words speak to another time, to another sensibility."[172] The poem's sensibilities, though, crossed religious, race, class, and cultural bounds. Each time it was reimagined, Sharpe's original text was bent to suit a new sensibility, including a Canadian one.

The "Book of Rules" was covered several times, including by reggae artists Inner Circle, Desmond Dekker, Pluto Shervington, and Grateful Dead singer-guitarist Bob Weir with his outfit Bobby and the Midnites.[173] For Weir, "Book of Rules" was one of his favourite reggae songs, but he was ignorant of its lineage when he recorded it in 1981. Not long after he released his version, Weir was amazed to find out that it was an American poem co-opted by a Jamaican band that had then returned to him – a reggae fan – in America: "That's an example of what happens when you send a lyric through the Caribbean and back: you get some transfiguration ... I had no idea there was the original poem. I knew there was something I liked about that song beyond the lyrics that were there."[174] Art behaves like this when its broadcast to the world. Transmitters, tradition bearers, improvers, collectors, and even original songwriters draw from a global pool and, from there, mimic, reimagine, or reinvent (though not always on purpose) what they've heard. Weir chose to retain the Heptones' own final stanza, which they had added to the Sharpe original.[175] As in the great balladeer tradition, the original text and melody was fashioned into something new while retaining a part of the old. This is how music works.[176] The agency of place in this process is almost as important.

The Frontline Mecca: The Bamboo

Reggae could draw from the past, but its message dovetailed nicely with the political activism of the punk and postpunk era. Queen Street West was perhaps the most politically charged and active corridor in the city. On any given week in the 1980s one could participate in an anti-cruise-missile-testing demonstration, attend an African National Congress gathering to beseech the Botha regime to release Nelson Mandela from prison, or dine at an event to show support for Dr. Henry Morgentaler and the pro-choice movement. Some events were galas held in ballrooms that drew out the city's glitterazzi.[177] Others were large-scale demonstrations, pitched on the lawn of Queen's Park. Others were more intimate affairs held in nightclubs. In the vanguard of these politico-music venues was the Bamboo Club at 312 Queen Street West. The club was a veritable bastion for activism and sometimes attracted divergent groups, including Jamaican reggae musicians and the city's gay activists.[178] The Bamboo was the most important space for Canadian reggae in its golden age.

Queen Street West seamlessly replicated the vibrant music and political activism that had been the preserve of Yorkville in the 1960s. By the 1980s, the spirit of the folky youth subculture had migrated south by a few blocks. Instead of Aran sweaters and "long-hairs" there were punks in Doc Martens and dreadlocked Rastas sporting bright ites, gold, and green attire.[179] The strip was lively and full of countercultural boutiques and radical bookstores interrupted only by some of the country's most important musical venues: the Rivoli, the Horseshoe and, most importantly for reggae musicians and fans, the Bamboo. It was at the latter that Toronto's reggae alchemists – if they were good enough – performed for a multicultural crowd. Indeed, many of Queen Street West's best young bands began employing a cross-genre approach to articulate their rebel stance, which greatly appealed to the city's music-savvy youth culture.[180] Yet the Bamboo was also a place for Jamaican Canadians to enact ethnicity in the downtown core and space for non-Jamaicans to observe, and if they chose, participate in Toronto-style Jamaicanness. In so doing, many non-Jamaicans explored something that was outside of their material reality. To set the scene, the club magically replicated, at least in part, the blues dance, with its mood lighting, thundering bass, and demonstrable sexuality, and over time the club developed into the nation's premier nightclub for reggae and world music.

The Bamboo opened on August 26, 1983, and was owned and operated by Canadian-born Patti Habib and Richard O'Brien. While it may have been a bastion for what some middle-class Torontonians considered radical activity (pro-choice rallies, African National Congress fundraisers, the scent of marijuana in the air, and so on), the music and its Caribbean and Thai cuisine allowed the club to compete with the strip's other top venues for the entertainment dollars of a new generation. Inside, patrons were transported to a tropical, beachfront bar, replete with bamboo furniture, wall-mounted fishing paraphernalia, and brightly coloured decor instead of the usual dim lighting. On a summer night, you could almost believe you were in Jamaica.

On a Friday or Saturday night, people lined up down Queen Street, sometimes with little hope of getting in. As Toronto music critic Peter Goddard raved in a piece on the Bamboo in a theatre magazine in 1985, the club trumped the city's other hip venues:

> The Elmo, the old champ, sold heat – it radiated not warmth as much as the kind of steam heat that generates sweat. The Bamboo, the new champ, hustles cool. Its colours are cool. Its crowds try to be cool ... you can find jazz at the Bamboo, along with salsa, rock and just about everything else. But mostly you'll find reggae.[181]

With its multiracial demographic, the Bamboo was, as SCTV and Hollywood actor Catherine O'Hara exclaimed, "the U.N. of groove."[182] West Indian migrant acts such as Messenjah, Truths and Rights, and Lillian Allen shared duties with multiracial bands such as the Sattalites, 20th Century Rebels, Sunforce, Tabarruk, Fujahtive, Culture Shock, Bonconganistas, and countless others who called the Bamboo home and collectively gave form, perhaps for the first time, to a legitimate downtown Toronto reggae scene. If the 1980s was the golden age of Canadian reggae, then the Bamboo surely was its Mecca.

Valentine's Day 1984 was a particularly busy one for the Toronto music scene. That night the Horseshoe Tavern held its "Calling All Sweethearts Ball," featuring American singer-songwriter and later Canadian radio DJ

Bob Segarini, Canadian folk icon Willie P. Bennett and, four years before the critically acclaimed release of her *Miss America,* Mary Margaret O'Hara.[183] Hard rocker Lisa Hart was playing five minutes up Spadina at the El Mocambo; the death-rock band Alien Sex Fiend was at Larry's Hideaway on Carlton Street; and Pan-Am Dance were at the Rivoli.[184]

Less than a minute's walk eastward along Queen, Leroy Sibbles provided the Bamboo's patrons with Canadian-style reggae, rocksteady, and lovers rock.[185] When the tall Jamaican and former welder sang the Heptones' hit "Book of Rules," the approving Toronto crowd – black, white, and all shades in between – jubilantly belted out the chorus along with him. Sibbles' rendition of the "Book of Rules" not only accessed an existing memory of Jamaica but also inscribed a brand new one that suited the Canadian context. Sharpe's poem was once again given a new interpretation. Although he was some seventeen hundred miles away from home, Sibbles did not have to explain the text to the crowd. To paraphrase Phil Vassell, though the crowd didn't look like him and didn't talk like him, they knew the words to his song and that meant something. Sibbles' audience was in the ken.[186]

Critically, the Bamboo played its own role. The immediacy of the local surroundings greatly informed the memory-making processes of the club's patrons.[187] Those in attendance that night and many nights thereafter, when the singer opened up the "Book of Rules," were linked not just to Sibbles, reggae, and Jamaica but also to the sights, sounds, and smells of Queen Street – Spadina Avenue's hot dog vendors, punk rockers with colourful mohawks en route to see a show, big-haired "new romantics" lined up at the Rivoli, the frosty snap of the winter weather, the dull roar and bright horns of drivers jockeying for parking, the crush of a Valentine's embrace and, crucially, the diverse crowd at the club itself.[188]

Inside, punkers, rockers, new wavers, ragamuffins, Rastas, and even the odd Bay Street suit intermingled. But certain areas were unofficially claimed by different pockets of the Bamboo's clientele. Lovers would freely rub-a-dub on the main dance floor directly in front of the stage, closely adhering to the blues dance aesthetic. Fringing the side of the Bamboo's awkward stage (the bulk of the patrons' view was obstructed by a post on stage left) were those musicians and singing hopefuls who were at the ready lest they be summoned up to "touch a piece" of a song. Behind this group stood the cool dreads, whose affection was pursued by many of the younger bands performing. If those dreads – who held up the club's easternmost flank – "bawled out" in approval, the rest of the club followed suit, and the performers were injected with a new-found confidence. If, however, the dreads were unmoved, the band's momentum often ground to a halt (Sibbles, of course, never had this problem).[189]

Upstairs, the side room directly attached to the dressing room was reserved for the elite members of the Toronto reggae scene. To get in, you had to get by an enormous bouncer who stood guard at the bottom of the stairs. The very few who could talk their way into the side room might find some animated character holding court amidst a dense fog of free-flowing weed. So heavy was the ganja haze that you didn't have to smoke yourself to get high. The room replicated basement side rooms at blues dances, where dreads might "reason" and share a spliff. It was a delightful juxtaposition to the more "refined" dining room downstairs, just off of the main dance floor, where people enjoyed a Caribbean curry chicken while nursing a Dragon Stout and effectively reliving their Mo Bay holiday. Yet all these spaces and people were somehow united through the music, and these varied and fleeting frames added to the richness of this Canadian reggae vignette.

The patrons worked out their own ideas of what the music meant to them at the Bamboo. To them, reggae could be music from home, the rebel's backing track, the music they'd heard at school, a spiritual meditation, a seductive one-drop beat that made girls dance, the sounds they'd heard on holiday, or the soundtrack to smoking marijuana. They were different experiences, but they were all Canadian reggae music.[190] The Bamboo was the blues dance, the church gathering, the high school corridor, the Summer of Love, the holiday beach, and the nightclub all rolled into one. The collective memory of Sibbles' performance, then, was not made in but rather with the Bamboo and its surroundings.[191] The future memory of this event was a Canadian one.[192] While the song meant different things to different people, who were responding to multiple sets of circumstances, Sibbles performed the text in one place for all in attendance. And while the nature of the Canadian reggae music fan can only be spectrally defined, "Bag of Tools" – the song, the lyric, the performance, the memory – meant the Bamboo.

The proliferation of meanings that Sharpe's poem has taken on demonstrates how place and time can alter a given text. We'll never know the true authorial intent of "Bag of Tools," but the sentiment was as valid to Sharpe, the son of a Confederate soldier, as it was to so many others. From the Jamaican-born musician on the stage, to his Jamaican- and Canadian-born side men, to the dreads who heartily belted out every word, to the wallflower who quietly swayed in the darkness near the club's coat check, each version of "Bag of Tools" was an authentic expression of a valid experience engineered by reggae music and crafted in Canada.

The Prodigal Son Returns

Leroy Sibbles moved back to Jamaica in 1994 and now looks back on his years in Canada, at least as an artist, with some regret.[193] Although he once believed that *Evidence* was a good strategy to access Canadian radio, he is now less enthusiastic about his Canadian-produced body of work:

> I was never totally satisfied with much Canadian recording, unless it was one I did for myself. The stuff that I played with other people was never satisfactory to me. You know, I wasn't feeling it, like the stuff that would be done in Jamaica ... Not everyone can play reggae ... Anyone can try, but it's not anyone that can play it.[194]

Perhaps he wasn't feeling it all along. A year after *Evidence,* Sibbles went to Jamaica to record *On Top.*[195] For this album, the Heptones singer used Jamaican musicians, including Sly and Robbie and Marcia Griffiths, to satisfy his muse. The *Globe and Mail*'s Mark Miller saw *On Top* as a return to form for Sibbles: "Sibbles produced this album himself, and recorded it in Jamaica with Jamaican musicians; not surprisingly, the results are definitely more convincing than the crossover album he attempted last year with the misplaced all-Canadian cast."[196] Miller's criticism spoke to a growing consensus – at least among journalists – that good reggae or "real" reggae could not be made in Canada.

This line of criticism weighed heavily on a lot of Canadian artists on the reggae scene who hoped that theirs was real reggae. Compounding this anxiety, and despite all the gains that pioneers such as Sibbles had made towards accessing the mainstream, reggae still languished in terms of broad acceptance throughout the nation. First, the total Jamaican population in Canada was small, mostly urban, and centred largely in Toronto.[197] Moreover, the Canadian music industry was a really small fish in the world market. The movers and shakers had only limited resources to commit to a precious few acts. While indigenous Canadian reggae acts such as the Sattalites and Messenjah did the unthinkable by getting signed to major record labels, the record companies involved didn't really know how to market reggae nationally.[198]

To be fair to Canadian music industry, there was a lack of cohesion within the Canadian reggae community itself. Many of the grassroots promoters did little to help reggae's cause. Big-time Jamaican acts may have been advertised on the bill, but they ended up being no-shows at the last minute.[199] Impossibly late starts for some concerts confused everyone except the real hard-core reggae community. It was not uncommon for the main act to take the stage at 2 or 3 a.m. While this habit was consistent with the all-night Jamaican party, many patrons, who were perhaps unused to this schedule, grew tired of waiting and simply left or, at the very least, thought twice about attending the next reggae event.[200]

In addition, rebel rockers and rub-a-dub lovers were not drawn to the more aggressive dancehall reggae of the late 1980s, which was accompanied by violence and gunplay. In 1988, for instance, the *Toronto Star* reported that TTC drivers were growing increasingly worried about late-night shifts up and down Yonge Street: "One of the danger zones on their list is outside the Masonic Temple, just north of Bloor St., where hundreds of hyped-up fans spill out of weekend reggae concerts."[201] This new atmosphere was at odds with the "one love" vibe of an earlier time and kept the "curious-but-not-that-curious" away from the gate. Popular Jamaican artist Bob Andy's theory about this transition is that the ska era of the 1960s was fuelled by white rum; the reggae era of the 1970s and early 1980s, by marijuana; and the dancehall era from the mid-1980s onward, by cocaine.[202] The parameters for the casual reggae fan had changed.

The bands in reggae's epicentre were also frustrated by a protracted lack of radio presence and wounded by accusations of inauthenticity. They chose a strategy of mimicking the type of reggae coming out of Jamaica instead of charting their own Canadian course. While the top British reggae acts of the day were brimming with confidence and winning international acclaim, their Canadian cousins lacked confidence in their own unique hybrid.[203] While the youth subculture of the late 1970s built common bridges for Jamaican migrants, their Canadian-born children, and other non-Jamaicans to cross, many retreated back into their own enclaves in the late 1980s.

The issue of the appropriation of voice in Toronto's literary world at the end of the decade also spilled over to influence the city's music forms or, at the very least, the vocabulary of journalists charged with reviewing Canadian reggae.[204] Anything deemed inauthentic – not "real" Jamaican reggae – was regarded with suspicion. Nor did Canadian reggae benefit from underground reggae DJs; rare was the Canadian-produced reggae song that found its way onto a turntable at a Jane-Finch blues dance. Even with a home field advantage, Canada's reggae hybridists had little chance. And they knew it.[205]

Sibbles' flight home to Jamaica heralded an ominous turn for Canadian reggae. The singer was clear about his perceived misstep: "I think that [moving to Canada] was the worst thing that I ever did, because I just went so far and couldn't go no further there. I was trying my best to keep up as much as I could, but I lost touch with what was happening here in Jamaica."[206]

While the Canadian chapter of his career may not have turned out as he had hoped, Sibbles had nothing but fond memories of the Bamboo: "Oh, yeah, man, we had some good vibes there. You remember that? Yeah, man, I had some good times at the Bamboo Club, real good, strong, healthy, wicked vibes."[207] To be sure, the Bamboo was itself a historical agent that informed the history made within its walls. As a place it remains – regardless of whether someone is today living in Kingston, Jamaica, or suburban Toronto – central to the very memory of the countless reggae parties that occurred twenty or thirty years prior. But it wasn't enough.

If the man who had helped put reggae into Toronto's musical vernacular "couldn't go no further," what chance did the next generation of Canadian reggae makers have? When Britain retained so many Jamaican greats, why couldn't Canada keep its "grand old man of reggae"?

5

The Bridge Builders

When Hilda Neatby said "No country is enriched by the co-existence of two cultures, if one half of the population cannot appropriate the cultural product of the other half," the great Canadian historian was speaking of the two solitudes: French and English Canada.[1] Yet Neatby's assertion could just as easily be applied to the broader concept of multiculturalism, which was just gaining traction in the Canadian consciousness when Neatby made the observation in the late 1950s. During the golden age of Reggae Canadiana, metaphorical bridges were being built all along the ethnic frontlines of the city. In some cases, Toronto's Jamaicans personally introduced reggae to non-Jamaicans. They did so through various means: being classmates at school, lending records, attending reggae concerts or dances together, or simply sharing a spliff. At the same time, many young non-Jamaicans were likewise being influenced by British musical trends, some of which were responding to the United Kingdom's own Jamaican population. Punk music, the two-tone movement, and the popularity of English reggae bands such as Aswad, Steel Pulse, and UB40 were trends that had great currency with Toronto's youth culture, Jamaican and otherwise, in the 1970s and 1980s.

Some non-Jamaicans were also profoundly affected by the international rise of Bob Marley and his music. It was, after all, Marley's image that came to serve as reggae's archetype. Through Marley, others were drawn to reggae's deeper spiritual side. A few non-Jamaicans turned to Rasta, some for a spell and others for a lifetime. Others still were attracted to reggae's endorsement of marijuana, which reflected the recreational drug culture found in other popular musics of the day. These various bridge-building activities in the leisure and private spaces along the frontline opened up the possibility, at least in some cases, for deeper, more meaningful relationships between migrant and host.

Toronto via London via Kingston

The allure of reggae captured the interest of young non-Jamaican Torontonians, many of whom had a formidable and transnational connection to either British culture or Caribbean culture, or sometimes both. This connection made them predisposed to Jamaican music. Jamaican culture came, for instance, to the white, Canadian-born reggae singer Andru Branch when his mother started dating a black Jamaican man. Because Branch was only six years old at the time, Bruce Johnson became something of a father figure to him for the next fifteen years, and he learned about Jamaican culture first-hand through his stepfather. Although Johnson did not listen to reggae, he did impart a great deal of Jamaican culture to Branch in his formative years: "At Christmas, he would take us around his relatives, and so we'd spend Christmas with some of his Jamaican family, and I started trying sorrel at Christmas time, and Jamaican cake, and started eating curry goat and those kinds of things."[2] It was much the same for the white reggae keyboardist Sam Weller. Weller was an adopted child, and Children's Aid provided different people to look after him while he was growing up. For several years (from age eight to twelve), he was cared for by a Jamaican woman and her family in Toronto. Sam's father had also worked in Jamaica for several years, so Sam was exposed to Jamaican culture from an early age.[3]

Sometimes, the Jamaican music literally came knocking at the door. Son of legendary Canadian jazz organist Bill King, Jesse King (a.k.a. Dubmatix) recalled one instance. During the 1970s, Bill King played with some Toronto reggae stalwarts, including Jackie Mittoo, guitarist Wayne McGhie, and Jamaican drummer Everton "Pablo" Paul. Paul loaned the young Jesse some reggae records and turned him on to dub music, a subgenre of reggae that changed his musical life:

142   *The Bridge Builders*

> It was really when he loaned me [Augustus Pablo's] *King Tubby Meets the Rockers Uptown.* He said, "Just listen to this." And I put this on, and I had never heard dub. I didn't know it existed, and when I heard that album, that was all I listened to pretty much then on ... I'd play it all the time. I would go over to parties and put it on ... and that kinda led really getting into dub and wanting to play reggae. And that was the defining moment.[4]

With a Juno award and six nominations under his belt, and nearly 3 million followers on SoundCloud, this non-Jamaican is now certainly one of Canada's premier reggae artists and has Paul to thank for introducing him to reggae.

For others, simply travelling to Jamaica was enough. This was the case for future Sattalites' bassist Bruce McGillivray, who went to Jamaica in 1978 with fellow Moonfood bandmate Eric Gamble. While there, McGillivray and Gamble played in a north coast Jamaican band in Montego Bay. The experience turned McGillivray on to reggae bass. Upon their return, McGillivray and Gamble began to write reggae melodies.[5]

One of the Sattalites' cofounders, singer Fergus Hambleton, joined their band in the early 1980s. Hambleton, however, had already begun his reggae voyage years earlier, playing with the likes of Leroy Sibbles. The white multi-instrumentalist was taken with the striking parallels between Jamaican and British popular musics, as he later explained in an interview with *Canadian Musician:* "There are more similarities than differences, I think, between Jamaican and Canadian culture. Obviously, there are some incredible differences, but at the same time, because of the British colonial thing, there's a lot of threads that run through everything."[6] This was also true for white photographer and avid reggae fan Greg Lawson: "You're in a very exotic place all of a sudden ... to me exotic, there [are] palm trees. I'm in a different country; I'm on an island in the Caribbean. Yet there's a familiarity, and that was the UK influence, the English influence, right. So it's very exotic, yet it's very familiar, therefore very comfortable at the same time."[7] The Canadian, then, exposed to British culture in Canada, recognized the same British influence in Jamaica. Penetrating the language of reggae was, in this way, a little easier for those familiar with British sensibilities.

White David Kingston, a Canadian reggae DJ, similarly believed that reggae was disguised in Jamaican Patois but transcended a strictly Jamaican listenership:

> Britain was the old country, and there was still that element, that quality comes from the old country. And you'd hear references in Jamaican songs like "frocks." So there's that whole British thing ... [Jamaica] remained more British than England did in some ways, you know – "entertainments," plural, "Will there be many entertainments tonight?," love of cricket. So all of that kind of resonated ... There was always that connection, so it didn't feel foreign, it didn't feel like it was from a different planet, it didn't feel like it was that far away.[8]

Hambleton concurred: "I found things that were very, very similar because of the British thing, and some things ... that seemed far away, seemed to be rooted in some other area that I didn't have any life experience with or real knowledge of. But by and large, people's lives went on the same."[9]

Rich was the tapestry woven into reggae, but the popular music culture of Great Britain remained one of its stronger threads. This fact was discernible to those up-and-coming Toronto reggae artists who were attuned to the genre's British connections. While the United Kingdom may have been the chief custodian of the colonial "Babylon system," the commonalities found in Jamaica, Britain, and Canada engendered an unspoken sense of unity and bridge building between cultures.

Some of Toronto's non-Jamaican champions of reggae were actually born or lived in England. Mark Matthews (a.k.a. Prince Blanco) was born on the Isle of Wight in 1965 and grew up in London.[10] Freelance journalist and CBC radio personality Errol Nazareth was born in Kuwait in 1964, schooled in India (from the age of nine until seventeen), and later went to school in Plymouth, England, at the height of the punk and two-tone movements, before coming to Canada in 1981.[11] Nicholas Jennings, freelance journalist, music critic, cofounder of the Canadian chapter of Rock Against Racism, and chief writer for the CBC Television documentary series on Canadian music *This Beat Goes On,* was born in London and also spent a couple of years in Malaya with his father, a British colonial who had been born there.[12]

Other members of Canada's reggae movement had serious Jamaican and British connections. Jeffrey Holdip, Canadian reggae's premier sound engineer, was one such person. On one side, Holdip's great-grandparents were from Scotland, England, and Ireland. On the other, his black father was of Bajan descent and born in Canada in 1930. Holdip's grandmother had come from Barbados to Toronto in 1927 and worked as a domestic. For a time, Holdip's father lived in the same household as future judge George E. Carter, who was also Bajan and became the first Canadian-born black judge in Canada.[13]

Tomaz Jardim, a professor of history and reggae musician, was born in London, England.[14] Jardim's English mother grew up in Jamaica, and he became interested in Jamaican culture because of his mother's connection and also because of his close association with young Toronto reggae bands such as Jericho.[15] Jardim felt, however, that his mother's white Jamaican British background both resembled and differed slightly from the black Jamaicans he would one day befriend:

I think the Jamaican culture of my mother was the Jamaican culture of my grandmother, which, in other words, was white Jamaican culture of Mandeville in the 1940s and '50s. So I think there was correspondence, but then, at the same time, it was a kind of old-time correspondence. So I think the people that I met [later] and were musicians and Rasta people, I don't think there was a great deal of overlap, although, clearly, there was some, and I felt comfortable with it.[16]

These concrete associations with Jamaica and Britain made it easier for some non-Jamaicans to connect with the city's Jamaican migrant musicians. Certainly, all the main players in Toronto's nascent reggae scene had a watchful eye on the musical waves washing into town, up from Jamaica and across the Atlantic from Britain. From these cues, Toronto's own reggae scene evolved.

Young Rebel

The Toronto scene, at least in non-Jamaican communities, developed mainly within the city's youth culture. The confrontational nature of some ska and reggae artists appealed to a good portion of Toronto's rebellious teenage set. These genres were oppositional, a fact that dovetailed nicely with the attitude towards hegemonic society that so many of the city's young reggae fans shared. Ska legend Prince Buster himself confessed: "It's protest music, protest against injustice ... [Young whites] saw me as a rebel and identified themselves as such. So there was some compatibility there, I think so, because you shoulda seen them [white kids]."[17] From the early 1970s and right through the 1980s, rude boys, raggamuffins, rockers, punkers, and new wavers adopted for themselves, to various degrees, elements of the ska and reggae oppositional aesthetic. The protest music of Queen Street West – the strange land where Reggae Canadiana had been delivered – bubbled and boiled over into the mainstream, harkening back to the days when the city's folk music scene vibrated outwards from Yorkville.[18]

Sartorially, though, the flower-children attire of Yorkville was replaced, first, with the rude boy's high-cuff pants, suspenders, and Doc Marten boots; then with the punk rocker's safety pins and Mohawks; and finally with the new waver's androgynous hair and eyeliner. But it was the rude boy persona in particular that persisted into the reggae era and experienced something of a renaissance when the second wave of ska hit Britain in the late 1970s. As Dick Hebdige recalled:

> At the Ska Bar in London, the white reggae fans began mixing with the black rudies and copying their style. And out of this contact emerged the white British skinhead – close-cropped hair, Ben Sherman shirt, braces, Crombie coat and the trousers ending high above the ankle to reveal a great polished pair of Dr. Marten boots. The style caused a sensation. The newspapers were filled with outraged headlines about skinhead violence, and soon the craze was sweeping through the nation's poorer areas.[19]

Indeed, a few Jamaican artists began targeting the white British skinhead audience. Not least of them was Desmond Dekker, whose "Israelites" had been an international hit, including in Canada: "Shirt them a-tear up, trousers are gone / I don't want to end up like Bonnie and Clyde / Poor me, the Israelite."[20] Jamaican music was inspiring not only England's

West Indian community but also its working-class white mods and skinheads.[21] Through labour migration and, in particular, the touring Jamaican musician, the rude boy image was exported abroad to the black communities of London, Birmingham, Manchester, and Coventry and then to Toronto directly from Jamaica or via Britain.[22] Britain's two-tone generation was noteworthy for its aggressively multiracial youth culture, which utilized the rude boy persona as a means of social rebellion.[23]

It could be legitimately argued that following the death of Bob Marley the British version of reggae, with bands such as Aswad, Steel Pulse, and UB40, reenergized the Jamaican reggae text and saved the genre in the 1980s. As black author Klive Walker attested, "British-Caribbean reggae bands ... were a crucial aspect of reggae's second wave of the early '80s."[24] For many young Canadian musos growing up in the '70s and '80s, British musical trends were vital and often dictated what the in crowd should be listening to through British music trade magazines. Brian Robertson, a reggae fan and future EMI Canada royalties manager, for instance, took a Grade 12 music course (when he was in Grade 10). His new friends got him into punk and British music magazines such as *New Musical Express*: "You know there were lots of other types of music going on, but there was certainly a lot of reggae covered in those publications."[25] The generation of British reggae artists that appealed to Robertson and others like him were willing to think outside of circumscribed notions of what reggae should sound like or, indeed, look like.

Yet while Canada's reggae movement responded to and in some measure replicated the vibrant British scene during the 1980s, it paled in comparison. Canada simply could not compete with biracial and multiracial British bands who were taking the interpretation of Jamaican music to the next level. The two-tone movement included the Selecter, Madness, the Bodysnatchers (later Belle Stars), the Specials, the Beat, and Bad Manners. Coupled with the success of UB40, the second biggest selling reggae act of all time, these bands normalized the biracial and multiracial experiences and collective expressions of musicians and audiences alike.

Some Jamaican Canadians noticed a difference between the way white Brits and white Canadians responded to ska and reggae. Jamaican-born Adrian Miller, for example, felt that "white British boys are a lot different from white Canadians ... I'm listening to [Ron Wood] on Q107, and nobody had the fucking balls ... this is my thirty-sixth year in Canada ... and nobody had the fucking balls to play Gregory Isaacs or Horace Andy ... "Skylarking" on fucking Q107!"[26] Miller's point was that it took a Rolling Stones guitarist, the English-born and reggae-savvy Ron Wood, to go beyond the successful commercial reggae hits *du jour* to play deep roots tracks such as Andy's "Skylarking." While some white Canadian DJs on commercial radio may have had an interest in reggae, the will to play it often, or to dig deeper into the reggae canon, simply wasn't there.

There were other noticeable differences between the British reggae audience and the Canadian one. Black Jamaican JuLion King, like Miller, felt that "the white people in Canada celebrate reggae different than the black people, whereas, in England, black and white celebrate reggae the same."[27] Similarly, Mark Matthews, who is white and grew up in London before moving to Toronto, saw a clear difference between the way the races mixed in England and how the same mixing transpired in Canada:

> Since the UK had been a destination for Caribbean immigrants for a longer time, the Windrush generation and all that, there always seemed to be a better "connection." In Toronto, the relationships I cultivated with first-generation Jamaicans tended to start with music, which can be a huge icebreaker, and then we took off from there ... Being English does help connect me with older Jamaicans. We had all our stuff there until 1962 after all.[28]

The English Windrush generation was simply older than the Canadian Trudeau-Manley one. The former required fewer icebreakers.

Moreover, the racially mixed unemployed and underemployed youth subculture was far more cohesive in the United Kingdom than it ever was in Canada. The depth of the relationships forged in the urban centres of Britain simply could not be replicated in Canada. For Adrian Miller, the Canadian reggae scene did not receive the same respect as did its British counterpart: "It's not like in England. England is a little bit different, because people respect their Aswad, their Matumbi, their Steel Pulse, their Black Slate, so on and so forth. People respect them, and they support them ... In Canada we never really kind of get that respect and support."[29]

148   *The Bridge Builders*

This may be a fair assessment. Because the English host had a different and older relationship with Jamaican migrants than did the Canadian one, reggae had more invested English champions: the Who's Pete Townshend bought reggae band Misty in Roots new equipment after theirs was stolen; Elton John wanted to sign Toots to his own record label; Peter Tosh lived for a time with Keith Richards in his Jamaican mansion; Robert Palmer published records for Desmond Dekker; the Spencer Davis Group had a number one hit in 1966 with Jamaican songwriter Jackie Edwards's "Keep on Running"; and Paul McCartney helped the Cimarons (the United Kingdom's first reggae band) get off the ground. And these are just a few examples.[30] In fact, outside of Bruce Cockburn, one is hard-pressed to find reggae champions in Canada's mainstream music scene. Sadly, many within the mainstream simply ignored the genre altogether.

Soul Rebel

Reggae's king, Bob Marley, however, was difficult to ignore. Although he transcended many musical spheres of influence, Marley was *the* rebel in an era of rebels. He was emblematic of the oppositional Jamaican archetype that appealed to so many Jamaicans and non-Jamaicans the world over.[31] Black British filmmaker, DJ, and reggae and punk historian Don Letts described the impact Marley had on black Britain: "There was a duality to being black and British at the time that Bob's lyrics bridged. That gig [the *Lyceum* in London, 1975] was the nearest to a religious experience I've ever had."[32] Marley had, as Klive Walker attested, "drilled way below the surface of Western popular tastes. Marley's reggae burrowed so deep that its rhythms and words erased barriers of language and culture, so that even the globe's most marginalized citizens embraced the Rastaman's vibration."[33] For so many non-Jamaicans, Marley was an entry point into reggae. As Tomaz Jardim confessed: "I think it actually had to do with Bob Marley the person and not with the art form [of reggae] more broadly. And I think there's something about his captivating and transformative presence and character that even as a child I could relate to."[34] Jardim's love affair with Marley began with his mom and dad's eight-track cassette of Marley Perry:

I remember "Mr. Brown" as a child so well. My mother, I wouldn't say she listened to reggae ... but I think she liked it. My older brother started listening to it a little bit ... I remember for instance ... that when *Mama Africa* [Peter Tosh] came out ... that "Maga Dog" [when it] was on in the house, I remember my mother saying she loved it. So, it [reggae] was kind of around, but I wouldn't say I got it from my mother, I'd say I got it more from my brothers.[35]

Today, Jardim's collection is one of the most complete collections in the world. His individual pieces of Marley's music – live and otherwise – number in the hundreds.[36]

Marley's rebel charm infiltrated the youth culture of Toronto and its suburbs. White music journalist Sebastian Cook recalled his introduction to Marley while living as a small child in Newmarket, Ontario: "My father was a big Bob Marley fan. A cassette of the seminal live recording *Babylon by Bus* was the first recording I listened to on my own frequently."[37] Sound engineer Jeffrey Holdip likewise recalled that although he attended high school faithfully, he was willing to make an exception for Marley: "That's the only time I ever skipped off school. I went to Maple Leaf Gardens, and I stood in line and bought the tickets and got to see him play on the *Survival* tour."[38] Marley's cross-racial and cross-generational appeal found believers all over the city.

Jamaican migrants in Canada began to notice that Marley was stirring up an interest in reggae among non-Jamaicans. Klive Walker remembered how a white colleague of his, whom he had been working with at Coca Cola at the time, was delighted to have seen Marley at Maple Leaf Gardens in 1979.[39] Friendship waited across Marley's bridge for both migrant and host, as Walker explained:

I'm living in the diaspora, and you and I are friends. You happen to be Scottish Canadian. It just kind of flames right out: I'm going to take you to a show, or you're going to come with me to something. You know, that's what I mean by "it" not being able to happen without the diaspora. It's those people that took the music in their suitcases, that when they opened their suitcase up, everybody was able to hear, not just them.[40]

150   *The Bridge Builders*

Many frontline bridges were rendered operational on the heels of Marley's immense success. The sheer volume of Jamaican migrants – with yawning suitcases – kept the bridges in good working order.

Punky Reggae Party

Marley further galvanized Britain and Canada's youth subculture through his open approval of punk music. But it was England – not Canada – that hosted the cultural earthquake that brought punk and reggae together, and London's Roxy was the epicentre. It was there that Don Letts spun reggae records in between the sets of various fledgling punk bands that had yet to record.[41] Subsequently, these embryonic punkers would incorporate elements of the reggae idiom into their own expressions.[42] The mixing of genres, however, was a reciprocal affair. Lee "Scratch" Perry, for instance, began to incorporate the edginess of punk into his productions, perhaps most notably on Junior Murvin's "Police and Thieves." Then, the Clash – gods in punk's pantheon – covered the song.

In many ways, the Clash helped establish reggae as another viable, underground rebel music in England. The band's incorporation of reggae did not resemble Clapton's breezy take on "I Shot the Sheriff": it was raw, poignant, and powerful. Lee Perry was delighted when the Clash embraced the Jamaican music form:

> If we could have some more white band play reggae, that woulda suit me even more. Me no criticize the way dem do it as long as dem don't alter words. Because they do it inna feel of how dem feelin', and as long as dem a tell the story right – that's movement. I feel them a try earth movement. I like the move.[43]

The Clash called on the services of Jamaican DJ Mikey Campbell (a.k.a. Mikey Dread) more than once. Dread played a key role on the Clash's *Black Market Clash* album (most notably on the track "Bank Robber") and later appeared on several tracks on the band's *Sandinista!* album.

These tributes from the trendsetters of the punk movement were not lost on reggae artists. After all, as Vivien Goldman suggests, "When you get right down to it, punks and dreadlocks are on the same side of the fence."[44] For the Clash's bassist Paul Simonon, it was literally so. Simonon was the only white kid in the school he attended and was enveloped by ska and reggae. He recalled: "Reggae, punk, it's not like most of the stuff you hear on the radio, it's something you can relate to kids your own age. Black people are being suppressed, we're being suppressed, so we have something in common."[45] Crucially, Marley himself saw an analogous relationship between the two groups: "The punks are the outcasts from society. So are the Rastas. So they are bound to defend what we defend ... In a way, me like see them safety pins and t'ing ... Me no like do it myself, y'understand, but me like see a man can suffer pain without crying."[46] The two seemingly disparate sounds of the city had actually, in effect, been corresponding with each other. While punks declared "London's Burning," reggae heads answered with "Concrete Slaveship."[47] Both groups were united in being, as Marley sang, "rejected by society."[48]

The linkages were galvanized when Marley and the Clash began tipping their hats to each other. The Clash's Joe Strummer and Mick Jones, for instance, name-checked several of their reggae heroes in their track "White Man in Hammersmith Palais," which was released as a 7-inch single in 1978:

> Dillinger and Leroy Smart
> Delroy Wilson, your cool operator
> Ken Boothe for UK pop reggae
> With backing bands sound systems
> And if they've got anything to say
> There's many black ears here to listen.[49]

Marley and Perry also spoke of the union of the two rebel sounds when they name-checked several punks and mods in "Punky Reggae Party," a B-side to the single "Jamming," released in 1977: "The Wailers will be there, the Jam, the Damned, the Clash – Maytals will be there, Dr. Feelgood too."[50] Two years later, the Clash referenced *The Harder They Come* in the reggae-based "Guns of Brixton":

152   *The Bridge Builders*

> You see, he feels like Ivan
> Born under the Brixton sun
> His game is called survivin'
> At the end of the harder they come.[51]

The world's biggest punk band and the world's biggest reggae star acknowledged and drew attention to each other's respective genres.[52] Young Canadians watched and listened with interest.

Rebels Respond to Racism

Reggae and punk bands in the United Kingdom and Canada were responding to the racism in both countries. Despite the liberal mixing of races in its urban centres, Britain remained largely racist with its "sus law," which allowed the police to arrest anyone on suspicion; the rise of the National Front; and the pervasive fear of the immigrant – as articulated by Conservative then later Ulster Unionist MP Enoch Powell – that had great currency with many Brits of an older generation.[53] Formed in 1967, the National Front provided an umbrella for several fascist British organizations whose chief desideratum was to "Keep Britain White."[54] Terrifyingly, by 1976 the National Front had become the fourth largest political party in Britain.[55] The infamous 1976 instalment of the Notting Hill Carnival in West London's Ladbroke Grove area was scarred by violence, but also signified a turning point – for some – in race relations. It was during this time that disenfranchised punkers began harmonizing with the marginalized black community. These sweet overtures no doubt threatened the establishment, and charged-up bobbies policing the 1976 event only aggravated the situation. It was the beginning of a rash of violent episodes between the police, blacks, and punkers that would continue through the 1970s and into the 1980s with the famous Brixton Riot of 1981. Frontline cultural collisions in Ladbroke Grove and Brixton and then in Handsworth, in Birmingham, resonated – though perhaps to a lesser degree – with Canadians who lived in similar multiracial neighbourhoods in Toronto.

But perhaps the salient moment that conjoined the musical cultures of punk, reggae, and new wave came in the summer of 1976 in Birmingham, when a blind-drunk Eric Clapton came out in support of Enoch Powell while on stage. Clapton declared that he would "stop Britain from becoming a black colony ... the black wogs and coons and fucking Jamaicans don't belong here."[56] One wonders if Clapton played his US chart-topping cover of Marley's "I Shot the Sheriff" that night. Clapton's tirade began a serious musical movement that united distorted guitars and bubbling organs, skinheads and dreadlocks, whites and blacks.

Rock Against Racism focused on the rise of the National Front and included both black and white bands within the rock and reggae communities.[57] Led by Tom Robinson, the organization brought reggae bands such as Matumbi and Aswad together with punk bands such as Stiff Little Fingers and Sham 69 and new wavers such as Elvis Costello. At Victoria Park in London's East End, a Rock Against Racism concert that featured the Clash, Steel Pulse, and the Tom Robinson Band played to a crowd of over eighty thousand people.[58] It was a staggering success that united the discourses of punk and reggae in the fight against racism. Rebel musics came together to form a viable political weapon that could not be ignored in the United Kingdom.[59]

Young Canadians couldn't ignore it either. Toronto had its own satellite division of Rock Against Racism. When the Ku Klux Klan opened a chapter on Dundas Street east of Broadview in 1981, music journalist Nicholas Jennings and some of his close friends began their own Canadian version of the organization.[60] Jennings explained the KKK's strategy:

> What [the KKK] started doing is, they started showing up on high school campuses, leafleting at lunch time and after school to try and get young people to buy into their agenda, which was, basically, of course, that immigrants were the source of all the problems in Toronto and Canada at the time.[61]

In response, Rock Against Racism put on several events, including one massive show at St. Lawrence Market North that was headlined by Leroy Sibbles.[62]

Rock Against Racism Canada also published its own newsletter, *Rebel Music*.[63] The journal not only featured stories about pressing political issues but also reviewed the performances and recordings of the participating bands in the Rock Against Racism family. The organization also had political speakers at its events from various communities, including Jamaican Canadian Dudley Laws.[64] According to Jennings, part of the mandate for the organization was that all events had to include a punk band and a reggae band. As he remembered: "In the interest of racial unity and promoting that kind of message ... that's what the optics should be. Every Rock Against Racism show: punk band, reggae band."[65] As a consequence, the profiles of the 20th Century Rebels, Bloodfire, and Truths and Rights were raised as they shared the stage with punkers such as the Young Lions and L'Étranger.

The labour movement reached out to Rock Against Racism Canada for entertainment for some of their events, including one large convention in 1982 that featured Truths and Rights. The organization was also called upon to provide the entertainment for a "Ban the Bomb" peace conference in Montreal. It was there that 20th Century Rebels and the Young Lions not only shared the bill but also the school bus that took them up the 401 from Toronto to Montreal. Had it not been for the musical intersection of punk and reggae, this journey, which included such a seemingly disparate collection of musicians, would not have occurred.[66]

Perhaps the most significant Canadian tie to the "Jah Punk" movement, however, arrived when the Clash decided to cover Jamaican Canadian Willi Williams's "Armagideon Time" on the B-side of their "London Calling" single. The song was also featured on the *Black Market Clash* album.[67] As a result, there was renewed interest in Williams's original version, which was later featured in the film *Ghost Dog: The Way of the Samurai* and on the *Grand Theft Auto: San Andreas* soundtrack.[68] Williams and his anthem – a Jamaican migrant living in Canada and a hit song courtesy of an English punk band – perfectly articulated the multicultural and transoceanic nature of Jamaican music as it continued to evolve.

Though it happened to a much lesser extent in Toronto than it did in Britain, some Jamaicans wound up embracing punk's aesthetic. Adrian Miller, for example, believes that it was a matter of timing for him:

The Bridge Builders   155

> Had I come to Canada a bit later ... older, [punk] probably wouldn't
> have been something I would have embraced. But it was an age when
> I was still a teenager, and it was at an age you're making that transition
> from teenager into adulthood. So, it was at an age where I could still
> appreciate other stuff outside of the dominant mode ... you know, a
> "rootical" culture versus North American pop culture.[69]

Sharing the stage with Toronto punk bands, Miller retained some punk characteristics in both his image and his art, including cutting guitar and a visceral singing approach. Similarly, R. Zee Jackson and Johnny Osbourne recorded and released "Rock Yu Punky." Jackson explained that "Bob Marley played the root of reggae music. I play rock-reggae. It's a sound for this country – the second generation of reggae."[70] In 1978, *Globe and Mail* journalist James Hill observed that "musically, the two forms couldn't be further apart ... However, both punk and reggae relish in insolence, in the barbed-wire rudeness of a guitar string cutting the throat of the 'downpressor man.'"[71] While unifying black and white youth subculture around concepts such as poverty, revolt, and "down-pression" was more challenging in the Canadian context, many young non-Jamaican Canadians were introduced to reggae through the bridge of punk and, later, the two-tone explosion.

Natasha Emery, a former publicist and manager for several Toronto-based reggae artists whose musical tastes drifted towards anything rebellious, was, at sixteen, fully indoctrinated in the punk scene when she was introduced to the music of Peter Tosh by a friend:

> I was attracted to the message of punk, which was not only rebellious
> but kinda spoke out against the monarchy and spoke out against
> things that were a waste of money. I was a socialist. I've always been
> a socialist, so it's kinda natural that you gravitate towards message
> music. Punk was definitely a lot more aggressive. Where reggae gets
> the message out with love, punk gets it out – often – with violence. I
> was part of the group that was more about social change and social

protest ... so I don't think I consciously drew the parallel [between reggae and punk]. But looking back now, I say, "Oh, yeah, that's why I was into it [reggae], that's why it meant something to me."[72]

Nicholas Jennings bore further witness to the intersection of punk and reggae in the city: "We in RAR, [reggae] really was just right up our alley. That spoke to us, that the Clash were recording a song by Willi Williams who was right here in Toronto."[73] As *The Observer*'s Neil Spencer concluded: "Punk may have got all the headlines, but reggae proved vital in ending the rift between black and white teenagers and introducing cross-pollination to the charts."[74] Toronto was mimicking British responses towards punk and Jamaican music.

Some white Torontonians ended up preferring the reggae vibes. Brian Robertson, for example, walked to reggae across the punk bridge:

Some of the punk bands would cover reggae songs – the Clash definitely did that – and when the whole ska thing happened in the 80s and the very late 70s, that kinda got me thinking ... I just found that reggae was so much more interesting than punk music ... There wasn't a lot of positive messages [in punk]. I found that reggae was just a little bit more colourful. I found it a little bit more accessible. And I guess because reggae existed a lot longer than punk at the time, so reggae had so many subgenres already. You know, rocksteady, dub – just even finding out about dub – listen to all this stuff, this is just mind-blowing.[75]

Some were aware of the punk scene and saw the connections to reggae but chose to bypass punk and head straight to reggae. Photographer Greg Lawson, for instance, did not like punk:

I didn't like the aggressiveness of the punk music. I liked the aggressiveness of the reggae, of the Rastafarian element of Jamaican music. All Jamaican music is not Rastafarian music by any stretch, but there's a social justice element that I didn't see in punk rock ... They're playing the same venues, and both groups are rebels ... but you can be disenfranchised and have a very positive goal, or you can be disenfranchised and just be angry.[76]

Lawson preferred Toronto new wavers Martha and the Muffins over the local Viletones and, more importantly, was inspired by the ska-punk-reggae fusion coming out of Britain in the late 1970s.[77]

This crucial fusion was led by the 2 Tone record label, which heralded the second wave of ska. Two-tone coincided with punk's zenith and also with the emergence of various indigenous British reggae bands such as Steel Pulse, UB40, and Aswad. Yet it was the two-tone bands that shared – at least aesthetically – the greater overlap with punk music. In the emotionally and politically charged atmosphere of late 1970s Britain, bands such as the Specials, Madness, Bad Manners, the Bodysnatchers, the Selecter, and the Beat began expressing their own sociopolitical viewpoints on the strength of the music they had been exposed to. The essence of Prince Buster, Desmond Dekker, the Skatalites, and various other Jamaican originators was liberally mixed with punk sensibilities in the updated second-wave sound.[78]

While most two-tone bands included some first-generation Brits with West Indian heritage, the Specials and the Beat went one step further by employing a resident first-wave black ska musician in each of their lineups. Playing and recording as he had done with Prince Buster, Laurel Aitken, and Desmond Dekker, Lionel Augustus Martin, a.k.a. Saxa, brought an impressive resume to his new gig with the Beat.[79] Similarly, Alpha Boys' School graduate Rico Rodriguez, who was often a guest musician with the Skatalites, helped the Specials break through with one of their biggest hits, "Rudie," which was buoyed by Rico's memorable trombone motif.[80]

In *Black Culture, White Youth,* cultural historian Simon Jones discusses the multiracial roots of the two-tone movement and how the music resonated with both the black and white communities of England's West Midlands:

> The multiracial composition of bands such as the Selecter, the Specials, the Beat and UB40 reflected the unprecedented degree of rapport

that had been built up between black and white youth in those areas, their music premised on the experience of a whole generation of young people who had been to school together and shared the same streets, communities and leisure activities ... As a result of these concrete social ties and links, the cultural lives of both black and white communities have become harmonized around the shared spaces and cross-cutting loyalties of street, pub and neighbourhood. Multiracial kinship and supportive neighbourhood networks, produced by mixed marriages, friendships and dating patterns, have progressively eroded the boundaries between black and white.[81]

The same process would occur in Toronto, accelerated by the success of the British model.

UB40 was particularly popular in Toronto. The band was somewhat removed from the two-tone movement in that it was a straight-up reggae band.[82] The eight-member multiracial group had set out to popularize reggae and, more broadly, the Jamaican reggae artists they had loved and listened to growing up. The band succeeded beyond all expectations and took reggae to places that it had never been.[83] UB40's first Toronto show at the Concert Hall in 1983, for instance, sold out in twenty minutes. A second show was added for the same night, and it, too, sold out the same day it was announced. Thus began a love affair with the city. UB40's near-annual Toronto shows were some of the most anticipated concerts in the city.

Because of punk's championing of reggae, the popularity of two-tone bands, and the mainstream breakthrough of bands such as UB40, many rock and R&B musicians in Toronto began to adopt the reggae aesthetic into their sound, repertoire, and even image. For these musicians, reggae was a new source of inspiration.[84] In terms of international appeal, integration through the two-tone movement and even the indigenous British reggae style may very well have saved the genre in the post-Marley era. Importantly, the music built a bridge between migrant and host for many young Torontonians. The more commercially successful reggae bands and two-tone bands served as a conduit for many fans who chose to explore other Jamaican bands.[85] English-born Mark Matthews reflected on this special era in British ska and reggae:

[It was] probably a combination of radio (reggae was fairly common on Top 40 radio in the United Kingdom in the '70s), schoolmates who had Jamaican parents, and via punk rock groups like the Clash and also the two-tone UK ska explosion in 1980 for the music side of things. The music led me to the culture and going 'round to my friends' parents for an oxtail dinner or some goat.[86]

Likewise, dub artist Jesse King can now, in retrospect, see the development of his reggae palette, which began with punk and was followed by two-tone: "I was listening to the Clash in '79 ... and then it went into the Specials and the English Beat ... I think it was a progression into [reggae], not necessarily wanting to go, 'Oh, I've got to learn about it,' but coming into it that way."[87] It was an organic and oceanic progression: Jamaican popular music was exported to and recontextualized in the British context and sent back across the Atlantic to Canada.

The musical quotient of this journey, however, does not fully explain reggae's allure. For many young Torontonians, the two-tone movement (and British reggae in general) served as a political forum in which matters of truth and justice could be explored. The political messages in reggae were analogous with those found in punk and mod. For Jeffrey Holdip, it was vital that the music he listened to spoke to his own material reality: "Being able to state your case and story, politically through the music ... that became very important to me."[88] Similarly, keyboardist Todd Britton was charmed by the duality in reggae's message: "I loved the idea that it was 'gospel music for the revolution.' The lyrics spoke of love and war simultaneously!"[89] Music journalist Errol Nazareth, who was in high school in England before he moved to Canada, recalled:

I mean, being one of four south Asian kids in this school of all white kids, and the stuff that we heard, the name calling, that died down when we stood up to it, all the things that people would say, the attitudes that you were kind of exposed to. England really politicized me. When I was in England not only did I get into, like, my love of black music, more towards edgy, some LKJ and political stuff, like the Specials and the Beat and what they were saying, and the Clash and what they were saying.[90]

Nazareth said he believed he was at the right place at the right time and that the dread poetry of the UK-based Jamaican Linton Kwesi Johnson, along with the ska and reggae fusion of Coventry's Specials and Birmingham's Beat, hastened his political awakening.[91]

The rebellious aesthetic of punk transferred neatly onto reggae and provided one of the sturdier bridges along Toronto's ethnic frontline. Youth culture in North America and Europe, through subversive means such as punk and reggae, reclaimed the original spirit of good old rock and roll.[92] Punk and reggae simply made sense together.[93] The rebel texts of punk and reggae awakened a political sensibility in many young Torontonians. Tomaz Jardim, for instance, felt that reggae kick-started his personal journey of critical thinking, which eventually led him to a career as a university professor. Because of reggae, the twelve-year-old Jardim "was totally engaged in thinking about issues like justice and equality and all of those kinds of things."[94] In short, reggae sharpened political awareness and a sense of the other in Jardim and other young Torontonians like him.

Play I Some Music

While people were drawn to the aesthetic and message of reggae music, the music itself, reggae's irresistible heartbeat, drew many suitors across Toronto's cultural bridges. In June 1975, for instance, *Globe and Mail* journalist Robert Martin was sent to review a Bob Marley concert at Massey Hall. Sitting beside him at the show was, according to Martin, "a young white man with bare feet, long hair, full beard and blue jeans, the standard appearance for any middle-class freak kid from Mississauga."[95] Martin was sure that the man could not possibly decode the patois in which Marley was singing and therefore could not know that he "was supposed to be a member of the oppressor class. All he understood was that beat. He clapped his hands, snapped his fingers, stamped his feet and hollered for pure joy. Marley was right. Music has no prejudice."[96] Two days after Martin's concert review, the *Globe and Mail*'s third page contained a litany of articles that, to put it mildly, raised concerns about Rastafarians and their message. The *Globe* told readers that Rastafarians were called the "most violent crime group in New York," that "the sect uses marijuana as an aphrodisiac," that a Toronto lawyer had deemed them "walking time bombs," and that they were "basically anarchists."[97]

Three years later, the tone of some Toronto journalists had hardly improved. Watching *Canada AM*'s Sandie Rinaldo interview Bob Marley before his 1978 concert at Maple Leaf Gardens through a twenty-first-century lens makes for uncomfortable viewing. Rinaldo is, to be charitable, provocative with Marley, and her approach reflects a less culturally sensitive time:

Rinaldo: Rastafarianism is very popular in Jamaica. Yet in Canada and the United States it has a bad reputation: people are associated with drugs and the trafficking of marijuana and violence, and police arrests ...

Marley: Yeah, man, they crucified Christ, remember? Christ was a Christian, and them crucified Christ, say him is not a ...

Rinaldo: No, but let's go back to the facts. People have been arrested, and Rastafarians in Toronto, for instance, have a bad reputation.

Marley: I wouldn't say that the Rastafarians had a bad reputation; I would say people give the Rastafarians a bad reputation. Because the Rastafarians, I mean, you know what I mean, all of these things happen before the Rastafarians coming to Canada anyway [*laughs amiably*].

Rinaldo: But the things that are very obvious are things like the way that you look, right? To most people who are very conservative in dress, you look quite strange. Plus the fact you advocate smoking marijuana.

Marley: Dig this. I wanna show you this now: could you tell God that it's not legal?

Rinaldo: No. But you're ...

Marley: You couldn't tell God that it's not legal?

Rinaldo: You have a very strong religious belief, but other people don't necessarily share that, and what they see are

162 *The Bridge Builders*

> the obvious things. And isn't it in fact true that many
> Jamaican people get involved in the trafficking of
> marijuana and therefore get the bad reputation associated
> with Rastafarians?
>
> *Marley:* [*Arms folded.*] "People get trafficking," you see, well,
> really, I don't really know anything about those parts
> of life. All I know is about Rastafari, and I'm try[ing]
> bringing this truth to the people. What the people do
> with them life, I don't know, but I know about my own.
>
> *Rinaldo:* Okay, but what is your own? What's your music to you?
>
> *Marley:* Music is more than music to me. It goes further than
> music, you know?[98]

To be fair to Rinaldo, her piece was, on balance, a positive review of how popular Marley and reggae had become in the city. Coded language, however, permeated the segment, particularly when Marley and his Wailers were introduced to viewers as a "raggle-taggle tribe of Jamaican musicians."[99]

While some attacks on Rasta and reggae were misplaced, there was one particular aspect of reggae and its culture that was hard for many to accept. A noticeable air of misogyny had permeated the genre since its inception. As the *Toronto Star*'s Garry Steckles rightly observed in 1980 when assessing whether local reggae singer Carlene Davis (of black, Indian, and Scottish descent) had a shot in the reggae world: "Unlikely, because Carlene Davis is a female, competing in a male-dominated area where girls sing the backing vocals if they're lucky."[100] Though this issue was not unique to the genre, the female singer in reggae had only limited access to an infrastructure that was largely commandeered by men. As Klive Walker explained: "Inequality within the island's music industry ... seems to have meant that a female artist's career was not adequately shaped, supported, and properly promoted. A record company that had a complete disregard for the specific circumstances of its female singers, in relation to family and children, was an obstacle impeding the progress of the women on its roster."[101] Moreover, the biggest female names in the reggae game – Rita Marley, Judy Mowatt, and Marcia Griffiths – had the clear advantage of having been backing vocalists for the "King of Reggae."

Yet while men may have driven reggae's commercial success internationally, they also saddled the genre with its greatest obstacles. As Steckles suggested:

> Reggae's big three [Marley, Tosh, and Cliff] are hardly likely to become appealing on a strictly personal level with the great record-buying public, who may be put off by the dreadlocks of Marley and Tosh, their uncompromising public stand in favour of marijuana, their association with the controversial (and usually wrongly-maligned) Rastafarian religion, which worships the late Emperor Haile Selassie of Ethiopia as a living god and believes in black re-patriation to Africa.[102]

This was written, of course, twenty years before *Time Magazine* chose Marley's *Exodus* as the album of the century and before the BBC chose Marley's "One Love" as the song of the millennium.[103]

Fear-mongering or even skeptical journalists, however, could not deny the pure joy of reggae music, the musical building blocks of which appealed to an older demographic. The Sattalites' Fergus Hambleton, for instance, found in reggae what he felt was vanishing from popular music in the 1970s:

> So this is the time of Yes, King Crimson, the beginning of Black Sabbath, and the beginning of all that stuff, the prog rock ... and metal, and to me rock music lost several of the things that I loved it for and which I love reggae for, which is group singing ... tasty use of the horns, and good songwriting ... concise ... popular songwriting. And rock kind of drifted away from that, and not to say that it didn't go in some interesting directions, because I liked a lot of that kind of singer-songwriter things, but it lacked a certain kind of joy that you could hear in the reggae.[104]

164 *The Bridge Builders*

At the root of that joy was the beat, the one drop, and the spaces that it created, which allowed the voice and the other support instruments the necessary time to state their musical claims.

The puzzle of reggae served as a bridge that attracted many non-Jamaicans interested in decoding the music. Some slightly older, white, Canadian musicians were attracted to Marley and his music but had trouble understanding how Jamaican reggae behaved in musical terms. For instance, while writing for *Beetle Magazine,* the future Bloodfire guitarist Paul Corby received a copy of Marley's *Natty Dread* album.[105] Corby had been aware of reggae through its presence on Top 40 radio and insofar as it had influenced other bands that he liked, including Steely Dan.[106] The musical mystery, coupled with the rebellious and contentious nature of an album such as *Natty Dread,* forever changed Corby's life:

> It was all wrong. The bass wasn't where it should be; the guy was yodelling ... He said he'd "feel like bombing the church now that he knows the preacher is lying." There's no excuse for that kind of talk ... "A hungry man is an angry man," I mean, that's not exactly "All you need is love" ... It took me a while to understand what the music was doing ... I couldn't play along with it ... As far as what the bass and drums were doing, it took my direct experience with Jamaican people to understand that.[107]

Future Sattalites' keyboardist David Fowler had a similar experience. Fowler remembered seeing Marley at the University of Montreal in 1976: "My then fiancée loved it, and I was saying, 'But the bass is in the wrong place. Don't you get it? The bass player is playing everything backwards. It doesn't make any sense.' But, really, I was completely intrigued. How could this music work when all the accents are in the wrong place?"[108] Todd Britton likewise found himself on a steep learning curve when he chose reggae keyboards: "Musically, I learned of the subtle tapestry of very simple rhythms to create very complicated and consuming rhythms. There was always a 'deceptive' quality to it; it seemed 'way laid back' because of the way the beats are accented, but in reality a player has to be very 'on top' of the rhythm."[109] These confessions bring to mind Walter Jekyll's assessment of the Jamaican "pulse" seventy-odd years earlier:

whites beat with the time and blacks beat against it.[110] Indeed, for many non-Jamaicans, reggae's seemingly upside-down structure, in which the bass behaves as a separate melody from the vocals and the one drop falls on what most rock musicians would consider beat three and not on beats two and four (which were, bizarrely, filled instead by the guitar chuck and piano skank), was irresistible to the curious who yearned to solve its puzzle and to "beat against it."

It was reggae's beat and the polyrhythmic possibilities in the genre that hooked non-Jamaican Sam Weller: "The first thing that attracted me was the rhythm. And, more specifically, what really hit me was ... the clavinets, the rhythm of the clavinets."[111] The rhythm also captured the attention of a young Jeffrey Holdip:

> I remember going to a school dance. And, now, the school I went to, Oakwood, there weren't that many Jamaicans in the school, but there were a few, and they were strong and mighty. And at one school dance, somebody put on some 7 inch, and you'd see all the guys lined up on the wall, and this was like foreign to us. We're watching this go down, and we're, like, "What is this?" But the rhythm really got to me, and I remember that.[112]

Andru Branch was likewise intoxicated by the music: "I think it's the hypnotic quality, frankly. There are other musics that are hypnotic, too, but the lull of the bass guitar and the repeated polyphony, there's something about it ... and certainly there's a spiritual quality that always moved me."[113] It was the same for Perry Joseph:

> The trancelike quality of reggae was very similar to the Arabic music I heard as a child and also similar to the Motown music my older siblings listened to. It started with Bob Marley for me and Jimmy Cliff, as I happened to catch *The Harder They Come* (with subtitles, thankfully) on late-night TV. As my education continued, I grew to love Aswad and Steel Pulse and UB40. Later, while touring with Jeffrey Holdip (who taught me a lot while we rode the van together) as our sound man, I learned more about artists like Ken Boothe, Dawn Penn, Alton Ellis, and many more.[114]

166   The Bridge Builders

There were also other musics referenced within reggae, which was perhaps part of its appeal. While most non-Jamaicans consciously knew that they had never heard anything like it, reggae was somehow still familiar. Because it heavily referenced American R&B of the 1950s and 1960s, reggae resonated with non-Jamaicans who had a special interest in black American musical traditions. Isax InJah (a.k.a. Richard Howse), Scarborough-born and trained as a jazz saxophonist in Texas and New York, was intrigued by the reggae he heard on the radio. In particular, Hortense Ellis's "Love Comes from Unexpected Places" caught his attention when he was going to school in New York:

> I had never really heard it before. You know, I really needed to know what it was. I really enjoyed it because I'd always liked the heavy funk from the south in the States, so there's something about the heaviness of the bass in the reggae that I started hearing that really drew me to it. And the way the music sat within the feel; it reminded me a lot of the baddest funk.[115]

Although he thought he would pursue a jazz career in New York, Isax instead gravitated to the reggae scene in Toronto, where he began to play with musicians such as Kwame, Iwata, drummer Raffa Dean, and the British Jamaican keyboardist Bernie Pitters. It was there that Isax said to himself, "These are the guys I want to play with."[116]

Rock aficionados and record collectors such as Fergus Hambleton saw Jamaican reggae as a parallel universe. In many ways, the vitality in reggae had been sapped out of rock, as Hambleton observed:

> It was exciting to find that whole scene going on ... It was a pop-music scene and, you know, in the Jamaican charts you get a novelty song, a love song, a song about some guy's sexual prowess ... a fairly filthy song about something else, or a really spiritual kind of song, and sometimes all those things can be in the same song, but you'd get all that stuff on the charts and that's the way the charts used to be here, but now they're so monochromatic ... You kind of know what to expect.[117]

For Hambleton and other music lovers and musicians like him, the exotic music culture of Jamaica could be accessed through their Jamaican migrant friends who kept their finger on the pulse of their homeland. They presented them with a brand-new musical planet to explore, replete with its own charts and stars that orbited outside of the mainstream pop galaxy.

The International Herb

Though called various names – weed, sleng teng, cannabis, hashish, ganja, sensimilla, and pot, to name a few – marijuana proved to be a very successful access point that facilitated bridge building between Jamaicans and non-Jamaicans in Canada long before it was legal. As *Globe and Mail* journalist (and non-Jamaican) Paul McGrath noted in 1979: "Reggae music itself has more than a little to do with marijuana. Both are used freely by the Rastafarian communities in the West Indies and throughout America in the pursuit of their religion. In fact, it's close to impossible to find a reggae artist who does not admit to and advocate the regular use of the drug."[118]

The white non-Jamaican Natasha Emery saw connections between the Rasta's and the hippie's love of weed: "Being an island girl, a BC girl, natural lifestyles were common. Smoking weed was very common growing up for me as a teenager ... It's part of the natural, hippie lifestyle. And the hippie lifestyle and the Rastafari lifestyle are very similar."[119] The connection was just as obvious to the Sattalites' white keyboardist David Fowler, who grew up in North Vancouver. Fowler left British Columbia at seventeen with the band the Family Dog, an early blues and psychedelic outfit, to go to Expo 67 in Montreal.[120] When Fowler finally got to Toronto he found that smoking marijuana was a beneficial bridge-building activity.[121] But Fowler's initiation into reggae and Jamaican culture had occurred on the road. Remarkably, Fowler was already on tour with the Sattalites when he came to terms with how reggae music was affecting him: "I guess the endless trips in the van where everybody was playing their favourite reggae songs and possibly imbibing certain herb substances, I suddenly realized what was really compelling about the music and how it was hypnotic and spoke directly to your solar plexus, made you really want to move. It was absolutely infectious in the body."[122] Likewise, music publicist Sebastian Cook felt that "having a marijuana addiction" actually helped and accelerated his introduction into Toronto's reggae world.[123]

Reggae music could sometimes be shared, though perhaps not by design, while sharing a friendly spliff, as the Jamaican-born JuLion King attested:

> I didn't feel the need to go and bring the music to the people, but through social gatherings ... and then because they were curious about what we were smoking ... True dem deh a smoke dem ting, and we smoke and dem get curious about wha we a smoke. We introduce them to some reggae music – Dennis Brown, Robert Nesta Marley, Studio One, whatever – and they introduce us to Led Zeppelin ... and I still believe to this day that some of the best music was written in the '70s.[124]

Weed broke down some of the social barriers. King, for one, felt that the sharing of ganja had a significant effect on the culture at his own high school:

> [Ganja] changed the culture of George S. Henry at that time somewhat ... As Jamaicans, you know, our motto is "Out of many, one people," so we don't really rate nobody about we black, white, brown, or green. And we no gwarn like we better than nobody either, but everybody is everybody. So, the culture really changed, and it surprised a lot of people back in the day.[125]

In essence, the use of marijuana opened up dialogues between some Jamaican migrants and non-Jamaicans that might not have occurred otherwise.

Children of Zion

Shared faith or an interest in spirituality also brought people together. Certainly, a lot of reggae has a strong spiritual sensibility. Jamaican-born singer Wayne Hanson spoke of the depth of his mystical experience in singing reggae: "Music for me is like a mystical thing, especially reggae music; it's very spiritual. For example, whenever I sing, it reminds me of my breath; it's so deep. The breath to me is life. So, whenever I take a breath, I remember; I experience being alive. It's some kind of a divine thing. Music does help my everyday living."[126] Reggae music is often unapologetic in talking about or praising God, as JuLion King attested: "The only time I hear about God is in reggae music. Reggae music is truthful; reggae don't romp; reggae just brings it."[127]

Exposure to these themes in reggae led some non-Jamaicans to adopt the Rastafarian religion – or elements of it – as their own. The Bajan Canadian Jeffrey Holdip, for example, "nattied" up in 1981. His parents were generally fine with his embrace of the reggae culture: "My dad, he was okay with it, because, you've gotta understand, coming from an interracial relationship, being married [in] 1960, they're rebels to begin with. And the majority of the music I'm playing in the house is rebel music, so my dad could deal with [me having dreadlocks], and my mother could understand it."[128]

However, the young black members of Trinidadian and Guyanese descent that made up Truths and Rights, whom Holdip was working with at the time, needed a little help convincing their parents. A meeting between the band members, the parents of the band members, and Holdip and his mom and dad was arranged at an Ital restaurant on Dundas Street. The dreadlocked musicians pleaded their case to their parents and tried to demonstrate that they were serious about their craft. Holdip explained: "So, we all had a little meeting there to show that we're not hoodlums, and this is what we're trying to do. You know my parents were cool. They were just happy as long as I was happy and hopefully not doing anything wrong."[129] The band, having cleared the considerable hurdle of winning their parents' approval, went on to pen, perhaps more so than any other Canadian reggae band, poignant commentaries on the social injustice and inequality that dogged the city.

Some young white Torontonians also embraced Rasta. Tomaz Jardim was, for a time, Rastafarian, an experience that he viewed as being extremely positive. Interestingly, Jardim felt that the negative attention he received during his time as a Rasta emanated more from white people than from black Jamaicans: "In some ways, to them [Rastas] it was almost like I – to a degree – legitimized what it was that they were doing because it was showing that it was catching on more broadly."[130] In retrospect, Jardim said he was amazed at how accepting most Jamaicans were:

> I think back to it and think, oh my God, me and my friend Doug, we were like fifteen-, sixteen-year-old kids from Lawrence Park with dreadlocks and parents at home ... Why were they accepting us with such open arms? ... Two white kids, and these old Rasta guys would come to the house and hang out in my high school bedroom when my mom was downstairs. We'd just kind of hang out and talk. And I think they had, that in a way they were imparting wisdom that clearly we wanted.[131]

For other whites, Rasta was a choice for life. Photographer Greg Lawson was introduced to Rasta when he met the Toronto reggae band Truths and Rights. The band raised Lawson's curiosity: "What is it about these people? These people have something that is extremely positive, and you can feel it."[132] Lawson transcended in Jamaica in the early 1980s while he was on a photographic shoot: "I started to get deeper and deeper into the Rastafarian faith, realizing that it's a Judeo-Christian faith, that it's not any hocus-pocus thing, that it is bona fide."[133] Greg started growing dreadlocks in his mid-thirties. As a white Rasta, Greg today feels that while he has been tested, he has always been supported by black Rastas.[134]

Receiving family support, however, was a different story, as Paul Corby attested: "I wasn't making any money. I was espousing things that made people uncomfortable. Even to explain a day in my life at a Christmas party, for instance, people would be shocked. But, you know, it was the life at the time, and I thought I was doing something important, so I wasn't ashamed."[135] Corby had dreadlocks in 1980, an extremely rare choice for whites at the time:

> They were totally not happy about it. There's no way [for Paul's parents] to explain it. How do you explain it? You can't explain that.

They came out of the '50s; they came out of World War II. How can you explain that? There was no way they were listening to my explanation, because it just didn't make any sense.[136]

The day Paul trimmed his locks, his father bought him a television set.[137]

Others were slightly more accepting. The first Rastafarian Natasha Emery met was her future husband, Wayne Hanson. They were married in 1989 and had two girls.[138] Emery's mom was accepting but was surprised by her special interest in Jamaican music and culture. To prepare her mother for what her new husband looked like, Emery's brother told her "to go to the record store ... Ask the shopkeeper for a Bob Marley album, and then she could pick it up and look, and then she would see: that was a Rastaman."[139] Emery's bridge building extended to the lives, musical tastes, and habits of those in her circle. Her brother, for instance, subsequently became a Peter Tosh fan.[140]

For some musicians, their journey to Jah was rooted squarely in their musical career. Saxophonist Isax InJah, for instance, came to Rastafari through jazz and reggae:

> I was already coming from the land of Coltrane, "A Love Supreme," so, then, to hear about the "one love" message of the reggae, and from Rastafari, too, that was kind of very resonant with me. I was already kind of into that ... When I started to hear people say "Selassie I" all the time, I started asking people, "What's up? Who's this Selassie guy?" And then my friends growing up who had become Christian, and I tried to listen to what they were saying and even I've gone to church many times, and it never, ever clicked with me. But then when I started to read about Haile Selassie, and ... instead of thinking about God up in the sky, but just thinking about ... God being a man, then that kind of made sense.[141]

His mom and dad thought it was a fad, but they eventually accepted that he had embraced reggae and Rastafari.

Still, having locks was sometimes not an easy choice for anyone living in Toronto. InJah's experiences were generally positive:

172   *The Bridge Builders*

> From my experience ... pretty much everybody just welcomes me
> and has nothing but respect and love for the whole thing ... Not to
> say every single person, but the people that are the real musicians or
> the real Rastafari ... when they recognize in somebody else that the
> person is sincere and really loves it and is really bringing something
> good to the table ... I think they go and accept it. As far as I know,
> that's how it is.[142]

Despite this general acceptance, in 2010 InJah was politely bumped from
a gig during the Toronto International Film Festival because the organizers
had been hoping for a more "clean-cut" sax player. Some Torontonians
still had issues with dreadlocks and what they might mean. The very
existence of white Rastas such as Isax InJah, Paul Corby, and Greg Lawson
challenged the upper-crust tastes of the TIFF's champagne-swilling
glitterati.

Many young non-Jamaican Torontonians had, nevertheless, earnestly
crossed over into the Jamaican community. Moreover, many Jamaican
migrants in Toronto had personally facilitated their crossing in various
spaces around the city. These metaphorical bridges were, more often than
not, anchored at both ends by an interest in music. Although smoking
marijuana, having sex, falling in love, getting married, talking God, con-
verting to Rasta, and forging lifelong friendships helped them along,
it was usually Bob Marley, Jimmy Cliff, punk, two-tone, and UK reggae
that served as the entry points. While crossing the bridge was clearly
possible, there were many roadblocks along the way.

The Mighty Pope, Lucea, Jamaica, 1960s. | Courtesy of Earle Heedram

JuLion King with his sister and mom before coming to Canada. | From the private collection of JuLion King

Facing page, top to bottom:

Many Jamaican families came to Canada piecemeal. Such was the case with Mike Smith and his family, seen here reunited in Toronto. | From the private collection of Mike Smith

The Harvey boys' first winter in Canada, 1966. | From the private collection of Carl Harvey

In 1969, reggae's keyboard king, Jackie Mittoo, left Jamaica for Toronto. | Photo: Erin Combs, courtesy of Getty Images

Metro's grand old man of Canadian reggae, Leroy Sibbles, live in Toronto. | Photo: Isobel Harry

Canada's reggae champions keyboardist Jackie Mittoo, artist manager Karl Mullings, and guitarist Lynn Taitt. | From the private collection of Tanya Mullings

Prior to his appointment as Toots and the Maytals' bandleader, Carl Harvey developed a good reputation as a session player in both Jamaica and Toronto. | From the private collection of Carl Harvey

Ernie Smith and Roots Revival (*left to right:* Paul Corby, Ernie Smith, Clive Ross, Tony Nicholson, and Wadi Daniel), Toronto, 1979. | Photo: Isobel Harry

Chalawa with Stranger Cole *(in knit hat),* 1979. | Photo: Isobel Harry

Facing page, bottom:

Truths and Rights, Kensington Market, Toronto. | Photo: Isobel Harry

Carlene Davis, Toronto, March 1980. | Photo: Isobel Harry

Fergus Hambleton and Jo Jo Bennett's Sattalite School of Music brought many Jamaican and non-Jamaican musicians together in Toronto. | From the private collection of Fergus Hambleton

The Sattalites, promo shot. | From the private collection of Fergus Hambleton

Rupert "Ojiji" Harvey, Messenjah's powerful frontman. | From the private collection of Rupert "Ojiji" Harvey

Messenjah, promo shot. | From the private collection of Rupert "Ojiji" Harvey

Earth, Roots and Water and 20th Century Rebels' inimitable frontman, Adrian "Sheriff" Miller. | From the private collection of Adrian Miller

Sunforce frontman Michael Garrick, live. | Courtesy of Michael Garrick

Various bands from Reggae Canadiana were featured at the Bamboo every month. | From the author's personal collection

Bonconganistas live at the Waterfall Stage, Harbourfront, Toronto, 1991. | From the private collection of Paul Corby

Fujahtive, promo shot. | Courtesy of Anthony Goldstein

Facing page, top to bottom:

For some, crossing the metaphorical bridge between migrant and host had far-reaching and often happy ramifications, as it did for Wayne Hanson and Natasha Emery. | Courtesy of Natasha Emery

Canada promised a better life for many Jamaican migrants, and education was the top goal. This was true for reggae trombonist and now educator Mike Smith. | From the private collection of Mike Smith

The talented and versatile DJ Friendliness. | From the private collection of Tanya Mullings

Andru Branch, promo shot. | Photo: Greg Lawson. From the private collection of Andru Branch

The royal family of the queen of Canadian reggae, songstress Tanya Mullings, live. | From the private collection of Tanya Mullings

Canadian reggae's iconic saxophonist Isax InJah. | From the private collection of Richard Howse

Bruce Robinson (a.k.a. "Preacher") and the Sattalites live at the Forum, Ontario Place, Toronto. | From the private collection of Fergus Hambleton

6

Blackness and Whiteness

Non-Jamaican and nonblack participation in reggae music has generally troubled perceptions of the genre's musicians. However, new forays in cultural or global history and ethnomusicology are challenging essentialized and stereotypical notions of blackness and whiteness.[1] These notions have been upheld by gatekeepers as often as they have been deconstructed by bridge builders within the Canadian reggae scene. Given the growing field of research on human DNA, scholars from the social sciences can no longer have the confidence (or, at least, shouldn't have the confidence) to speak of race as purely a construction.[2] Nevertheless, constructions of blackness and whiteness, insofar as they apply to social groupings, persist. These outmoded notions informed how the two biggest-selling reggae artists of all time were perceived, and they influenced whether Canadian reggae artists were deemed "black enough" or "too white."

Forgiving Captain Marley

Scholars have recently addressed how lighter-skinned musicians have negotiated trials of authenticity in hip hop.[3] Indeed, some white-skinned reggae artists have utilized similar approaches to secure a stamp of authenticity within Canadian reggae. One approach has been fully embracing the Rasta faith system. Another has seen artists tacitly declaring their whiteness in a quest to write and sing about their own Canadian-centric experiences on top of a reggae groove. Both approaches problematize the original reggae text, as it is perceived. On the one hand, Selassie is a black

God, and some feel his message, which dovetails with the prevailing Pan-Africanist sentiment, is remote from the white Canadian experience. On the other, singing about Canadian experiences divorces the musical message of reggae from its perceived cultural origins. Nevertheless, most white-skinned Canadian reggae musicians felt accepted by other, black-skinned reggae musicians, provided they were able to play the music. For the musician, then, the extramusical quotients of appearance and ethnic background rarely had a place in the actual music making.[4]

Internationally, whiteness has been an impediment for various reggae musicians, including the most famous one of all. Having a lighter skin tone did not help the young Robert Nesta Marley. The racial balance in Jamaica at the time of the island's independence in 1962 was roughly 77 percent black and 20 percent brown.[5] At the time, the brown-skinned Marley constantly faced racism from both sides. Whites did not see him as their equal while blacks were deeply suspicious of his "caste." Marley was often harassed for having a white father.[6] His mother, Cedella Booker, recalled one instance when Bob was enamoured with a young black girl from his yard in Trenchtown. While the feelings may have been mutual, the girl's family intervened, as Cedella explained: "Her brother say to Bob, 'we don't want no white man in our breed.'"[7] For some, Marley was a misfit who did not belong in the Trenchtown ghetto because his skin tone troubled others' preconceptions of Jamaica's mulatto middle class. Future bandmate Bunny Wailer recalled seeing Marley for the first time in Trenchtown: "He was the only little, what do you call it, red pickney in the place, because everybody else was black people ... Teased is not the word; we call it rejected."[8] These encounters with antimulatto racism perhaps exacerbated Marley's disdain for and disassociation from the father who named him.

Norval Sinclair Marley has mostly been portrayed as a deadbeat dad who abandoned Marley and his mother.[9] This portrayal suits the facts: the fifty-something-year-old colonial supervisor of English heritage impregnated a seventeen-year-old girl from the country. Yet this depiction lacks nuance. First, Captain Marley intended to marry Booker, but his plans were waylaid, in part because of his relocation to Kingston (a chronic hernia caused him to change jobs) but, more plausibly, because of the Marley family's reservations. As Bob Marley's mom explained: "He told me he loved me, and I believe that he did. He was always honest with me in that time. He told me he was the black sheep of his family, because the Marleys did not like black people, but Norval liked them very much."[10] At least for a time, Captain Marley made monthly visits to St. Ann to visit Cedella and their son, Bob, but these visits grew increasingly infrequent as Bob got older. The captain's absence from Marley's life profoundly affected his psyche and shaped the future King of Reggae's attitudes towards race.[11]

To be sure, Marley harboured a lifelong resentment towards his largely absent white father that manifested in several ways, including his early identification with countercultural and sometimes criminal rude boy behaviour, his rejection of his white heritage in favour of Rasta, his embrace of black consciousness, and the steadfast Pan-Africanist sensibilities in his later lyrics.[12] In the end, Marley denied every part of his whiteness except, of course, the one part that he could not.

At the same time, Marley saw himself as a missionary, and while his body of work may have championed Pan-Africanism, it also held out the promise of a utopian community that transcended the language of race.[13] As Marley himself said: "My father was a white, and my mother black, now them call me half-caste, or whatever. Well, me don't *deh pon* nobody's side. Me don't *deh pon* the black man's side nor the white man's side. Me *deh pon* God's side, the man who create me and cause me to come from black and white."[14] While the child might not have been black enough for Trenchtown, the dreadlocked man was black enough for the rest of the world and became the face of reggae. With Marley's unparalleled success, Rastafarian musicians assumed the role of reggae's custodians, despite the great number of non-Rasta writers, producers, and performers making reggae in Jamaica.[15] Rastafari and its polemics therefore became the authentic reggae text for the gatekeepers – the majority of journalists and ethnomusicologists around the world.[16]

The "Marley mould" was adopted as a strategy for commercial success by record labels and other reggae bands, including ones outside of Jamaica.[17] The United Kingdom's Aswad was one example. Like most other young black Britons growing up in London in the late 1960s and early 1970s, Aswad's frontman, Brinsley Forde, loved Marley and became a personal friend of his during Marley's time in England. But Forde was

English and was therefore influenced by pop music, as he explained: "For the most part, we heard the sounds and watched all the popular rock/ pop bands and artists such as the Beatles, Stones, Presley, et cetera ... and saw all the advertising and imagery used in their promotional campaigns, TV appearances. So our influences were taken from our surroundings."[18] The high-end production quality of Marley's albums elevated reggae to an international level, where it had a chance to compete with the top rock and pop acts of the day, and Marley's success opened up an international touring circuit for future reggae acts.[19]

Other young Brits were profoundly influenced by Marley. Ali Campbell – the son of Ian Campbell, the popular folk singer and proud card-carrying member of the Communist Party of Britain – saw Marley perform live in London when he was just a teenager. For Campbell, it was the nearest thing he had had to a religious experience in his life.[20] Not long afterwards, Campbell, his brother Robin, and six other friends – all of whom were unemployed – formed what would become one of the most important reggae bands of all time. Yet UB40 have long been the whipping boy of reggae journalists and historians. Few scholars have discussed the real motivations behind the original eight members' meteoric rise to fame. Fewer still have discussed the two and a half members who are of Afro-Jamaican descent. Instead, scholars have focused on how UB40's interpretation of reggae can't be taken seriously because they hit the proverbial commercial jackpot.[21] Only a few bands such as the Beatles and Queen have had more charted singles in the history of British music, and in terms of reggae, only Bob Marley has sold more albums than UB40's 70-plus million.[22] Yet the perception of UB40 created by a few music journalists has altered – for the worse – reggae scholarship.

Discussing reggae history and addressing UB40 only tangentially is akin to discussing the Second World War without mentioning Roosevelt.[23] UB40 had a profound influence on reggae music internationally and, indeed, on the lives of the Jamaican reggae artists to whom UB40 paid tribute.[24] Ranking Miss P, a British Jamaican DJ, observed that UB40 "made a lot of reggae artists a lot of money and UB40 are highly respected in Jamaica because of this." As far as documentary filmmaker Don Letts is concerned, because of UB40, a good number of Jamaican reggae artists whose songs were covered by the English band "have got a new lease of life and everybody wants their song to be covered by UB40."[25] In 2010, Jamaica's biggest daily, *The Gleaner,* posited that the greatest tribute to reggae music of the 1960s and 1970s could be found in UB40's *Labour of Love* album series.[26] A few years earlier, in 2002, Sly and Robbie, the Mighty Diamonds, Ken Boothe, Max Romeo, Toots Hibbert, John Holt, Gregory Isaacs, Alton Ellis, Bob Andy, Leroy Sibbles, and many other famous reggae artists took part in a project that returned the tribute. In a reverse of the band's *Labour of Love* series, these seminal Jamaican musicians sang original UB40 songs.[27] So while their place in reggae's history has been questioned by some of the genre's critics, Jamaican journalists and the actual makers of the music have celebrated the band's significant contributions and role as a bridge builder.

Despite their success with cover songs, UB40's original lyrics are oppositional, a fact that has warranted reconsideration from some reggae journalists.[28] The band's name referred to Unemployment Benefit, Form 40. The members only began playing music on their native instruments some six months before their first gig, and they got some of their first pieces of equipment from a disability cheque that Ali Campbell, the lead singer, received after being glassed in the eye in a barroom fight.[29] The members stole the rest of their gear.[30] Moreover, the Campbell brothers were the red-diaper babies of a communist, a fact that complicates some critics' assessment of UB40's motivations.

Clearly stated from the outset, UB40's aim, like Marley's, was to become ambassadors for reggae music. In fact, the band wanted to record the first set of its *Labour of Love* series as their debut album but decided instead to record and release *Signing Off,* which became the highest-charting independent release in UK history.[31] The platinum album featured several politically charged songs that addressed, *inter alia,* nuclear war, lynching, Thatcherism, and the wrongful conviction of black American Gary Tyler. What critics choose to ignore is that UB40 never abandoned these sorts of themes. Although their biggest commercial successes have been cover versions, only four of the sixteen proper studio albums released by the band were cover albums.[32] It is true that not all UB40's cover attempts have been – at least artistically – unqualified successes. But the same can be said of a vast number of Jamaican reggae artists who have, at some point or another, offered up an ill-conceived rendition of a cover song (e.g., the Wailers' "What's New Pussycat?"). Yet these "violations" have not resulted in their being excluded from the history of reggae.

The case of UB40 is important when considering the Canadian reggae scene of the late 1970s and 1980s. UB40 helped fan the flame of reggae internationally and especially in Jamaican outposts such as Toronto. With this in mind, it must be asked: If British reggae bands such as UB40 have not been officially recognized by the genre's chroniclers, what chance do Canadian reggae bands have? Despite producing valid and varied reggae texts that suited their own unique Canadian sensibilities, both the Jamaican migrant musician and the non-Jamaican musician struggled to wrest themselves free from the tightly circumscribed conception of what reggae "ought to be."

Fortunately, some scholars are now pressing beyond such stereotypes and misperceptions.[33] New ideas regarding the construction of whiteness have begun to challenge the so-called authenticity of the reggae text. In 2003, Jeff Chang paid his respects to the recently deceased Clash frontman, Joe Strummer, calling his trailblazing fusion of punk and reggae an emblem of radical whiteness.[34] Radical whiteness, according to Chang, both sees and rejects white privilege within the context of a multicultural society.[35] Yet this is hardly a new idea, at least as far as Jamaica is concerned. From nineteenth-century abolitionists such as the English Baptist minister William Knibb to early twentieth-century internationalists such as Walter Jekyll, Jamaica had several worthy examples of people who challenged normative constructions of whiteness.[36]

The Appropriation of Voice

The human body has become a primary text.[37] The popular idea of the dreadlock-flashing, Babylon-busting reggae musician have, for some, made the non-nattied-up, non-Rasta, non-Jamaican, and even nonblack authenticities that exist in reggae illegitimate. Still, many non-Jamaican musicians felt that their acceptance by Jamaicans in Toronto's reggae scene was easily gained. Fergus Hambleton, for example, said that he achieved it by remaining true to himself: "I think that Jamaicans appreciate ... you know, you're coming to their culture, but you're not saying, 'Oh, mine's rotten. I love yours.' It's basically [that] I love the beautiful things that are in both the cultures."[38] Nevertheless, people often reacted dramatically to the mixing of races and cultural expressions.[39] Isax InJah, who had a child with a black Jamaican woman, spoke of his own experience as a white Rasta:

> Lots of people outside of Jamaican culture, when they would look at us, or look at me, a lot of people think that I'm just a space cadet, straight up, like, people, say, that would have known me before I ever went away to the States ... I know now they still respect me as a musician, but I know lots of them. They really think I'm just, like, in my own world ... They're still nice to me, and everything, but that's just a feeling. I know how it is right, like, "What the fuck are you doing?," right?[40]

The most dramatic, and perhaps the most disingenuous, reactions to whites playing reggae in the Toronto scene have come not from Jamaican musicians or even Jamaicans but rather from other whites.

These negative reactions were at their height during the late 1980s, when extramusical identity politics began to slow the growth of the genre in what was deemed an exclusively black Jamaican art form. To be sure, these criticisms did not emanate from within the actual reggae community itself but rather from the periphery, in the media where journalists or "purveyors of cool" chose to ignore much of the reggae being crafted in Toronto. Beginning at Toronto's Women's Press in 1987, the Canadian literary community experienced a plague, whereby certain writers and then visual artists and musicians were held suspect if their art reflected or appropriated the voice or experience of the other. In short, the old adage that you should write about what you know was horrifyingly expanded to designate *who* you could write about. This stance emerged in response to white writers who had written about black women. Nonblacks were accused of cultural imperialism, and almost the entire Toronto arts community felt they were walking on eggshells. Neil Bissoondath deconstructed the reasoning behind the argument:

> Not only must whites not write about blacks, but men must not write about women, non-natives about natives, and so on, all based on the

claim that if you haven't lived the life, you don't have the right to write about it. And the writer who dares to explore the territory deemed not his or her own becomes a thief, open to charges of racism, sexism, imperialism from people who object to being portrayed in ways other than they would portray themselves – and self-portraits, let us face it, tend to be free of blemishes.[41]

The most troublesome aspect of the argument was that it was implicitly racist. UB40 was, for example, an obvious target because of their whiteness and non-Rasta lyrics, as the *Globe and Mail*'s Chris Dafoe demonstrated:

It must cause reggae purists no end of consternation that UB40, the Birmingham, England[,] band that played Kingswood Music Theatre last night, is generally recognized as the most popular reggae act in the world. The band has numerous strikes against it, not the least of which are the facts that it is not Jamaican and that most of the band, including frontman Ali Campbell are white. On more substantive points, UB40 has stripped reggae of its spiritual elements, winning their success with a light-stepping pop-reggae that doesn't threaten suburban teens. And while the band has written some songs that, for lack of a better term, might be called socially relevant, most of their hits have featured lyrics that praise romantic, rather than religious love.[42]

Dafoe made no mention of the fact that UB40's "romantic love" songs had originally been written by what he would have called "real" Jamaican reggae artists (or were adaptations of their songs) and that these artists were only too delighted that UB40 had chosen to pay tribute by covering them.[43]

Toronto journalist Liam Lacey was equally willing to ignore UB40's socialist and oppositional lyrics and black and Rasta members: "In this distinctly Anglo-fied reggae music, the aggression and rhythmic bite have been exchanged for sweet, almost coy melodies to catch the ears of a mainstream audience. Compared to the relative mastery of Toots and the Maytals ... UB40's pasteurized reggae lacks something vital, what Rastas call *ital*."[44] Certainly, this pithy critique of "italness," or purity, was not reserved for Brits, and Canadian reggae acts soon began to feel the heat, as James Marck's review of the Sattalites' live album in *NOW* attested: "Fans of the Sattalites may appreciate this record because it has a good live mix and represents the band's sound well. But the excitement is vastly more contrived than real."[45] This generation of music reporters began to use racialized language to denote what – according to them – was and wasn't authentic reggae.

NOW, the most important music weekly in Toronto, surreptitiously equated "white" with light, weak, watered-down, and contrived. Marck, for instance, appraised white rocker Christopher Ward's self-titled album in 1987 in the following way: "This stuff is like Wonder-bread – light, white and lacking in anything but artificial additives."[46] Fellow *NOW* writer Christopher Jones also employed "white" in the pejorative, even in positive reviews, one of which began: "As white soul/funk singers go."[47] Despite its overall complimentary tone, an article by Kim Hughes classified the Toronto ska outfit the Hopping Penguins as a "watered-down reggae-by-white-people-for white people."[48] Similarly, according to *NOW*'s Helen Lee, Syren, two white sisters who played reggae in the city along with their multiracial band, were "a bland facsimile of Caribbean spirit" who had, in concert, "ambled through a selection of studiously topical songs, undisturbed by the context of singing about strife, war and 'Third World Woman' to a predominantly white audience."[49]

These essentialized ideas applied to blackness as well. All-black bands such as Messenjah were asked by certain promoters in advance of their gigs if they were, indeed, all-black acts.[50] This trend forced Messenjah's hand in terms of which musicians they considered for the bandstand. Adrian Miller said he was well aware that his art – created in Canada – was a fusion that included non-Jamaican influences:

> You have a lot of Jamaicans who just think Burning Spear and Culture and Abyssinians is ... king and everything else sucks. I've always thought that every culture has its own genius and, for me, I'd be cheating myself if I locked myself into a little box and listened to Burning Spear and Culture for fucking 365 days a year. I couldn't

do that, because I'm a great lover of all kinds of music. You have a lot of reggae artists who talk about how they listen to *that* music and they listen to *that* music, but you could never find it in their own music that they play. Whereas, someone like me, now, if people listen to my music, you might have the odd one or two songs that are more straight-ahead reggae, but at some point you're going to get some fusion happening there ... "Why can't I do a song that has nothing to do with Jamaican roots reggae?" The only problem with that is you're going to have a backlash, "Buoy, Adrian Miller, than man soundin' white these days, mon."[51]

By virtue of what he added to his own mix, Adrian Miller's blackness might very well be called into question by some gatekeepers.

The issue of appropriation cast a grey shadow on the Canadian reggae scene. It effectively meant that Isax InJah, Paul Corby, and a variety of other white-skinned musicians who had given themselves wholly to reggae music for decades would henceforth be considered illegitimate on the grounds of not looking the part. It meant that all-black bands had to remain so. Black artists straying too far from the understood norm might be accused – as in the case of Adrian Miller – of "soundin' white."[52] And as for mixed-race bands, the perpetual media question of authenticity beset their hard-won successes. Fergus Hambleton discussed how these issues had affected the Sattalites in *Eye Magazine* in 1992: "We've faced resistance to reggae, and then resistance from people who thought we weren't black enough to play reggae."[53] So although reggae music was informing new forays in the world's musical conscience on the international stage, Canadian reggae bands struggled to maintain a commercially competitive profile within the nation's mainstream musical culture.

Actual musicians in Toronto's reggae scene hardly thought this way, as long-time reggae DJ David Kingston observed: "People who are musicheads, like anyone who is involved with music, never really questions all that ... Whereas you've got politicizers who are saying, 'You know, you can't do this and that.'"[54] Keyboardist Sam Weller echoed Kingston's point: "Musicians are operating outside the confines of their culture ... People of different backgrounds have always been playing music together, and it all comes down to that [musical] language thing ... [Some] try to make big connections between music and culture, and sometimes I don't think those connections are as big as people think they are."[55] These artists, however, were forced to swim upstream against the "purveyors of cool," who foregrounded skin colour over musical competence in terms of who was supposed to play reggae.

Exacerbating this trend was the fashion of "not cheering for the home team," which was endemic in certain strains of Canadian music journalism. Music critics who had been long-time champions of homegrown reggae were frustrated with the cynicism of some of their colleagues, as Errol Nazareth, who has written many reggae pieces for *Eye Magazine* and the *Toronto Sun* explained: "If I don't like a record I just won't review it. But these guys ... you can almost watch them rubbing their hands with glee: 'I'm going to trash this.'"[56] Similarly, Nicholas Jennings, who has covered reggae in *Maclean's,* the *Toronto Star,* and the *Globe and Mail,* resisted the purist approach:

> No matter what the genre, anyone who sets themselves up as the police to determine what is "pure" or "impure," "right" or "wrong" is anathema to me, because I basically believe that music is a constantly evolving force that is always incorporating other influences and blending and evolving in an ongoing way. To try and set up gates or boundaries and say that it was only "true" or "real" for this very specific period, it's just wrong, it's just weird, and I think it's unhealthy.[57]

Ironically, this very blending and evolving of the hybrid reggae text threatened the purists' apparatus.

One Love

Perceptions of cultural authenticity aside, Toronto's uniqueness and diversity fostered the possibility of cross-cultural harmony. The city's Jamaican community, for instance, played a direct role in shaping the musician and person that the talented Isax InJah would become. As he explained:

> Maybe if I never came back to Toronto, I would have just stayed in New York and been just within the jazz thing. But coming back to Toronto and how it all went ... Whatever I had done with jazz and learned about with jazz, I started to look at reggae, Rastafari, and one love as being where I'm supposed to put my energy in, what my true work is.[58]

Others felt that reggae was central to building bridges between cultures in the city, as David Kingston recalled: "All of a sudden, it's a common platform ... It's a way for [people] to communicate ... It's like people start to trust the immigrants when they eat [their] food, and it's okay, there's an element of that ... Music just does powerful things."[59] And multiracial bands playing to multiracial audiences was symbolic and powerful for so many of the people involved in the city's reggae scene.

Cross-cultural dialogue flourished at the Bamboo, as Patti Habib observed:

> The Bamboo Club helped bring Jamaican music and culture to the mainstream audience, [to] young Torontonians who got turned on to a different way of living than being brought up in a middle-class home that tended to be of one ethnicity. White. Greek. Portuguese. Everyone mixed, and the music brought them all together, and I used to love watching everyone getting along on the dance floor and coming to make Jamaican friends.[60]

Bamboo regulars the Sattalites witnessed and helped facilitate bridge building in the city and elsewhere, as bassist Bruce McGillivray explained: "Spreading this music through Canada, we feel that we've been a rather important source of getting this music across to Canadians. And once Canadians totally embraced it – we would hope more than they have – it certainly opened up reggae music to all Canadians."[61] Charged with the nationwide ambassadorship of reggae, the multiracial Sattalites reflected the multiracial audiences they performed for.

Strides towards further cultural fusion were made offstage, as in the case of Rock Against Racism. Organizer Nicholas Jennings bore witness to the collaborative effort put into the organization's events: "Having put on ... let's say several dozen concerts in Toronto, I know that every single audience that was at those events was totally and wonderfully mixed. It was very much a multicultural audience and, thus, I think it's safe to say that reggae music has helped to break down racial barriers in this city."[62] Sound engineer Jeffrey Holdip also felt that, at least during Canada's golden age of reggae, that the music and movements such as Rock Against Racism found some success in evoking harmony between the races:

> [Reggae] used to promote it big time ... When I first got into it, there wasn't the racial harmony that there is perceived to be today. So they tried to bring it together ... but remember, that era, too, they had started with the two-tone, so a lot of the bands from Britain were mixed anyways. But the Canadian bands were trying with Rock Against Racism, a lot of the bands were involved with that organization ... so, you know, they tried.[63]

Reggae events in the city at the very least offered a place where discussions might begin.

Reggae's effect on racial boundaries developed in many spaces around the city over time. Reggae singer David Matthews, a second-generation Jamaican born in Canada, recalled the reggae-inspired paradigm shift that he witnessed between elementary school and high school in Scarborough in the late 1980s:

> You could clearly see the difference ... You know, [people] sort of intermixed, but it wasn't so much of a gel. Now, by the time I was into high school I noticed that you found everybody with everybody. My best friend growing up was an Italian guy. I hung out with a Newfie. So we all pretty much gelled, and it was all more because of our interest, and a lot of it was based around reggae music.[64]

What might have been deemed bold behaviour by the migrants of a previous generation had become commonplace.

Many first-generation migrants were unequivocal about reggae's success in bringing black and white together, as Jamaican-born concert promoter Denise Jones attested:

For our shows that we'd do downtown, our audience was 50 percent to 60 percent nonblack. I think the music is quite the integrator. I think the music really opens doors to people knowing about Jamaica, learning about Jamaica, loving Jamaica. The basis of reggae ... even if it has not been acknowledged, played a significant role in informing the world about apartheid ... It's through that music that we heard that stuff.[65]

Calgary ReggaeFest director Leo Cripps concurred: "I witness this every year at Calgary ReggaeFest: people of every nationality and culture, under one umbrella to enjoy reggae music. You play reggae music, and whatever walls that were surrounding, whatever dividing, groups crumble."[66] Reggae possessed the power to both sooth and disarm its audience.

While Toronto was certainly the epicentre of the Canadian reggae explosion, the appeal of the Jamaican migrants' music travelled across the country in the aftershocks and took root in the most unusual places. Black Jamaican trombonist Mike Smith witnessed bridge building in Saskatchewan:

One time ... in Saskatoon, I was able to go into a pub and heard a ska band, and it was all white kids, all punk rockers, playing ska. I was just blown away, and I was so happy to see that they were doing that ... Music is not stagnant, and you have to keep changing it. You have to go back to the roots at times, but the roots have different branches, you know.[67]

By 1990, reggae had taken root across Canada.

Reggae could be a serious business. The urgency of some of Canadian reggae's messages, for instance, pushed people to revaluate their personal beliefs. Some migrant musicians felt that reggae shows gave expression to various issues of the day and added to the broader conversation, as Willi Williams observed:

Reggae is a podium for social change and justice regardless of who, or what, the nationality of the individual is. Because, as we go back again and say "We're all family" ... this is something, that we're here on Earth, and we promote racial harmony ... And that was the motive for reggae music and still is the motive for reggae music.[68]

Jamaican guitarist Rannie "Bop" Williams echoed Williams' point: "We get a good response, we share together, we dance together, we do a lot of things together. So, in every way, it's the music that brings us together."[69] Having established reggae in Toronto, these migrant musicians had seen first-hand how reggae promoted unity.

Others, however, felt that reggae had changed prevailing attitudes in only a small measure. Jamaican-born bassist Peter Holung, for instance, felt that reggae perhaps brought harmony between musicians but no further.[70] While Sebastian Cook conceded that Toronto was perhaps a more tolerant and racially open city because of the large-scale immigration of Jamaicans, he was unsure as to what role reggae had played: "There is no question that reggae/ska has helped many Canadians and Jamaicans connect and build lasting friendships, but I am not sure that is the same thing as eroding racial lines and promoting harmony on a truly societal scale."[71] The English-born Mark Matthews was similarly unconvinced:

Sadly, I believe it will take a lot more than music to do this. If music, as it did to some degree in my case, can lead a person to understanding Jamaican culture a little better, then that's great. Although reggae music lyrics can be loaded with unity and positivity and all, I think we'd be fooling ourselves into thinking that any real change can occur from music alone.[72]

Change, for some, had occurred only incrementally and usually not in the broader, mainstream consciousness but rather in an intimate, one-on-one setting.

Cook, Matthews, and Holung may have been unsure, but others were certain that reggae had not brokered significant gains in terms of promoting citywide racial harmony. For the Jamaican-born JuLion King, reggae music had broken down some barriers, but it suffered because the small reggae community was divisive, and systemic racism was, as far as JuLion was concerned, "as big and bad and broad as it ever was."[73] The Canadian-born guitarist Paul Corby agreed:

> I think probably, superficially, you could say yes, but as far as the depths of racism, no. That is a very deep well. I think possibly in Toronto – and I can only speak [for] Toronto – I think it has only exacerbated the situation, because it's forced people to draw lines and to choose sides, which is a good thing in the long run but a bit painful for a lot of people.[74]

Reggae is an oppositional music. Consequently, some of the messages found within its lyrical content challenged the status quo and may have made some members of the cultural hegemony uncomfortable. The Jamaican-born Adrian Miller spoke about how the music's boldness sometimes isolated it from the mainstream:

> Reggae music is anticolonial, anti-oppression; it's saying stuff that people don't always want to hear about. When they speak the truth, the truth is an impediment, because it means you have to be introspective, evaluate your actions and think a lot, and people don't want to do that ... Just because someone likes Bob Marley, doesn't mean that they're not racist ... Music won't really change anything really ... because music is just music. Its sole purpose is to entertain you.[75]

Some people felt that reggae actually limited non-Jamaicans' understanding of Jamaican culture, as second-generation Jamaican Canadian Dalton Higgins explained:

> The racism in Canada is crippling, and so subtle. So I find that Canadians think in this linear, myopic way when they try to understand Jamaican culture. The amount of times one gets asked if they know Bob Marley is mind-numbing, as if that's all Jamaica is about. Jamaica has produced world-class leaders in many disciplines, from literature and science to athletics, arts, and culture, so it would be good if these other tenets of Jamaican culture were used as bridges too.[76]

While reggae may have brought many individuals together, enduring and pervasive attitudes limited the reach of the music.

Cultural Divide

The cultural mixing could also be a little untidy for some people. Some reggae-loving non-Jamaicans, for example, found it hard to reconcile certain aspects of Jamaican culture with their own belief structures. David Fowler, for one, felt that Jamaican culture was fundamentally very different from the way he had been raised:

> No one ever raised their voices in my house. And I know lots and lots of other people that grew up the same way. It just didn't happen. If it did, you'd better get out of there. And yet Jamaicans seem to raise their voice every two or three minutes, and it was either in hysterical laughter or frightening anger.[77]

Mark Matthews struggled with other aspects of Jamaican culture:

> It was difficult to stay with my Jamaican ex, and it was often a challenge sometimes in the past to form a long-term relationship with Jamaican women due to my atheism, as religion is a huge part of their culture. Also, my stance on homosexuality, being that I'm not homophobic and have gay and lesbian friends, does not always sit well with many of my Jamaican acquaintances.[78]

Reggae may have brought some people together, but deeper cultural disconnects were not always so easily reconciled.

Perhaps the further erosion of racial lines lies in the future. Carrie Mullings is known to many as the ambassador of Canadian reggae. Mullings' father, Karl, was a seminal figure in the Canadian scene, though not as a musician. He had travelled with the Sheiks and became that band's tour manager for their 1963 American tour before settling in Toronto. Importantly, he convinced Jackie Mittoo to stay in Toronto in 1969.[79] Carrie Mullings maintained that better must come and that reggae can and will break down barriers:

206   *Blackness and Whiteness*

> Is it happening here in Canada? I can say I see that in certain circles;
> it's been very beneficial. I can also see the change that's been hap-
> pening with more Canadian content on air has improved the content,
> improved the quality of the recording ... which has obviously helped
> our Caribbean community and are non-Caribbean community [to]
> respect what's coming out.[80]

As a Jamaican Canadian who has been fully immersed in the Canadian reggae scene since birth, Mullings was uniquely positioned to witness the coming together of migrant and host. Indeed, her father met her mother, a Canadian, in the late 1960s at the WIF Club in Toronto and began to have a family that included Mullings' multiple-award-winning sister, reggae songstress Tanya Mullings. Her family could rightly be considered the royal family of Canadian reggae.[81]

Despite its limitations, reggae has been at the root of these cross-cultural relationships, of both the fleeting and more long-lasting kind. Early exposure to Jamaicans and Jamaican culture led many young non-Jamaicans in the city on a path of discovery, not only of reggae music but also of the migrants themselves. In this sense, music was, for so many, the bridge, the point of entry, and the very reason for contact. Errol Nazareth felt reggae in Canada already has the advantage of a healthy intercultural environment: "[Reggae] fosters that relationship that's already healthy ... When you go to a show, like this big mix of people having a good time ... So you might be black chatting up a white bird ... or a white guy starts chatting an Indian woman, or whatever ... I think it adds to more of that harmony that's there."[82] Music simply trumped other considerations time after time, as the Sattalites' Jamaican-born Neville Francis attested: "It happens a lot with jazz musicians, whenever people come together across racial lines. I don't think it necessarily means people have resolved issues to do with race, but the music becomes what's important, what pulls people together and binds people together."[83] While it might not have "resolved issues," reggae started a much-needed conversation between people along the city's ethnic frontlines.

At the same time, reggae encourages musicians to recognize the existence of a pan-musical identity. Musical collaboration necessitates that participants be open. It follows that openness might allow for deeper cross-cultural experimentation and, possibly, greater sensitivity to the other.[84] Performing in the limelight as they did, Jamaican migrant musicians were – necessarily – open to the host community. So, too, were non-Jamaicans open to listening and learning the migrant's music. Learning to play reggae for non-Jamaicans in Toronto required equal portions of humility and sincerity, but throughout the process there remained an unflappable faith in a positive result.

Indeed, many non-Jamaicans believe that without reggae music there would have been no opportunity to develop relationships of any kind with Jamaicans. David Fowler, who has maintained long-term relationships with a few Jamaicans, believes that music was the sole bridge: "I think that it was the only way those relationships could have developed. Without music, there wouldn't have been those relationships."[85] It was the same for Jeffrey Holdip: "It's only because of the music, really ... because that's what keeps me ingrained in that community, otherwise ... we [would] never really have met."[86] Perhaps reggae in Canada only managed to superficially alter prevailing attitudes towards race. The genre nevertheless made inroads into the Canadian musical mainstream. In so doing, reggae opened up minds in various, sometimes unusual places. As Natasha Emery noted, "Look at little Ladysmith, BC, having a reggae festival. Pure white town, you know."[87] There are now annual reggae or ska festivals in, among other places, Calgary, Winnipeg, Victoria, and Saskatoon. For many, there was no doubt that the cross-generational, cross-racial divide had been bridged. Isax InJah remarked, "Sometimes, when I'm feeling very depressed, and I feel like, 'What the hell am I doing, man, like, what am I doing?,' and I got down to Wire's store, and there'll be a few of the older guys into music there, and just the way that they greet me and everything. I leave out of there, and I say, 'Yes, man, we're alright now. We're alright.' And go back home and get to work."[88]

7

In Search of the Canadian Sound

At times, the Canadianness of the music coming out of Toronto's reggae scene both helped and hindered the progress and proliferation of Canadian reggae. Many people within the scene could articulate the sonic quality of Canadian reggae and identify how this sound differed – for better or for worse – from the Jamaican and British forms. Thematically, the lyrics prevalent in Toronto-made reggae in the 1980s often addressed Canada-specific subjects. The question is whether this approach served local reggae artists making music in Toronto.

More often than not, Canadian reggae artists were compelled to chase the Jamaican sound and looked to Jamaica for inspiration and, importantly, validation. Some brave acts such as Messenjah, Lillian Allen, 20th Century Rebels, Messenjah, and the Sattalites, however, sought to articulate a Canadian-centric experience within their songs and found some success in doing so. These groups featured Jamaican migrants and non-Jamaicans from the host society. Young immigrant musicians from neighbourhoods such as Malton, Jane-Finch, Eglinton West, and Regent Park teamed up with young members of the dominant society. Often these youths were from the same neighbourhoods, but sometimes young whites from more "traditional" and affluent communities such as Lawrence Park, North Toronto, and the Beaches took a keen interest in playing reggae. Their sound successfully conveyed a multiracial expression that reflected the experiences of those on stage and those in the audience, resulting in the golden age of Canadian reggae.

Maple Leaf Reggae

There are certain keynote sounds in Canadian reggae music that differ slightly from both Jamaican reggae and its British branch.[1] Understanding these keynotes is essential to appraising those sounds that have been contested, negotiated, and adapted to the Canadian environment. Tempo, bass volume, organ drawbar settings, the space where the piano/guitar skank falls, the use of certain amps, and the velocity used on the various instruments are among the keynotes that make up reggae's aural aesthetic. These keynotes are as important to the artist as lyrical content, back phrasing, the use of harmony, and singing in Jamaican Patois. Through these sounds – agreed upon and executed in a Canadian setting first by transplanted Jamaicans and then by non-Jamaican Canadians – we can hear the results of frontline bridge building.

The hallmark sounds of reggae can act as a calling card, a sonic authentication that declares how closely the music approximates the genre's point of origin. For some, it is important that the music sounds like it is from Yard. It was the desideratum for many Canadian reggae artists (and remains so today) to attain that authentic Yard sound. If the bass was not mixed loud enough, if the guitar didn't cut like a razor, if the piano "naw ring out," if the organ shuffle was clumsy, then it didn't sound like it came from Yard and was therefore inferior.

One of Toronto's first multiracial bands to attempt to replicate the Jamaican sound was Chalawa. Formed in 1975 by John Forbes and Alex King, Chalawa's original lineup featured a multiracial mix of musicians, including Leroy Sibbles on bass before he concentrated on his solo career. A later lineup also featured Jamaican drumming veteran Anthony "Benbow" Creary, whose sprawling resume included sessions with Lee Perry, the Mighty Diamonds, and Augustus Pablo. The band's 1977 album, *Exodus Dub,* a dub tribute to Marley's *Exodus* album, saw some success in the European pop charts. Likewise, their 1978 album, *Capture Land,* also featured significant contributions from Jamaican migrant musicians in Toronto such as Stranger Cole and Johnny Osbourne.[2] Chalawa introduced the notion of meaningful musical collaboration between migrant and host and anticipated the city's popular reggae acts of the 1980s by ten years.

A decade later, Dave Tulloch discussed the fledgling Canadian brand of reggae in an article that appeared in *The Spectrum: Making Minorities Visible*. In it, Tulloch cleverly coined the local version of the Jamaican music as "maple leaf reggae."[3] To be sure, the idea of maple leaf reggae as a fusion or a hybrid of the original Jamaican hybrid was one that had currency even among Jamaican migrant musicians. Adrian Miller, for example, characterized 20th Century Rebels' sound as very eccentric.[4]

It was similar for the Sattalites. In an interview from 1987, Fergus Hambleton discussed the band's live album and confessed that their brand of reggae could only have happened in Canada:

> Without really thinking about it, we've achieved a genuine cross-cultural synthesis, something that's a reflection of Canada's ethnic mix. That's what I love about *Live via Sattalites*. It sounds like authentic reggae, all right, but there's a lot more going on. Even in New York, where we played last year, the locals said we had something different, something very Canadian. Now all we have to do is convince Canadians of that.[5]

Some were, indeed, convinced. Empowered, fans of Canadian reggae in the middle of the 1980s harboured great hope for future successes.

Led by the Sattalites, Messenjah, and 20th Century Rebels, who made the cover of *NOW* magazine in 1984, Toronto reggae elbowed its way into the nation's print media, onto the dance floors, and onto the airwaves on stations such as CFNY and Q107.[6] Canadian reggae bands made it to the big league too. Messenjah became the first Canadian reggae band to sign with a major label when WEA picked them up in 1983.[7] The Sattalites also found their way to the majors when they signed to WEA Records via Risqué Disque in 1989.

Despite these gains, describing the Canadian sound, for even those within the genre, proved to be a difficult task, as Mark Matthews attested: "I do think there is a special Canadian sound to some reggae, though I can't put my finger on it – it's likely the influence of other music styles in the mix. But then there are others who are just mimicking the Jamaican sound."[8] Others, felt that there was no unifying Canadian sound. According to Willi Williams,

We never did get our Canadian reggae sound because most of the people at the studios here ... didn't invest their time in reggae music. So they didn't get a chance to [learn] like when I go to England ... Just name any studio [in England], and them know about reggae, and they play reggae. And it's not just black people who play reggae or Jamaican.[9]

Canadian reggae DJ David Kingston could not put his finger on the local style either:

I don't know if there's a consistent sound, where you'd say, "More treble on top," "More bass on bottom" ... I think of Earth, Roots and Water. I think of their kind of dry and heavy militancy. So I think there are a lot of sounds ... but it's hard to play a record, and you say, "That's Toronto," the same way you would ... with British reggae. It's got a warmth and Jamaica too, [where] the mastering is hot.[10]

If those within the scene could not precisely characterize the Canadian sound, there was little chance that those on the outside looking in were going to do it.

Others were less charitable and believed that Canadian reggae artists lacked that necessary fire in the belly. JuLion King opined, "Other artists in other places in the world tend to blaze fire or something in wha them a do. We need that here."[11] Carrie Mullings likewise recognized a lack of passion in many Canadian reggae artists, whose desire to chase down opportunities lagged behind that of Jamaican or English reggae music makers.[12] Jamaican-born bassist Peter Holung observed:

The reason why Jamaica has the sound that it does is because the whole culture lives on the edge, so the music is edgy. Canada, in their rock and roll, in their jazz, in their R&B, hip hop, and reggae, it does not have a face. It does not have a sound because it is borrowed from and emulated by ... Now if you ask me if Europe does, then, yes, it does ... [Canadian reggae] is watered down, "soft" as we put it. And the reason why is that Canada is a place that has great health care, has a great standard of living and makes people very complacent.

212 *In Search of the Canadian Sound*

> And everything that morphs from that complacency breeds absolutely
> no identity ... But I still think it's one of the best place in the world
> to live.[13]

This alleged softness of Canadian reggae has also polarized musicians
within the scene.

Some musicians agreed with Holung that Canadian reggae paled in
comparison to Jamaican reggae and cited differences within the specific
sounds of reggae's chief instruments and approach. According to Paul
Corby, "Musically, I think the Canadian reggae guitar is a bit limp, holding
the chords too long ... I think that's characteristic of reggae in Canada,
and our refusal to go slow enough."[14] Rannie "Bop" Williams, who played
guitar on Marley's original versions of "Trenchtown Rock" and "Rock
My Boat," also heard it in the guitar sound. For Rannie, it was the Fender
amplifier in Jamaica that sharpened the guitar skank: "Over here, they
use the treble to get [the sound]. Because I'm used to the real thing
at home, and I know this is slightly different. Anytime Canadians start
to leave out a little of the treble, they're going to sound like Jamaican
reggae."[15]

Reggae concert promoter Denise Jones addressed the ubiquitous
issue of pushing the low-end envelope in the Canadian studio – that is
to say, the volume and placement of the bass guitar in the mix:

> There was always an issue about that needle going in the red. And
> musicians would always tell me that that was a struggle in the
> [Canadian] studio. That thing [the needle] lives in the red in reggae.
> I don't think people sort of saw it, when the music was being created,
> as a bad thing, that was, in fact, part of the good thing about the
> music.[16]

Trombonist Mike Smith had heard several times that the Canadian take
on Jamaican music was "not as 'bouncy,' or it doesn't have that feel as
when you're in Jamaica. As a little joke, some people attribute it to the
cold."[17] Carrie Mullings recognized that the Canadian sound differed
even from the English sound: "Lovers rock in England compared to our
lovers rock here: two different sounds ... Lovers rock in England tends to

lay back on the rhythm more, where our lovers rock ... [we] lean forward."[18] In this sense, the Canadian sound was sometimes viewed as inferior to the Jamaican or British reggae, sometimes even by those within the community.

To find legitimacy within both the reggae community and within Toronto's often cynical music press, some young Toronto reggae artists felt compelled to chase and bottle the Jamaican brand, as David Kingston observed: "They always felt they had this Yard sound; they had to get to be liked and to be authenticated. So, if somebody is trying to do something that's true to them in their musical vision, it's going to be stilted."[19] Phil Vassell saw first-hand just how imperative capturing the Jamaican sound was for some Canadian reggae artists: "I've seen guys that will save every last penny of theirs to go to Jamaica and sit in the Jamaican studio and produce the record there because they think they're going to get a certain kind of sound and a certain kind of feel and perhaps get away from what they perceive as a 'Canadian' sound."[20] Dalton Higgins concurred that some artists believed "that the only way to achieve a more authentic and gritty sound, they have to work in the reggae motherland of Jamaica, something about the engineers in Jamaica knowing how to turn them knobs."[21] With the hard-won successes of bands such as Messenjah, Truths and Rights, and the Sattalites now in the rear-view mirror, many Toronto reggae artists increasingly drifted away from even attempting to craft a unique maple leaf brand.

Yet the uniqueness of the Canadian reggae sound had its champions. Even those who were critical of the sonic quality of the scene's recorded products believed that several quality Canadian reggae bands existed, especially in the live context. Canada's big three as far as Jeffrey Holdip was concerned were Bloodfire, Truths and Rights, and 20th Century Rebels. The latter two, according to Holdip, "carried the 'swing' because they had a unique sound and style."[22] Natasha Emery identified the Sattalites, Leejahn, Wayne Hanson, Fredlocks Asher and the Ultra Flex Crew, Revelation, Culture Shock, Friendlyness, and Whitey Don as representing

> a distinct Canadian reggae sound that had the driving bass and drums, because, more often than not, the bass[ist] and drum[mer] were

214   *In Search of the Canadian Sound*

Jamaicans, but it was all the flavour, and the lyrics, and the delivery that was Canadian ... I think that our delivery, our cadence, doesn't come out the same way ... whether it's Fergus [Hambleton] singing or Rupert [Harvey] from Messenjah, even though he's Jamaican, there's still a Canadian softness, covering gentleness about it. Where I find Jamaican singers are more boisterous.[23]

Paul Corby chose, *inter alia,* Leroy Sibbles and the Reggae Cowboys.[24] JuLion King listed Ibadan, Dream Band, Mountain Edge, Tabarruk, Andru Branch, and Souljah Fyah.[25] A multiplicity of reggae sounds informed the local Canadian reggae text.

One question that few dared to ask was: Why should Canadian reggae have to sound like it comes from Jamaica? Some believed that the best indigenous reggae faithfully reflected the authentic Canadian experience instead of trying to bottle the Jamaican sound. Klive Walker reflected:

The Canadian reggae that I liked really sounded like it came from here. If you're trying to sound like Jamaica, then what's the point? Jamaican reggae already exists ... When [someone is] going to play reggae, they have to bring with them their experiences, their musical experiences and their life experiences, to the music and, in doing so, the flavour of their country, of their city, and of their region should come out in the music. I think that's what makes it genuine and what makes it honest.[26]

Rupert Harvey talked about Messenjah's open defiance of pressure to conform to the pure Yard sound: "We were brave ... A lot of guys wanted to see what [was] accepted by Jamaica or the Jamaican community. Where Messenjah [was concerned], we didn't care about that and people gravitated towards it."[27]

Isax InJah felt that perhaps the Toronto sound was developing only now:

You know, maybe for a lot of years ... we would all be trying just to copy the Jamaican style exactly. And I think the Toronto style, just because it's a different place and there are different kinds of influences, it's only naturally going to have a different sound, and it could have quite a different sound, and maybe we don't even know what that sound is going to be.[28]

For Walker, Harvey, InJah, and others like them, the fact is that Canadian reggae will never sound like Jamaican reggae. Crucially, they also believed that it should never have to.

Sounding Canadian

Apart from the sonic nature of the music, it took time before Canadian reggae bands felt comfortable enough to introduce the Canadian experience into their lyrical themes. While the earlier generation of Jamaican musicians living in Toronto (such as Leroy Sibbles, Carlene Davis, Stranger Cole, and Jackie Mittoo) may have brought reggae's musical framework to the Great White North, they weren't necessarily articulating the Caribbean Canadian experience in their songs. It was the musical environment created by the next generation of reggae music makers – including members of the Caribbean diaspora – that allowed for meaningful critiques of the sociopolitical condition of blacks living in Canada and other cross-cultural themes in Canadian reggae.[29]

Even then, and for a variety of reasons, only a few artists fully threw themselves into rendering the Canadian experience within the Jamaican art form. Adrian Miller, for instance, said that the Canadian reggae artist in general did not believe that "writing songs that can relate to the Canadian experience is going to give him any kind of leverage. So, he has to emulate what comes out of Jamaica, because, well, that's what he assumes, to the max, that's what is going to give him his props."[30] Some believed that Canadian reggae artists chose to delve less into sociopolitical themes than their Jamaican or British counterparts. According to Dalton Higgins, "The cold climate might have some effect on outing the 'fire' themes so prevalent in reggae. And there is a lot of copycat mechanisms at play (i.e., Canadian reggae artists feel this need to mimic reggae music productions coming from Jamaica, to make it)."[31] Paul Corby also felt that politics had been bled from the music: "There's a lot less politics in Canadian reggae ... I think, largely, it was steering towards utopianism over rebellion."[32]

Although artists struggled to find a voice that suited the Canadian experience, some musicians wanted a certain level of honesty within the lyrical expression of homegrown Canadian reggae, as Jamaican-born Mike Smith explained:

> It would be strange for me to sit here and talk about hunger when I'm always full. It's hard for me to talk about the violence or the political situation when it's not the same as in Jamaica ... I can't write a song about a storm because the only storm I've had is maybe a snow storm, whereas they're experiencing a tropical hurricane ... Of course, I can talk about a girl in both places.[33]

Phil Vassell echoed Smith's observation:

> Talking about the "ghetto" when you're from Regent Park, or from some other part of Toronto, Jane and Finch or some other place in Scarborough, it just doesn't ring as truthful as it might in certain places in the States ... I mean it just kind of sounds hollow ... Some things aren't going to ring as being authentic outside of Jamaica, where there are real ghettos and real poverty.[34]

Many Canadian reggae artists were caught choosing between the seemingly disingenuous replication of Jamaican or Rasta themes and the uncharted – and not necessarily rewarding – waters of Canadian topics.

A few chose the latter option. Faithfully rendering the Canadian experience in their songs was a high priority for Messenjah, Truths and Rights, 20th Century Rebels, Lillian Allen, and the Sattalites. Thematically, Truths and Rights were in the vanguard of Toronto's socially conscious music-making scene, tackling, as they did, questions of racial discrimination, police violence, and – long before it was fashionable – the environment, in their classic 1980 recording "Acid Rain":

> Acid rain, falling from our skies
> It would fall down on I
> What are they doing to man, woman, and child
> Messing with our lives and the environment.[35]

The band's "Metro's No. 1 Problem" was another self-penned song, conspicuous for its exposé on racial tension that transcended Toronto's black community: "Trouble down in Rexdale, Pakistani family battered ... / Metro's number one problem: racial tension."[36]

Certain significant moments in the Jamaican migrant experience were also interpreted by various reggae acts. The 1979 shooting death of Jamaican Canadian Albert Johnson, for instance, was a subject treated by more than one Canadian reggae artist. Lillian Allen's "Riddim and Hard Times" references the infamous shooting by Toronto Police, as does Rupert "Ojiji" Harvey's track "Albert Johnson."[37] Harvey, in particular, was one Jamaican-born artist who held the torch particularly high for incorporating the Canadian experience into reggae song: "We're not living in Jamaica; we're living in Canada ... We have to adjust to this. Reggae is the voice of the people in Jamaica. When we play it here [in Canada], it's the voice of people here."[38]

Some non-Jamaican Canadians responded favourably to Messenjah's efforts to incorporate Canadiana into their reggae, as Brian Robertson observed: "They did bring in some of their Canadian experiences into their lyrics."[39] 1984's "Jam Session," for example, name-checked Canadian themes:

> Canada jamming in a parliament style,
> Call the house in session mek them boogie for a while.
> Some of them jam it in a local government,
> Dubbing with the people that they represent.[40]

The official video even included footage of a parliamentary debate. Similarly, Lillian Allen's dub poetry addressed, from a feminist perspective, a variety of Canadian issues that immigrants from the Caribbean constantly faced.[41] In "I Fight Back," a track featured on *Revolutionary Tea Party* (1986), Allen cleverly critiques the realities facing domestic servants and nannies brought to Canada to care for its more affluent members: "Here I am in Canada, bringing up someone else's child / While someone else and me in absentee, bring up my own."[42]

The artists of this era, however, could not sustain their output of Canadian-centric, homegrown reggae. As Adrian Miller suggested, many local reggae artists instead retreated to garden-variety Jamaican reggae topics: Jah, Babylon, and weed. Believing that the reggae genre was being lost or diluted, some Jamaican Canadians adopted, as Klive Walker maintained, a "fortress mentality."[43] Part of the problem was the umbrella term "reggae," which confused the individual elements (and different subgenres, for that matter). Rannie "Bop" Williams, who had played reggae from its inception, cited the six different ages of modern Jamaican music, which most people simply call reggae: (1) mento, (2) ska, (3) rocksteady, (4) reggae, (5) dancehall, and (6) dub.[44] Indeed, Vybz Kartel could hardly be mistaken for the Jolly Boys, just as Mad Professor seems worlds away from Eric "Monty" Morris. Yet they all supped from the same broth that created Jamaican popular music. Engineer Jeffrey Holdip maintained, nevertheless, that "there's a definite reggae that's Jamaican, everything else is a derivative. I love [the English band] Aswad, but it's something different to me than reggae from Jamaica, a Jacob Miller or whatever. So, a non-Jamaican, whatever they're doing as a form of reggae, it's a different grape, making a different wine."[45] Though the tannins may have differed, the northern reggae vine still flowered and found success in Jamaica.

The Jamaican audience is considered by many to be among the toughest. Sunray Grennan – whose father, Winston Grennan, pioneered reggae's signature one-drop beat, provided drums on Toots and the Maytals' most essential tracks and also appeared on Paul Simon's "Mother and Child Reunion" and "Cecilia" – spoke of fickle Jamaican audiences and how they could dismiss Canadian reggae artists: "Jamaican [audiences] tend to be a little prejudice against Canadian artists ... They think we don't know reggae, but we *do* know reggae. It's just that we're not doing it like them. And how could we? Our experiences are different."[46] Holdip concurred: "Look it, there are Jamaicans that have a hard time dealing with their own audience. You know they stoned Bunny Wailer ... I mean the Jamaican audience is not easy, by any stretch."[47] Consequently, it was usually only those artists with extreme confidence and talent who could succeed in that environment.

Some Canadian acts did take on the Jamaican audience. In 1985, Messenjah appeared at Reggae Sunsplash. Rupert "Ojiji" Harvey recalled the palpable feeling emanating from a group of young, skeptical Jamaican

In Search of the Canadian Sound   219

men awaiting the performance. One young ruffian threatened: "Unno better play good tonight."[48] Kicking off with their bold religious anthem "Abraham's Children," Messenjah quickly won the crowd over, and the young man who had warned the Canadians before the show apologized and then asked Harvey if he would sponsor him to come to Canada![49]

The Sattalites likewise played Reggae Sunsplash. The experience was a mixture of triumph and terror, as keyboardist David Fowler recalled:

> Reggae Sunsplash scared me to death. Once the sun went down, all there was was a ring of fire around the fence. And total blackness out there. And thousands and thousands of Jamaicans – most of them in bare feet – out there in a compound surrounded by men with guns and dogs. Sunsplash was one of the strongest experiences in my entire life in terms of extremes.

The experience was similar for bassist Bruce McGillivray: "When we played in Jamaica, here's a North American bunch of folks that can actually play reggae. That created quite a wave in Jamaica. You know, there was some initial snickering, but once it all came down, they loved our variations on what their music was."[50] Lead singer Fergus Hambleton observed that people naturally respond well to others who take a special interest in their culture: "Musicians, especially, but just generally Jamaican people ... If you show any interest in Jamaican culture, they're just so cheered by that, you know, they're just so hospitable and so supportive. So I've had nothing but tremendous support all the time."[51]

Natasha Emery also spoke about the favourable results that can come when you demonstrate a sincere interest in another's culture:

> When you can speak intelligently about someone else's music, when it's very culturally specific, I think that there's an automatic appreciation, an acceptance of you. It's, like, "Wow, you're interested." It's like going to a country where you don't speak the language but you've learned a few phrases; there's a real appreciation that you've made the attempt ... So I think it's sort of the same when discussing music or feeling music: if you're showing interest in it, people love that.[52]

220 *In Search of the Canadian Sound*

Despite the odds, Canadian reggae acts fared well in Jamaica.

The Jamaican press generally approved of the Sattalites. In one instance, the band performed at a high-profile event put on by the St. Andrew Corporation to celebrate its presentation of the keys to the city to the island's most famous folklorist, Louise Bennett, at the Ward Theatre in Kingston. This pressure cooker of a gig might have gone all wrong for the Canadian side, but Kingston's *Weekend Star* raved, "The band played quality reggae music which made a lot of fans for them."[53] Similarly, Kingston's *Daily Gleaner* raved about the band's debut album in 1985: "The band has masterfully blended some heavy 60s rock sounds with roots reggae takes and have come up with a winner."[54] It must be noted, however, that the journalist was careful to affix the "reggae-pop" categorization to the Sattalites.

Nevertheless, this stamp of approval, especially since it was from the Jamaican press, gave the Sattalites a leg up with Toronto's own widely read Jamaican community newspapers. Upon the release of *Sattalites,* for example, a reviewer for *Share,* under the pseudonym "Diskreet," gave the album a positive review: "The Sattalites' professionally independent approach to the LP is something of a benchmark for other club-circuit artists, and, at the same time, shows that the simplicity of black and white can make a new, and very attractive, shade of grey."[55] The reviewer, however, had previously classified the amalgam of Jamaican Jo Jo Bennett's "all-round musician-arranger" with Hambleton's "white Canadian folk roots" as "somewhat awkward."[56] Although they received a stamp of approval, like Britain's two-tone acts, multiracial bands such as the Sattalites, Sunforce, Culture Shock, and Fujhative strove to entertain and reflect the attractive "grey" audiences they played for in the city.

White Man Can Dub

Learning reggae was difficult for those who had already mastered their instruments and different genres before taking up Jamaican music. In many ways, these musicians had to unlearn some of their musical habits to approach an "authentic" reggae sound. For the most part, they were able to do so. Jamaican journalist Gerald Reid, for example, singled out

Sattalites bassist Bruce McGillivray for his reggae-savvy approach during a performance in Kingston: "['The Enemy'] is a heavy song with some good bass by Canadian Bruce Mack, who seems to be well familiar with reggae."[57] Given the centrality of the bass to the reggae sound, McGillivray's whiteness often drew attention when the Sattalites performed. As Ottawa journalist Dave Tulloch observed, the bass

> is so fundamental to reggae music that most reggae bands tend towards a bassist of the Jamaican persuasion. Not so with the Sattalites. Bruce Mack, on bass, is as Canadian as the Maple Leaf. Bruce, who has been playing music for over 20 years, happened to visit Jamaica in 1978. On this visit he began to play a different tune. He now pulls out the kind of heavy bass lines which tell you that this man has somehow grown some "roots."[58]

Some Jamaicans, however, took exception to oversimplified appraisals of what a roots sound meant. Messenjah's Rupert Harvey, for instance, challenged that "no one can look inside of your heart and tell you that you can't feel this music ... Like, I hear, 'Oh, a white man cyant play roots.' That's nonsense; we all have roots. So you're trying to tell me that one tree grows above the ground, and then one grows beneath it?"[59] To be fair to Tulloch, given its unique feel, it is harder to "grow" into reggae if you've played other musical forms before picking up reggae at a more mature age, as was the case with McGillivray.

Before the Sattalites orbited, however, McGillivray was fortunate to have been taught reggae bass by Leroy Sibbles, so he learned from one of the best:

> My mentor, Leroy Sibbles, was my man. He was not critical at all. He just saw that I loved the music, and he set it out for me – what it should be, where you should rest, where you should be relaxed behind the groove ... And Leroy changed my way of looking at bass, even when I would play a rock gig. You know, in the studio doing some rock stuff, I would always think about how Leroy would think behind the beat.[60]

222 *In Search of the Canadian Sound*

This was primary bridge building in operation: the Canadian-born McGillivray, of Scottish heritage, being mentored by legendary Studio One Jamaican reggae bassist Leroy Sibbles.[61] This frontline encounter had serious ramifications on the Canadian reggae scene and its sound. Yet, in some respects, it is what players such as McGillivray did not unlearn that added to the distinctiveness of the Canadian sound; the residue of McGillivray's rock upbringing made him a wholly unique reggae bassist.

While the bass in reggae is privileged and perhaps, along with the drums, plays the most crucial role, the keyboard skank (or off-beat, which usually lands on beats two and four) is also extremely important and deceptively difficult, as one of the Sattalites' two long-time keyboardists, the classically trained David Fowler, explained:

> In our case, the keyboard player who handles just the rhythmic aspects is Jamaican and grew up with reggae music and he does a much better job of it than I can, even though I have a lot more technical training that he does. It's very difficult for me to get that exact feeling into the rhythmic parts, and himself, having lived reggae music all his life, it's part of him. He doesn't think, "am I in the groove or am I out of the groove?," he just thinks, "am I playing my part?" Whereas for me, I have to say "am I slightly ahead of the beat or should this be pushed a bit?" It's difficult for me to reduce myself to the same level of perfection that he achieves without even thinking about it.[62]

Sam Weller, another non-Jamaican keyboardist, confessed: "I've seen a lot of really fabulous musicians struggle to play with reggae ... One of the things about reggae is that, technically, it's not that difficult, but it's the feel. You have to get the feel."[63] Likewise, Isax InJah said that he believed that "it takes a grown man all of his effort to do that [keyboard] skank, to play the skank properly, and when you hear the one guy, the guy who can really do it ... right away you start to hear the hypnotic vibes of reggae."[64]

But before the non-Jamaican could transcend, they had to crack the code, and the only way to do that was with time. Certainly, the genre's sonic nuances confounded many of reggae's non-Jamaican suitors, as Jamaican JuLion King observed:

They used to tell us that reggae was simplistic ... a very simple beat, blah, blah, blah. So me seh, "Eh, if it's so simple, how come unno cyant play it? Unno cannot play it." It's the simplest beat in the world, and Stevie Wonder and Prince have tried and cyant do it ... If you cyant walk with a skank, you cyant play reggae music. You hav e have a lean pon your left hand and walk like a bad man, and that is reggae music.[65]

For Denise Jones, reggae's feel reflected far more than notes on a staff: "Reggae music is a deeply spiritual thing ... Music is an integral part of culture, and when you feel it in that way, the way it really ricochets through your body, through your mind, then you can play it if you're a player of instruments."[66] Capturing reggae's elusive touch and understanding the behaviour of individual instruments could come, but only for those with patience.

Paul Corby was patient. Although he did not abandon all his previous rock sensibilities, his reggae expertise was such that he could pass it on to other non-reggae musicians:

The problem I used to have with teaching white musicians how to play reggae was that this beat happens here, this beat happens a long time after that, and you have to have faith that you're going to get to that next beat ... And I'm not including children, children get it. But as far as adults, who have learned ... semiquavers and function on that level, are unable to maintain the faith that it takes to get from one beat to the next.[67]

Corby believed that it took ten years for him to get that reggae sound.[68]

While a keyboardist or bassist might tuck himself behind other musicians, singers were up front, centre stage, and therefore far more exposed. But as vulnerable as they may have been, the possibility of approval for a non-Jamaican lead singer was great. The *Globe and Mail*'s Liam Lacey believed that he knew why so many people were attracted to the Sattalites:

Part of the appeal of the Sattalites, for Jamaicans, may be the simple oddity of the act. The studio where Jo Jo and Fergus recorded in

Kingston was usually crowded with onlookers, most of whom were fascinated by the idea of a white singer who sounded Jamaican. Jamaicans have called Hambleton "the white Gregory Isaacs," the Jamaican singer known as the Cool Ruler, for his gracefully understated vocal style.[69]

Hambleton did not, of course, take offence to such assessments and admitted: "I've copped so much from those singers that the comparisons don't really surprise me ... The little 'oohs' and 'ahs' and trills – are all things I learned from reggae records, and, of course, they show."[70] That Hambleton approximated Gregory Isaacs was probably a good thing for the Sattalites. Hambleton, however, could only approximate Isaacs, and his own previous nonreggae vocal experiences necessarily crept in. This fact further distinguished the Sattalites as a Canadian and not a Jamaican reggae band.

The process of learning reggae was altogether different for the next generation of non-Jamaican reggae musicians. Quite simply, the next generation was exposed to it for a longer period of time and started playing it earlier. By the mid-1980s, Jamaican popular music had penetrated the world's musical consciousness. Through direct and indirect exposure (including radio airplay, rap, hip hop, punk, television commercials, and children's programming), it was easier for the younger generation of non-Jamaicans to learn how to play reggae because they had heard so much of it already, including the Canadian version of it. As David Kingston declared:

> It's just exposure that makes you able to do things. I don't believe you're born with different blood or DNA ... You grow up listening to the Police and the Clash, and the way you drum is going to be different than if you grew up in the era when it was all glam rock and 4s. It's what's normal to you is your points of reference, so when they change, everything changes.[71]

Someone born in the 1970s and exposed to reggae from an early age therefore found "beating against the time" familiar.

This generational distinction was apparent to concert promoter and publicist Sebastian Cook: "Two of the three most talented reggae artists I know are non-Jamaicans. If one grows up surrounded by a musical style, or is immersed in it, for any length of time, it is just as easy for them to excel at that music as it would be for a native."[72] Moreover, as some reggae artists have noted, many Jamaicans cannot play reggae. Mark Matthews stated: "I know Jamaicans who can't play reggae/ska, as I know non-Jamaicans who can't either. Like any music style, you've gotta go into it with big ears to understand it properly, though it probably helps if you are Jamaican."[73] Still, reggae, like any other music, is there for anyone to play. And, like other musics, the audience is usually the best litmus test to see whether your interpretation is laudable and sincere, as journalist Errol Nazareth explained:

> If you're coming at it from a place of a deep knowledge of the music, a respect for the roots, and being genuine, like you being you and bringing your own voice, your own vibe to the thing ... So, I don't think anything can be a barrier to you, other than the negativity you hear from other people. But you gotta come correct, man![74]

Most audiences believed that band such as the Sattalites were "coming correct."

The Canadian Reggae Institution

Leroy Sibbles – Canada's grand old man of reggae – set one of the key bridge-building moments in Reggae Canadiana into motion when he introduced the white Canadian Fergus Hambleton to Alpha School alumnus and horn man Jo Jo Bennett. Hambleton had been working steadily with Sibbles as a saxophonist, guitarist, and singer while Sibbles lived in Canada.[75] Connecting the two had a profound effect on the way that Canadian reggae was disseminated among Torontonians who attended the Sattalite Music School, founded in 1981. Bennett and Hambleton's meeting also helped define the sound of Canadian reggae.

By their very nature the Sattalites produced a form of reggae that represented the experiences of both migrant and host within a multiracial context. For his part, Hambleton had tried to emulate the Jamaican sound in various outfits that predated the Sattalites: "You know, we really liked Sibbles' band, so we used to go and see them a lot, and the band I had, a little rock band, tried to imitate [Sibbles] ... We got to know members of the band and got to know R. Zee [Jackson]."[76] Jackson hired Hambleton for some session work, and by 1978 Hambleton was part of Sibbles' band.[77] At the same time, the former Dragonaire Jo Jo Bennett, who was finding regular work with his band Jo Jo and the Fugitives, began to slowly assemble the parts that would one day morph into the Sattalites.[78]

With a mission to further raise the profile of reggae music in the city, Bennett and Hambleton put their heads together and organized the Sattalite Music School. The school catered to Torontonians who shared a desire to learn to play music but who might have lacked access to traditional music educational trajectories or the funds to realize their artistic aspirations. The school opened in a small basement in the heart of Toronto's West Indian community at the corner of Eglinton Avenue West and Winona and operated on a "pay what you can" basis. Most important, the school allowed for the cultural collision between Jamaican migrant and Canadian host. This significant extramusical function was, as the Sattalites' Neville Francis confirmed, just as important as the musical equation:

> The school ... meant different things to different people. But more than anything else the Sattalite Music School provides us with an intriguing and positive example of the meeting of two cultures ... Students and visitors to the school were Jamaican and Canadian. They were serious musicians as well as hobbyists. When Fergus Hambleton joined Jo Jo Bennett to teach at the school, the partnership was a tangible symbol of the intermingling and comingling of the two cultures that had been going on all along.[79]

The effects on the local reggae scene were far-reaching. Wayne Hanson, for example, had performed in a school band and church plays back in Jamaica but hadn't performed professionally until he came to Canada. It was at Bennett and Hambleton's school of music that Hanson improved his craft.[80]

Essentially, the Sattalites flowered out of the school, providing one of the earliest and perhaps best examples of a reggae band that combined Jamaican-born musicians with non-Jamaican Canadians to achieve a Canadian sound. The school, as a symbol of intermingling, brought would-be reggae stars of all ages and ethnicities together. To be sure, not all the school's members were hobbyists, as Bennett explained:

> Professional musicians were coming in there to learn just the reggae thing, to incorporate it into what they're doing. The kids and stuff, they didn't pay. It just keep them off the street, they hang out, learn about music. It's not just Rasta Man, or dreadlocks or Jamaicans, there are a lot Canadians there too. Everything mix up man, no separation.[81]

One year after the school opened its doors, a collection of seasoned professionals and fledgling upstarts assembled themselves as the first incarnation of the Sattalites.

As a business, the school made very little money and was ultimately closed at the end of 1983. But by then, the Sattalites – including two Sattalite school alumni – were now a real band whose unique take on reggae began to draw attention. The multicultural aspect of the band reflected Canadian society as it was, black and white together, and it earned the band a half-page story in the *Toronto Star,* even though the band had only yet played to seven people at the Isabella Hotel. The story nevertheless captured the imagination of the newspaper's readership, accelerating the band's success.[82]

The *Globe and Mail* also noticed the Sattalites' Canadian sound: "[They] have created a gentle hybrid pop-reggae that has dignity, warmth, great musicianship and style. They're one of the few bands on the Toronto scene that really shouldn't be missed."[83] Through their early efforts, the band secured its first gig, in 1984, at the Bamboo Club, which had just opened.

The band's name paid homage not only to Jamaican legends and pioneers of the ska genre the Skatalites but also to an Abyssinian hymn

228 *In Search of the Canadian Sound*

"Satta," which means "holy."[84] Philosophically, the members of the Sattalites subscribed to the tenet of understanding.[85] The band's MC, Bennett, introduced the song/philosophy to every mixed crowd they performed for in the following manner: "You see dreadlocks, baldheads, whities and blackies, but what it takes is understanding."[86]

Despite the band's departure from the norm, the Sattalites felt that their first recorded material needed to be grounded in a Jamaican process. Bennett persuaded the legendary reggae rhythm section Sly and Robbie to help with their first official recording. The album, which took nearly two years to complete, finally saw the light of day in 1985. The self-titled debut, *Sattalites,* was released on Axe Records, a label owned by Fergus Hambleton's older brother Greg.[87] *Sattalites* had the support of CBC Radio and the cutting-edge station CFNY 102.1 FM. The album was warmly received and helped introduce the band to a nationwide audience.

The band's goal was to break into the Canadian mainstream and, going by the tone of the earliest reviews, it certainly made some inroads. Veteran music critic Nicholas Jennings reviewed the album for *Maclean's* and spoke of the band's potential: "The album is a determined effort to convince Canadian record companies and radio stations of reggae's commercial potential ... When the Sattalites attain a joyful reggae-pop sound, it is hard to imagine radio being able to resist."[88] The *Globe and Mail* sang similarly high praises: "Don't be dissuaded by the budget cover, or the reggae dub versions of the Beatles' She Loves You and band member Fergus Hambleton's own Wild; these aren't filler, they're integral to a well-integrated album, a painstaking, infectious blend of sixties' pop melody with reggae-wise rhythms."[89] The sincerity of the Sattalites' take on Jamaican reggae was apparent to even the most critical musos in the Canadian press. *NOW Magazine's* notoriously tough critic James Marck, for example, observed: "[The Sattalites] have a quality that can't be expressed by any musical equation – something that's germinated in the heart and soul of the music and made material by the band's embodiment of reggae's most trenchant values – harmony, unity and purpose."[90] And Jamaicans came to the Sattalites' shows.

The Sattalites were selling out three-nighters at the Bamboo Club and playing hundreds of shows across North America at festivals and nightclubs. Most significantly, they performed at California's prestigious Reggae on the River festival and at Jamaica's famed Reggae Sunsplash. As far as *Globe and Mail* rock journalist Liam Lacey was concerned, 1985 had "launched the Sattalites" in Canada.[91]

Reggae Canadiana was now in full bloom, and the Sattalites were the centrepiece. From the mid-1980s through the early 1990s, Ontario Place Forum held a near-annual reggae show featuring local reggae acts. On one unseasonably cold Tuesday night in June 1987, the Sattalites, alongside Messenjah and Sunforce (led by powerful frontman Michael Garrick), drew roughly seven thousand fans. Despite the weather, it was sunny skies for the band, as it was for the city's reggae scene at large.[92]

A second album followed on Axe Records. Titled *Live via Sattalites,* it had been recorded at the Bamboo in 1987 and was received warmly in the mainstream press. *The Globe and Mail,* for example, trumpeted the arrival of album with the headline: "Sattalites beam down a beauty."[93] The *Toronto Star*'s Greg Quill wrote of the important strides that the live album was making for the band, "[*Live via Sattalites*] is gradually helping the band reach a new and larger audience with airplay on college and some 'progressive' music stations across the country."[94] The album also cracked the top ten on the nation's campus stations.[95]

Building on this success, the band set up an impressive touring circuit, were picked up by the Act management agency, and, when they signed with WEA Records through Risqué Disque, became only the second Canadian reggae band to sign a major record deal (Messenjah was the first, in 1983). Videos followed, including for "Gimme Some Kind of Sign" and "Too Late to Turn Back Now," a track featured on the their first full-length Risqué Disque release, *Miracles* (1989). The song won the Sattalites their first Juno Award for Best Reggae/Calypso Recording in 1990.[96]

By the end of the 1980s, the Sattalites had become a household name in Canada, at least among those who enjoyed live music. The nation's Toronto-based reggae scene had successfully exploited the global successes of British reggae acts. If Messenjah was Canada's Steel Pulse, and 20th Century Rebels were its Aswad, the Sattalites were its UB40. This was in the band's favour, as a *NOW Magazine* journalist observed: "The group mixes classy originals with some truly offbeat cover choices that ensure aural attention. Anyone who's ever bought a UB40 album is a potential fan of the band, and that's a sizeable base on which to build a career."[97] Betsy Powell, journalist with the *Toronto Star,* noted the Sattalites' advantage over other reggae acts: "Like Britain's UB40 and Ziggy Marley (Bob's son), the Sattalites' brand of reggae – a mixture of easygoing lover's rock and dancehall style – is more radio friendly than hardcore reggae."[98]

The problem with these compliments is that they undermined the Sattalites' legitimacy as a reggae act. It is true that the Sattalites enjoyed radio success with cover songs (for example, Eddie Cornelius's "Too Late to Turn Back Now" and Katrina and the Waves' "Walking on Sunshine"), but so too did many other reggae bands of this era, including Jamaican ones. This was also true of all-black Canadian reggae bands such as Messenjah who, for example, found success with the Spinners' radio-friendly hit "Could It Be I'm Falling in Love."[99] Yet it was the Sattalites who had "pop" prepended to their brand of reggae. Despite the importance of the cover-song tradition in Jamaican reggae music, these distinctions perpetuated the whispers of nonconfidence that circulated around Canadian reggae.

The Sattalites, nevertheless, persevered. It has been over thirty years since the Sattalite Music School first opened its door. The band that was born out of that institution became itself an institution of Canadian reggae. Despite a couple of lineup changes and the untimely death of keyboardist Bruce "Preacher" Robinson, the Sattalites continue to perform live and have a solid core of fans that are always willing to relive Canada's golden age of reggae.

The Reggae Museum

Unfortunately for the Toronto scene, reggae as a genre began to stagnate in the early 1990s. With an overreliance on tried-and-true musical commodities of an earlier age, reggae artistry was nearing bankruptcy. Despite a new worldwide market for dancehall – one of reggae's many offshoots – reggae proper failed to regenerate or evolve and was poised to become a museum curiosity.

Some of those who lived through the golden age continue to defy the circumscriptions of what a powerful minority felt reggae must be. Surely all reggae artists should have the freedom to imagine what the music can be. Otherwise, reggae may very well experience the same unfortunate fate as polka music. In 2009, the Recording Academy deemed that polka was no longer relevant or responsive, and retired the genre's Grammy award.[100] Polka had ceased to evolve, and it paid the ultimate price on one of the world's biggest music platforms.

In Canada, concerns about cultural appropriation did much to stifle freedom in the arts community, and reggae suffered. Many Jamaican migrants believe that the gains earned on the frontlines had been won despite the official multiculturalism, not because of it. In this context, notions of what Canadian reggae should sound and look like managed to stint the proliferation of the genre for a time.

Other factors slowed its growth. The possible death of reggae was accelerated by the dire state of the music industry in general. People simply stopped buying music as much as they used to, and reggae record store and record labels closed up shop around the world.[101] The reggae industry, as British reggae DJ David Rodigan confessed in 2010, was gone: "Record sales are really poor and record shops are finding it hard to survive as a result ... We're now at the point where some artists are releasing their music for free."[102]

The slow regeneration and post-1980s evolution of reggae was also partially to blame. As the British reggae artist Soloman, son of Aswad's Drummie Zeb, observed:

> I think people feel that in order for reggae to be authentic, it needs to sound like it was made at Studio One 20 years ago. I think that's rubbish. Hip hop has changed, R&B has changed, and even dancehall has changed, but reggae, to me, is stuck in this old sound. I think that's part of reggae's problem – it's not evolving.[103]

Canadian reggae DJ David Kingston echoed this opinion:

> Things haven't changed to the same degree in Jamaican music. It's more of a regurgitation. But that first twenty-five years is so magic, and that's why you've got to appreciate it as a special time ... If something doesn't evolve, it dies ... You can love the pure, pure, purist forms that only existed with the originators, but if people don't keep it living and evolving, it just becomes some kind of museum piece.[104]

232   *In Search of the Canadian Sound*

Even today's Canadian reggae artists can foresee the genre's impending doom. For multiple Juno Award winner Jesse King, the majority of today's reggae is mostly

> heartless. It's got no soul ... There's nothing; there's no groove. It's the same stuff ... The modern "roots" is even the worst, you know, because it's basically the synthetic one drop ... And everybody's going to do the same hi-hat shuffle ... We have to leave that behind ... I mean, I go to Europe, and I'm hearing music coming out of these guys that far surpasses anything coming out of Jamaica.[105]

Tomaz Jardim concurred:

> I think there is this common phenomenon with the evolution of all music once their peak has passed and they're essentially dead as an art form is that either ... you have an immense amount of vision, you take it in a new and interesting direction, which generally doesn't happen, or you are left to try to and re-create its greatest moments as faithfully as possible, which also is very useful.[106]

Jardim lamented that the politically charged, halcyon days of meaningful reggae and ska have been replaced by frivolous and often irrelevant party music that recalls the holiday music of an earlier age:

> The thing that drives me crazy is when people are, like, "Oh, I like reggae too," and they instantly have this big smile on their face, like it is Club Med music, which I think is the most unfortunate direction that the legacy of reggae has gone, you know, this perception that reggae is all about being happy and everything. And it's so fucking ironic, and I don't think it was that way when we were into it in the 1980s. Back then, it was perceived much more truly as what it was at the time, which was the music of suffering and the oppressed.[107]

For those of us who have been in the reggae game for over two or more decades, it seems as if few alternatives exist outside of tired, formulaic songs about weed, Jah, and Babylon, anodyne pop, or R&B-flavoured frat-party pap. Most modern reggae has ceased to advance and may very well be, at least to a critical mass, irrelevant.

While reggae today has obvious problems, the question remains: Why was Canada's golden age of reggae not as resplendent as it could have been? JuLion King pondered this question:

> It was always a shock to me, especially in the early days of the Bamboo, with the Sattalites, Leroy Sibbles, Willi Williams, and those guys, that generation, how the place would be corked, ram every Friday and Saturday night. So if it's that popular, why isn't getting airplay? I didn't see any other club, except for the Horseshoe when big-name artists used to show up from abroad, that could pull that kind of power every single weekend.[108]

To be sure, Canada's mainstream music industry has at times been suspicious of – or, at the least, uncharitable towards – indigenous Canadian reggae acts, which makes the successes of Messenjah and the Sattalites all the more impressive.[109] As one anonymous local reggae producer said in 1980: "If the big companies are stupid enough to ignore the fact that there are almost 200,000 West Indians living in Toronto, man, well that's their problem ... But there's money to be made out there."[110] In one particular instance, when a record company representative looked at the credits of the Sattalites' debut album and saw heavyweights Sly and Robbie listed, he snidely quipped: "These guys are playing with everybody these days, aren't they?"[111] This was during the years when Sly and Robbie were laying tracks for Bob Dylan, Mick Jagger, Grace Jones, and Serge Gainsbourg, but it truly was a typically Canadian commentary on the home team. As Hambleton asked in 1985: "So, if [Sly and Robbie] are playing with a Canadian band, it couldn't possibly be because they also consider them good, could it? I can tell you one thing: it wasn't for the money. We paid Jamaican studio rates, which are embarrassingly low."[112] It could be argued that lack of support permeated the entire Canadian music industry, even after the implementation of CRTC guidelines had proven to be effective in raising the Canadian game. The suspicion that some musos held towards indigenous reggae persists today.

234   *In Search of the Canadian Sound*

The comparatively small Canadian music industry also explains why the reggae scene in Canada did not enjoy the same successes as its British counterpart. It was a matter of infrastructure. Britain, for instance, could boast two successful companies with a mission to put Jamaican music on the map. Both companies – Chris Blackwell's Island Records and Lee Gopthal's Trojan – were run by British Jamaicans. Canada had no equivalent. As Klive Walker observed, "There were no record companies, independent or otherwise, that believed in the music enough to consistently and aggressively promote Canadian reggae."[113] Only a few companies gambled on homegrown Canadian reggae. GRT tendered Ishan People a two-album deal in 1977, while WEA had those brief encounters with the Sattalites and Messenjah.[114] Despite penetrating the commercial airwaves, major releases such as Sibbles' *Evidence* or Messenjah's *Jam Session* or even the Sattalites' *Miracles* all managed, at best, modest sales. Though Ishan People's two albums with GRT had encouraging sales, they were not sufficient enough for the label to justify resigning the band.[115] While the record labels did sign Canadian reggae acts, they didn't successfully convince Canadian mainstream radio to play homegrown reggae. Not surprisingly, mainstream record companies shied away from future reggae signings.

Most Canadian reggae acts relied heavily on underground channels, including community radio shows dedicated to reggae music. The mainstream print media was also somewhat receptive to Canadian reggae, as were community-based Caribbean newspapers such as *Share* and *Contrast*. More mainstream arts-and-culture weeklies such as *NOW* and *Eye* magazines were sometimes supportive of the Toronto reggae scene, but like community-based papers, they tended to privilege Jamaican and other international reggae acts over local ones. For a few bands, television provided the highest-yielding exposure. Messenjah and the Sattalites were regularly featured on MuchMusic, CBC, and Citytv, and the latter's *Breakfast Television* provided a fairly regular outlet for several Toronto reggae acts, including Adrian Miller, Jay Douglas, and Tabarruk in the late 1980s and early 1990s.

There were also problems within the scene itself. Perpetual bickering and lack of unity among promoters and musicians often dragged down the scene's tempo. As Frances Henry observed, struggles and disputes that began in Jamaica were sometimes transplanted to Toronto.[116] Carrie Mullings spoke of the sometimes crippling bitterness that existed within the reggae community:

> The problem is is that there's been a huge breakdown in the structure of how the industry should run. And that breakdown has come from an imbalance: too much ego and not enough hard-working people, people that are here for fame and growing their name ... The scene for a while has been bitter: "I've been doing this for so many years, and I'm not getting anywhere with this." It's hard when the elders have very little positive to say to the new generation.[117]

For many outside the reggae community, these divisive dynamics were a turnoff.

Music publicist Sebastian Cook, who was born in Newmarket, Ontario, spoke of the difficult nature of promoting reggae: "I have worked with or alongside many Jamaican Canadians (both immigrants and second-generation). This experience has been overwhelmingly positive, but there certainly have been times when elements of the Jamaican business culture – machismo, lack of formal structure or agreements – were frustrating and challenging."[118] The lack of confidence emanating from within the scene itself begat disorganization, poorly promoted and attended shows, nonexistent or confusing contractual agreements and, ultimately, a meagre payday for everyone involved. A series of late starts, no-shows, and even gunplay kept reggae fans away in droves.[119]

Another major problem was that many Jamaican migrants were uninterested in Canadian reggae. While the demographic certainly suggested a potential market, the truth of the matter was that the community did not support local music. Jamaican-born artists recognized this massive obstacle. Adrian Miller illustrated the lukewarm attitude of Toronto's Jamaican community:

> For the past thirty years, me living in Canada playing reggae, [be]cause I'm talking pre-Bamboo, our audience was always 75 percent Caucasian ... But we never really have that respect. It's almost like [Jamaican] people would rather stay home and wait until ... Freddie

McGregor and Culture comes to Toronto, before they got out and spend their forty-five dollars to see them. So there was always a displacement. You know what I mean.[120]

Dalton Higgins, Harbourfront artistic director and second-generation Jamaican, witnessed first-hand this tepid response: "There are few Canadian reggae acts that get genuine respect from Jamaican audiences. There are a few groups that get some supports from mainstream non-Jamaican audiences, but by and large the response is not good. And the track record of Canadian reggae artists trying to make a living in Canada supports this theory."[121] Indeed, there are precious few Canadian reggae artists who have been able to sustain a living exclusively from reggae music in Canada. The local community, musicians notwithstanding, has consistently undervalued the local artist.

This fact is all the more regrettable when one considers the wealth of stellar reggae pioneers that have, at one time or another, resided in the city, as Nicholas Jennings confirmed:

> I've always been in awe of the fact that my hometown was where people such as Jackie Mittoo and Stranger Cole and Lord Tanamo and Jay Douglas ... and then later Leroy Sibbles and from Trinidad Mojah ... and on and on [called home]. So, we had the Oakwood and Eglinton hub, we had the Malton hub, and we had your hub Keele and Finch, Jane and Finch. All of that music was – from my perspective, as a music fan but also as a music journalist – I just thought that we were just so fortunate to have all of that going on in the city.[122]

Unfortunately, Jennings was one of the few mainstream journalists who devoted ink to the city's reggae community.

Perhaps Toronto's reggae scene was simply a microcosm of so many other artistic disciplines and endeavours in Canada in which the local girl or boy has to go abroad to make it big.[123] Phil Vassell, whose magazine has been one of the only Toronto publications to keep its finger on the local reggae scene, lamented the fact that so many quality artists were compelled to leave Canada to ply their trade in greener pastures: "If you look at their address and acknowledge the fact that that address was a Canadian address at one point ... People get to a point where they say, 'You know what? If this is what I want to pursue, maybe I need to be elsewhere.'"[124] It was not a lack of talent. Britain may have been blessed with Jamaica's Jackie Edwards, Owen Gray, and Laurel Aitken, but Canada had Leroy Sibbles, Jackie Mittoo, Stranger Cole, Johnny Osbourne, Delroy Wilson, Prince Jammy, Carlene Davis, Lord Tanamo, Alton Ellis, and so many other veritable legends of Jamaican popular music, individuals who imparted their knowledge to generations of Canadian reggae artists.

8

A Strange Land

Move ahead to 2017. On May 14, the eccentric Jamaican legend Lee "Scratch" Perry performed at Toronto's Danforth Music Hall on Danforth Avenue. Canadian reggae musicians, in typical fashion, were called upon to open the show: the Sattalites' Fergus Hambleton and Bruce McGillivray, alongside keyboardist Sam Weller, drummer Sunray Grennan, trombonist Chris Butcher, singers RaLion and Papa Levy, and the House of David Gang's King Selah, Jay Cleary, and Snappy Homefry rounded out the home side. Not quite a month later, on June 7, two-tone legends the Specials brought their second-wave ska to the same venue.

A week later, on June 15 and due west on Sherbourne Street, the Wailers performed the best of Marley's canon at the Phoenix Concert Theatre. Toronto's the Human Rights, featuring reggae veterans Friend-lyness, Tréson, and the inimitable keyboardist Bernie Pitters, opened. On July 21, Beres Hammond played a summer reggae blockbuster to the south at Massey Hall, and on September 5, UB40 returned to Toronto for its seemingly annual sold-out Canadian reggae party.

In between those two colossal shows, Nathan Philips Square at Toronto's City Hall had a Canada Day weekend party that featured the Kingston All-Stars, fronted by Jamaican icons Sly Dunbar, Robbie Lyn, and Mikey Chung. The show also featured several Jamaican expats from Toronto's reggae scene, including Stranger Cole, Anthony "Bassie" Hibbert, Noel Ellis, Carol Brown, and Rannie "Bop" Williams, all of whom joined the Kingston All-Stars on stage during the show.

It was 2017, but it felt like 1987. Reggae's legacy on the city of Toronto and Canada at large was undeniable, though some things weren't quite the same.

With the advent of rap and hip hop in the 1980s, reggae's popularity had begun to wane. Reggae, for all its popularity in mainland Europe, Britain, and her former colonies, struggled to make significant inroads into the American mainstream. Although it had a massive influence on rap and hip hop, American black radio stations in avoided jumping on the reggae bandwagon.[1] As early as 1985, rock critic Alan Niester, attending Reggae Sunsplash at Toronto's Massey Hall, prophetically observed the obvious issue of reggae's audience: "Anyone looking would have been hard-pressed to find someone under 20. These were predominantly older fans, people who grew up with reggae before coming north. Today's black youth, those in school instead of the workforce, is more interested in Grandmaster Flash or the Fat Boys – New York rap – than in the spirit of Bob Marley."[2] Predictably, younger Jamaican Canadians by the early 1990s were disinclined to embrace the music of their parents. Young white reggae fans were also thinning.

Moreover, modern reggae, in Toronto and elsewhere, did not resonate with the rebel youth subculture as it once had. The punk-reggae alliance was broken. As Stephen Duncombe and Maxwell Tremblay assert in *White Riot: Punk Rock and the Politics of Race,* "Most punks wouldn't be caught dead with a Bob Marley record, as reggae as a whole has come to signify a kind of collegiate bohemianism (or worse: frat boys partying on spring break) and is incompatible with punk's serious politics and no-bullshit aesthetic."[3] While this is a sweeping assertion, they are correct that reggae holds a different meaning for white youth subculture today than it did for the previous generation.

Even in its golden age, Canadian reggae could not compete with the British scene, which continues to value and develop its own British reggae star system. Willi Williams, who lives in Pickering but has made much of his living from music in Europe and Britain, opined: "You have to understand that Britain is a world leader. Canada is not really a world leader. Canada is a colony of Britain ... They'll follow everybody else ... I'm not knocking the place as a country, because Canada is a beautiful place."[4] Blacks and whites in Brixton, for instance, were more readily able to identify with each other along class lines and, for many, class association trumped racial considerations. Unemployment in the heart of the Thatcher era was a great leveller, galvanizing different sorts of relationships between blacks and whites of the working and underclasses. Class behaved differently in Canada and was far less unifying, even in urban centres. As journalist Peter Goddard observed in 1980, Canadian reggae had "less to do with revolution than recreation."[5] Perhaps because of this the Canadian rude boy lacked the aggression found in the UK variant.

Jamaican enclaves in Britain were also older than Canada's by two generations. As early as the 1960s, West Indians and white Brits who lived in the poorer areas of Britain's inner cities were, through simple propinquity, obliged to accept and even adopt part of each other's culture. While the essence of movements such as Rock Against Racism rang true for Canadians, Toronto did not experience the intensely physical riots that plagued Britain in the late 1970s and 1980s, riots where black and white youths fought the police side by side.[6] During a particularly violent week in the summer of 1981, when black and white youth clashed with the police in various parts of Britain, the Specials' "Ghost Town" served as the movement's anthem and was number one on the British charts:

> This town, is coming like a ghost town
> Why must the youth fight against themselves?
> Government leaving the youth on the shelf
> This place, is coming like a ghost town.[7]

It was in this atmosphere that ska and reggae came to be the sound of a disenfranchised and proudly multiracial generation in Britain. As tough as the "struggle" in Toronto might have been, the city simply never got hot enough to cook up the same results.[8]

Reggae in Canada was localized, grounded mainly in the Toronto experience and only in particular parts of it. While the same might be said about British reggae, London had satellite scenes in Coventry, Birmingham, Bristol, Manchester, Glasgow, and various other urban areas. These satellites informed the larger UK scene. In Toronto, the Sattalites and a handful of other bands were the scene, and in terms of infrastructure, the Canadian scene paled in comparison to the British one. Several British reggae record companies moved thousands of units and experienced sustained chart success first with Jamaican-born artists such as Millie Small, Desmond Dekker, John Holt, and Dave and Ansell Collins, and then with indigenous British artists such as Matumbi, Aswad, Steel Pulse, UB40, and Maxi Priest. British record companies also had the gumption and resources necessary to stare down and persuade stiff-necked programmers at the BBC to play reggae music, as London-based Trojan Records executive Chips Richards recalled:

> I was pushing a record called "Everything I Own" by Ken Boothe, which finally became No. 1, and I was in the BBC offices when it was being played over the radio by Tony Blackburn. Then half-way through playing the record, he stopped it and said something like: "Oh, utter rubbish! How can anyone in his right mind go out and buy something like this, after listening to the David Gates *real* version?" That got me absolutely mad. I no longer respected anybody. I stopped knocking on doors. I pushed doors and I entered. And I reminded them that they were public servants representing the public, and I was a member of the public. I no longer used the soft smiling attitude. I began to demand. I used to compile scrap-books showing them the demand for reggae. I wrote letters to them telling them that our records were in the breakers in the British Market Research Board (BMRB), and that our records used to outsell a lot of pop records, and it was because of lack of radio support that we could not have progressed further.[9]

Perhaps Canada had needed a Chips Richards to push doors open and enter the belly of commercial radio stations, demanding that reggae be played.

Canadian reggae nevertheless made some gains and profoundly impacted the lives of many Canadians, especially in the mid- to late 1980s. As Messenjah's Rupert Harvey noted:

We were on the vanguard; we were the tip of the spear that helped to create that. A lot of the times, when we went to a town in "prairie someplace," we were the first dreads anyone ever saw. And I think people initially came out of curiosity to check out these freaky guys, and then they started to say, "Wait a second, we can dance to this."[10]

The Sattalites enjoyed the same elevating experiences, as Bruce McGillivray explained:

We put black and white people together in this country, and it is these types of art forms that are, unfortunately from, say, a government level ... are forgotten ... They should be supported, because that's one of things that develops a society, is music, art ... I think that's probably what – I think we've accomplished most for doing this all of these years as the Sattalites is to draw people together.[11]

Though real commercial success lay mostly out of reach, Canadian reggae bands won cultural and personal successes, especially when artists opted for a Canadian-centric approach and were not overly focused on chasing the Yard, or even British, sound. The golden age of Canadian reggae may have been ephemeral, but the legacy of those Queen Street West bands that got Toronto jamming remains intact, in Toronto and elsewhere.

Of course, flashes of Canadian-based reggae burst on the music scene following the golden age of the 1980s. In 1994, Snow (a.k.a. Darrin O'Brien), who was born and raised in Toronto's Allenbury Projects, became, for a time, the most commercially successful white DJ in the world.[12] Snow's "Informer," which he sang completely in Jamaican Patois, was an international hit, including in Jamaica.[13] Five years later, in 1999, Big Sugar's "Turn the Lights On," which featured veteran reggae bassist Garry Lowe, was a significant radio hit that proved just how impressive reggae's influence on popular Canadian musical currents had been.[14]

Toronto's reggae pioneers, though, live on, or "survive," in various ways, not necessarily in how reggae is approached but rather in the genre's offshoots. Reggae has directly influenced and informed, *inter alia*, American rap, hip hop, British jungle music, and Puerto Rican reggaeton.

Canadian hip hop, in particular, has always had a fair quotient of reggae within its brand.[15] As Klive Walker explained, "rap artists such as Toronto's Kardinal Offishall and MC Collizhun (formerly of Nefarius) and Vancouver's Rascalz fuse heavy doses of reggae and reggae vocal style into hip-hop laced with lyrics that sometimes offer incisive social commentary about the Caribbean diaspora in Canada."[16] New, talented, and socio-politically active songwriters who might have, in an earlier time, been streamlined into the reggae sphere now find different ways to articulate their message.

There were those, however, who still found success using the reggae blueprint. In 2005, Toronto-based rock-reggae hybrid Bedouin Sound-clash scored a success on the Canadian, Scottish, and English charts with their single "When the Night Feels My Song."[17] The band's *Sounding a Mosaic* album went platinum and climbed to number nine on the US Billboard Reggae Chart.[18] The band – formed when members Jay Malinowski and Eon Sinclair met at Queen's University – has since built on its early success and continues to develop an international audience.

The twenty-first century has also rekindled interest in Toronto's reggae past. Perhaps unsurprisingly, it took an American label to identify the need to rescue a true Canadian story. Light in the Attic, a record label out of Seattle, began a campaign to shine a light on the important impact that popular Jamaican music has had on the city of Toronto. Issued between 2004 and 2008, the label's Jamaica to Toronto series included six albums that captured an earlier time in Jamaican Canadian music history. The project celebrated several works by Jamaican Torontonians, including, among others, Bob and Wisdom; Jo Jo and the Fugitives; Eddie Spencer; Lloyd Delpratt; Johnny Osbourne; Earth, Roots and Water; Wayne McGhie; the Hitch-Hikers; the Mighty Pope; the Sheiks; Noel Ellis; the Cougars; and, of course, Jackie Mittoo. The series exceeded all expectations.

The project materialized as a result of the positive waves caused by the label's 2004 rerelease of *Wayne McGhie and the Sounds of Joy*. Following this success, Light in the Attic's Matt Sullivan called on Canadian music historian, DJ, and Grammy-nominated producer Kevin Howes (a.k.a. Sipreano) to provide the context for the Toronto scene from which Wayne McGhie had emerged. As Howes explained:

244   *A Strange Land*

Having grown up in North York and learning as much as I could about Jamaican and Canadian music, I was able to fill in some of the blanks about the Toronto scene and [bring] even more Jamaican and Caribbean-Canadian records, like Jackie Mittoo's *Wishbone,* to their attention ... When Matt and I connected with Wayne McGhie and his family for the first time in Toronto in the winter of 2003 (thanks to some detective work by Jay Douglas), I brought with me a box of 7-inch singles and a portable turntable that I had bought in Japan. One by one we listened to the records. Wayne, who had gone missing and had been dealing with significant mental health issues since the late 1970s, hadn't heard his music, nor that of his peers, for many years. Needless to say, it was a very emotional experience. There wasn't a dry eye in the house. It was then when Matt and I looked at each other and realized that we had to do much more than simply rerelease *The Sounds of Joy.* The Jamaica-Toronto series was born that day.[19]

Toronto enthusiastically embraced the series' artists and albums. The project received national coverage, including gracing the cover of *NOW.*[20] There were several performances, though perhaps none as spectacular as the one in front of six thousand people at Harbourfront Centre in the summer of 2006.[21] The series was, as far as Jay Douglas was concerned, "one of the best things that happened for music, not just in Canada, or just in Toronto, but worldwide, because it introduced what he have and what we had here in Canada to the rest of the world."[22] The Jamaica to Toronto experience would be, for many of the artists involved, the most magical chapter of their career.

The magic did not end with Jamaica to Toronto. In 2014, Magic!, a self-styled pop-reggae band from Toronto, enjoyed enormous success with the single "Rude." The song hit number one on both the US and UK charts.[23] While Magic!'s success brought on the naysayers (not only because there were no black Jamaicans in the band but also because they were somewhat removed from the city's established reggae community), it also reawakened interest in earlier Toronto reggae acts.[24] After "Rude" hit big, various media, including CBC's *The National* and the *Globe and Mail,* decided to gaze backwards to a time when Messenjah and the Sattalites held sway on Queen Street.[25]

The City of Toronto also began to recognize its reggae roots and routes. A once unnamed roadway that runs off Oakwood Avenue on the southside of Eglinton Avenue in Toronto's Little Jamaica community was officially named Reggae Lane. Josh Colle, chair of the Toronto Transit Commission, led the nomination committee (which included several members of the city's reggae community) to have the roadway named to honour Toronto's reggae past. The talented visual artist Adrian Hayles was commissioned to paint a wall mural on Reggae Lane that captures some of Toronto's famous reggae music makers, including Jo Jo Bennett, Bernie Pitters, and Leroy Sibbles. Perhaps unsurprisingly, Bob Marley and Haile Selassie are also featured.[26]

There is, of course, still a vibrant reggae scene in Toronto, though the bands are perhaps less widely known than those of the golden age. Indigenous Canadian reggae is still being made by a diverse base of artists such as the Filipina, Anglo-Indian, and Canadian singer Elaine Shepherd and the Australian Canadian artist RaLion.[27] Ammoye, Kafinal, and the multiple Juno Award-winning Exco Levi have also kept reggae on the nation's musical map.

The efforts of DJ Carrie Mullings are particularly laudable. Mullings took it upon herself to reenergize the Canadian reggae scene. Instead of following the CRTC guidelines to play 30 percent Canadian content, Mullings reversed the quota. Yet even this was not enough for the ambassador of Canadian reggae. Mullings did the unthinkable and changed her show to 100 percent Canadian reggae music, a bold move, even for a confident DJ in the new millennium:

> When I made the switch, I'm, like, "Oh my God, they're going to crucify me. They're going to call in. They're going to hate the show." Because I felt that 30 percent, I felt, was what was keeping the show alive. And it really wasn't. It was how you deliver the music to the people and how you perceive that music as a radio DJ and what you say to [listeners].[28]

With her show streaming on internet radio, Mullings has listeners all around the world and regularly gets messages from Kuala Lumpur, Bangkok, Sierra Leone, Kuwait, Germany, Denmark, and various other places.

246   *A Strange Land*

She uses an online translator to reach out to all the people that are listening to new Canadian reggae.[29]

Yet old Canadian reggae continues to exact its long-deserved due. In 2016, Jay Douglas was visiting friends and family in the United Kingdom. In an HMV record shop in London, he introduced himself to the staff: "They treated me royally and gave me huge discounts because of the Jamaica to Toronto project ... The people in London – they still think that the CD release should have taken place there! That was really something to hear."[30] The triangular, transoceanic musical conversation between Jamaica, Britain, and Canada continues to endure.

Reggae music did indeed facilitate a cultural dialogue between Jamaican migrant and Canadian host in Toronto during the 1970s and 1980s. Musical and cultural exchanges occurred in various places along the city's ethnic frontier. From basement blues dances and the nightclubs of Queen Street West to large venues such as Massey Hall, the Forum at Ontario Place, and Maple Leaf Gardens, reggae united sometimes strange bedfellows and brought black and white youth together in a sometimes highly politicized, "oppositional" movement that rebelled against the status quo.

Migrants could enact their Jamaican ethnicity within these reggae venues, while non-Jamaicans could satisfy their curiosity about Jamaican music and culture. So ubiquitous was the reggae sound in Toronto that by the 1980s it had become a part of the city's musical vernacular. Yet Jamaican migrants in Canada were not a homogeneous group. Likewise, members of the city's non-Jamaican (mostly white) youth culture were attracted to reggae and Jamaicans for a diversity of reasons. Considering these two shifting variables, the reggae texts crafted in Toronto ultimately held different meanings for different people. In fact, sometimes the only thread that tied people's experiences together was that Toronto was the place where reggae happened.

At the same time, the hybrid that is reggae music evolved outside of place. That is to say, reggae, as a transnational popular music form, was made by a people in motion, and it was constantly informed by influences that ping-ponged back and forth across the Atlantic Ocean. Between the seventeenth and nineteenth centuries, the musical cultures of Africa and

Europe fused in the ports of Jamaica, creating a creolized Jamaican sound. In the twentieth century, however, technology accelerated the musical conversation that was occurring across the black Atlantic. It was an organic process: while Jamaican migrants, labourers, domestics, and musicians carried the island's popular musics with them wherever they went, radio and sound systems broadcast British and American musics back to Jamaica, updating the new musics being created there. Simultaneously, ska, rocksteady, and reggae were being reimagined by Brits and Canadians living in urban centres that boasted healthy Jamaican populations. A few of these artists were lucky enough to complete the circle by taking their hybrid of a hybrid back to Jamaica via both performances and recordings.

These successes were, at least for the Canadian reggae brand, hard won. Despite the significant amount of reggae texts crafted by non-Rastas, non-Jamaicans, and even nonblacks, it was the black, dreadlocked Rastafarian that became the normative iconography for the genre. This was in part because of Bob Marley, who, despite being biracial, gave reggae music its essentialized look. Though he raised the profile of reggae, Marley's image assembled an artificial apparatus within the media that subsequently dictated what reggae should sound and look like. The Marley effect limited – at least as far as some journalists were concerned – reggae's authenticities, making mischief for multiracial bands such as Britain's UB40 and Canada's Sattalites. It also set limitations on black reggae musicians in Canada who wanted to push the reggae envelope. Both groups were circumscribed by what reggae was "supposed to be" and by restrictive constructions of blackness and whiteness. This fact obliged many musicians to chase an authentic Jamaican sound at the expense of fully realizing a Canadian one.

As popular as it may have been, Reggae Canadiana never reached the heights it might have, given the wealth of talent, Toronto's large Jamaican population, and the multicultural makeup of some of its acts. The scene fell well short of the successes realized in Britain. Still, a majority of Jamaican migrants believed that their association with reggae music gave them a psychological advantage in the acculturation process. In short, reggae was part of their strategy for success. The music from home strengthened their own sense of self, helped them to build successful lives and meaningful relationships with non-Jamaican Canadians in Toronto, and encouraged them to sing King Alpha's song in this, their new strange land.

Across the metaphorical bridge, non-Jamaican Torontonians were summoned to reggae by a variety of signifiers. Whether it was matters of spirituality, the oppositional aesthetic of the reggae text, marijuana, or simply the infectious Jamaican hybrid of melody and rhythm that struck a sympathetic, if subconscious, chord, reggae was central to a process that coupled host to migrant in various places around Toronto. Many non-Jamaicans said they believed that, without reggae, they would have had little cause to connect with the Jamaican migrant community. Bridge building and bridge crossing transcended music. Reggae provided an important social space where differences between migrant and host were negotiated and, for some, where long-lasting relationships were forged. Theirs was an earnest form of interculturalism that bore little resemblance to the governmental brochure version of multiculturalism. One can only hope that new reggae artists will continue to trumpet the Canadianness in their sound and text and that they will recognize, as Jo Jo Bennett reminds us, that "understanding is the key to it all."[31]

Notes

Preface and Acknowledgments

1 David Rider, "Toronto declares Saturday 'Titans of Reggae Day,'" *Toronto Star*, March 1, 2019, GTA Edition.

2 See Mark Suppanz, "Review: Jason Wilson, *Perennials*," *Big Takeover* 79 (2016): 37; The Insider, "Remember the BamBoo? Exploring Toronto's reggae roots," *Globe and Mail,* August 1, 2014; Deana Sumanac, "Magic! tops Billboard chart with Rude, exposing Canada's reggae roots," *The National,* CBC, August 1, 2014; Ken Hunt, "Review: Wilson & Swarbrick, *Lion Rampant*," *fRoots,* April 2014; Nannie Bootles, *When the Doodle Was the Most Wonderful Doodle in the World: And Makes the Bestest Music in the Whole Wide World,* a reggae memoir (Stouffville, ON: publication pending, 2010); Ted Boothroyd, "Album Review: *The Peacemaker's Chauffeur*," *Beat* (Los Angeles) 28, 1 (2009): 51–52; "Jason Wilson," *Guelph Mercury,* June 26, 2009; Colin Irwin, "Rebel Music: Dave Swarbrick, Jason Wilson and David Francey," *Penguin Eggs,* Summer 2009, 22–24; Errol Nazareth, "Tribute to late reggae great Mittoo," *Toronto Sun,* March 14, 2008; Nicholas Jennings, "Album Review: *The Peacemaker's Chauffeur*," *Inside E Canada* 7, 6 (2008): 108; Errol Nazareth, "Songs of war and peace: Jason Wilson," *Toronto Sun,* October 3, 2008, E5; Sebastian Cook, "Jason Wilson," performance review, *The Live Music Report,* September 25, 2008; John Jason Wilson and Kevin Shea, *Lord Stanley: The Man behind the Cup* (Toronto: Fenn Publishing, 2006); John Jason Wilson, "UB40's Got Plenty More," *Word Magazine,* April 2006, 18; Greg Quill, "Two musical icons, one heartfelt style: The two Bobs," *Toronto Star,* January 25, 2006, E2; CBC Television, "The Grateful Dread: Jason Wilson," *The National,* with Peter Mansbridge, August 19, 2004; Kevin Shea, "Big Shinny Tunes: Jason Wilson," *Legends Magazine,* Fall 2003, 74, 76–78; Stuart Bearman, "Rastaman Variations: Jason Wilson and Tabarruk," *Eye Magazine,* May 21, 1998, 21; and Jane Stevenson, "Alanis vocal fires interest in local band," *Toronto Sun,* March 25, 1996.

250   *Notes to pages 3–5*

Introduction: King Alpha's Song

1 Peter Edwards, "Black history looms large at busy corner," *Toronto Star,* January 26, 1998, B3.

2 Colin Grant, *Negro with a Hat: The Rise and Fall of Marcus Garvey* (London: Vintage Books, 2009), 442–43, 503.

3 Ibid., 442–43.

4 Bob Marley and the Wailers, "Redemption Song," Island Records WIP 6653, 1980. Marley most likely was aware of the speech, which had been transcribed in the Sydney, Nova Scotia, journal *Black Man* (alternatively, *Blackman*). For further discussion, see Jon Tattrie, *Redemption Songs: How Bob Marley's Nova Scotia Song Lights the Way Past Racism* (Lawrencetown Beach, NS: Pottersfield Press, 2017); Elizabeth Patterson, "Iconic song had basis in Whitney Pier: Writer details history behind Bob Marley classic in new book," *Cape Breton Post,* February 16, 2017.

5 I use "oppositional" to represent the articulated response of the counterculture. This counterculture, however, still operates within a larger dominant culture, as historian Stuart Henderson explains: "Counterculture is best defined not as an alternative system of social interactions and ideologies existing *outside* the expected, dominant culture but rather as the shifting sets of responses, refusals, and acceptances performed by actors in the cultural process." See *Making the Scene: Yorkville and Hip Toronto in the 1960s* (Toronto: University of Toronto Press, 2011), 5.

6 See Hazel V. Carby, *Cultures in Babylon: Black Britain and African America* (London: Verso, 1999); Penny Von Eschen, *Race against Empire: Black Americans and Anti-colonialism, 1937–1957* (Ithaca, NY: Cornell University Press, 1997); and Joseph Heathcott, "Urban Spaces and Working-Class Expressions across the Black Atlantic: Tracing the Routes of Ska," *Radical History Review* 87 (Fall 2003): 183–206.

7 This was perhaps done most famously by Paul Gilroy. See Paul Gilroy, *The Black Atlantic: Modernity and Double Consciousness* (Cambridge, MA: Harvard University Press, 1994). See also Arjun Appadurai, *Modernity at Large: The Cultural Dimensions of Globalization* (Minneapolis: University of Minnesota Press, 1996); Heathcott, "Urban Spaces and Working-Class Expressions," 183; and Linda Basch, Nina Glick Schiller, and Christina Szanton Blanc, *Nations Unbound: Transnational Projects, Postcolonial Predicaments, and Deterritorialized Nation-States* (Luxembourg: Gordon and Breach, 1994).

8 For examples, see James Opp and John C. Walsh, *Placing Memory and Remembering Place in Canada* (Vancouver: UBC Press, 2010), 6. See also Roxann Prazniak and Arif Dirlik, eds., *Places and Politics in an Age of Globalization* (Lanham, MD: Rowman and Littlefield, 2001); Geert De Neve and Henrike Donner, eds., *The Meaning of the Local: Politics of Place in Urban India* (London: Routledge, 2006); Arturo Escobar, "Culture Sits in Places: Reflections on Globalism and Subaltern Strategies of Localization," *Political Geography* 20 (2001): 139–74; and Steven Hoelscher and Derek H. Alderman, "Memory and Place: Geographies of a Critical Relationship," *Social and Cultural Geography* 5, 3 (2004): 347–55.

9 This line of inquiry is not, however, altogether new. As early as 1973, Clifford Geertz articulated his semiotic approach to culture, which demonstrated how people are

Notes to pages 5–7 251

forever spinning webs of significance to make sense of and give meaning to the human experience. Establishing systems of meaning is, as Geertz observed, "as real and pressing as the more familiar biological needs." These systems of meaning produce culture and so become the collective property of a particular people in a particular place at a particular time. See Clifford Geertz, *The Interpretation of Cultures: Selected Essays* (New York: Basic Books, 1973), 5, 140, and *Local Knowledge: Further Essays in Interpretive Anthropology* (New York: Basic Books, 1983), 22. For more recent examples, see William Turkel, *The Archive of Place: Unearthing the Pasts of the Chilcotin Plateau* (Vancouver: UBC Press, 2007); and Julie Cruikshank, *Do Glaciers Listen? Local Knowledge, Colonial Encounters, and Social Imagination* (Vancouver: UBC Press, 2005).

10 For further discussion, see Michel de Certeau's enduring and valuable musings on spatial encounters in *The Practice of Everyday Life* (Berkeley: University of California Press, 1984). For a more recent work on the usefulness of place as a historical tool, see Tim Cresswell, *Place: A Short Introduction* (Malden, MA: Blackwell, 2004).

11 "Frontline" is a term often used by Jamaicans when referring to the imaginary (and sometimes not so imaginary) ethnic boundary separating migrant from host. London's Aswad referred to such a boundary in their tune "Cool Runnings inna W11 Area" from 1983. "W11," or West 11, is the postal code representing London's Notting Hill neighbourhood. Notting Hill was home to two historical race riots: one in 1958 that involved belligerent teddy boys and recent black Caribbean immigrants, and one in 1976 that involved the police fighting both black *and* white kids at the conclusion of that year's Notting Hill Carnival. Aswad had been performing there before the riot broke out, an event that inspired their song that called for peace: "Cool runnings in a W11 area, / Frontline a' carry the swing 'bout ya." The Clash's Joe Strummer and Paul Simonon also participated in the riot, which inspired their "White Riot" track. See Aswad, "Cool Runnings inna W11 Area," *Aswad: The BBC Sessions,* Strange Fruit SFRCD 002, 1997; and the Clash, "White Riot," CBS S CBS 5058, 1977.

12 See George Beckford and Michael Witter, *Small Garden, Bitter Weed: The Political Economy of Struggle and Change in Jamaica* (London: Maroon Publishing House, 1980).

13 For an excellent discussion on ska's role in these routes, see Heathcott, "Urban Spaces and Working-Class Expressions."

14 Ibid., 187.

15 Dick Hebdige, *Cut 'n' Mix: Culture, Identity and Caribbean Music* (London: Comedia, Methuen, 1987), 91, 93.

16 Lorenzkowski, in part building on Rogers Brubaker, helped identify the fleeting character of ethnicity as an event: "Everyday encounters, practical categories, common-sense knowledge, cultural idioms," and so forth express the performance-like behaviour of doing ethnicity. See Barbara Lorenzkowski, *Sounds of Ethnicity: Listening to German North America, 1850–1914* (Winnipeg: University of Manitoba Press, 2010), 6–10; and Rogers Brubaker, "Ethnicity without Groups," *Archives européennes de sociologie* 43, 2 (2002): 167–68.

17 For other works that see ethnicity as something that is practised or enacted, see Jordan Stranger-Ross, *Staying Italian: Urban Change and Ethnic Life in Postwar Toronto and Philadelphia* (Chicago: University of Chicago Press, 2009) and Carolyn Whitzman,

252 *Notes to pages 7–10*

> *Suburb, Slum, Urban Village: Transformations in Toronto's Parkdale Neighbourhood, 1875–2002* (Vancouver: UBC Press, 2009).

18 Klive Walker has been extremely helpful to me throughout this journey. He described an insider as "a writer who has an intimate understanding of the social, political, and cultural conditions that gave birth to Jamaican popular music through actual experience with Jamaican culture. An insider is someone who has been a participant or witness to the unfolding history and development of the music. The insider perspective is a view that fuses the writer's lived experience with the music together with interviews, secondary sources, and other forms of research and analysis": *Dubwise: Reasoning from the Reggae Underground* (Toronto: Insomniac Press, 2005), 260.

19 CBC Television, "The Grateful Dread: Jason Wilson," *The National*, with Peter Mansbridge, August 19, 2004.

20 For the facade of multiculturalism, see Neil Bissoondath, *Selling Illusions: The Cult of Multiculturalism in Canada* (Toronto: Penguin, 2002). For further discussion of the concept of interculturalism, see Milton J. Bennett, *Basic Concepts of Intercultural Communication* (Boston: Intercultural Press, 1998); and Craig Storti, *Cross-Cultural Dialogues* (Boston: Intercultural Press, 1994).

21 Nineteen of the twenty-one Jamaican respondents were born in Jamaica. Author Klive Walker is the lone exception. Walker was born in England to Jamaican parents but spent what he described as his "formative years" in Jamaica before moving to Toronto. See interview, Klive Walker, Pickering, ON, September 9, 2010.

22 These anthropological terms differentiate between observations of cultural behaviour. An *emic* account is one that emanates from within the group or culture in question, for instance, Jamaicans observing Jamaicans. An *etic* account is one that emanates from outside the group in question, for instance, white Torontonians observing Jamaican migrants.

23 Robert Burns, "To a Louse: On Seeing One on a Lady's Bonnet at Church," in *The Works of Robert Burns* (Ware, UK: Wordsworth Editions, 1994), 138–39.

24 Connected as I am with the Canadian reggae scene, I was able to arrange many of the interviews by simply lifting the telephone. Yet I also interviewed a few key members of Toronto's scene with whom I had no prior relationship. This closeness to the subject, however, produces both pros and cons for the historian. One of the issues I had to tackle with the oral reports was the question of "me" in the history of Canadian reggae (although my band, Tabarruk, only really began to take off in 1989, a fact that helped in determining the closing date for the project). Although I asked my interviewees to avoid discussing me too much in the history, I inevitably "came up" in the discussions. In one respect, my decades-long connection to Toronto's Jamaican community and reggae scene afforded me with access that would likely not be available to other historians and musicologists in pursuit of the same answers. The bulk of my interviewees were comfortable and familiar with me, and I with them. On the other hand, this familiarity might have led some of the interviewees to tailor some of their responses. This is not to say that my subjects avoided vexatious topics to spare my feelings. On the contrary, such familiarity allowed for some exploration and, sometimes, sensitive dialogue. Still, there was, as far as professional historical research goes, an unusual familiarity and comfort level with the interviewees that needs to be declared.

25 I had the pleasure of regularly working with these particular artists for the last several years. During this time, I engaged these icons in several illuminating discussions on the evolution and state of reggae.

26 Interview, David Swarbrick, Coventry, UK, November 8–11, 2010.

27 See the Melodians, "By the Rivers of Babylon," Summit/Trojan SUM-6508, 1970. Many of the subtitles are also gleaned from various reggae songs that speak to elements of the work at hand.

28 As Burning Spear himself rightly asked: "What could be better than to sell your own music, and get paid?": Winston Rodney (a.k.a. Burning Spear), "Wisdom to Do What Is Right," *Burning Spear Blog,* August 23, 2009.

29 Quoted in Peter Goddard, "He's Metro's grand old man of reggae," *Toronto Star,* May 29, 1982, F3.

30 For good examples, see Garth White (a.k.a. Razac Blacka), "Master Drummer," *Jamaica Journal* 11, 1–2 (1977): 16–17, and "Rudie, Oh Rudie!," *Caribbean Quarterly* 13, 3 (1967): 39–44; Gordon Rohlehr, "Some Problems of Assessment: A Look at New Expressions in the Art of the Contemporary Caribbean," *Caribbean Quarterly* 17, 3–4 (1971): 92–113; and Verena Reckford, "Rastafarian Music: An Introductory Study," *Jamaica Journal* 11, 1–2 (1977): 3–13. For a strong and more recent review, see Barry Chevannes, *Rastafari: Roots and Ideology* (Syracuse, NY: Syracuse University Press, 1995).

31 Indeed, a separate historiography section could be written to cover the popular literature on Bob Marley alone. If, however, we restrict the number of entries to only some of the very best, then Timothy White's brilliant *Catch a Fire: The Life of Bob Marley* (New York: Henry Holt, 1983) would be a very good place to begin. Jamaican American Malika Lee Whitney and broadcaster-author Dermott Hussey produced an intriguing piece of Wailer literature titled *Bob Marley: Reggae King of the World* (Kingston, Jamaica: Kingston Publishers, 1984), which should also be considered among the stronger works on reggae's king. Kwame Dawes's *Bob Marley: Lyrical Genius* (London: Sanctuary, 2002) and *Natural Mysticism: Towards a New Reggae Aesthetic* (Leeds, UK: Peepal Tree, 1999) are likewise very good works that transcend the journalistic approach. Finally, and most recently, Colin Grant's *The Natural Mystics: Marley, Tosh and Wailer* (London: Random House, 2011) is superb not only for its detailed analysis of the career trajectories of the three main Wailers but also for its assessment of the role of Rastafari in the construct of the Wailer image.

32 See US Department of State, *July–December, 2010 International Religious Freedom Report: Jamaica* (Washington: Bureau of Democracy, Human Rights, and Labor, 2011).

33 Howard Campbell, "Carlene Davis focuses on 'best of glory,'" *Gleaner* (Jamaica), August 4, 2009.

34 Paul McGrath, "Davis proves there is life after reggae," *Globe and Mail,* August 5, 1981, 15.

35 Ibid.

36 Keith Tuber, "Reggae's Carlene Davis Sends a Message from Jamaica," *Orange Coast Magazine,* January 1983, 88–90.

37 Hopeton Lewis, *Take It Easy: Rocksteady with Hopeton Lewis,* Island UK ILP 957, 1967.

254 *Notes to pages 15–16*

38 Debates around racial interpretation in music have long been waged in the literature of other genres such as jazz and blues. In terms of the latter, there are those at one end of the spectrum, such as Amiri Bakara and, more recently, Guthrie Ramsey, who argue that blues music is a vernacular articulation of the racial experience. Still, a number of scholars have positively blurred the racialist binaries of folk-commercial and black-white. The notion that blues was neither purely "black" nor purely "white" is not, however, a new argument. Newman White raised this point as early as 1928 with his *American Negro Folk Songs,* and many scholars such as Paul Oliver (who formerly argued for the racialist perspective), David Evans, and Elijah Wald have since added nuance to White's argument. Similarly, jazz scholars (perhaps more so than any other genre) have tackled issues of race within the evolution of that music. In general, much of jazz scholarship, with some notable exceptions, has demonstrated an integrationist perspective, that is, a colour-blind approach. See, for examples, Amiri Baraka, *Blues People* (New York: Morrow Quill, 1963); Christopher Small, *Music of the Common Tongue: Survival and Celebration in Afro-American Music, 1927–2011* (London: J. Calder/New York: Riverrun Press, 1987); Houston A. Baker Jr., *Blues, Ideology, and Afro-American Literature: A Vernacular Theory* (Chicago: University of Chicago Press, 1984); Henry Louis Gates Jr., *The Signifying Monkey: A Theory of Afro-American Literary Criticism* (New York: Oxford University Press, 1988); Guthrie P. Ramsey, *Race Music: Black Cultures from Bebop to Hip-Hop* (Berkeley: University of California Press, 2003); Newman I. White, *American Negro Folk-Songs* (Hatboro, PA: Folklore Associates, 1965 [1928]); Paul Oliver, "That Certain Feeling: Blues and Jazz ... in 1890?," *Popular Music* 10, 1 (1991): 11–20; David Evans, "Introduction," *American Music* 14, 4 (1996): 397–401; Elijah Wald, *Escaping the Delta: Robert Johnson and the Invention of the Blues* (New York: Amistad, 2004); Rudi Blesh, *Shining Trumpets: A History of Jazz* (New York: Da Capo Press, 1975); James Lincoln Collier, *The Making of Jazz: A Comprehensive History* (New York: Dell, 1978); Scott Saul, *Freedom Is, Freedom Ain't: Jazz and the Making of the Sixties* (Cambridge, MA: Harvard University Press, 2003); and Scott DeVeaux, *The Birth of Bebop: A Social and Musical History* (Berkeley: University of California Press, 1997). For a recent exception to the integrationist approach, see Jon Panish, *The Color of Jazz: Race and Representation in Postwar American Culture* (Jackson: University Press of Mississippi, 1997).

39 See Richard Cook and Brian Morton, *The Penguin Guide to Jazz Recordings,* 9th ed. (London: Penguin Books, 2008).

40 While attention might have been drawn, for instance, to the Scandinavians that made up Oscar Peterson's European rhythm section, it would take a bold soul to question Ulf Wakenius and Niels-Henning Ørsted Pedersen's proficiency, much less their motives for playing America's musical art form. It should also be noted that Jamaican jazzers – of various hues – have likewise been accepted by the jazz intelligentsia.

41 In 1982, Musical Youth, a young black reggae outfit from Birmingham, England, hit the big time with their single "Pass the Dutchie." Partly because of its incredible success and partly because it was performed by a young boy band, "Pass the Dutchie" was criticized for being an inauthentic articulation of the original reggae text. This reading, which suggests that the band was solely the manufactured product of a white-dominated recording industry, lacks some vital details. The young Birmingham band

Notes to page 16 255

was made up of schoolboys of Jamaican descent. Frederick Waite, father to two of the boys in the band, was an original member of the popular ska and rocksteady outfit the Techniques. The boy band built its song on Jamaica's Mighty Diamonds' 1981 hit "Pass the Kouchie," which had been voiced on top of an existing riddim (instrumental track) called "Full Up," which was originally released in Jamaica in 1968 as an instrumental by the session band Sound Dimension for Coxsone Dodd's Studio One label. The principal writers for this instrumental version were future Jamaican Canadians Jackie Mittoo and Leroy Sibbles (two other Sound Dimension musicians, Headley George Bennett and Robbie Lyn, are also credited on the original). Adding their own melody and lyrics to "Full Up," Mighty Diamonds' singers Lloyd Anthony Ferguson and Fitzroy Simpson amended the existing Jamaican text first authored by Mittoo and company thirteen years prior. Mittoo, who worked with Musical Youth while he was in England before returning home to Canada, suggested that the word "kouchie," referring to marijuana paraphernalia, should be replaced by "dutchie," a Jamaican colloquialism for "cooking pot." While most of the world might not have been able to tell the difference between "kouchie" and "dutchie," it was important, at least for the Jamaicans involved, to have the young band sing something more age-appropriate. So, the involvement of Jamaicans at every level of crafting the "Pass the Dutchie" track hardly reconciles with a reading that the song was somehow disconnected from the genre's "organic" roots. Yet these dull arguments persist. See George Lipsitz, *Dangerous Crossroads: Popular Music, Postmodernism and the Poetics of Place* (New York: Verso, 1994), 97–114; Musical Youth, "Pass the Dutchie," MCA Records Canada MCA–13961, 1982; the Mighty Diamonds, "Pass the Kouchie," Island Records 12WIP 6838, 1982; and Jackie Mittoo and Sound Dimension, "Full Up," Studio One, 1968. See also Alexis Petridis, "Famous for 15 months," *The Guardian,* March 21, 2003.

42 Fortunately, a few scholars have addressed the multiple meanings of reggae and its attendant culture. Timothy Rommen, for instance, compares the parallels between the Rastafarian messages in reggae with those found in the fledgling genre of Christian reggae in North America in his 2006 article "Protestant Vibrations? Reggae, Rastafari, and Conscious Evangelicals," *Popular Music* 25, 2 (2006): 235–63. Similarly, Jorge Giovannetti explores the curious use of reggae by white Puerto Ricans to articulate an expression or symbol of that island's elite culture in his 2003 article "Popular Music and Culture in Puerto Rico: Jamaican and Rap Music as Cross-Cultural Symbols," in *Musical Migrations: Transnationalism and Cultural Hybridity in Latino America,* ed. Frances R. Aparicio and Candida F. Jáquez (New York: Palgrave, 2003), 81–98. Likewise, Timothy Taylor's section on reggae in *Global Pop: World Music, World Markets* (New York: Routledge, 1997), 155–68, is another scholarly work that successfully considers the emerging pluralistic authenticities in reggae-dancehall-bhangra fusions in Britain, as evidenced by the highly successful South Asian Brit Apache Indian.

43 For some exceptional examples, see Carolyn Cooper, *Sound Clash: Jamaican Dancehall Culture at Large* (New York: Palgrave MacMillan, 2004); Heathcott, "Urban Spaces and Working-Class Expressions"; Robert Witmer, "'Local' and 'Foreign': The Popular Music Culture of Kingston, Jamaica, before Ska, Rock Steady, and Reggae," *Latin American Music Review* 8, 1 (1987): 1–25; and Daniel T. Neely, "'Mento, Jamaica's Original Music': Development, Tourism and the Nationalist Frame" (PhD diss., New

256 *Notes to pages 16–21*

York University, 2008), 96–100. See also Denis Constant, *Aux sources du reggae: Musique, société et politique en Jamaïque* (Roquevaire, France: Parenthèses, 1982); Erna Brodber and J. Edward Greene, *Reggae and Cultural Identity in Jamaica* (Mona, Jamaica: Institute of Social and Economic Research, University of the West Indies, 1988); Olive Lewin, *Rock It Come Over: The Folk Music of Jamaica* (Mona, Jamaica: University of the West Indies Press, 2000); Marylin Rouse, *Jamaican Folk Music: A Synthesis of Many Cultures* (Lewiston, NY: Edwin Mellen Press, 2000); Kenneth M. Bilby, "Gumbay, Myal, and the Great House: New Evidence on the Religious Background of Jonkonnu in Jamaica," *ACIJ Research Review* 4 (1999): 47–70; Daniel T. Neely, "Long Time Gal! *Mento* Is Back!," *The Beat* 20, 6 (2001): 38–42.

44 Erna Brodber, "Reggae as Black Space" (opening plenary delivered at the Global Reggae Conference, University of the West Indies, Mona, Jamaica, February 18, 2008).

45 Erna Brodber, as quoted in Basil Walters, "Reggae rinsed the word black and made it a sweet-smelling rose," *Jamaica Observer*, February 20, 2008.

Chapter 1: Hybridity and Jamaican Music

1 Walter Jekyll, ed., *Jamaican Song and Story: Annancy Stories, Digging Sings, Ring Tunes, and Dancing Tunes,* with an introduction by Alice Werner (London: David Nutt/Folk-Lore Society, 1907; repr., Mineola, NY: Dover, 2005 [1966]).

2 The Dragonaires and Sattalites' Jo Jo Bennett, for example, was an Alpha School alumnus; Lucea (Jamaica)'s Earle Heedram has a unique connection to folklorist Walter Jekyll; and the English-born historian Tomaz Jardim is the great-nephew of folklorist Astley Clerk.

3 See the chapter titled "The Melody of Europe, the Rhythm of Africa" in Rex M. Nettleford, *Mirror Mirror: Identity, Race and Protest in Jamaica* (Kingston, Jamaica: LMH, 1998, [1970]), 185.

4 See Caroline Muraldo, "The Caribbean Quadrille," https://www.muraldodc.com, 2007. Similarly, Hugh Paget, an English civil servant and Jamaican folk-song historian, said of the island's traditional music: "In the opinion of such students of folk music ... the tunes of most of the Jamaican songs derive ultimately from Europe and mainly from the British Isles; the rhythm, however, is African in origin, while the blend is essentially Jamaican." See Hugh Paget, as quoted in Noel Hawks, liner notes, various artists, *Take Me to Jamaica: The Story of Jamaican Mento,* Pressure Sounds, PSCD 51, 2006.

5 Neely correctly observed that the most egregious example of the African-European binary within Jekyll's collection was not, in fact, Jekyll's language but rather that found in Werner's, Broadwood's, and Myers's appendixes. See Daniel Tannehill Neely, "'Mento, Jamaica's Original Music': Development, Tourism and the Nationalist Frame" (PhD diss., New York University, 2008), 96–100.

6 Ibid., 7.

7 Kenneth M. Bilby, "The Caribbean as a Musical Region," in *Caribbean Contours,* ed. Sidney W. Mintz and Sally Price (Baltimore, MD: Johns Hopkins University Press, 1985), 181–218.

8 For examples, see Martha Beckwith, "The English Ballad in Jamaica: A Note upon the Origin of the Ballad Form," *Publications of the Modern Language Association of America*

39 (1924): 455–83, and *Jamaica Folk-Lore* (New York: American Folk-Lore Society, 1928). See also Helen Roberts, "Some Drum and Drum Rhythms of Jamaica," *Natural History* 24 (1924): 241–51; "A Study of Folk Song Variants Based on Field Work in Jamaica," *Journal of American Folk-Lore* 38, 148 (1925): 149–216; and "Possible Survivals of African Songs in Jamaica," *Musical Quarterly* 12, 3 (1926): 340–58.

9 In her work, Deborah Thomas discusses the "creole multiracial nationalist project" that existed in Jamaica's official policy-making at this time. This approach incorporated, as Thomas explains, "previously disparaged Afro-Jamaican cultural practices in order to foster a sense of national belonging among Jamaican's (majority black) population." See *Modern Blackness: Nationalism, Globilization and the Politics of Culture in Jamaica* (Durham, NC: Duke University Press, 2004), 4. See also Chris Gibson and John Connell, *Music and Tourism: On the Road Again* (Tonawanda, NY: Channel View Publications, 2005); John Urry, *The Tourist Gaze*, 2nd ed. (London: Sage, 2002); and Neely, "Mento, Jamaica's Original Music," 19.

10 As mentioned earlier, British bands, especially multiracial bands such as UB40, are afforded only a cursory mention, if they are treated at all, in many of these "authoritative" works. See Steve Barrow and Peter Dalton, *Reggae: The Rough Guide* (London: Rough Guides, 1997); Lloyd Bradley, *Reggae on CD* (London: Kylie Cathy, 1996) and *Bass Culture: When Reggae Was King* (London: Viking, 2000); Kevin O'Brien Chang and Wayne Chen, *Reggae Routes: The Story of Jamaican Music* (Philadelphia: Temple University Press, 1998); Michael De Koningh and Laurence Cane Honeysett, *Young, Gifted and Black: The Story of Trojan Records* (London: Sanctuary Publishing, 2003); Lou Gooden, *Reggae Heritage: Jamaica's Culture and Politics* (Kingston, Jamaica: Olivier Printery, 2003); Brian Jahn and Tom Weber, *Reggae Island: Jamaican Music in the Digital Age* (New York: Da Capo, 1998); David Katz, *Solid Foundation: An Oral History of Reggae* (New York: Bloomsbury, 2003); Colin Larkin, ed., *The Virgin Encyclopedia of Reggae* (London: Virgin Publishing, 1998); David Moskowitz, *Caribbean Popular Music: An Encyclopedia of Reggae, Mento, Ska, Rock Steady and Dancehall* (Westport, CT: Greenwood Press, 2006); Chris Potash, ed., *Reggae, Rasta, Revolution: Jamaican Music from Ska to Dub* (New York: Schirmer Books, 1997).

11 Hans Sloane, *Voyage to the Islands Madera, Barbados, Nieves, S. Christophers and Jamaica ...*, 2 vols. (London: B.M. for the author, 1707), lxviii–lvii.

12 For an excellent overview of the musical quotient of Sloane's visit to Jamaica, see Richard Cullen Rath, "African Music in Seventeenth-Century Jamaica: Cultural Transit and Transition," *William and Mary Quarterly,* third series, 50, 4 (1993): 700–26.

13 Sloane, *Voyage to the Islands,* xlviii–xlix, lii.

14 For further discussion, see J.H. Kwabena Nketia, *The Music of Africa* (New York: W.W. Norton, 1974) and *African Music in Ghana* (Evanston, IL: Northwestern University Press, 1963); Arthur M. Jones, *Studies in African Music* (Oxford: Oxford University Press, 1959); and Rose Brandel, *The Music of Central Africa* (The Hague: Martinus Nijhoff, 1962). For Kromanti drumming and a more recent discussion on the music of the Maroons, see Kenneth M. Bilby, "Kromanti Dance of the Windward Maroons of Jamaica," *Nieuwe West-Indische Gids* 55, 1–2 (1981): 52–101; Kenneth M. Bilby, liner notes, various artists, *Drums of Defiance: Maroon Music from the Earliest Free Black Communities of Jamaica,* Smithsonian/Folkways Recordings SF 40412, 1992.

258 *Notes to pages 23–25*

15 Patterson and Brathwaite took their cues from the mid-twentieth-century ethno-cultural debate known as the Herskovits and Frazier problem, associated with African survivals in the culture of the United States. See Edward Franklin Frazier, *The Negro Family in the United States,* rev. and abr. (Chicago: University of Chicago Press, 1966 [1948]); and Melville J. Herskovits, *The Myth of the Negro Past* (New York: Harper and Brothers, 1941).

16 Orlando Patterson, *The Sociology of Slavery: An Analysis of the Origins, Development and Structure of Negro Slave Society in Jamaica* (Cranbury, NJ: Associated University Presses, 1969).

17 Edward Brathwaite, *The Development of Creole Society in Jamaica, 1770–1820* (Oxford: Oxford University Press, 1971).

18 The Patterson-Brathwaite argument was refined further by anthropologists Sidney W. Mintz and Richard Price, who combined linguistic conceptions with cultural conceptions of creolization, as identified by Brathwaite. See Sydney W. Mintz and Richard Price, *The Birth of African-American Culture: An Anthropological Perspective* (Boston: Beacon Press, 1992).

19 Bilby, "Kromanti Dance," 52–101.

20 Rath, "African Music in Seventeenth-Century Jamaica."

21 Olive Lewin, *Rock It Come Over: The Folk Music of Jamaica* (Mona, Jamaica: University of the West Indies Press, 2000); Bilby, "The Caribbean as a Musical Region," 185; Olive Lewin, "Jamaican Folk Music," *Caribbean Quarterly* 14 (1968): 49–56; Neely, "Mento, Jamaica's Original Music," 68.

22 For further discussion of the relationship between the oppressor and the oppressed and how music behaved within it, see Norman Stolzoff, *Wake the Town and Tell the People: Dancehall Culture in Jamaica* (Durham, NC: Duke University Press, 2000); Bilby, "The Caribbean as a Musical Region"; Garth White, "Traditional Music Practice in Jamaica and Its Influence on the Birth of Modern Jamaican Music," *African Caribbean Institute of Jamaica Newsletter* 7 (1982); and Neely, "Mento, Jamaica's Original Music," 70.

23 For a further discussion on how mimicry was a means of survival in the Caribbean, see Michael Taussig, *Mimesis and Alterity* (New York: Routledge, 1993); and Richard Price, *The Convict and the Colonial* (Boston: Beacon Press, 1998).

24 Nyabinghi was a warrior princess from the area in Africa presently known as Rwanda. A cult was developed around her by those Ethiopians who faced off against Mussolini during Italy's invasion of Rwanda during the 1930s. Oswald Williams, a.k.a. Count Ossie, with his inimitable burru hand drum, is among the most famous Nyabinghi drummers. See Klive Walker, *Dubwise: Reasoning from the Reggae Underground* (Toronto: Insomniac Press, 2005), 118, and Vivien Goldman, *The Book of Exodus: The Making and Meaning of Bob Marley and the Wailers' Album of the Century* (New York: Three Rivers Press, 2006), 72.

25 Interview, Earle Heedram (a.k.a. the Mighty Pope), Richmond Hill, Ontario, December 13, 2010.

26 Jekyll, *Jamaican Song and Story.*

27 See C. Kitchener, "Letter to the editor," *Gleaner* (Jamaica), February 15, 1910, 4; Anonymous, "Bad blood disease," *Gleaner,* April 17, 1916, 4; Robert Craig, "The social

evil," *Gleaner,* April 18, 1916, 4; and Walter Jekyll, "Mr. Walter Jekyll and the matter of supernatural darkness," *Gleaner,* October 19, 1916, 11.

28 Jekyll was buried in the churchyard in Lucea, and his tombstone bears the epitaph "Musician, gardener, philosopher, teacher, and writer, he lived 34 years in this Island of his adopting, where he gave himself to the service of others and was greatly beloved by all who knew him." See John Archibald Venn, comp., *Alumni Cantabrigienses* (London: Cambridge University Press, 1922–54), s.v. "Jekyll, Walter." See also Archdeacon Simms, as quoted in Frank Cundall, "In Portrait Gallery of the Institute," *Gleaner* (Jamaica), August 19, 1929, 21.

29 Quoted in Cundall, "In Portrait Gallery," 22.

30 Jekyll's life passions drifted across larger currents such as the fledgling domain of folk-art collecting; the scientific theories of Charles Darwin, John Lubbock, and Edward Tylor; the "higher criticism" of the German philosophers; Spencerian rationalism; and, by virtue of his close relationship with McKay, questions about race in Jamaican society and elsewhere. Of all these various movements, however, Jekyll was most concerned with stemming the flow of modernity and its presumed attack on the folkways of the "peasantry" around the world. And just as his famous garden-designing sister, Gertrude Jekyll, documented the folkways of West Surrey, Jekyll, who moved to Jamaica in 1895, would do the same for people in the hilltops of Jamaica's Port Royal Mountains. See Gertrude Jekyll, *Old West Surrey: Some Notes and Memories* (London: Longmans, Green, 1904). The book was updated and retitled *Old English Household Life: Some Account of Cottage Objects and Country Folk* in 1939.

31 As far as I know, no comprehensive overview of Jekyll has been undertaken. Certain misapprehensions of the man are evidenced in the work of scholars such as Michael North, Paul Jay, and Rhonda Cobham. See Michael North, *The Dialect of Modernism: Race, Language and Twentieth-Century Literature* (New York: Oxford University Press, 1994); Paul Jay, "Hybridity, Identity and Cultural Commerce in Claude McKay's Banana Bottom," *Callaloo* 22, 1 (1999): 176–94; and Rhonda Cobham, "Jekyll and Claude: The Erotics of Patronage in Claude McKay's Banana Bottom," in *Queer Diasporas,* ed. Cindy Patton and Benigno Sánchez-Eppler (Durham, NC: Duke University Press, 2000), 55–78. For more charitable interpretations of Jekyll's role in McKay's life, see Josh Gosciak, "Between Diaspora and Internationalism: Claude McKay and the Making of a Black Public Intellectual" (PhD diss., City University of New York, 2002); and Wayne F. Cooper, *Claude McKay: Rebel Sojourner in the Harlem Renaissance – A Biography* (Baton Rouge: Louisiana State University Press, 1987).

32 Even Pope was pleased with the contract, which he found to be fair and good. There was a significant advance. See interview, Earle Heedram.

33 George Mullins, a Jamaican contemporary of Heedram, looked forward to Jekyll's daily performance. At precisely 1 p.m. each day, and with the windows wide open, Jekyll played his only luxury, a grand piano. Mullins was among the people Peter Kiernan and Janet Morgan interviewed during their search for Jekyll's lost garden. See Peter Kiernan, "Walter Jekyll and His Jamaica Garden" (slide show lecture delivered at Garden History Society, Winter Lectures, the Gallery, London, February 2, 2005); and Cundall, "In Portrait Gallery," 21. Rusea's High School was founded by

260 *Notes to pages 26–27*

Martin Rusea, a Frenchman who loved Lucea and left a handsome amount of money to the school named for him. See interview, Earle Heedram.

34 Cundall, "In Portrait Gallery," 21; and Kiernan, "Walter Jekyll and His Jamaica Garden."

35 Today, *Jamaican Song and Story* still commands space on the reading lists of folklore, ethnomusicology, Caribbean, and black Atlantic courses throughout the world. Wisconsin, Berkeley, St. Andrews, Oxford, Utah State, City University of New York, University of Florida, and, of course, University of the West Indies are among the many universities currently offering courses that have Jekyll's work on the reading list.

36 There are many "Empire-First" examples that serve as antitheses to Jekyll's life and influence in Jamaica. For a useful work on the Indigenous peoples of New Zealand and their introduction to the British Empire – a topic that parallels the complexities of the Jamaican experience in many ways – see Tony Ballatyne, "Mr. Peal's Archive: Mobility and Exchange in Histories of Empire," in *Archive Stories: Facts, Fictions, and the Writing of History,* ed. Antoinette Burton (Durham, NC: Duke University Press, 2005), 87–110.

37 For further discussion, see Gosciak, "Between Diaspora and Internationalism"; and Cooper, *Claude McKay.*

38 In his author's note, McKay declares that Gensir was the only nonimaginary character in his book. Almost all the passages that illustrate Gensir's manner, opinion, and general way of being ring true with existing historical documents about Jekyll. Consider McKay's recollection of the real Jekyll alongside the passage quoted here: "When I sent them on to Mr. Jekyll, he wrote back to say that each new one was more beautiful than the last. Beauty! A short while before I never thought that any beauty could be found in the Jamaica dialect. Now this Englishman had discovered beauty and I too could see where my poems were beautiful." See Claude McKay, *My Green Hills of Jamaica* (Kingston, Jamaica: Heinemann Educational Books, 1979), 69; and *Banana Bottom* (New York: Harper and Row, 1933; repr., London: Serpent's Tail, 2005), author's note. Michael North, however, believes that Gensir is a composite, a "mixture of the Jekyll of 1912 and the McKay of 1932." See North, *The Dialect of Modernism,* 122.

39 Between 1864 and 1866, Jekyll was educated at Harrow, and while he openly rebelled at school, he proved to be an exceptional scholar who spoke six languages and was at the top of his class. Jekyll later completed a bachelor of arts and a master of arts at Trinity College, Cambridge, and graduated with honours. Jekyll continued on a respectable path and was ordained as a deacon in 1874. Later still, he became a priest and was curate of Heydon from 1874 until 1877. Soon afterwards, he was placed in a minor canonry at Worcester Cathedral, followed by a short stint as a chaplain in Malta in 1879. It was around this time that Jekyll's skepticism overrode any desire to remain in the service of the church or to follow his family's wishes. For further discussion, see Susan Budd, *Varieties of Unbelief: Atheists and Agnostics in English Society, 1850–1960* (London: Heinemann Educational Books, 1977).

40 According to Peter Kiernan and Janet Morgan, Jekyll likely visited North's Jamaican exhibit at Kew Gardens in the 1880s. See Kiernan, "Walter Jekyll and His Jamaica Garden." See also Royal Botanic Gardens, Kew, *Marianne North at Kew Gardens* (Exeter: Webb and Bower/Royal Botanic Gardens, Kew, 1990); and Marianne North,

Recollections of a Happy Life: Being the Autobiography of Marianne North, edited by her sister, Mrs. John Addington Symonds (Charlottesville: University Press of Virginia, 1993 [1894]).

41 Annabel Freyburg, "Edward and Julia Jekyll and Their Family," in *Gertrude Jekyll: Essays on the Life of a Working Amateur,* ed. Michael Tooley and Primrose Arnander (Durham, NC: Michaelmas Books, 1995), 41.

42 Cooper, Cobham, North, Gosciak, and Jay have, however, chosen to take Jekyll's homosexuality for granted. This leap of faith is likely based on Jekyll's relationship with Colonel Ernest Boyle. Jekyll spent many summer months in Norway fishing for trout with Boyle, and the colonel moved to Jamaica to be near Jekyll in 1908. On a visit back to England during the First World War, Boyle rejoined his regiment and was killed at the front in 1917. See Cundall, "In Portrait Gallery," 21.

43 McKay's biographer, Wayne Cooper, offered Sir Richard Burton, Cecil Rhodes, and Lord H.H. Kitchener among his antithetical examples to Jekyll. Cooper, *Claude McKay,* 31.

44 Julia Jekyll died in 1896, and with the inheritance money, Jekyll was able to permanently settle in Jamaica's Blue Mountains. The earthquake of 1907, however, claimed Jekyll's first Jamaican house in the hills, and according to his brother Herbert, he was lucky to escape death in the ensuing landslide. Following the quake, Jekyll gave his headman his property and moved to Mavis Bank near Kingston. Later still, he moved to Hanover and, finally, to Bower Hill near Riverside, where he lived in a house built for him by his niece Millicent von Maltzahn. Millicent, the daughter of Jekyll's eldest brother, Edward, moved to Jamaica in the late 1920s to take care of Jekyll following the death of her husband, Baron Erich von Maltzahn. See Cundall, "In Portrait Gallery," 21; Freyburg, "Edward and Julia Jekyll," 34; and Kiernan, "Walter Jekyll and His Jamaica Garden."

45 McKay, *My Green Hills,* 71.

46 Both Walter and Gertrude were close to William Robinson, founder of the Arts and Crafts movement that so inspired the siblings' horticultural approach. Walter contributed several articles to Robinson's journal, *The Garden,* which Gertrude edited. From an "our man in Kingston" approach, Jekyll addressed all manner of issues regarding the Jamaican garden. He wrote some 37,000 words on Jamaican plant life for both local and British publications and also cultivated an herbarium collection that boasted over 8,125 specimens. See "Searching for hidden gardens: Morgan and Kiernan in Ja," *Jamaica Gleaner,* October 10, 2004, 26–27; Kiernan, "Walter Jekyll and His Jamaica Garden"; Charles Dennis Adams, *Flowering Plants of Jamaica* (Mona, Jamaica: University of the West Indies, 1972).

47 Jekyll, however, resisted the musical-nationalism debate. According to McKay, Jekyll "hated the British Empire." See McKay, *My Green Hills,* 71.

48 Internationalism had currency among Fabian socialists, suffragettes, and pacifists. See Gosciak, *Between Diaspora and Internationalism,* 3.

49 Stuart Hall, "Introduction: Who Needs 'Identity'?," in *Questions of Cultural Identity,* ed. Stuart Hall and Paul du Gay (London: Sage, 1996), 1–17.

50 Colin C. Eldridge, *The Imperial Experience: From Carlyle to Forster* (London: Macmillan Press, 1996), 142.

51 Scientific racism was a concept developed by James Hunt, who founded the Anthropological Society of London in 1863. See ibid., 158. See also Claude McKay, *A Long Way from Home* (New York: Arno Press/New York Times, 1969), 14.

52 See Edward B. Tylor, "Wild Men and Beast Children," *Anthropological Review* 1 (1863): 21–32; Margaret T. Hogden, *The Doctrine of Survivals* (London: Allenson, 1936), 57; and Laavanyan Ratnapalan, "E.B. Tylor and the Problem of Primitive Culture," *History and Anthropology* 19, 2 (2008): 131–42.

53 For an antithetical view on the superiority of the Anglo-Saxon race, see Eldridge, *The Imperial Experience,* 141.

54 In reference to the caste system at play in Jamaica, Jekyll confessed that "white gentlemen" count "many points in the estimation of the Negro." In his field notes reviewing the digging sing "Sambo Lady," Jekyll demonstrates his intimacy with the island's caste system: "A Sambo is the child of a brown mother and a black father, brown being a cross between black and white. The Sambo lady, very proud of the strain of white in her blood, turns up her nose at the black man. She wants a white man for a husband. Failing to find one, she will not marry at all." Jekyll also observed that "Blacks do not mind calling themselves niggers, but a White man must not call them so. To say 'black nehgher' is an offence not to be forgiven." He also warned that it is "a mistake to suppose that the black man is either stupid or lazy." See Jekyll, *Jamaican Song and Story,* 76, 176–77, 189, 227.

55 There are some paternalistic overtones in Jekyll's appraisal of the island and its people: Ledhu is his "coolie" gardener; Headlam, his "head man." Cobham's reading of Jekyll is particularly interesting, circumscribed as it is by her predetermined suppositions about the man and how they support an accepted orthodoxy about white men in the far reaches about the Empire. But as Cooper counters, "Walter Jekyll surely ranked among the more interesting Englishmen found in Queen Victoria's far-flung possessions." Moreover, while the ethnographer was in pursuit of the "primitive," he was already home. And when Victoria had been dead for nearly thirty years, Jekyll remained there, in the hilltops of Jamaica. See Cobham, "Jekyll and Claude"; Cooper, *Claude McKay,* 22–23; and Walter Jekyll, "In the Port Royal Mountains, Jamaica," *The Garden: An Illustrated Weekly Journal of Gardening in All Its Branches,* September 14, 1901, 180, and "Aloe Vera," *The Garden: An Illustrated Weekly Journal of Gardening in All Its Branches,* September 7, 1901, 160.

56 Robert Huttenback identifies the significance of the Natal formula for the immigration policies of the self-governing British colonies in *Racism and Empire: White Settlers and Coloured Immigrants in the British Self-Governing Colonies, 1830–1910* (Ithaca, NY: Cornell University Press, 1976) and "The British Empire as a 'White Man's Country': Racial Attitudes and Immigration Legislation in the Colonies of White Settlement," *Journal of British Studies* 13, 1 (1973): 108–37.

57 Alistair Bonnett, "Whiteness in Crisis," *History Today,* December 2000, 38–39.

58 Ibid., 39.

59 Lord Alfred Milner, "Address to the Municipal Congress, Johannesburg," May 18, 1903, in *The Milner Papers: South Africa,* vol. 2, *1899–1905,* ed. Cecil Headlam (London: Cassell, 1933), 467.

Notes to pages 30–32   263

60 Jekyll, *Jamaican Song and Story,* liii.
61 The dressing up of objectionable lyrics and themes in so-called rescued folk songs was something that most collectors were aware of. See Vic Gammon, "Folk Song Collecting in Sussex and Surrey: 1843–1914," *History Workshop Journal* 10 (1980): 71; and Jekyll, *Jamaican Song and Story,* liii.
62 Jekyll, *Jamaican Song and Story,* liii.
63 See Cheryl Ryman, "Astley Clerk 1868–1944: Patriot and Cultural Pioneer," *Jamaica Journal* 18, 4 (1985–86): 17–26; and Peta Gay Jensen, *The Last Colonials: The Story of Two European Families in Jamaica* (London: Radcliffe Press, 2005), 1.
64 Astley Clerk, *The Music and Musical Instruments of Jamaica: A Lecture Delivered at: Edmondson Hall (Wesley Guild), 19 November 1913; and Jamaica Institute (Kingston Athenaeum), 15 December 1913* (Kingston, Jamaica: self-published, 1914). See also Ryman, "Astley Clerk," 17; Jensen, *The Last Colonials,* 68.
65 Clerk, *The Music and Musical Instruments of Jamaica,* dedication page; Ryman, "Astley Clerk," 22.
66 Ivy Baxter, *The Arts of an Island: The Development of the Culture and of the Folk and Creative Arts in Jamaica, 1494–1962 (Independence)* (Metuchen, NJ: Scarecrow Press, 1970).
67 For an example, see Neely, "Mento, Jamaica's Original Music," 91–94.
68 See Ryman, "Astley Clerk," 22; Jensen, *The Last Colonials,* 70.
69 "On Our Jamaican Poets," *Daily Gleaner* (Jamaica), April 16, 1917.
70 See Ryman, "Astley Clerk," 24; Jensen, *The Last Colonials,* 70.
71 Joseph G. Moore, George Eaton Simpson, and Tamara and Josef Obrebski were among the foreign anthropologists who worked independently (or, as was the case with the Obrebskis, for the United Nations) and greatly informed the cultural aspect of Jamaica's developmental movement. See Neely, "Mento, Jamaica's Original Music," 23.
72 Ibid., 85. Jekyll's work influenced both Martha Beckwith and Helen Roberts, who were in search of the English ballad in Jamaican music. Later, Jamaican scholars and folklorists such as Philip Sherlock, Louise Bennett, and Rex Nettleford expressed their gratitude, through prefaces, to Jekyll for his ethnographic work in *Jamaican Song and Story.*
73 At Cambridge, Jekyll had been a member of the Cambridge University Musical Society. The famous Irish composer Sir Charles Villiers Stanford served as the society's conductor. It was there that Jekyll, as a member of the male chorus, took part in the English debut of Brahms's "Rhapsodie, Opus 53" and Stanford's "The Forty-Sixth Psalm, Opus 8." Jekyll's father, Edward, had been a virtuosic flautist, and his mother, Julia, possessed a strong contralto. As the Jekylls were very well connected, the composer Mendelssohn often accompanied Julia on piano at the Jekyll home. In Milan, Jekyll studied voice with the Italian master and singing teacher Francesco Lamperti. In 1884, Jekyll translated one of Lamperti's treatises on the traditional *bel canto* approach to singing. Henceforth, Jekyll's knowledge of the Italian libretto would inform not only the way he taught music but also the way he collected his ethnographic data. Jekyll marked the Italian soundings of certain words in Jamaican Patois: "The *o's* have the open sound of Italian, and not the close sound of English." Upon returning from

264 *Notes to pages 32–33*

the Continent, Jekyll settled in London but then moved to Birmingham, where he taught music and gave "penny singing lessons" to the poor. Jekyll then moved to Bournemouth and befriended Robert Louis Stevenson, who might have, as the family's plausible legend goes, asked Jekyll if he could use his name for his book *The Strange Case of Dr. Jekyll and Mr. Hyde*. Jekyll's final English home was in Newton Abbott, in Devonshire, where he lived for several years before leaving for Jamaica. See "Charles Villiers Stanford," *Musical Times and Singing Class Circular* 39, 670 (1898): 785; Cambridge University Musical Society, "Concert Programme," May 22, 1877, and December 3, 1877; Primrose Arnander, "Jekyll Family History," in Tooley and Arnander, *Gertrude Jekyll*, 18; Freyburg, "Edward and Julia Jekyll," 25; and Giovanni Battista Lamperti, *The Art of Singing: According to Ancient Tradition and Personal Experience – Technical Rules and Advice to Pupils and Artists*, translated by Walter Jekyll (London: G. Ricordi, 1884).

74 McKay, *Banana Bottom*, 240–41.

75 Jekyll, *Jamaican Song and Story*, liii.

76 McKay, *Banana Bottom*, 120.

77 Gammon, "Folk Song Collecting in Sussex and Surrey," 83.

78 Lucy Broadwood, "Songs from the Collection of Lucy E. Broadwood," *Journal of the Folk Song Society* 1, 4 (1902): 140. Ralph Vaughan Williams, too, was documenting the songs of the "more primitive people of England," whom the composer regarded as vanishing ghosts. See Ralph Vaughan Williams, as quoted in Ursula Vaughan Williams, *R.V.W: A Biography of Ralph Vaughan Williams* (London: Oxford University Press, 1965), 88; and Gammon, "Folk Song Collecting in Sussex and Surrey," 83.

79 Jekyll, *Jamaican Song and Story*, 5–6.

80 Ibid., preface.

81 Perhaps the two most famous pieces from Jekyll's collection are "There's a Black Boy in the Ring" and "Linstead Market." Boney M.'s "Brown Girl in the Ring" was a B-side to their version of "Rivers of Babylon," and it became one of the best selling singles in UK chart history. "Linstead Market" remains an unofficial anthem of Jamaica's slavery days. See Stephen Thomas Erlewine, *All Music Guide*, July 5, 2009; Jekyll, "There's a Black Boy in the Ring" and "Linstead Market," in *Jamaican Song and Story*, 208, 219; and Boney M., "Rivers of Babylon"/"Brown Girl in the Ring," Hansa Records/ Sire Records/Atlantic Records, 1978.

82 Slavery came to an end in Jamaica in 1834. See Philip Sherlock, "The Living Roots," in Jekyll, *Jamaican Song and Story*, vii–viii.

83 Frank Cundall, a contemporary of and friend to Jekyll, also discussed various aspects of Jamaican folk songs and stories in the journal *Folklore*. Cundall was appointed the secretary and librarian of the Institute of Jamaica in 1890. Frank Cundall, "Folk-Lore of the Negroes of Jamaica," *Folklore* 15–16 (1904–5): vol. 15: 87–94, 206–14, 450–56; vol. 16: 68–77.

84 "Anansi" is the Tshi (the language of the Ashanti) word for spider, and a character heavily featured in the folk traditions of Africa's west coast. For further discussion, see Alice Werner, introduction, in Jekyll, *Jamaican Song and Story*, xxiii–lii.

85 Rex Nettleford, "Jamaican Song and Story and the Theatre," in Jekyll, *Jamaican Song and Story*, xiii.

86 "Little Sally Water" or "Sally Water" was the most common of the dancing tunes. See Jekyll, *Jamaican Song and Story,* 190–91. See also Alice B. Gomme, *The Traditional Games of England, Scotland and Ireland: With Tunes, Singing Rhymes and Methods of Playing according to the Variants Extant and Recorded in Different Parts of the Kingdom* (London: Nutt, 1894), 149.

87 McKay suggested that "minto" may be a native name for the minuet, which raises the question of the relationship between mintoes and mento music. See McKay, *Banana Bottom,* 123–24.

88 Ibid., 124. North argues that the real Jekyll would not have endorsed borrowing or stealing for art's sake. Gosciak, however, disagrees, suggesting that the team of Jekyll and McKay viewed borrowing, through their training in Annancy, as something that was "second nature, particularly when transcribing the songs of a culture from the oral tradition." See North, *The Dialect of Modernism,* 122; and Gosciak, *Between Diaspora and Internationalism,* 76.

89 Jekyll also lamented that Jamaican blacks had "adopted many of the most trivial of English superstitions." See Jekyll, *Jamaican Song and Story,* 261–62, xlix, 87.

90 Ibid., 216.

91 In the mid-1990s, Robert Young, for example, called for a model to review the cultural commerce that transpired between different cultures to "map and shadow the complexities of its generative and destructive processes." Yet Tylor had located some of these same "degrading and destroying influences" in his work 130 years earlier. See Robert J.C. Young, *Colonial Desire: Hybridity in Theory, Culture and Race* (London: Routledge, 1995), 5; and Edward B. Tylor, *Researches into the Early History of Mankind and the Development of Civilization* (London: John Murray, 1865).

92 Jekyll, *Jamaican Song and Story,* 216. Charles Samuel Myers confirmed Broadwood's assessment that Jamaicans had learned many of the songs via sailors' shanties but was careful to stress that "a community does not adopt exotic music without at the same time exercising selection." Charles Samuel Myers, "Traces of African Melody in Jamaica," in Jekyll, *Jamaican Song and Story,* 284.

93 Neely, "Mento, Jamaica's Original Music," 35.

94 Ibid., 104.

95 Ibid., 108–9. See also Beckwith, "The English Ballad in Jamaica," and *Jamaica Folk-Lore*; and Roberts, "Some Drum and Drum Rhythms of Jamaica," "A Study of Folk Song Variants Based on Field Work in Jamaica," and "Possible Survivals of African Songs in Jamaica."

96 See Lucy E. Broadwood, "English Airs and Motifs in Jamaica," in Jekyll, *Jamaican Song and Story,* 285–88. In his work, Neely aptly illustrates the dangers associated with the racialization of musical influences in Jamaican musicology. His claim that the melody of Europe – though touted in the spare body of literature relating to Jamaican musics – was not present within "the corresponding historical consciousness among its practitioners" is less convincing. See Neely, "Mento, Jamaica's Original Music," 109.

97 The eleven are "Yung-kyum-pyung," "King David," "Blackbird and Woss-Woss," "Mr. Bluebeard," "Man-Crow," "Saylan," "Tacoma and the Old-Witch Girl," "The Three Pigs," "Pretty Poll," "Open Sesame," and "The Three Sisters." See Werner, introduction, in Jekyll, *Jamaican Song and Story,* xxvi.

266   *Notes to pages 35–38*

98   In *Banana Bottom,* Gensir, for instance, explains to Bita that he thinks some of the "famous European fables have their origin in Africa." Alice Werner clarified that "The Three Sisters," along with "Gaulin," "Yellow Snake," "John Crow," and "Devil and the Princess," shared an obvious African prototype. See ibid., xxvi, xxx, 1; and McKay, *Banana Bottom,* 124.

99   The main players in the West African version of "The Hare and the Tortoise," for example, were replaced by a toad and a donkey, largely owing to the fact that Jamaicans, at least at the turn of the twentieth century and before, would not have been familiar with the land tortoise and the sea turtle. See Werner, introduction, in Jekyll, *Jamaican Song and Story,* xxxv, xxxviii.

100   Charles Samuel Myers, "Traces of African Melody in Jamaica," in Jekyll, *Jamaican Song and Story,* 283–84.

101   Ibid., 284.

102   Some of the respondents here do talk of the European, or at least British, quotient in reggae.

103   Interview, Peter Holung, Newmarket, ON, February 3, 2011.

104   Goldman, *The Book of Exodus,* 34.

105   Ibid.

106   Interview, Leo Cripps, Calgary, January 9, 2011. See also Goldman, *The Book of Exodus,* 34.

107   Hawks, liner notes, *Take Me to Jamaica.*

108   "Sansa" is a generic term for instruments that have wooden or metal keys attached to a sounding board and are plucked or sometimes struck with the finger. See Astley Clerk, "Extract from the *Music and Instruments of Jamaica," Jamaica Journal* 9, 2–3 (1975): 59–67; and Rath, "African Music in Seventeenth-Century Jamaica," 718.

109   Muraldo, "The Caribbean Quadrille."

110   Ibid.

111   Tom Murray, ed., *Folk Songs of Jamaica* (Oxford: Oxford University Press, 1951); and Hawks, liner notes, *Take Me to Jamaica.* Bahamian goombay and the Dominican Republic's merengue are examples of other musics in the Caribbean that approximate the rudiments of mento. More commonly, mento has been called Jamaica's calypso. See Marjorie Whylie, *Mento: The What and the How* (Kingston, Jamaica: Whylie Communications, 2000), 2. For an incredibly detailed discussion of mento, see www.mentomusic.com.

112   This same attitude would occur with the rise of ska music in the 1960s. Ernest Ranglin told me that he used a pseudonym on his early ska recordings for fear that his parents would find out what he had been up to. See John Jason Collins Wilson, "The Fast Bowling Ernest Ranglin," *Word Magazine,* Caribana edition, July 2006; and "Ernest Ranglin: Reggae Pioneer," *Word Magazine,* December 2005.

113   Indeed, the music also found currency with British and American tourists, who often mistook the music to be calypso. See Stephen Davis and Peter Simon, *Reggae Bloodlines: In Search of the Music and Culture of Jamaica* (New York: Da Capo Press, 1992 [1977]), 9–14; and Heathcott, "Urban Spaces and Working-Class Expressions," 188.

114   Interview, Fergus Hambleton, Toronto, July 10, 2010.

115   Interview, Jeffrey Holdip, Toronto, January 20, 2011.

Notes to pages 38–41 267

116 Nettleford, "Jamaican Song and Story and the Theatre," xiv.
117 For just a sample of the many examples, see Yellowman, "Zungguzuggugguzungguzeng," *Yellowman Most Wanted,* Greensleeves, 2007 [1982–87]), 12-inch mix; Bob Marley and the Wailers, "No Woman, No Cry," *Live!,* Tuff Gong/Island Records, 1975; Eric "Monty" Morris, "Penny Reel," *Intensified: Original Ska, 1962–66,* Mango Records, 1979 [1964]; and Derrick Harriott, with Audley Williams and Combo, "John Tom," *Dip and Fall Back: Dr. Kinsey to Haile Selassie, Classic Jamaican Mento,* WIRL Records, 1965/Trojan Records, 2005.
118 Broadwood, "English Airs and Motifs in Jamaica," 14, 286; and Francis James Child, *The English and Scottish Popular Ballads* (New York: Dover Publications 1965 [1904]).
119 Broadwood, "English Airs and Motifs in Jamaica," 26, 286. See also Lucy E. Broadwood and J.A. Fuller Maitland, "There Was a Lady in the West" and "Scarborough Fair," *English County Songs* (London: Leadenhall Press, 1893); and Frank Kidson, *Traditional Tunes: A Collection of Ballad Airs* (Wakefield, UK: S.R. Publishers, 1970). See also "The Lover's Tasks," in Sabine Baring-Gould and H. Fleetwood Sheppard, *Songs of the West: Folk Songs of Devon and Cornwall Collected from the Mouths of the People,* vol. 48 (London: Patey and Willis, 1889–91/Methuen, 1895), 96–97.
120 Broadwood, "English Airs and Motifs in Jamaica," 96, 287. See also John Stokoe and Samuel Reay, *Songs and Ballads of Northern England,* collected and edited by John Stokoe; harmonized and arranged for pianoforte by Samuel Reay (Darby, PA: Norwood Editions, 1973 [1892]).
121 Broadwood, "English Airs and Motifs in Jamaica," 54, 59, 287. See also Broadwood and Maitland, *English County Songs*; and Child, *The English and Scottish Popular Ballads,* 346.
122 Broadwood, "English Airs and Motifs in Jamaica," 65, 287. See also Broadwood and Maitland, *English County Songs*; and Baring-Gould and Sheppard, *Songs of the West.*
123 Broadwood, "English Airs and Motifs in Jamaica," 187, 288.
124 Ibid., 267, 288.
125 Ibid., 209, 218, 288.
126 Ibid., 227, 264, 288.
127 "Gee Oh Mother Mac," in Jekyll, *Jamaican Song and Story,* 173.
128 Rombas, the story's hero, kills the whale that has swallowed the girl and cuts out the mammal's tongue. See "Man-Crow," in Jekyll, *Jamaican Song and Story,* 54.
129 Broadwood offers 1876 as the date when "La Mandolinata" was composed. Broadwood, "English Airs and Motifs in Jamaica," 91, 271, 287. See also Alfred Moffat and Frank Kidson, *Children's Songs of Long Ago* (London: Augener, 1905), 42.
130 Broadwood, "English Airs and Motifs in Jamaica"; and Jekyll, *Jamaican Song and Story,* 225, 288.
131 Jekyll, *Jamaican Song and Story,* 6.
132 Lewin, *Rock It Come Over.*
133 Jekyll, *Jamaican Song and Story,* 158.
134 A thorough rereading of Jekyll's collection reveals linkages between digging sings such as "Me Know the Man," "Oh John Thomas!," and "Rub Him Down Joe" with modern Jamaican theatre. See Nettleford, "Jamaican Song and Story and the Theatre," xv.

268 *Notes to pages 41–46*

135 "Little Sally Water," in Jekyll, *Jamaican Song and Story,* 190–91. See also Gomme, *The Traditional Games of England, Scotland and Ireland,* 149.
136 Jekyll, *Jamaican Song and Story,* 256.
137 Neely, "'Mento, Jamaica's Original Music," 80–81.
138 Clerk dated it as c. 1857. See Astley Clerk, unpublished manuscript, c. 1910s, National Library, Kingston, Jamaica; and Neely, "Mento, Jamaica's Original Music," 81.
139 Interview, Ranford Williams, Toronto, January 20, 2011.
140 "Give us the Queen!," *Gleaner* (Jamaica), June 28, 2011. See also Kenyon Wallace, "Most residents think Jamaica 'better off as a British colony,' poll suggests," *Toronto Star,* June 29, 2011.

Chapter 2: Music of the Black Atlantic

1 See Robert Witmer, "'Local' and 'Foreign': The Popular Music Culture of Kingston, Jamaica, before Ska, Rock Steady, and Reggae," *Latin American Music Review* 8, 1 (1987): 18–19.
2 The resultant religious music arrived at what Heathcott classified as a wholly new Afro-Caribbean sound. See Joseph Heathcott, "Urban Spaces and Working-Class Expressions across the Black Atlantic: Tracing the Routes of Ska," *Radical History Review* 87 (Fall 2003): 188.
3 Witmer, "'Local' and 'Foreign.'"
4 As Walker confirmed, "It was virtually impossible for a child to grow up in Jamaica during the '50s, '60s, and '70s and not be intimately familiar with Bennett's work in creating art out of the people's language." See Klive Walker, *Dubwise: Reasoning from the Reggae Underground* (Toronto: Insomniac Press, 2005), 68, 73.
5 Louise Bennett, "Bans A' Killin," in Louise Bennett, *Aunty Roachy Seh,* edited by Mervyn Morris (Kingston, Jamaica: Sangster's, [1944] 1993), 4–5; Walker, *Dubwise,* 70–72.
6 "War Down a Monkland," c. 1865, in *Jamaican Song and Story: Annancy Stories, Digging Sings, Ring Tunes, and Dancing Tunes,* ed. Walter Jekyll, with an introduction by Alice Werner (London: David Nutt/Folk-Lore Society, 1907; repr., Mineola, NY: Dover, 2005 [1966]), 187; Bob Marley and the Wailers, "Blackman Redemption," *Confrontation,* Tuff Gong/Island Records 422–846 207–1, 1983.
7 Louise Bennett, "Me and Annancy," in Jekyll, *Jamaican Song and Story,* xi.
8 Walker, *Dubwise,* 74.
9 As Klive Walker explains in his essay "Rain a Fall, Dutty Tuff: The Relationship between Louise Bennett's Mento Verse and Bob Marley's Reggae Poetry," "Bob Marley's poetry, in some ways, is like the post-colonial successor to Bennett's mento poetry." See Walker, *Dubwise,* 68.
10 Interview, Rupert "Ojiji" Harvey, Toronto, September 6, 2010.
11 Ibid.
12 Messenjah, "Emanuelle Road," *Cool Operator,* Version VLP-001, 1987; Louise Bennett, "Manuel Ground," *Children's Jamaican Songs and Games,* Folkways Records FW07250/ FC 7250, 1957.
13 Interview, Rupert "Ojiji" Harvey.

Notes to pages 47–50   269

14 Heathcott, "Urban Spaces and Working-Class Expressions," 188.

15 Interview, Carol Brown, Bolton, ON, January 30, 2011.

16 Interview, Mike Smith, Brampton, ON, July 15, 2010.

17 Central Intelligence Agency, "Jamaica," *The World Factbook* (Washington, DC: CIA, 2013–14). See also CARICOM Capacity Development Programme, *2000 Round of Population and Housing Census Project: National Census Report, Jamaica* (Greater Georgetown, Guyana: Regional Statistics Sub-Programme Information and Communication Technologies Caribbean Community, 2000); and US Department of State, *July–December, 2010 International Religious Freedom Report: Jamaica* (Washington, DC: Bureau of Democracy, Human Rights, and Labor, 2011).

18 Vivien Goldman, *The Book of Exodus: The Making and Meaning of Bob Marley and the Wailers' Album of the Century* (New York: Three Rivers Press, 2006), 71–72, 76.

19 Adebayo Ojo, *Bob Marley: Songs of African Redemption* (Lagos: Malthouse Press, 2000), 39.

20 Gregory Stephens, *On Racial Frontiers: The New Culture of Frederick Douglass, Ralph Ellison, and Bob Marley* (Cambridge: Cambridge University Press, 1999), 149.

21 See Goldman, *The Book of Exodus,* 70–76.

22 See Willi Williams, "Armagideon Time," Studio One SO 0099, 1978; the Clash, *Black Market Clash,* Epic WPE38540, 1980.

23 The "obeah-man" or "bush doctor" dealt in Jamaican voodoo, or magic, and sorcery. See Jekyll's field notes, *Jamaican Song and Story,* 241.

24 See Werner, introduction, in Jekyll, *Jamaican Song and Story,* xxvi.

25 See, for example, "Oh Selina!," in Jekyll, *Jamaican Song and Story,* 174.

26 Ernie Smith, "Duppy or a Gunman," various artists, *Original Wild Flower Reggae Hits,* Federal/Wildflower LP 367, 1974.

27 Wolfgang Laade, *Die Situation von Musikleben und Musikforschung in den Laendern Afrikas und Asiens und die neuen Aufgaben der Musikethnologie* (Tutzing, Germany: Hans Schneider, 1969), 214; and Witmer, "'Local' and 'Foreign,'" 3.

28 Heathcott, "Urban Spaces and Working-Class Expressions," 188.

29 "History," http://alphaboysschool.org.

30 Compiled from Mark Williams, liner notes, various artists, *Alpha Boys' School: Music in Education,* Trojan Records 06076–80550–2, 2006.

31 Interview, Jo Jo Bennett, Toronto, October 19, 2010; and Williams, liner notes, *Alpha Boys' School.*

32 The Alpha Boys Band served as a feeder for larger Jamaican wind ensembles, including the Jamaican Constabulary Band, the Jamaican Regiment Band, the West India Regiment Band, and, perhaps most famously, the Jamaica Military Band. For further discussion, see "Seventy-Five Years Helping to Build Jamaica," *Gleaner* (Jamaica), August 29, 1965, 13; Ivy Baxter, *The Arts of an Island: The Development of the Culture and of the Folk and Creative Arts in Jamaica, 1494–1962 (Independence)* (Metuchen, NJ: Scarecrow Press, 1970); and Williams, liner notes, *Alpha Boys' School.*

33 "History," http://alphaboysschool.org.

34 As Trojan Records' Mark Williams confessed: "Alpha would give us the deepest sense of Jamaica's boundless musicality, the essential ingredient in all that was to

270   *Notes to pages 50–52*

come from its studios during the ensuing decades." See Williams, liner notes, *Alpha Boys' School.*

35 Abyssinians, "Forward on to Zion/Satta A Massagana," Klik KL 631, 1977; and Burning Spear, "Marcus Garvey," Capo Records CA-070, 1974.

36 Interview, David Kingston, Toronto, September 1, 2010.

37 See Williams, liner notes, *Alpha Boys' School.*

38 Sonny Bradshaw, quoted in ibid.

39 For further discussion on the importance of Australian-born Pamela O'Gorman and how her pedagogical approach influenced the musical instruction of indigenous Jamaican music during the 1970s and 1980s, see Anne Hickling-Hudson, "Postcolonialism, Hybridity and Transferability: The Contribution of Pamela O'Gorman to Music Education in the Caribbean," *Caribbean Journal of Education* 1–2 (2000): 36–55.

40 See Witmer, "'Local' and 'Foreign,'" 11.

41 Harriott was able to realize his vision through the help of the St. Vincent-born trumpeter Shake Keane, Scottish pianist Pat Smythe, English drummer Phil Seamen, and fellow Jamaican and bassist Coleridge Goode, who was still gigging in and around London right up until his death in 2015 at the age of 100. See Coleridge Goode and Roger Cotterrell, *Bass Lines: A Life in Jazz* (London: Northway Books, 2002); and Alan Robertson, *Joe Harriott: Fire in His Soul* (London: Northway Publications, 2012). See also Joop Visser, liner notes, Joe Harriott, *The Joe Harriott Story,* Proper Properbox160, 2011.

42 The Small Faces even recorded a song in Eddie's honour titled "Eddie's Dreaming." See Small Faces, *Small Faces,* Immediate IMLP 008, 1967; and the Beatles, "Got to Get You into My Life," Capitol Records 4274, 1976.

43 Desmond Dekker, "Israelites," Green Light GLS 411, 1969.

44 Bryan has also played with the London Philharmonic, Ziggy Marley, Ray Charles, and Earth, Wind and Fire. See interview, Jo Jo Bennett.

45 Ibid. See also Williams, liner notes, *Alpha Boys' School.*

46 Interview, Jo Jo Bennett.

47 Baxter, *The Arts of an Island*, 261; and Witmer, "'Local' and 'Foreign,'" 4.

48 As boys were required to leave the school by sixteen, Bennett was reintroduced to his mother before leaving Alpha for good. Musical performances, competitions, and talent contests or "hunts," as they were called, had been part of Kingston's urban musical culture from as early as 1927 and were vital to the nascent musician trying to make his or her mark. Bennett was no exception. On seeing him perform, Byron Lee actually asked one of the sisters at Alpha if he could take Bennett from the school for his own band. Headhunting was normal practice at such performances and competitions, which were in themselves important in introducing new singing stars and musicians to the Jamaican public. Rannie "Bop" Williams was discovered by Skatalites legend Tommy McCook in much the same manner long before he headed north to Canada. For further discussion, see Witmer, "'Local' and 'Foreign,'" 9; Baxter, *The Arts of an Island,* 328; interview, Jo Jo Bennett; and interview, Ranford Williams, Toronto, January 20, 2011.

49 Witmer, "'Local' and 'Foreign,'" 7, 11. See also Noel White, "Forty-One Years on the Lighter Side of Jamaican Life," *Gleaner* (Jamaica), February 19, 1972, 2–3.

50 For further discussion, see Witmer, "'Local' and 'Foreign,'" 2.

51 Ibid., 7. See also Heathcott, "Urban Spaces and Working-Class Expressions," 189.

52 Interview, Jay Douglas, Toronto, June 7, 2017.

53 For further discussion, see Witmer, "'Local' and 'Foreign,'" 16.

54 Harry Hawke, "Over and Over," *Record Collector,* Christmas 2001, 62–64, 66. In particular, Rosco Gordon's piano style was highly influential on the ska and reggae genres.

55 As Goldman confirmed: "The gentle folk shuffle of mento, with its raunchy 'Big Bamboo' innuendo, [is] performed by small groups of men in straw hats playing painted bamboo percussion and square-bodied guitars called rhythm boxes." See Goldman, *The Book of Exodus,* 36–37.

56 Herbie Miller, describing Klive Walker, in Walker, *Dubwise,* 7–9.

57 Interview, Natasha Emery, Toronto, December 29, 2010.

58 Various members of the Jamaica to Toronto project spoke of their love of the country and western music they were exposed to via Jamaican radio. See Tim Perlich, "Jamaica to Toronto: Lost stars of the city's vibrant 60s R&B scene finally get their chance to shine," *NOW,* July 13, 2006, cover story.

59 Interview, Klive Walker, Pickering, ON, September 9, 2010.

60 Interview, Earle Heedram (a.k.a. the Mighty Pope), Richmond Hill, December 13, 2010.

61 Ibid.

62 Interview, Ranford Williams.

63 Johnny Nash, *Tears on My Pillow,* CBS S 69148, 1975.

64 See Walker, *Dubwise,* 106.

65 See Herbie Miller's preface, ibid., 7.

66 For further discussion, see Heathcott, "Urban Spaces and Working-Class Expressions."

67 Though definitive claims of this nature are always fraught with pitfalls, the consensus among most of the ska musicians I have worked with is that Laurel Aitken's "Boogie in My Bones" is the first ska record. See Laurel Aitken, "Boogie in My Bones"/"Little Sheila," Starlite [UK], ST.45 011, 1960.

68 As Heathcott explains, "Ska music formed part of a broader Jamaican urban youth culture anchored by the so-called 'rude boy,' a suit-and-tie hooligan bent on turf protection and the defiance of adult authority." See Heathcott, "Urban Spaces and Working-Class Expressions," 193.

69 Interview, Earle Heedram.

70 Terence Young, dir., *Dr. No,* produced by Harry Saltzman and Albert R. Broccoli, based on the novel by Ian Fleming (London: EoN Productions/United Artists, 1962).

71 Interview, Jo Jo Bennett.

72 Al Caiola, "The Guns of Navarone," *Solid Gold Guitar,* United Artists Records ULP 1003, 1962.

73 Goldman, *The Book of Exodus,* 38.

74 See Wailing Wailers, *The Wailing Wailers,* Studio One SOCD 1001, 1996 [1965]. See also Vivien Goldman, "Another Bright Saturday," *Sounds* (London), April 30, 1977.

75 Holung also name-checked Deep Purple, Carlos Santana, Yes, Led Zeppelin, T-Rex, and Uriah Heep among his favourite bands. He learned rock and roll songs from his affluent friends in semi-private school in Jamaica. See interview, Peter Holung, Newmarket, ON, February 3, 2011.

272 *Notes to pages 56–60*

76 Goldman, *The Book of Exodus,* 61.

77 Maureen Sheridan, *Bob Marley: Soul Rebel – The Stories behind Every Song, 1962–1981* (Cambridge, MA: Da Capo Press, 1999).

78 Wayne Perkins, quoted in Jeremy Marre, dir., *Bob Marley and the Wailers: Catch a Fire,* Classic Albums (Los Angeles: Image Entertainment, 1999).

79 Paul Gilroy, *There Ain't No Black in the Union Jack: The Cultural Politics of Race and Nation* (Chicago: University of Chicago Press, 1987), 170–71.

80 Bunny Lee, in Jeremy Marre, dir. and prod., *Reggae Britannia* (London: BBC Four, 2011).

81 Colin Larkin, ed., *The Virgin Encyclopedia of Reggae* (London: Virgin Publishing, 1998).

82 Dick Hebdige, *Cut 'n' Mix: Culture, Identity and Caribbean Music* (London: Comedia, Methuen, 1987), 93; Sebastian Clarke, *Jah Music: The Evolution of the Popular Jamaican Song* (London: Heinemann Educational Books, 1980), 140; David Van Biema, "The Legacy of Abraham," *Time,* September 30, 2002; and Goldman, *The Book of Exodus,* 14, 47.

83 Walker, *Dubwise,* 80.

84 10CC, "Dreadlock Holiday," *Bloody Tourists,* Mercury 9102 503, 1978; Kate Bush, "Kite," *The Kick Inside,* EMI America SW17003, 1978; the Eagles, *Hotel California,* Asylum Records AS13084, 1976; Led Zeppelin, "D'yer Mak'er," *Houses of the Holy,* Atlantic SD 7255, 1973; Steely Dan, "Haitian Divorce," ABC Records ABC 4152, 1976, 7 inch. Paul Simon's effort comes a little closer to a Jamaican sound, recorded as it was in Jamaica with reggae session players, including drummer Winston Grennan, father of Jamaican Canadian drummer Sunray Grennan. See Paul Simon, "Mother and Child Reunion," Columbia 4–45547, 1972.

85 Eric Clapton, "I Shot the Sheriff," *461 Ocean Boulevard,* RSO 2394 138, 1974; Neil Spencer, "Reggae: The sound that revolutionised Britain," *The Guardian,* January 29, 2011.

86 Johnny Nash, "I Can See Clearly Now"/"Stir It Up," Epic 15–2329, 1972.

87 Bob Andy, in Marre, *Reggae Britannia.*

88 For further discussion, see Bigga Morrison, as quoted in Jeremy Marre, "Reggae Britannia," *BBC Music Blog,* February 7, 2011, https://www.bbc.co.uk/blogs/bbcmusic/2011/02/reggae_britannia.html; and Marre, *Reggae Britannia.*

89 Burning Spear, *Burning Spear Live,* Island Records/Mango B000003QH8 (1990 [1977]).

90 Bob Marley and the Wailers, "One Love/People Get Ready"/"So Much Trouble in the World"/"Keep on Moving," Tuff Gong 12 TGX 1 (1984 [1977]).

91 Dennis Brown, "Promised Land," Simba SM003, 1979.

Chapter 3: Jamaica to Toronto

1 Ninette Kelley and Michael Trebilock, *The Making of the Mosaic: A History of Canadian Immigration Policy* (Toronto: University of Toronto Press, 1998).

2 See Anne Milan and Kelly Tran, "Blacks in Canada: A Long History," *Canadian Social Trends* 72 (Spring 2004): 4–5.

Notes to pages 61–63   273

3   Bob Marley and the Wailers, *Exodus,* Island 9123 021, 1977.

4   The concept for the album was based entirely on Marley's leaving Babylon (read Jamaica) following an assassination attempt. See David Van Biema, "The Legacy of Abraham," *Time,* September 30, 2002; and Vivien Goldman, *The Book of Exodus: The Making and Meaning of Bob Marley and the Wailers' Album of the Century* (New York: Three Rivers Press, 2006), 14.

5   The Melodians, "By the Rivers of Babylon," music and lyrics by Brent Dowe and Trevor McNaughton, later updated by Frank Farian and Reyham, Summit/Trojan: SUM-6508, 1970.

6   The album, titled *Calypso,* was the first full-length LP to sell a million copies. For simplicity's sake (and likely for American sales after the success of the Andrews Sisters' calypso hit "Rum and Coca Cola"), the record company chose to call Belafonte's music calypso and not mento. The melody to "Jamaica Farewell" was taken from the classic mento song "Iron Bar." Harry Belafonte, "Jamaica Farewell," RCA Victor 47–6663, 1956.

7   Statistics Canada, *Census of Canada, 1881,* Library and Archives Canada, Statistics Canada Fonds, Record Group 31-C-1, microfilm C-13162 to C-13286.

8   Milan and Tran, "Blacks in Canada," 1.

9   For further discussion, see Donald H. Avery, *Reluctant Host: Canada's Response to Immigrant Workers, 1896–1994* (Toronto: McClelland and Stewart, 1995); and Valerie Knowles, *Strangers at Our Gates: Canadian Immigration and Immigration Policy, 1540–2006* (Toronto: Dundurn Press, 2007).

10 Kelley and Trebilcock challenge Freda Hawkins's claim that Canada was a "nation of immigrants" in *The Making of the Mosaic.* See also Freda Hawkins, *Canada and Immigration: Public Policy and Public Concern* (Montreal: McGill-Queen's University Press, 1972); and Jorgen Dahlie and Tissa Fernando, eds., *Ethnicity, Power and Politics in Canada* (Toronto: Methuen, 1981).

11 *An Act Respecting Immigration,* SC 1910, c 27, s 38(c).

12 See James W. St. G. Walker, *"Race," Rights and the Law in the Supreme Court of Canada: Historical Case Studies* (Toronto and Waterloo: Osgoode Society for Canadian Legal History/Wilfrid Laurier University Press, 1997). See also Lisa M. Jakubowski, *Immigration and the Legalization of Racism* (Black Point, NS: Fernwood Publishing, 1997); and Kathryn Blaze Carlson, "'Canada's Rosa Parks,' Viola Desmond, posthumously pardoned," *National Post,* April 14, 2010. In 2018, Viola Desmond replaced Sir John A. Macdonald on the ten-dollar bill.

13 Editorial, "How Can We Keep Our British Racial Balance?," *Saturday Night,* December 11, 1943, 6–7.

14 See Paul R. Magocsi, ed., *Encyclopedia of Canada's Peoples* (Toronto: University of Toronto Press, 1999); and Jean Burnet and Howard Palmer, *"Coming Canadians": An Introduction to a History of Canada's Peoples* (Toronto: McClelland and Stewart, 1988), vii–xi.

15 See Robert A. Huttenback, "The British Empire as a 'White Man's Country': Racial Attitudes and Immigration Legislation in the Colonies of White Settlement," *Journal of British Studies* 13, 1 (1973): 108–37, and *Racism and Empire: White Settlers and Coloured Immigrants in the British Self-Governing Colonies, 1830–1910* (Ithaca, NY:

274 *Notes to pages 63–65*

Cornell University Press, 1976). Perhaps none have suggested it more plaintively than sociologist Vilna Bashi. See "Globalized Anti-blackness: Transnationalizing Western Immigration Law, Policy, and Practice," *Ethnic and Racial Studies* 27, 4 (2004): 584–606. See also Janice Monk, "Race and Restrictive Immigration: A Review Article," *Journal of Historical Geography* 4, 2 (1978): 94.

16 See Vilna Bashi, "Neither Ignorance nor Bliss: Race, Racism, and the West Indian Immigrant Experience," in *Race, Migration, Transnationalism, and Race in a Changing New York*, ed. Hector R. Cordero-Guzman, Ramon Grosfoguel, and Robert Smith (Philadelphia: Temple University Press, 2001), 212–38; and "Racial Categories Matter Because Racial Hierarchies Matter: A Commentary," *Ethnic and Racial Studies* 21, 5 (1998): 959–68.

17 Bashi, "Neither Ignorance nor Bliss," 212–38.

18 "Toronto Negro Citizenship Association protests discrimination," *Canadian Unionist*, May 28, 1954, 181.

19 "Britain Puts the Pressure on Canada," *Saturday Night*, May 13, 1961, 37–38.

20 "Brief Presented to the Prime Minister, the Minister of Citizenship and Immigration, and Members of the Government of Canada by the Negro Citizenship Association," Ontario Labour Committee Papers, vol. 19, April 27, 1954, Library and Archives Canada; and Walker, *"Race," Rights and the Law*, 419. See also "Toronto Negro Citizenship Association Protests Discrimination," 181.

21 See Don Moore, *Don Moore: An Autobiography* (Toronto: Williams-Wallace, 1985). Other significant biographical works have rendered the lives of certain pioneer agents for change within the black community in Canada. See, for example, Bromley Armstrong and Sheldon Taylor, *Bromley: Tireless Fighter for Just Causes* (Pickering, ON: Vitabu Publishing, 2000); Donna Hill, ed., *A Black Man's Toronto: The Reminiscences of Harry Gairey* (Toronto: Multicultural History Society of Ontario, 1981); and Agnes Calliste, "Race, Gender and Canadian Immigration Policy: Blacks from the Caribbean, 1900–1932," *Journal of Canadian Studies* 28, 4 (1993–94): 131–48.

22 Throughout her study "'The Movement of 100 Girls': 1950s Canadian Immigration Policy and the Market for Domestic Labour," *Zeitschrift Für Kanada-Studien* 19, 2 (1999): 131–46, Christiane Harzig analyzes the political gamesmanship and economic evolution of the program of bringing domestics from the West Indies. She then calibrates this analysis with the social and psychological ramifications of the program's operations.

23 Douglas's mother also had to fib about having children (she had four) to be considered eligible for entry into Canada. She encountered some bizarre questions on her interview, including "How would you roast a leg of lamb?" See interview, Jay Douglas, Toronto, June 7, 2017.

24 Leo Cripps and Mike Smith are among the Jamaican Canadians interviewed for this study whose mothers – like Jay Douglas's – had come to work in Canada before their children were sent for (or allowed in).

25 See Karen C. Flynn, "Experience and Identity: Black Immigrant Nurses to Canada, 1950–1980," in *Sisters or Strangers? Immigrant, Ethnic, and Racialized Women in Canadian History*, ed. Marlene Epp, Franca Iacovetta, and Frances Swyripa (Toronto:

University of Toronto Press, 2004), 381–98, and "Race, Class, and Gender: Black Nurses in Ontario, 1950–1980" (PhD diss., York University, 2004). On gender roles as they apply to West Indian immigrant labour, see Dionne Brand, *No Burden to Carry: Narratives of Black Working Women in Ontario, 1920s–1950s* (Toronto: University of Toronto Press, 1989). Though less central to the Caribbean case study, see also Agnes Calliste and George Dei, *Anti-racist Feminism, Critical Race and Gender Studies* (Halifax: Fernwood, 2000).

26 See Flynn, "Experience and Identity."

27 Gordon Donaldson, "How We Cover Up Our Racial Abuses," *Saturday Night,* February 15, 1958, 11–12, 46.

28 Ibid.

29 Ibid.

30 Ontario towns such as Dresden, Wallaceburg, and Chatham boasted sizeable black populations, and approximately nine thousand blacks lived in the Maritimes. The urban centres of Toronto and Montreal also had comparatively large numbers of blacks. For a classic study on the various black populations in Canada, the first of its kind, see Robin W. Winks, *The Blacks in Canada: A History* (Montreal: McGill-Queen's University Press, 1971); see also Donaldson, "How We Cover Up Our Racial Abuses," 11–12, 46.

31 Donaldson, "How We Cover Up Our Racial Abuses," 11–12, 46.

32 Milan and Tran, "Blacks in Canada," 4–5.

33 In the 1962 reforms, Conservative MP Ellen Fairclough called for de-emphasizing the role of sponsored relations and privileging education and skills over ethnic background. These initiatives still restricted the migration of underqualified immigrants from Europe (particularly Italy) who were being sponsored by Canadian relatives. See Applied History Research Group, *The Peopling of Canada, 1946–1976* [online tutorial] (Calgary: Applied History Research Group, 1997).

34 Among them was my uncle Sid Virtue, who was first a bus driver, then worked for the British Gas Board for thirty years. "Britain Puts the Pressure on Canada," 37–38.

35 Ibid.

36 Ibid.

37 Ibid.

38 Ibid. A separate Jamaican High Commission was established in August 1962 to coincide with securing independence from Britain. Pyne would later become press officer of the Jamaican High Commission.

39 For two strong arguments that hold official policy-making and its attendant language to account, see Vic Satzewich, "Racism and Canadian Immigration Policy: The Government's View of Caribbean Migration, 1962–1966," *Canadian Ethnic Studies* 21, 1 (1989): 77–97; and Ian Mackenzie, "Early Movements of Domestics from the Caribbean and Canadian Immigration Policy," *Alternate Routes: A Journal of Critical Social Research* 8 (1988): 124–43. Satzewich poses a gutsy challenge to the notion that a meaningful deracialization of Canada's official immigration policies occurred in 1962. Differing slightly from Satzewich's findings, K. Wayne Taylor presents two alternative theories of racial discrimination as it applied to Canada's official governmental

276 *Notes to pages 68–70*

policy on immigration. See "Racism in Canadian Immigration Policy," *Canadian Ethnic Studies* 23, 1 (1991): 1–20.

40 "Immigration: Tabling of White Paper on Government Policy," *House of Commons Debates,* 27th Parl., 1st sess., vol. 8 (October 14, 1966), at 8651–54 (Hon. Jean Marchand).

41 Ibid.

42 Ibid.

43 Milan and Tran, "Blacks in Canada," 3.

44 Ibid. In 2006, 783,795 blacks were living in Canada, constituting roughly 2.5 percent of the total population: see Statistics Canada, "Ethnocultural Portrait of Canada Highlight Tables," *2006 Census,* 97–562-XWE2006002, 2008.

45 Elizabeth Thomas-Hope, *Migration Situation Analysis, Policy and Program Needs for Jamaica* (Kingston: Planning Institute of Jamaica, PIOJ, and UNFPA, 2004).

46 Milan and Tran, "Blacks in Canada," 4–5.

47 George E. Eaton, "Jamaicans," in Magocsi, *Encyclopedia of Canada's Peoples,* 833–41.

48 Milan and Tran, "Blacks in Canada," 3.

49 Statistics Canada, "Census Profile: 2016 Census," Toronto, 98–316-X2016001. For earlier reports, see Statistics Canada, "Profile for Census Metropolitan Areas and Census Agglomerations, 2006 Census, 94–581-XCB2006004, 2008; and "Population by Selected Ethnic Origins, by Census Metropolitan Areas, 2006 Census."

50 In terms of a ward-by-ward breakdown: 12.7 percent of Metro Toronto's Jamaicans were (as of 2003) living in Etobicoke North (Ward 1); 9.5 percent were in Scarborough Rouge (Ward 42); 8.5 percent were in the Jane-Finch Corridor (Ward 8); 7.5 percent were in Scarborough East (Ward 43); and 6.7 percent were in Eglinton-Lawrence (Ward 15). See Mahogany Saunders, "Where Jamaicans Live," *Jamaicans.com: Out of Many One People Online,* August 1, 2003, https://www.jamaicans.com.

51 Ibid.

52 Interview, Jo Jo Bennett.

53 See Toronto, *City of Toronto Priority Neighbourhoods: Overview of Demographics and Community Services, Jane-Finch – #2* (Toronto: City of Toronto Social Development, Finance and Administration Division, 2006).

54 John Sakamoto, "How Jane-Finch was born," *Toronto Star,* November 30, 1986, F01.

55 As of 2005, Jamaicans accounted for approximately 9 percent of the Jane-Finch population. See Toronto, *City of Toronto Priority Neighbourhoods.* See also Rosie DiManno, "Jane-Finch: Perceptions and realities," *Toronto Star,* November 30, 1986, F01; and the Jane-Finch Corridor's website, http://jane-finch.com.

56 Goldman, *The Book of Exodus,* 66.

57 A graduate of the London School of Economics, Manley had the "people's touch," aligned as he was with the Rasta movement. Selassie himself presented Manley with a staff upon his visit to Jamaica in 1966, a staff that was later christened the "Rod of Correction." The prime minister's good looks and sophistication gained him many friends and supporters, including, significantly, Africa's fledgling leaders, which won him further credibility with a big portion of Jamaica's black population. See Goldman, *The Book of Exodus,* 69. The PNP counted on reggae singer Delroy Wilson and his "Better Must Come" song to provide the soundtrack for Manley's drive to power. See Delroy Wilson, "Better Must Come," Jackpot JP 763, 1971.

58 Darrell E. Levi, *Michael Manley: The Making of a Leader* (Athens: University of Georgia Press, 1990).

59 Seaga was accused of having links with the CIA (which spawned an unfortunate, at least for him, nickname: CIAga). See Goldman, *The Book of Exodus,* 82.

60 Castro had won favour on the island by helping Jamaica build durable roads and improve school buildings in the 1970s. See ibid., 85.

61 Levi, *Michael Manley.*

62 Euclid A. Rose, *Dependency and Socialism in the Modern Caribbean: Superpower Intervention in Guyana, Jamaica and Grenada, 1970–1985* (Boston: Lexington Books, 2002).

63 Goldman, *The Book of Exodus.*

64 James Hill, "Backbeat for Jah Jah," *Globe and Mail,* April 5, 1978, 10–11.

65 Klive Walker, *Dubwise: Reasoning from the Reggae Underground* (Toronto: Insomniac Press, 2005), 23.

66 Interview, Denise Jones, Toronto, February 8, 2011.

67 Eaton, "Jamaicans," 833–41.

68 Ibid.

69 Recent works have added nuance to the findings of earlier scholars such as Subhas Ramcharan and Vic Satzewich: see Amoaba Gooden, "Community Organizing by African Caribbean People in Toronto, Ontario," *Journal of Black Studies* 38, 3 (2008): 413–26; Dwaine Plaza, "The Construction of a Segmented Hybrid Identity among One-and-a-Half-Generation and Second-Generation Indo-Caribbean and African Caribbean Canadians," *Identity* 6, 3 (2006): 207–29; Alwyn D. Gilkes, "Among Thistles and Thorns: West Indian Diaspora Immigrants in New York City and Toronto" (PhD diss., City University of New York, 2005); and Terry-Ann Jones, "Comparative Diasporas: Jamaicans in South Florida and Toronto" (PhD diss., University of Miami, 2005).

70 See Subhas Ramcharan, "The Adaptation of West Indians in Canada" (PhD diss., York University, 1974); and, more recently, Frances Henry, *The Caribbean Diaspora in Toronto: Learning to Live with Racism* (Toronto: University of Toronto Press, 1994).

71 Henry, *The Caribbean Diaspora in Toronto.*

72 Alwyn Gilkes, for example, compared a sample of twenty West Indian migrants who had immigrated to New York with twenty others who had immigrated to Toronto. See Gilkes, "Among Thistles and Thorns."

73 Perhaps one of Gilkes's most interesting discoveries, however, was that these restrictions were more acute for the West Indian group in Toronto. See ibid., 85–88. See also Gooden, "Community Organizing by African Caribbean People in Toronto"; and Plaza, "The Construction of a Segmented Hybrid Identity."

74 For a further discussion on acculturation stress, see Gilkes, "Among Thistles and Thorns," 88–93.

75 The JCA's first committee was composed of Roy G. Williams, Bromley Armstrong, E.S. Ricketts, Miss Phyllis Whyte, Mrs. Catherine Williams, George King, Leyton Ellis and Kenneth Simpson. The JCA originally occupied 65 Dawes Road in the Danforth area of the east end; it later swung over to the city's west end at 1621 Dupont Street. Its most recent home is just west of Jane and Finch at 995 Arrow Road. See the association's website for more information, https://jcaontario.org.

278   *Notes to pages 73–79*

76 See ibid., and Eaton, "Jamaicans," 833–41.
77 See Jones, "Comparative Diasporas." See also Henry, *The Caribbean Diaspora in Toronto*; and Gilkes, "Among Thistles and Thorns." For a good discussion of approaches to black diasporas and transnationalism, see Michelle A. Stephens, "Reimagining the Shape and Borders of Black Political Space," *Radical History Review* 87 (Fall 2003): 169–82. Inversely, the role of the Jamaican Canadian Association in Toronto has in recent times transcended a strictly Jamaican community and now operates within the larger multicultural spectrum. See Vincent G. Conville, "The Jamaican Canadian Association in a Multiracial and Multicultural Society: Four Decades of Service" (PhD diss., University of Toronto, 2004).
78 Interview, Marcia Vassell, Brampton, ON, February 17, 2011; and interview, Phil Vassell, Brampton, ON, December 8, 2010.
79 Drummer Sunray Grennan, for one, felt that there was far less prejudice in Canada than there was in the United States. See interview, Sunray Grennan, Toronto, July 8, 2010.
80 Many Jamaicans feel that the overt racism that plagued an earlier generation of West Indian immigrants has, like the language of official immigration policy, transformed into a less visible but equally harmful version that duly prohibits full access to the dominant society. See Gilkes, "Among Thistles and Thorns," 85–88.
81 Interview, Mike Smith, Brampton, ON, July 15, 2010.
82 Interview, Sunray Grennan.
83 Interview, Peter Holung, Newmarket, ON, February 3, 2011.
84 Interview, JuLion King, Toronto, January 28, 2011.
85 Interview, Phil Vassell. See also interview, Marcia Vassell.
86 Interview, Mike Smith.
87 Interview, Rupert "Ojiji" Harvey, Toronto, September 6, 2010.
88 The Harveys of Jamaica were the central focus of Lorna Goodison's book *From Harvey River: A Memoir of My Mother and Her Island* (New York: HarperCollins Publishers, 2007). Rupert and Carl's younger brother, Richard, was born in Canada in 1968 and was, during his short time on earth, my best friend. Richard died in 1986.
89 Interview, Rupert "Ojiji" Harvey.
90 Interview, Denise Jones.
91 Interview, Earle Heedram (a.k.a. the Mighty Pope), Richmond Hill, December 13, 2010.
92 Interview, Jay Douglas.
93 Interview, Jo Jo Bennett.
94 Ibid.
95 Ibid.
96 Ibid.
97 Ibid.
98 Bob Marley and the Wailers, *The Complete Bob Marley and the Wailers, 1967 to 1972 Soul Rebels,* Fiftyfive Records FF 1389-2, 1998.
99 Interview, Ranford Williams, Toronto, January 20, 2011.
100 Interview, Willi Williams, Pickering, ON, February 19, 2011.

Notes to pages 79–82 279

101 Interview, Adrian Miller, Toronto, February 6, 2011.
102 Interview, Klive Walker, Pickering, ON, September 9, 2010.
103 Ibid.
104 Interview, Mike Smith.
105 Interview, Earle Heedram.
106 Ibid.
107 Interview, Leo Cripps, Calgary, January 9, 2011.
108 Interview, Paul Bennett, Toronto, August 17, 2010.
109 Interview, Rupert "Ojiji" Harvey.
110 Messenjah, *Cool Operator,* Version VLP-001, 1987.
111 Interview, Wayne Hanson, Toronto, December 30, 2010.
112 Interview, Marcia Vassell; and interview, Phil Vassell.
113 Interview, Earle Heedram.
114 Interview, Peter Holung.
115 The motto has naturally come under scrutiny from various political pundits. Perhaps most famously, the late Rex Nettleford characterized it as "little more than a pithy epigram for speeches of exhortation and official brochures, when it was really intended to describe and inform the spirit of multiracialism and cultural integration among the Jamaican people." See Nettleford, *Mirror Mirror: Identity, Race and Protest in Jamaica* (Kingston, Jamaica: LMH, 1998 [1970]), 178.
116 Interview, Klive Walker.
117 Interview, JuLion King.
118 For example, I remember the late 1970s, when Glenroy, a newly arrived Jamaican teenager, squared off against Eddie, a kid from the Maritimes in our townhouse complex at Keele and Finch in Downsview, in the northwest section of Toronto. I have a vivid memory of my mother pulling me back by my shirt for my own good as people emptied out of most of the forty townhouses to see the scuffle, and perhaps join in. It was these frontline collisions that were difficult to reconcile with government-endorsed brochures on multiculturalism or the footage that accompanied the national anthem when CBC Television signed off for the night. Perhaps it took a fight or two before any honest relationships could emerge. Dave, Glenroy's younger brother, and I were close all through elementary and high school. Glenroy would later lend me a microphone for rehearsals with my first band. It was the same microphone that he had used at his own blues dances, just ten townhouses down from my own.
119 Interview, Adrian Miller.
120 For further discussion, see Akua Benjamin, "The Social and Legal Banishment of Anti-racism: A Black Perspective," in *Crimes of Colour: Racialization and the Criminal Justice System in Canada,* ed. Wendy Chan and Kiran Mirchandani (Peterborough, ON: Broadview Press, 2002), 177–90.
121 For contemporary discussions, see Social Planning Council of Metropolitan Toronto and Urban Alliance on Race Relations, *Law Enforcement and Race Relations,* Urban Seminar Series 4 (Toronto: Social Planning Council of Metropolitan Toronto, 1976); and Frances Henry, *The Dynamics of Racism in Toronto: Research Report* (Ottawa:

280 *Notes to pages 82–89*

Group Understanding and Human Rights Program, Department of the Secretary of State, 1978).

122 For useful bibliographies on the literature on the crisis in race relations, see Harriet Seenath, Navin Joneja, and Antoni Shelton, *Race and the Canadian Justice System: An Annotated Bibliography* (Toronto: Urban Alliance on Race Relations, 1995); and Amy Evans, *Race Relations Bibliography,* compiled for the Urban Alliance Centre on Race Relations (Toronto: Urban Alliance on Race Relations, 1985).

123 Interview, Mike Smith.

124 For a good example of how old-country attitudes were transplanted to the new country, see Henry, *The Caribbean Diaspora in Toronto.*

125 Interview, Mike Smith.

126 Ibid.

127 Colin Lindsay, *Profiles of Ethnic Communities in Canada: The Jamaican Community in Canada, 12* (Ottawa: Statistics Canada, 89–621-XIE, 2007), 16. See also Jones, "Comparative Diasporas"; Gilkes, "Among Thistles and Thorns"; and Flynn, "Race, Class, and Gender."

128 Interview, Mike Smith.

129 Interview, Rupert "Ojiji" Harvey.

130 Ibid.

131 Interview, Marcia Vassell; and interview, Phil Vassell.

132 Interview, Sunray Grennan.

133 Ibid.

134 Interview, Phil Vassell.

135 For further discussion on the evolution of the Yorkville scene and its attendant political awareness, see Stuart Henderson, *Making the Scene: Yorkville and Hip Toronto in the 1960s* (Toronto: University of Toronto Press, 2011).

136 See Van Gosse, *Rethinking the New Left: An Interpretive History* (New York: Palgrave, 2005), 24; Theodore Roszak, *The Making of a Counterculture* (Garden City, NY: Doubleday Anchor, 1969), 1; and Henderson, *Making the Scene,* 15.

137 Wayne Hanson, for one, confirmed that when Marley "brings Jamaica internationally, that does really facilitate it." See interview, Wayne Hanson.

138 Interview, Denise Jones.

139 Interview, Marcia Vassell; and interview, Phil Vassell.

140 Interview, Phil Vassell.

141 Interview, Rupert "Ojiji" Harvey.

142 Interview, Sunray Grennan.

143 Interview, Paul Bennett.

144 Interview, Earle Heedram.

145 Interview, Wayne Hanson.

146 Interview, Adrian Miller.

147 Interview, Ranford Williams.

148 Interview, Willi Williams.

149 Lindsay, *Profiles of Ethnic Communities in Canada,* 16; and Statistics Canada, *Ethnic*

Notes to pages 89–95   281

Diversity Survey 2002 (Ottawa: Statistics Canada/Canadian Heritage, 89M0019XCB, 2003). See also Jane Badets, Jennifer Chard, and Andrea Levett, *Ethnic Diversity Survey: Portrait of a Multicultural Society* (Ottawa: Statistics Canada/Canadian Heritage, 89-593-XIE, 2003).

150 See Dennis Conway and Robert B. Potter, "Caribbean Transnational Return Migrants as Agents of Change," *Geography Compass* 1, 1 (2007): 25–45. For earlier discussions, see also Jorge Duany, "Beyond the Safety Valve: Recent Trends in Caribbean Migration," *Social and Economic Studies* 43, 1 (1994): 95–122; and Dawn I. Marshall, "A History of West Indian Migrations: Overseas Opportunities and 'Safety-Valve' Policies," in *The Caribbean Exodus,* ed. Barry B. Levine (New York: Praeger, 1987), 15–31.

151 Interview, Adrian Miller.

152 Interview, Earle Heedram.

153 Interview, Leo Cripps.

154 Interview, Sunray Grennan.

155 This is a belief that is examined in depth in recent Caribbean diasporic literature. See, for example, Conway and Potter, "Caribbean Transnational Return Migrants."

156 Interview, JuLion King.

157 Interview, Peter Holung.

158 Conway and Potter, "Caribbean Transnational Return Migrants."

159 Interview, Klive Walker.

160 Ibid.

161 Herbie Miller said of Klive Walker that he is able to play both sides, as it were, as an insider and an outsider. See Herbie Miller, preface, in Walker, *Dubwise,* 7–9.

162 Interview, Phil Vassell.

163 Henry, *The Caribbean Diaspora in Toronto.*

164 Interview, Denise Jones.

165 Interview, Willi Williams.

166 Interview, Ranford Williams.

167 Interview, Mike Smith.

168 Interview, Earle Heedram.

169 Interview, Marcia Vassell; and interview, Phil Vassell.

170 Interview, Sunray Grennan.

171 Interview, Rupert "Ojiji" Harvey.

172 Interview, Adrian Miller.

173 Interview, Denise Jones.

174 Interview, Leo Cripps.

175 Interview, Wayne Hanson.

176 Interview, Denise Jones.

177 Interview, Carol Brown, Bolton, ON, January 30, 2011.

178 Interview, Jay Douglas.

179 Interview, Marcia Vassell; and interview, Phil Vassell.

180 Interview, Mike Smith.

181 Interview, Ranford Williams.

282 *Notes to page 97*

Chapter 4: Place and Meaning in Toronto's Reggae Text

1 For examples, see Gaston R. Gordillo, *Landscapes of Devils: Tension of Place and Memory in the Argentinean Chaco* (Durham, NC: Duke University Press, 2004); Marlene Creates, *Places of Presence: Newfoundland Kin and Ancestral Land, Newfoundland, 1989–1991* (St. John's, NL: Killick Press, 1997); Andreas Huyssen, *Present Pasts: Urban Palimpsests and the Politics of Memory* (Palo Alto, CA: Stanford University Press, 2003), 11; and James Opp and John C. Walsh, *Placing Memory and Remembering Place in Canada* (Vancouver: UBC Press, 2010).

2 For further discussion, see Alan Gordon, *Making Public Pasts: The Contested Terrain of Montreal's Public Memories, 1891–1930* (Montreal: McGill-Queen's University Press, 2001). For examples of how place making can resist dominant narratives, see Steven High, "Placing the Displaced Worker: Narrating Place in Deindustrializing Sturgeon Falls, Ontario," in Opp and Walsh, *Placing Memory and Remembering Place in Canada*, 159–86; and Kirsten Emiko McAllister, "Archive and Myth: The Changing Memoryscape of Japanese Canadian Internment Camps," in Opp and Walsh, *Placing Memory and Remembering Place in Canada*, 215–46.

3 Environmental artist Marlene Creates observed that the land "is not an abstract physical location but a *place,* charged with personal significance, shaping the images we have of ourselves." See Creates, *Places of Presence,* 11.

4 This process was not, of course, unique to the Toronto reggae scene. Nor is the use of place as a historical approach particularly new to Canadian history. Donald Creighton's watershed work *The Commercial Empire of the St. Lawrence, 1760–1850* (Toronto: Ryerson Press/Carnegie Endowment for International Peace, Division of Economics and History, 1937), for instance, birthed the so-called Laurentian thesis, which posited that geography (in this case, the Laurentian waterway) could act as an historical agent, playing a significant role in the grand narrative of Canada's socioeconomic development. Seven decades after Creighton's work, historians have brought great nuance to the use of place as an approach. For an excellent example, see Opp and Walsh, *Placing Memory and Remembering Place in Canada.*

5 Gaston Gordillo believes that every memory is fundamentally a memory of a place. See Gordillo, *Landscapes of Devils,* 4. Likewise, in her work, Joan M. Schwartz speaks of the importance of the "cartographic illusions of the geographical imagination." See "Constituting Places of Presence: Landscape, Identity and the Geographical Imagination," in Creates, *Places of Presence,* 11.

6 Opp and Walsh believe that "in focussing closely on local practices and local understandings, we resist the tendency to frame the productions of place and public memory as simply overarching tools of exclusionary power": *Placing Memory and Remembering Place in Canada,* 14. For an example of how the "cultural production of tradition" can wield an exclusionary tool in terms of place making and memory, see Ian McKay, *Quest of the Folk: Antimodernism and Cultural Selection in Twentieth-Century Nova Scotia* (Montreal: McGill-Queen's University Press, 1994).

7 As a former speakeasy, the Bamboo, through its transition from an illegal underground establishment to one of the city's elite nightclubs, troubled the status quo through its very existence.

8 Studying collisions between different cultures along the frontline reveals the extent to which migrants adjusted to their adopted land and, in turn, influenced members of the host society. See Kathleen Neils Conzen, David A. Gerber, Ewa Morawska, George E. Pozzetta, and Rudolph J. Vecoli, "The Invention of Ethnicity: A Perspective from the U.S.A.," *Journal of American Ethnic History* 12, 1 (1992): 3–40; and Barbara Lorenzkowski, *Sounds of Ethnicity: Listening to German North America, 1850–1914* (Winnipeg: University of Manitoba Press, 2010), 6.

9 In her work, Barbara Lorenzkowski appraises the role of those nineteenth-century German immigrant gatekeepers who sought to preserve the purity of German music (and language) being performed in Canada and the United States. These aims, as Lorenzkowski observes, were often at odds with those of the vast majority of German immigrants living in North America, who were less fearful of cultural dilution. Franca Iacovetta also uses the gatekeeper analogy in her work to signify the attitudes of middle-class Canada and those institutions that defined citizenship in Cold War Canada. In this sense, gatekeepers profoundly shaped the lives of new Canadians. See Lorenzkowski, *Sounds of Ethnicity*; and Franca Iacovetta, *Gatekeepers: Reshaping Immigrant Lives in Cold War Canada* (Toronto: Between the Lines, 2006).

10 In locating the bridges and gates, then, I am less focused on testing the homogeneousness of the Jamaican migrant group than on apprehending the reciprocal cultural exchange that occurred in key places along Toronto's ethnic frontline. Moreover, scholars have begun to test the notion of "groupness" among ethnic groups. See, for example, Lorenzkowski, *Sounds of Ethnicity*; Jordan Stranger-Ross, *Staying Italian: Urban Change and Ethnic Life in Postwar Toronto and Philadelphia* (Chicago: University of Chicago Press, 2009); and Carolyn Whitzman, *Suburb, Slum, Urban Village: Transformations in Toronto's Parkdale Neighbourhood, 1875–2002* (Vancouver: UBC Press, 2009).

11 For anthropologist Frederick Barth, having a known boundary was essential to a given ethnic identity. Indeed, that precious imaginary bandwidth dividing one ethnic group from another was more important than the actual "culture" housed within the boundaries themselves. See Frederick Barth, introduction to *Ethnic Groups and Boundaries: The Social Organization of Cultural Difference* (Boston: Little, Brown, 1969), 9–37; and Lorenzkowski, *Sounds of Ethnicity,* 6.

12 Lorenzkowski, *Sounds of Ethnicity,* 8.

13 Rosie DiManno, "Jane-Finch: Perceptions and realities," *Toronto Star,* November 30, 1986.

14 For example, see "Followers called walking time bombs, lawyer says," *Globe and Mail,* June 11, 1975, 3.

15 Interview, Rupert "Ojiji" Harvey, Toronto, September 6, 2010.

16 Interview, Mike Smith, Brampton, ON, July 15, 2010; and interview, Rupert "Ojiji" Harvey.

17 Interview, Phil Vassell, Brampton, ON, December 8, 2010.

18 Interview, Mike Smith.

19 Vivien Goldman, *The Book of Exodus: The Making and Meaning of Bob Marley and the Wailers' Album of the Century* (New York: Three Rivers Press, 2006), 177.

20 Ibid., 179.

284 *Notes to pages 101–6*

21 Interview, Wayne Hanson, Toronto, December 30, 2010.

22 In Britain, for example, Boy George and the Clash, as Goldman confirmed, "would skank alongside Aswad and Steel Pulse." See Goldman, *The Book of Exodus,* 177.

23 James Hill, "Backbeat for Jah Jah," *Globe and Mail,* April 5, 1978, 11.

24 Interview, Mike Smith.

25 Interview, Sunray Grennan, Toronto, July 8, 2010.

26 Interview, David Kingston, Toronto, September 1, 2010.

27 For a good example of contesting public space, see Frances Swyripa, "Edmonton's Jasper Avenue: Public Ritual, Heritage, and Memory on Main Street," in Opp and Walsh, *Placing Memory and Remembering Place in Canada,* 81–106.

28 For further discussion, see de Certeau, *The Practice of Everyday Life* (Berkeley: University of California Press, 1984); and Tim Cresswell, *Place: A Short Introduction* (Malden, MA: Blackwell, 2004).

29 Neil Bissoondath, *Selling Illusions: The Cult of Multiculturalism in Canada* (Toronto: Penguin, 2002), 136. Matumbi's "Nothing to Do with You" and Tippa Irie's "Complain Neighbour" deal with these pitched battles of listening to reggae loud in a British context.

30 Interview, Phil Vassell.

31 See Dick Beddoes, "Reggae to rafters," *Globe and Mail,* May 28, 1979, 8.

32 Jack Batten, "100,000 blacks: And the sounds are all their own," *Globe and Mail,* March 8, 1975, "Entertainment" cover page.

33 Norman Otis Richmond, "Bathurst St. Has Always Been Part of Black Life in T.O," *Share* (Toronto), October 14, 2009.

34 See Kevin Howes, liner notes, various artists, *Jamaica to Toronto: Soul Funk and Reggae, 1967–1974,* Light in the Attic LITA019, 2006.

35 Hill, "Backbeat for Jah Jah," 11; Batten, "100,000 blacks"; Richmond, "Bathurst St."; and interview, Phil Vassell.

36 See Morris Duff, "150 calypso fans cram tiny room," *Toronto Star,* June 20, 1960; and Kevin Plummer, "Historicist: Sounds of home II; After-hours clubs and the West Indian music scene of the 1960s," *Torontoist,* December 28, 2013.

37 Kevin Howes, liner notes, Jackie Mittoo, *Wishbone,* Light in the Attic Records LITA021, 2006.

38 "For your night on the town," concert listings, *Globe and Mail,* April 30, 1975, 17.

39 See Donna Hill, ed., *A Black Man's Toronto: The Reminiscences of Harry Gairey* (Toronto: Multicultural History Society of Ontario, 1981); and Plummer, "After-hours clubs and the West Indian music scene of the 1960s."

40 Interview, Jay Douglas, Toronto, June 7, 2017.

41 Ibid. Manager Karl Mullings helped to put the Cougars together when he was residing with Everton "Pablo" Paul and Bobby Roseau on Keele Street. See Howes, liner notes, various artists, *Jamaica to Toronto.*

42 Interview, Earle Heedram (a.k.a. the Mighty Pope), Richmond Hill, ON, December 13, 2010.

43 Hill, "Backbeat for Jah Jah," 11.

44 Interview, Phil Vassell.

45 See Batten, "100,000 blacks."

Notes to pages 107–9 285

46 Noel Walker, as quoted ibid.

47 See, for example, Lewis, as quoted in Paul McGrath, "Island rhythms find new roots," *Globe and Mail,* January 10, 1981, 6; and interview, Ranford Williams, Toronto, January 20, 2011.

48 Previously, Tiger had been the co-owner of the Calypso Club on Yonge Street, which he opened with Harold Wintraub in 1960. See Plummer, "After-hours clubs."

49 Williams, who was also a member of Skatalites' Tommy McCook's band, appeared on the original version of Marley's "Trench Town Rock." See Bob Marley and the Wailers, "Trench Town Rock," Tuff Gong, 1970. See also Chapter 11 in Jon Masouri, *Wailing Blues: The Story of Bob Marley's Wailers* (London: Omnibus Press, 2009).

50 See Greg Quill, "For the record: T.O. shops lead world in spinning rare discs," *Toronto Star,* September 26, 1986, D20.

51 I was in Yahwedeh in 1987.

52 Quill, "For the record," D1, D20.

53 Ibid., D20.

54 CHWO's Willie Dee's midnight show was particularly popular. See Batten, "100,000 blacks."

55 Ibid.

56 Interview, David Kingston.

57 Given the number of albums bought, the youth subcultures of the punk and postpunk eras were perhaps among the most music-savvy connoisseurs in the history of the recording industry.

58 See Gary McGroarty, dir., *Rise Up: Canadian Pop Music in the 1980s* (Toronto: EMI Music Canada, 2009).

59 Adele Freedman, "Doing it: One heart, one love ... Amma," *Globe and Mail,* February 15, 1978, 3.

60 Ibid.

61 See Keith McCuaig, "Jamaican Canadian Music in Toronto in the 1970s and 1980s: A Preliminary History" (master's thesis, Carleton University, 2012); Plummer, "After-hours clubs"; and Howes, liner notes, various artists, *Jamaica to Toronto.*

62 Interview, Earle Heedram.

63 Lee also toured Canada many times, including performances at Expo 67 and the CNE. See interview, Jo Jo Bennett, Toronto, October 19, 2010.

64 "Rocksteady? Reggae? They go with jump-up at Caribana," *Globe and Mail,* May 18, 1971, 14.

65 Robert Martin, "Jimmy Cliff concert hits smooth stride after stumbling beginning," *Globe and Mail,* October 15, 1975, 15; Robert Martin, "Cliff delivers reggae in the mainstream," *Globe and Mail,* October 13, 1975, 15; and Paul McGrath, "Reggae's free spirit: Toots gives it his all," *Globe and Mail,* June 14, 1980, 3.

66 In 2006, *The Harder They Come* was translated from film to the stage. The play debuted at London's Theatre Royal Stratford East. Such was the success of the play that it later enjoyed two more London runs, at the Barbican in 2008 and the Playhouse Theatre, 2009, before coming to Toronto's Canon Theatre in 2009. Jan Ryan, the play's producer, had originally seen the film in a theatre in Brixton in the 1970s and was – some thirty years later – able to convince Perry Henzell, the filmmaker, to write a stage version

286 *Notes to pages 110–14*

of the movie. Just as the Jamaican movie, replete with thick patois, had resonated with audiences outside of Jamaica, so too did the play score successes in those centres that boasted significant Jamaican populations. See Jon Kaplan, "Rousing reggae: The stage version of the classic film *The Harder They Come* has a powerful beat," *NOW,* July 26, 2009; and CBC, "*The Harder They Come* hits Toronto: Musical is based on 1972 film that made Jimmy Cliff a star," *CBC News: Arts and Entertainment* (online), July 20, 2009. Not every critic, however, was as charitable. The *Star*'s Richard Ouzounian, for example, complained, "Boy, I've never seen a musical ostensibly in English that was in such desperate need of subtitles": "The play's harder to take than iconic film," *Toronto Star,* July 24, 2009.

67 Robert Martin, "A new sound from Jamaica and a new Clyde-style hero," *Globe and Mail,* August 25, 1973, "Entertainment" cover page.

68 Lawrence O'Toole, "Reggae the Jamaican pop," *Globe and Mail,* May 7, 1975, 17.

69 Stephen Brunt, "Sibbles' new sound dips into mainstream," *Globe and Mail,* July 10, 1982, 5.

70 Mittoo had been living in Toronto since 1969.

71 Dave and Ansell Collins, *Dave and Ansil Collins in Toronto,* G-Clef CLEF-0011, 1974.

72 CKFM's Carl Banas was a big supporter of Mittoo and often featured him on his popular evening show. See Howes, liner notes, Jackie Mittoo, *Wishbone.*

73 Jackie Mittoo, *Let's Put It All Together,* United Artists, 1975; *Reggae Magic,* Canadian Talent Library 477–5164, 1972; and *Wishbone.*

74 Howard Cable, as quoted in Howes, liner notes, Jackie Mittoo, *Wishbone.*

75 The issue with the sound or volume of the bass guitar would continue to plague Canadian recordings throughout Canadian reggae's golden age.

76 Jackie Mittoo, interview by I. Jabulani Tafari, *Reggae Report* 6 (1988): 8–9.

77 Earth, Roots and Water boasted Adrian Miller, whose future with 20th Century Rebels awaited him in the next decade. Noel Ellis was the son of legendary ska pioneer Alton Ellis. For an excellent overview of Summer Records, see Kevin Howes, liner notes, *Summer Records Anthology, 1974–1988,* Light in the Attic Records LITA029, 2007.

78 Klive Walker, *Dubwise: Reasoning from the Reggae Underground* (Toronto: Insomniac Press, 2005), 160.

79 Peter Goddard, "Olivia makes a play for T.O. reggae," *Toronto Star,* January 12, 1980, F1.

80 Ibid.

81 Rap Rose, as quoted in Hill, "Backbeat for Jah Jah," 10–11.

82 Interview, Mike Smith.

83 For further discussion on the CanCon and MAPL regulations, see Gary McGroarty, dir., *This Beat Goes On: Canadian Pop Music in the 1970s* (Toronto: EMI Music Canada, 2009).

84 Paul Hyde, ibid.

85 Hill, "Backbeat for Jah Jah," 10–11.

86 Ibid.

87 Interview, Phil Vassell.

88 Bruce Cockburn, *Dancing in the Dragon's Jaws,* True North Records TN37, 1979.

Notes to pages 114–19   287

89 The song's stock continues to rise. In 2005, Canadians voted "Wondering Where the Lions Are" twenty-ninth on a list of the fifty most essential tracks in English-language Canadian pop music history. See *50 Tracks with Jian Ghomeshi,* CBC Radio, 2005.

90 Bernie Finkelstein, in McGroarty, *This Beat Goes On.*

91 Ibid.

92 Bruce Cockburn, ibid.

93 Leroy Sibbles performed at the Horseshoe in 1978: see Ray Conlogue, "Jazz/folk," concert listings, *Globe and Mail,* March 29, 1978, 15.

94 Garry Steckles, "A reggae feast for Toronto," *Toronto Star,* October 11, 1980, F3.

95 "For your night on the town," concert listings, *Globe and Mail,* July 29, 1978, 34.

96 Kim Cameron, "Rock 'n' roll is a deep crack in civilization that can free the spirit," *Globe and Mail,* November 19, 1977, 6.

97 For his part, Cameron is now "dealing practically with the world" as Microsoft's chief architect of identity and has been called one of the fifty most powerful people in networking. See Jack Kapica, "Laws of identity: Interview, Kim Cameron," *Globe and Mail,* March 31, 2009.

98 Mary Walpole, "Dining around the town with Mary Walpole," event listings, *Globe and Mail,* September 21, 1974, 38.

99 "Sattalites perform," *Globe and Mail,* May 25, 1988, C10; and Steckles, "A reggae feast for Toronto," F3. See also "Starring at the Forum," *Toronto Star,* May 19, 1983, E7.

100 These acts include, but are in no way limited to, Lillian Allen; Leroy Sibbles; Ishan People; Chalawa; O. Travis; Earth, Roots and Water; the Mighty Mystics; the Fudge Brothers; the Dilliters; Tropical Energy Experience; Carlene Davis; Lorna Dixon; and, of course, Jackie Mittoo.

101 Adele Freedman, "Toronto reggae explodes despite security damper," *Globe and Mail,* October 20, 1980, 17.

102 Ibid.

103 Ibid.

104 Lewis, as quoted in McGrath, "Island rhythms find new roots," 6.

105 Interview, Andru Branch, Halifax, August 23, 2010.

106 This was a common route to reggae.

107 Paul McGrath, "The Selecter uses ska to leave 'em dancing," *Globe and Mail,* May 16, 1980, 20.

108 Paul McGrath, "The beat: Jumping ska rhythm and rock," *Globe and Mail,* October 4, 1980, 9.

109 William Littler, "Reggae star Sibbles rides the new wave," *Toronto Star,* July 28, 1980, D4.

110 Dill Pickles, as quoted in Paul McGrath, "Hot dub," *Globe and Mail,* March 6, 1982, "Entertainment" cover page.

111 Interview, Brian Robertson, Toronto, September 23, 2011.

112 Goddard, "Olivia makes a play for T.O. reggae."

113 Truths and Rights, "Metro's No. 1 Problem," Rhythm Discs RD-500, 1981.

114 20th Century Rebels, "Running from the F.B.I.," *Rebelution,* Rebelution REB001, 1983.

288 *Notes to pages 119–22*

115 UB40, "Red Red Wine," DEP International DEP 7, 1983; and Colin Larkin, ed., *The Guinness Who's Who of Reggae* (London: Guinness Publishing, 1994), 277–78.

116 The band has since made four in this series of albums of Jamaican covers. See UB40, *Labour of Love,* DEP International DEP 5, 1983; *Labour of Love II,* DEP International DEPCD 14, 1989; *Labour of Love III,* DEP International DEPCD 18/Virgin 7243 8 46469 29, 1998; and *Labour of Love IV,* Virgin CDV3072, 2010.

117 Larkin, *The Guinness Who's Who,* 277–78.

118 I was at the band's Kingswood performances on August 26, 1986; August 15, 1988; and August 9, 1993.

119 Adele Freedman, "Gladiators' reggae as tight as a fist," *Globe and Mail,* June 24, 1983, E6.

120 In 2001, there were approximately 1,270,400 Italians, 1,071,100 Ukrainians, and 713,000 East Indians living in Canada, compared to only 160,210 Jamaicans. See Colin Lindsay, *Profiles of Ethnic Communities in Canada: The Jamaican Community in Canada, 12* (Ottawa: Statistics Canada, 89–621-XIE, 2007); and Statistics Canada, "Profile for Census Metropolitan Areas and Census Agglomerations, 2006 Census," 94–581-XCB2006004, 2008.

121 Reggae shared a category with calypso from 1985 until 1993, before getting its own separate category in 1994. Only one calypso artist, however, won the award prior to 1994. For a review of the inaugural year for the reggae-calypso category, see Will Aitken, "Jolt of Juno power could do the trick," *Globe and Mail,* November 2, 1985, D3.

122 Peter Goddard, "He's Metro's grand old man of reggae," *Toronto Star,* May 29, 1982, F3.

123 William Burrill, "Why Jamaican reggae star Sibbles moved to Toronto – in January, yet!," *Toronto Star,* August 3, 1982, A2.

124 Goddard, "He's Metro's grand old man of reggae," F3.

125 Alan Niester, "Sibbles collects five awards," *Globe and Mail,* April 29, 1983, E4.

126 Goddard, "He's Metro's grand old man of reggae," F3.

127 Burrill, "Why Jamaican reggae star Sibbles moved to Toronto," A2; interview, Leroy Sibbles, Kingston, Jamaica, March 1, 2011.

128 Littler, "Reggae star Sibbles rides the new wave," D4.

129 Goddard, "He's Metro's grand old man of reggae," F3; see also Burrill, "Why Jamaican reggae star Sibbles moved to Toronto," A2. For further discussion on the issues of memory and experience, see Robert Perks and Alistair Thomson, eds., *The Oral History Reader* (Abingdon-on-Thames, UK: Routledge, 2006); and Alessandro Portelli's *They Say in Harlan County: An Oral History* (New York: Oxford University Press, 2011); "Oral History as a Genre," in *Narrative and Genre,* ed. Mary Chamberlain and Paul Thompson (London: Routledge, 1998), 23–45; and *The Death of Luigi Trastulli, and Other Stories: Form and Meaning in Oral History* (Albany: State University of New York Press, 1990).

130 Alan Niester, "Sibbles keeps his good-time reggae on the mark," *Globe and Mail,* February 19, 1981, 22.

131 Burrill, "Why Jamaican reggae star Sibbles moved to Toronto," A2.

132 On July 7, 1984, for instance, Sibbles, alongside Black Uhuru, Aswad, Dennis Brown, Musical Youth, and others, performed for twenty-five thousand people at London's

Crystal Palace. See Greg Quill, "Sibbles makes a splash in London," *Toronto Star,* July 26, 1984.

133 The lack of support or interest in the arts in Canada is an issue that has been raised in several key works. Among the best are Jonathan F. Vance, *A History of Canadian Culture* (Don Mills, ON: Oxford University Press, 2009); Mary Vipond, *The Mass Media in Canada* (Toronto: James Lorimer, 1989); and Maria Tippett, *Making Culture: English-Canadian Institutions and the Arts before the Massey Commission,* 3rd ed. (Toronto: University of Toronto Press, 1990).

134 Some Jamaicans were aware of this. As Phil Vassell explained, "Being Jamaican has always been cool ... gave me an edge." See interview, Phil Vassell.

135 Interview, Rupert "Ojiji" Harvey.

136 Various non-Jamaicans that I interviewed spoke of the feisty boldness and self-assuredness of their Jamaican friends and colleagues: interview, Andru Branch; interview, Natasha Emery, Toronto, December 29, 2010; interview, Isax InJah, Toronto, January 19, 2011; interview, Tomaz Jardim, Toronto, August 21, 2010; and interview, Jesse King, Toronto, February 15, 2011.

137 Norman Otis Richmond, "Film festival focuses on issue of racism," *Globe and Mail,* October 11, 1984, E5.

138 Jennifer Hodge and Roger McTair, dirs., *Home Feeling: Struggle for a Community* (Toronto: National Film Board of Canada, 1983).

139 Perhaps the most recent, if romanticized, appraisal of the Corridor was produced by *The Fifth Estate* in 2006. See Paul Nguyen, dir., "Lost in the Struggle," *The Fifth Estate* (Toronto: CBC, 2006).

140 Leroy Sibbles, *Evidence,* A&M SP-9075, 1982; and Brunt, "Sibbles' new sound dips into mainstream," 5.

141 Brunt, "Sibbles' new sound dips into maintream."

142 Ibid.

143 Liam Lacey, "Record review: Leroy Sibbles, *Evidence,*" *Globe and Mail,* June 5, 1982, 6.

144 Peter Goddard, "Toronto talent helps Jamaica salute youth," *Toronto Star,* March 31, 1985, G1.

145 Greg Quill, "Bruce Cockburn in tune with Jamaican audience," *Toronto Star,* April 8, 1985, D1.

146 Lorenzkowski, *Sounds of Ethnicity,* 103. See also Laura Mason's work on the French Revolution, *Singing the French Revolution: Popular Culture and Politics, 1787–1799* (Ithaca, NY: Cornell University Press, 1996), 3.

147 For music as a process and not a product, see Philip V. Bohlman, "On the Unremarkable in Music," *19th-Century Music* 16, 2 (1991): 214; Roger Chartier, *Cultural History: Between Practices and Representations* (Ithaca, NY: Cornell University Press, 1988), 40–41; and Lorenzkowski, *Sounds of Ethnicity,* 103. See also Simon Frith, "Music and Identity," in *Questions of Cultural Identity,* ed. Stuart Hall and Paul du Gay (London: Sage Publications, 1996), 109.

148 For many artists, simply surviving a Jamaican audience *in* Jamaica was a huge success. In 1980, the *Toronto Star*'s reggae specialist, Gary Steckles, illustrated the importance of Reggae Sunsplash in Montego Bay. The annual Jamaican music festival has come to be regarded as the ultimate test of a reggae artist's stature: if you can impress a

290　*Notes to pages 125–29*

critical crowd sated by more than two dozen top groups over four nights, you're on your way. Garry Steckles, "Carlene Davis could make break for reggae," *Toronto Star,* October 11, 1980, F3.

149 Peter Bailey, "Conspiracies of Meaning: Music-Hall and the Knowingness of Popular Culture," *Past and Present* 144 (1994): 138–70.

150 See Jacques Derrida, *Of Grammatology,* translated by Gayatri Chakravorty Spivak (Baltimore, MD: Johns Hopkins University Press, 1976), 158–63.

151 As American historian Saul Cornell wrote in 1995, for strong textualists such as Derrida and Foucault, "context is not a fixed background against which texts are read. Foreground and background are each textualized and the connections between them must be read inter-textually." See Saul Cornell, "Splitting the Difference: Textualism, Contextualism, and Post-Modern History," *American Studies* 36, 1 (1995): 57.

152 Updates, challenges, dismissals, and resurrections of Derrida's model aside, the philosopher's assessment of the chameleon nature of textual meanings still has currency. For those interested in the discourse on Derrida's philosophy, see Gertrude Himmelfarb, "Telling It as You Like It: Post-Modernist History and the Flight from Fact," *Times Literary Supplement,* October 16, 1992; Bryan D. Palmer, *Descent into Discourse: The Reification of Language and the Writing of Social History* (Philadelphia: Temple University Press, 1990); Steven Watts, "The Idiocy of American Studies: Post-Structuralism, Language, and Politics in the Age of Self-Fulfillment," *American Quarterly* 43 (1991): 625–60; and Cornell, "Splitting the Difference," 57–80.

153 See George Lipsitz, *Dangerous Crossroads: Popular Music, Postmodernism and the Poetics of Place* (New York: Verso, 1994), 97–114.

154 There are, as mentioned earlier, some strong exceptions, including Timothy Taylor's useful section on reggae in *Global Pop: World Music, World Markets* (New York: Routledge, 1997), 155–68.

155 See Goddard, "Olivia makes a play for T.O. reggae."

156 Born in 1872, Robert was Edwin and Annie Sharpe's third child.

157 Robert Lee Sharpe, "Bag of Tools," in *Best Loved Poems of the American People* (New York: Doubleday, 1936), ed. Hazel Fellerman, 99. "At Journey's End" and "The Illusion of Time" were two of Sharpe's elegiac offerings, but neither of them approached the place in the canon that "A Bag of Tools" would one day command.

158 Ibid.; A.L. Alexander, ed., *Poems That Touch the Heart* (New York: Doubleday, 1956 [1941]), 31; and James Dalton Morrison, ed., *Masterpieces of Religious Verse* (New York: Harper and Brothers Publishers, 1948), 306.

159 See Edwin R. Sharpe Papers, 1861–69, Georgia Historical Society, Savannah, Box MS 1485; and James C. Bonner, *Georgia's Last Frontier: The Development of Carroll County* (Athens: University of Georgia Press, 1971). See also Joel Chandler Harris, Brigadier General Clement A. Evans, and W.J. Northen, *Memoirs of Georgia: Historical and Biographical Containing Historical Accounts of the State's Civil, Military, Industrial and Professional Interests, and Personal Sketches of Many of Its People* (Atlanta: Southern Historical Association, 1895), 442.

160 For various citations of "Bag of Tools" in recent religious teachings, see W.F. Haynes, "Pastoral Reflections," St. Simons Island, Georgia, in *Lifeline: Sharing God's Love,* May

Notes to pages 129–30 291

22, 2011; Boyd K. Packer, "The Unwritten Order of Things," delivered at Brigham Young University, October 15, 1996, in Church of Jesus Christ of Latter-Day Saints, *Principles of Leadership: Teacher Manual* (Salt Lake City, UT: Church of Jesus Christ of Latter-Day Saints, 2001), 111; Judge Merl Code, "Black History Month Presentation" (presentation delivered at Christ Church Episcopal School, Greenville, SC, February 15, 2011); R.L. Sharpe, "Bag of Tools," *Age of Jahiliyah,* February 16, 2011, https://ageof jahiliyah.wordpress.com/2011/02/16/a-bag-of-tools-by-r-l-sharpe/; and *The Pastor's Page,* St. Paul's United Methodist Church, West Deptford, NJ, February 2006, https://www.spocala.org/pastors-page/.

161 While there is no evidence that Sharpe was actually initiated in the craft, an excerpt from his poem "The Illusion of Time" testifies to the poet's admiration of Freemasonry: "No, never again / Will you Feel the Grip / Of the Master Mason – / In good Fellowship ... / This Mortal Coil / You have set aside / For the Celestial Lodge – / Where you now Abide." See R.L. Sharpe, "The Illusion of Time," *The Theosophical Path* 39, 3 (March 1931): 222–24; and Carl Glick, ed., *A Treasury of Masonic Thought* (London: Robert Hale, 2003 [1950]).

162 Irish taoiseach Enda Kenny, for example, met with young entrepreneurs in Dublin Castle in April 2011 as part of his government's launch of the National Youth Entrepreneurship Strategy. Kenny chose to close his address with Sharpe's inspirational poem. See Enda Kenny, as quoted in "Taoiseach meets with young entrepreneurs," *Merrion Street: Irish Government News Service,* April 15, 2011. See also Neil French, dir., Maggie Smith reciting "A Bag of Tools," advertisement for the Union Bank of Switzerland, 1998.

163 The poem was, for instance, reimagined by Canadian composer Jack Lorne Hodd. A noted composer of nonsecular music, Hodd was also an organist and musical director at several churches in the Hamilton, Ontario, area, including St. Giles United Church. In 1988, the seventy-four-year-old Hodd composed a piece to fit Sharpe's poem titled "A Bag of Tools: For Voice and Piano." See Jack Lorne Hodd, "Obituary," *Hamilton Spectator,* October 11, 2005; and Jack Lorne Hodd and R.L. Sharpe, *A Bag of Tools: For Voice and Piano,* Leslie Vocal Series no. 7068 (Oakville, ON: Leslie Music Supply, 1988). Perhaps more famously, the British band Oasis used an excerpt of Sharpe's poem in their chart-topping track "Go Let It Out." The band, however, slightly altered some of Sharpe's original text: "Is it any wonder why princes and kings / Are clowns that caper in their sawdust rings / And ordinary people that are like you and me / We're the keepers of their destiny." The retooling of the lyrics worked in terms of commercial success: Oasis hit number one on both the UK and Canadian singles charts with the song. See Oasis, "Go Let It Out," *Standing on the Shoulder of Giants,* Big Brother RKIDCD 002, 2000.

164 Every single Jamaican interviewed for this work was brought up in the church. According to the US Department of State's report *July–December, 2010 International Religious Freedom Report: Jamaica* (Washington, DC: Bureau of Democracy, Human Rights, and Labor, 2011), the religious breakdown, by percentage, of the international (non-resident) Jamaican population (2.7 million) in 2010 was as follows: Church of God, 24; Seventh-Day Adventist, 11; Pentecostal, 10; Baptist, 7; Anglican, 4; Roman

292   *Notes to pages 130–31*

Catholic, 2; United Church, 2; Methodist, 2; Jehovah's Witnesses, 2; Moravian, 1; Brethren, 1; unstated, 3; other, 10; and no religious affiliation, 21.

165   Eric Doumerc, "Nuff Lyrics, the Heptones – 'Book of Rules,'" *Reggae Review.com*, April-May 2007. See also Stephen Davis and Peter Simon, *Reggae Bloodlines: In Search of the Music and Culture of Jamaica* (New York: Da Capo Press, 1992 [1977]).

166   Interview, Leroy Sibbles.

167   The film did not, however, reach Canadian shores until late 1980. See Steckles, "A reggae feast for Toronto," F3.

168   As film critic David Walker opined: "If *The Harder They Come* introduced reggae on the big screen, giving it a cinematic identity, then Ted Bafaloukos' *Rockers* gave it heart and soul." See David Walker, "DVD Review: *Rockers*," *DVD Talk*, June 21, 2005, https://www.dvdtalk.com/reviews/17242/rockers-25th-anniversary-edition/.

169   The first Heptones version of "Book of Rules" was featured on its eponymous full-length album released in 1973. Sharpe's original poem was appended with another verse and put into music by Heptones' harmonist Barry Llewellyn and legendary Jamaican producer Harry Johnson, a.k.a. Harry J (of African, Sicilian, and Scottish decent, no less). The song was a number one hit in Jamaica and even crept into the lower echelons of the UK pop charts when it was rereleased on the band's *Night Food* (1976) album for Island Records. The tune was also one of the few in the Heptones' catalogue that was not sung by Leroy Sibbles. Sibbles did, however, come to sing the song in a live setting throughout the course of his solo career, including the time he spent in Canada. See the Heptones, "Book of Rules," written by Barry Llewellyn, Harry Johnson, and R.L. Sharpe, as found on the Heptones, *Book of Rules,* Jaywax HJ 112/Island Records ILPS 9297, 1973; and *Night Food,* Island Records ILPS 9381, 1976; various artists, *Rockers,* original soundtrack from the film, Island Records ILPS 9587, 1979; and Jo-Ann Greene, review of "Book of Rules," *Allmusic.com,* 2011.

170   Jerry Johnson, "Various artists, *Rockers* soundtrack," album review, *Globe and Mail,* December 20, 1980, 7.

171   Citizen K., "The Heptones: Book of Rules," *Just a Song: Thoughts on Songs and Songwriters,* blog, April 28, 2009, http://justasong2.blogspot.com/2009/04/heptones-book-of-rules.html.

172   Interview, Fergus Hambleton, Toronto, July 10, 2010.

173   Bobby and the Midnites (a.k.a. Bob Weir), *Bobby and the Midnites,* Arista 204.175, 1981.

174   David Gans, *Conversations with the Dead: The Grateful Dead Interview Book* (Cambridge, MA: Da Capo Press, 2002), 130–31.

175   The third stanza added by Llewellyn and Johnson was as follows: "Look when the rain has fallen from the sky / You know the sun will be only with us for a while."

176   For an excellent overview of how the texts of Scottish ballads, for example, were "improved" and reimagined, see Valentina Bold, "'Nouther Right Spelled nor Right Setten Down': Scott, Child and the Hogg Family Ballads," in *The Ballad in Scottish History,* ed. Edward J. Cowan (Phantassie, UK: Tuckwell Press, 2000), 116–41; Edward J. Cowan, "Hunting of the Ballad," in Cowan, *The Ballad in Scottish History,* 1–18; Charles Duffin, "Fixing Tradition: Making History from Ballad Texts," in Cowan, *The*

Notes to pages 132–34   293

Ballad in Scottish History, 19–35; Christopher Harvie, "Ballads of a Nation," *History Today* 49, 9 (1999): 10–16; and Catherine Kerrigan, "Reclaiming History: The Ballad as a Women's Tradition," *Etudes Ecossaises* 1 (1992): 343–50.

177 One of the more elaborate and memorable affairs was "Afroheat: Sounds of the People," which included Bishop Desmond Tutu and Harry Belafonte alongside Queen Street West regulars the Parachute Club and Leroy Sibbles. The event took place on June 1, 1986, at Toronto's Massey Hall. See Tom Hawthorn, "Afroheat takes audience on trip around the globe," *Globe and Mail,* June 2, 1986, C12.

178 In 2006, human rights groups gave Jamaica the dubious distinction of being the most homophobic place on earth. See Tim Padgett, "The most homophobic place on earth?," *Time World,* April 12, 2006.

179 See Stuart Henderson, *Making the Scene: Yorkville and Hip Toronto in the 1960s* (Toronto: University of Toronto Press, 2011).

180 This fact was perhaps best evidenced in multiracial bands such as "V." Comprised of Truths and Rights' Mohjah, future Parachute Club lead singer Lorraine Segato, Canadian Aces' drummer Billy Bryans, and Rough Trade bassist Terry Wilkins, "V" was, according to Jennings, "nothing less than a collective supergroup," a supergroup that chose the Bamboo for its home. Mohjah, just as Sibbles had, wielded a powerful influence on the trajectory of many Queen Street West bands and was also a member of Big Sugar, with Gordie Johnson and stalwart reggae bassist Garry Lowe. See Nicholas Jennings, liner notes, various artists, *QSW: The Rebel Zone,* Columbia CK 80698, 2001; Liam Lacey, "Review of *Compass,*" *Globe and Mail,* October 19, 1983; and Walker, *Dubwise,* 173.

181 Peter Goddard, "Nightbeat," *Performance: Canada's Leading Theatre Magazine,* May 6–12, 1985, 29–30, 33.

182 Catherine O'Hara, as quoted in Richard O'Brien and Patti Habib, *The Bamboo Cooks: Recipes from the Legendary Nightclub* (Toronto: Random House, 1997), 9.

183 Mary Margaret O'Hara is sister to famous Canadian actor and comedian Catherine O'Hara. Their brother Marcus O'Hara was a partner with Richard O'Brien in the warehouse salon known as the Dream Factory before O'Brien opened the Bamboo in 1983. O'Brien and Habib, *The Bamboo Cooks,* 10.

184 Lacey, "Good news, music from Queen Street," *Globe and Mail,* February 14, 1984, 22.

185 "Entertainment guide," *Toronto Star,* February 9, 1984, 118. Though it was used by reggae musicians in Jamaica and around the world, lovers rock's reggae beat has its origins in England. From the late 1970s onward, lovers rock has mostly been used in songs associated with romantic themes.

186 The Valentine's Day show was one of Sibbles' first performances at the club, which had been open for only six months. Sibbles became the marquee act at the Bamboo in its early years.

187 See Brian Osborne, "From Patriotic Pines to Diasporic Geese: Emplacing Culture, Setting Our Sights, Locating Identity in a Transnational Canada," *Canadian Journal of Communication* 31, 1 (2006): 147–75; and Opp and Walsh, *Placing Memory and Remembering Place in Canada,* 6.

188 Memories collectively gleaned from the following interviews: Rupert "Ojiji" Harvey; Leroy Sibbles; Mike Smith; Andru Branch; Natasha Emery; Patti Habib, Toronto,

294   *Notes to pages 135–42*

February 28, 2011; Fergus Hambleton; Isax InJah; David Kingston; Errol Nazareth, Toronto, January 6, 2011; and Brian Robertson.

189   Ibid.

190   Ibid.

191   For a similar discussion involving Indigenous voices and glaciers, see Julie Cruikshank, *Do Glaciers Listen? Local Knowledge, Colonial Encounters, and Social Imagination* (Vancouver: UBC Press, 2005); and Opp and Walsh, *Placing Memory and Remembering Place in Canada,* 7.

192   For further discussion on personal and localized meanings, see Creates, *Places of Presence*; Steven High and David W. Lewis, *Corporate Wasteland: The Landscape and Memory of Deindustrialization* (Toronto: Between the Lines, 2007); Dolores Hayden, *The Power of Place: Urban Landscapes as Public History* (Cambridge, MA: MIT Press, 1995); and Opp and Walsh, *Placing Memory and Remembering Place in Canada.*

193   Interview, Leroy Sibbles.

194   Ibid.

195   Leroy Sibbles, *On Top,* Micron MICCAN-0052, 1983.

196   Mark Miller, "Sibbles' music spare, elegant," *Globe and Mail,* December 22, 1983, E5.

197   In 2001, over 70 percent of the country's total Jamaican population lived in Toronto. See Lindsay, *Profiles of Ethnic Communities in Canada.*

198   Interviews with Rupert "Ojiji" Harvey, Fergus Hambleton, and Nicholas Jennings (Toronto, January 17, 2011).

199   Gregory Isaacs, Dennis Brown, and Sugar Minott (more than once) were all infamous no-shows of the 1980s era.

200   Interviews with Mike Smith, Fergus Hambleton, David Kingston, and Brian Robertson.

201   "TTC's all-night Yonge St. bus terrorized by drunks and goons," *Toronto Star,* November 28, 1988, A4. See also "All-night dance ends in violence," *Toronto Star,* August 4, 1987, A2.

202   As told to David Kingston. A similar process occurred in Yorkville during the 1960s. See Henderson, *Making the Scene.*

203   Aswad, UB40, Steel Pulse, and Maxi Priest have all enjoyed successful international careers.

204   Bissoondath, *Selling Illusions.*

205   Interviews with Rupert "Ojiji" Harvey and Fergus Hambleton.

206   Leroy Sibbles, interview by Carter Van Pelt, https://www.leroysibbles.com, c. 2010.

207   Interview, Leroy Sibbles.

Chapter 5: The Bridge Builders

1   Hilda B. Neatby, "The New Century," in *The Canadians 1867–1967,* ed. J.M.S. Careless and R.C. Brown (Toronto: Macmillan, 1968), 137–71.

2   Interview, Andru Branch, Halifax, August 23, 2010.

3   Interview, Sam Weller, Toronto, July 29 and August 5, 2010.

4   Augustus Pablo, *King Tubby Meets Rockers Uptown,* Shanachie SH 1007, 1987. See interview, Jesse King, Toronto, February 15, 2011.

Notes to pages 142–48 295

5 The Sattalites' Fergus Hambleton worked with McGillivray on the former's solo work. Interview, Bruce McGillivray, Toronto, August 19, 2011.

6 Fergus Hambleton, as quoted in Jamie Kastner, "The Grand Ambassadors of Reggae Music in Canada: The Sattalites," *Canadian Musician* 18, 3 (1996): 45.

7 Interview, Greg Lawson, Toronto, February 7, 2011.

8 Interview, David Kingston, Toronto, September 1, 2010.

9 Interview, Fergus Hambleton, Toronto, July 10, 2010.

10 Interview, Mark Matthews, Toronto, January 12, 2011.

11 Interview, Errol Nazareth, Toronto, January 6, 2011.

12 Interview, Nicholas Jennings, Toronto, January 17, 2011.

13 Interview, Jeffrey Holdip, Toronto, January 20, 2011. Jeffrey's dad was a DJ at Toronto's UNIA Hall (Marcus Garvey Hall) in the 1950s.

14 Interview, Tomaz Jardim, Toronto, August 21, 2010.

15 Ibid. Jericho consisted of Andru Branch and future Tabarruk members Mike Taylor and myself.

16 The London-born Jardim can today meet an older Afro-Jamaican market lady and be reminded of his mother and his grandmother during a time that predated Jamaican independence. Some of Jardim's Jamaican family members are among those examined in Peta Gay Jensen's work on colonial families in Jamaica. See Peta Gay Jensen, *The Last Colonials: The Story of Two European Families in Jamaica* (London: Radcliffe Press, 2005); and interview, Tomaz Jardim.

17 Prince Buster, in Jeremy Marre, dir. and prod., *Reggae Britannia* (London: BBC Four, 2011).

18 For further discussion, see Stuart Henderson, *Making the Scene: Yorkville and Hip Toronto in the 1960s* (Toronto: University of Toronto Press, 2011).

19 Dick Hebdige, *Cut 'n' Mix: Culture, Identity and Caribbean Music* (London: Comedia, Methuen, 1987), 93.

20 Desmond Dekker, "Israelites," Green Light GLS 411, 1969.

21 Marre, *Reggae Britannia*.

22 Joseph Heathcott, "Urban Spaces and Working-Class Expressions across the Black Atlantic: Tracing the Routes of Ska," *Radical History Review* 87 (Fall 2003): 193.

23 Ibid., 184.

24 Klive Walker, *Dubwise: Reasoning from the Reggae Underground* (Toronto: Insomniac Press, 2005), 25.

25 Interview, Brian Robertson, Toronto, September 23, 2011.

26 Interview, Adrian Miller, Toronto, February 6, 2011.

27 Interview, JuLion King, Toronto, January 28, 2011.

28 Interview, Mark Matthews.

29 Interview, Adrian Miller.

30 Marre, *Reggae Britannia*; interview, Brinsley Forde, Coventry, UK, November 8, 2010; interview, Michael Virtue, Coventry, UK, November 8, 2010; and interview, Adrian Miller.

31 Vivien Goldman, *The Book of Exodus: The Making and Meaning of Bob Marley and the Wailers' Album of the Century* (New York: Three Rivers Press, 2006), 67.

32 Don Letts, as quoted ibid., 58–59.

296   *Notes to pages 148–53*

33 Walker, *Dubwise,* 43.
34 Interview, Tomaz Jardim.
35 Ibid.
36 Ibid. Jardim also has fifty-plus audio interviews that Marley gave.
37 Interview, Sebastian Cook, Toronto, February 11, 2011.
38 Marley played Toronto on November 1, 1979. Interview, Jeffrey Holdip.
39 Interview, Klive Walker, Pickering, ON, September 9, 2010.
40 Ibid.
41 Goldman, *The Book of Exodus,* 175.
42 One thinks of the Slits, the mostly all-female punk outfit, whose debut album, *Cut,* was produced by Dennis Bovell, from the pioneer UK reggae group Matumbi. The Slits also recorded a version of "Man Next Door," a song written by Jamaican lovers rock stalwart John Holt. Generation X, with Billy Idol and Tony James, also borrowed heavily from reggae's dub aesthetic for their early recordings. See the Slits, *Cut,* Island Records 200 874-320, 1979, and "Man Next Door," Y Records/Rough Trade Y 4, RT 044 UK, 1980; and Generation X, *Generation X,* Chrysalis PV 41169, 1978.
43 Lee "Scratch" Perry, as quoted in Goldman, *The Book of Exodus,* 185.
44 Vivien Goldman, "Interview, Bob Marley," *Sounds* (London), September 3, 1977; Goldman, *The Book of Exodus,* 186–87.
45 Paul Simonon, as quoted in Goldman, *The Book of Exodus,* 187–88.
46 Goldman, "Interview, Bob Marley"; and Goldman, *The Book of Exodus,* 186–87.
47 Aswad, "Concrete Slaveship," *Aswad,* Island Records ILPS 9399, 1976; and the Clash, "London's Burning," *The Clash,* CBS S CBS 82000, 1977.
48 From Marley's "Punky Reggae Party." See Bob Marley and the Wailers, "Jamming"/ "Punky Reggae Party," Island Records 109 072, 1977; and Hebdige, *Cut 'n' Mix,* 96.
49 The Clash, "White Man in Hammersmith Palais," CBS S CBS 6383, 1978.
50 Bob Marley and the Wailers, "Jamming"/"Punky Reggae Party."
51 The Clash, "Guns of Brixton," written by Paul Simonon, *London Calling,* Epic E2 36328, 1979.
52 Interestingly, "Guns of Brixton" was one of the few Clash songs written entirely by bassist Paul Simonon. Simonon, who as a white kid was in the minority when he attended school in London's Brixton area, explained that reggae for him and his other white friends "became our music, so to speak, because I suppose the lyrics and sentiment, was sort of like, well it was to do with the rebel stance which we all associated with." See Paul Simonon, in Marre, *Reggae Britannia.*
53 The "sus law" was, in the end, a free pass to harass members of Britain's black community. For further discussion, see Tom Terrell, liner notes, Linton Kwesi Johnson, *Independant Intavenshan: The Island Anthology,* Island Records 524 575-2, 1998, 8.
54 For further discussion, see Martin Walker, *The National Front* (Glasgow: Fontana Collins, 1978).
55 Walker, *Dubwise,* 189.
56 Neil Spencer, "Reggae: The sound that revolutionised Britain," *The Guardian,* January 29, 2011.
57 For a good overview of the evolution of the original Rock Against Racism movement in Britain, see Daniel Rachel, *Walls Come Tumbling Down: The Music and Politics of*

Rock Against Racism, 2 Tone and Red Wedge (London: Picador, 2016); and Ian Goodyear, "Rock Against Racism: Multiculturalism and Political Mobilization, 1976–81," *Immigrants and Minorities* 22, 1 (2003): 44–62. Another excellent examination can be found in David Widgery, *Beating Time* (London: Pluto, 1986).

58 Walker, *Dubwise,* 190.

59 Paul Gilroy praised the Rock Against Racism movement for its antiracist stance but warned that the movement may have superficially equated antiracism with black liberation. See Paul Gilroy, *There Ain't No Black in the Union Jack: The Cultural Politics of Race and Nation* (Chicago: University of Chicago Press, 1987).

60 For further discussion of Toronto's KKK chapter, see Julian Sher, *White Hoods: Canada's Ku Klux Klan* (Vancouver: New Star Books, 1983); and Ciaran O Maolain, *The Radical Right: A World Directory* (Burnt Mill, UK: Longman, 1987), 47.

61 Interview, Nicholas Jennings.

62 Ibid.

63 *Rebel Music* 1, June 1981, and *Rebel Music* 2, September 1982, newsletters from the private collection of Nicholas Jennings.

64 Interview, Nicholas Jennings.

65 Ibid.

66 Ibid.

67 The Clash, "Armagideon Time," *Black Market Clash,* Epic WPE38540, 1980. "Jah Punk" was a term coined by Vivien Goldman in the late 1970s in Britain, see Goldman, *The Book of Exodus,* 185.

68 Interview, Willi Williams, Pickering, ON, February 19, 2011.

69 Interview, Adrian Miller.

70 R. Zee Jackson, interview with James Marck, as cited in Nancy Gyokeres, "Jackson Fights the Reggae Cause," *Music Scene,* January–February 1984, 16.

71 James Hill, "Backbeat for Jah Jah," *Globe and Mail,* April 5, 1978, 11.

72 Interview, Natasha Emery, Toronto, December 29, 2010.

73 Interview, Nicholas Jennings.

74 Spencer, "Reggae."

75 Interview, Brian Robertson.

76 Interview, Greg Lawson.

77 Ibid.

78 As Klive Walker attested, "Buster's UK television appearance on the program *Ready Steady Go* was a defining moment for many young fans at the time." See Walker, *Dubwise,* 138.

79 The English Beat, *I Just Can't Stop It,* Go-Feet Records BEAT 1, BEAT 001, 1980.

80 The Specials, "Rudie," *The Specials,* 2 Tone Records CDL 1265, 1979.

81 Simon Jones's *Black Culture, White Youth: The Reggae Tradition from JA to UK* (Basingstoke, UK: Macmillan, 1988), 105, still ranks among the most important assessments of how reggae music operated as a bridge between black and white youth culture in British urban centres. Sebastian Clarke's *Jah Music: The Evolution of the Popular Jamaican Song* (London: Heinemann Educational Books, 1980) is likewise commendable for its consideration of the mixing of black and white youth subcultures in the urban centres of a nascent British reggae scene. Black and white youth and the

298 *Notes to pages 158–64*

intersection of the punk and reggae subcultures is also a feature of Dick Hebdige's important works *Subculture: The Meaning of Style* (London: Methuen, 1979) and *Cut 'n' Mix*. Hebdige was highly influenced by Roland Barthes's semiotic theory regarding cultural phenomena. See Roland Barthes, *Mythologies* (Paris: Editions de Seuil, 1957).

82 At their most uncharitable, music critics have called UB40 "cod reggae," referring to the music being bland and, crucially, white (despite the band's two Jamaicans, one half-Jamaican and one Arab member). See Colin Larkin, ed., *The Guinness Who's Who of Reggae* (London: Guinness Publishing, 1994), 277–78.

83 Jones, *Black Culture, White Youth,* 112.

84 Jones believed the same was true in the case of Britain's inner cities; see ibid., 104–5.

85 Ibid., 141.

86 Interview, Mark Matthews.

87 Interview, Jesse King.

88 Interview, Jeffrey Holdip.

89 Interview, Todd Britton, Guelph, ON, January 8, 2011.

90 Interview, Errol Nazareth.

91 Ibid.

92 Gary McGroarty, dir., *This Beat Goes On: Canadian Pop Music in the 1970s* (Toronto: EMI Music Canada, 2009).

93 Interview, David Kingston.

94 Interview, Tomaz Jardim.

95 Robert Martin, "Wailers get them dancing in the aisles," *Globe and Mail,* June 9, 1975, 14.

96 Ibid.

97 See "Rastafarians called most violent crime group in New York," *Globe and Mail,* June 11, 1975, 3; "U.S. report says sect uses marijuana as an aphrodisiac," *Globe and Mail,* June 11, 1975, 3; "Religion's members are basically anarchists," *Globe and Mail,* June 11, 1975, 3; "Reggae records the beliefs of the rudies and Rastas," *Globe and Mail,* June 11, 1975, 3; "Cultists believed Selassie would take them back to Ethiopia," *Globe and Mail,* June 11, 1975, 3; and "Church says troublemakers can't be Brethren," *Globe and Mail,* June 11, 1975, 3.

98 Sandie Rinaldo, "Interview, Bob Marley at Maple Leaf Gardens," *Canada AM,* CTV, June 9, 1978.

99 Ibid.

100 Garry Steckles, "Carlene Davis could make break for reggae," *Toronto Star,* October 11, 1980, F3.

101 Walker, *Dubwise,* 84–85.

102 Steckles, "Carlene Davis could make break for reggae," F3.

103 "Best of the Century," *Time Magazine,* December 31, 1999; and Jane Robins, "Yawns greet BBC millennium line-up," *The Independent,* December 3, 1999.

104 Interview, Fergus Hambleton.

105 Bob Marley and the Wailers, *Natty Dread,* Tuff Gong 422–846 204–1, 1974.

106 See, for example, Steely Dan, "Haitian Divorce."

107 Interview, Paul Corby, Toronto, January 26, 2011.

108 Interview, David Fowler, Toronto, September 22, 2010. Marley played the university's Centre Sportif on May 4, 1976, during his *Rastaman Vibration* tour.

109 Interview, Todd Britton.

110 Walter Jekyll, ed., *Jamaican Song and Story: Annancy Stories, Digging Sings, Ring Tunes, and Dancing Tunes*, with an introduction by Alice Werner (London: David Nutt/Folk-Lore Society, 1907; repr., Mineola, NY: Dover, 2005 [1966]), 6.

111 Interview, Sam Weller.

112 Holdip later heard Marley's "Jamming" on Q107 in Grade 10. After school, he went straight to Sam the Record Man and bought Marley's live album *Babylon by Bus*. See interview, Jeffrey Holdip.

113 Interview, Andru Branch.

114 Interview, Perry Joseph, Orangeville, ON, June 9, 2017.

115 Interview, Isax InJah, Toronto, January 19, 2011.

116 Ibid.

117 Interview, Fergus Hambleton.

118 Paul McGrath, "NORML's reggae rally serves joint purpose," *Globe and Mail,* July 26, 1979.

119 Interview, Natasha Emery.

120 Fowler had spent the summer of love in San Francisco and then moved to Montreal with the band that helped to bring the psychedelic phase to eastern Canada. Although he voted for the Parti Québécois, Fowler, like many other anglophones living in Quebec, was motivated to leave because of the contentious politics in the province in the 1970s. Fowler moved to Toronto in 1978, at the age of twenty-eight. Interview, David Fowler.

121 Ibid.

122 Ibid.

123 Interview, Sebastian Cook.

124 Interview, JuLion King.

125 Ibid.

126 Interview, Wayne Hanson, Toronto, December 30, 2010.

127 Interview, JuLion King.

128 Interview, Jeffrey Holdip.

129 Ibid.

130 Interview, Tomaz Jardim.

131 Ibid.

132 Interview, Greg Lawson.

133 Ibid.

134 Ibid.

135 Interview, Paul Corby.

136 Ibid.

137 Ibid.

138 Interview, Natasha Emery.

139 Ibid.

140 Ibid.

300 *Notes to pages 171–91*

141 Interview, Isax InJah.
142 Ibid.

Chapter 6: Blackness and Whiteness

1 Todd Fraley, "I Got a Natural Skill ... : Hip-Hop, Authenticity, and Whiteness," *Howard Journal of Communications* 20 (2009): 37–38.
2 Nicholas Wade, synthesizing scientific data, convincingly contends that human evolution is "recent, copious and regional": see *A Troublesome Inheritance: Genes, Race and Human History* (New York: Penguin Books, 2014), 4.
3 Fraley, "I Got a Natural Skill," 37–38.
4 More recent scholarship on hip hop has afforded some elasticity to this latter approach. Witness author William Perkins' endorsement of white rapper MC Serch, who was given approval for not "trying to be Black." See William E. Perkins, "The Rap Attack: An Introduction," in *Droppin' Science: Critical Essays on Rap Music and Hip Hop Culture,* ed. William E. Perkins (Philadelphia: Temple University Press, 1996), 36.
5 The remainder was 1 percent white and 2 percent Asian. See Gregory Stephens, *On Racial Frontiers: The New Culture of Frederick Douglass, Ralph Ellison, and Bob Marley* (Cambridge: Cambridge University Press, 1999), 167–68; and Scott Gurtman, "The Influence of Bob Marley's Absent, White Father" (essay for Rhetoric of Reggae Music, University of Vermont, Burlington, 2002), 3.
6 Stephen Davis, *Bob Marley* (London: Plexus, 1993 [1985]); and Vivien Goldman, *The Book of Exodus: The Making and Meaning of Bob Marley and the Wailers' Album of the Century* (New York: Three Rivers Press, 2006), 30. For further discussion on Norval Marley and Bob Marley's English relatives, see Ben Leach, "Bob Marley's long-lost cousins traced to Devon coastal town," *The Telegraph,* May 20, 2009; Trystan Jones and Genevieve Tudor, "World War One: Bob Marley's father 'neurotic and incontinent,'" *BBC.com,* August 4, 2014; and Glenys Roberts, "Revealed: The white ex-naval officer who fathered Bob Marley was a British captain from Essex," *Dailymail.co.uk,* April 18, 2012.
7 Cedella Booker, as quoted in Stephens, *On Racial Frontiers,* 169.
8 Bunny Wailer, in Kevin Macdonald, dir., *Marley* (New York: Magnolia Pictures/Universal Pictures, 2012).
9 Klive Walker, *Dubwise: Reasoning from the Reggae Underground* (Toronto: Insomniac Press, 2005), 45.
10 Cedella Booker, as quoted in Davis, *Bob Marley.*
11 For further discussion on Marley's father, see Gurtman, "The Influence of Bob Marley's Absent, White Father."
12 For an excellent overview of how Marley's "whiteness" affected his "blackness," see Colin Grant, *The Natural Mystics: Marley, Tosh and Wailer* (London: Random House, 2011), 40–48.
13 See Stephens, *On Racial Frontiers,* 149.
14 Marley, in Macdonald, *Marley.*
15 While it might not approximate hard science, I surveyed approximately fourteen websites boasting the "Top 100" reggae songs of all time. I found that between 65 and

Notes to page 191 301

72 percent of the songs listed did not have Rasta-related themes, and a little fewer than half of the artists were not Rasta. The results that emerged out of the University of the West Indies in Mona, Jamaica, are perhaps more compelling. In 2009, the university conducted a symposium centred on identifying the top one hundred Jamaican songs of the previous fifty years. The criteria for inclusion allowed for, as former Jamaican finance and planning minister Omar Davies explained, "any Jamaican genre of music recorded or produced whether in Jamaica or overseas – between 1957 and 2007." To qualify, the artists had to "be Jamaican born, a naturalised Jamaican or first generation Jamaican born elsewhere." The songs could be either originals or, given their importance to Jamaican music, cover songs. The panel was headed by Davies and included the coauthor of *Reggae Routes,* Wayne Chen; Jamaican musicologist Vaughn "Bunny" Goodison; broadcaster Francois St. Juste; journalist Basil Walters; and a variety of key Jamaican musicians, including Fab Five bandleader Frankie Campbell, Boris Gardiner, Dean Fraser, and Sly Dunbar (all of whom I've had the privilege of performing with). The top twenty were as follows:

1 "One Love/People Get Ready" (Bob Marley and the Wailers)
2 "Oh Carolina" (the Folkes Brothers)
3 "54–46" (Toots and the Maytals)
4 "Got to Go Back Home" (Bob Andy)
5 "My Boy Lollipop" (Millie Small)
6 "Many Rivers to Cross" (Jimmy Cliff)
7 "Israelites" (Desmond Dekker and the Aces)
8 "Cherry Oh Baby" (Eric Donaldson)
9 "Simmer Down" (the Wailers)
10 "Carry Go Bring Come" (Justin Hinds and the Dominoes)
11 "The Harder They Come" (Jimmy Cliff)
12 "No Woman No Cry" (Bob Marley and the Wailers)
13 "Rivers of Babylon" (the Melodians)
14 "Redemption Song" (Bob Marley and the Wailers)
15 "Easy Snappin'" (Theophilus Beckford)
16 "Girl I've Got a Date" (Alton Ellis)
17 "Satta Massagana" (the Abyssnians)
18 "Everything I Own" (Ken Boothe)
19 "Eastern Standard Time" (Don Drummond)
20 "Wear You to the Ball" (U-Roy)

Only seven of these songs can be considered Rasta-themed, and slightly fewer than half of the artists are Rastas (I counted the mento group the Folkes Brothers as Rasta – given the importance of Count Ossie's involvement – and Toots as not Rasta, which he wasn't when he recorded "54–46"). At the risk of sounding trite, I must once again stress that some, and maybe even most, of the best reggae is Rasta-reggae, and the best reggae artists may very well be Rastas. I'm only trying to highlight that while much of Jamaican reggae is oppositional, it is not all Rasta. Crucially, eleven of the top twenty songs were recorded by artists who, at least at the time of the recording, did not have dreadlocks. See Mel Cooke, "'One Love/People Get Ready' heads Jamaican

302 *Notes to pages 191–92*

Top 100: Criticism, congrats after list revealed at UWI," *Gleaner* (Jamaica), April 20, 2009, cover story.

16 Marley himself was not immune to criticism from those who believed he sold out to gain a wider appeal. As Mike Alleyne observed: "The commercially motivated dilution of a core element is alarming at the very least, and raises serious questions regarding authenticity and integrity ... Later Marley albums and, indeed, posthumous releases provide further evidence of this damaging trend." It is, however, hard to reconcile "Rastaman Chant," "Zimbabwe," "Africa Unite," "Babylon System," or "Talkin' Blues" – which has the lyric "I'm a gonna take a just one step more, 'cause I feel like bombin' a church, now that you know that the preacher is lyin'" – with a "damaging trend" that compromised reggae's oppositional text. The Wailers' 1965 rendition of "What's New Pussycat," on the other hand, seems far more dangerous. See Mike Alleyne, "White Reggae: Cultural Dilution in the Record Industry," *Popular Music and Society* 24, 1 (2000): 19–20. See also Mike Alleyne, "Resistance and Subversion in Caribbean Popular Music," *The Griot* 16, 1 (1997): 58–64, and Bob Marley and the Wailers, "Talkin' Blues," *Natty Dread,* Tuff Gong 422–846 204–1, 1974.

17 Mike Alleyne, for example, believes that major-label careers of later reggae acts such as Steel Pulse, Aswad, and Third World suffered because of Marley's success and were made to conform to his aesthetic. See Alleyne, "White Reggae," 19–20. Having had the privilege of working with Aswad's Brinsley Forde for years, I find it hard to imagine him conforming to any preconceived notion of what and how his art was going to emerge.

18 Interview, Brinsley Forde, Coventry, UK, November 8, 2010.

19 Forde addressed the quality of his and others' work as it applied to Marley's production sensibilities: "Bob said, 'I and I are the roots.' Break it down: the roots give sustenance to the tree with leaves and branches, which, in its turn, bears fruit, which bears seed to start the whole process. See the high-end production spread that seed so far around the world that the reggae influence can be found present in all genres of music, past or present." See ibid.

20 Interview, Ali Campbell, Cleveland, OH, April 8, 2006; Montreal, April 10, 2006; and Toronto, April 11, 2006.

21 For Dave Thompson, UB40's version of "I Got You Babe" was "truly, truly ghastly." Len J. McCarthy's flawed and awkwardly titled thesis compared "I Got You Babe" to what he, a self-confessed "dabbler" in reggae music, considered more authentic songs in an attempt to categorically dismiss UB40 as a "real" reggae band. Thompson and McCarthy may have missed the send-up that was intended. To be fair to them, the video for the song, which featured a caricature of Margaret Thatcher and Ronald Reagan embracing during a romantic dance, was banned by the BBC. See Len J. McCarthy, "The Significance of Corporeal Factors and Choreographic Rhythms in Jamaican Popular Music between 1957–1981 (Ska, Rocksteady, Reggae), with an Historical and Critical Survey of all Relevant Literature Dealing with Jamaican Folk, Religious and Popular Musics and Dance" (PhD diss., York University, 2007), and Dave Thompson, *Wheels Out of Gear: 2-Tone, the Specials and a World in Flame* (London: Soundcheck Books, 2004), 203–4.

22 As Dave Thompson rightly observed, "UB40 aren't simply established as the most successful reggae act outside of Bob Marley, they are also among the most successful bands in British chart history." See Thompson, *Wheels Out of Gear,* 203.

23 In what was otherwise an exceptional journalistic history of reggae, Lloyd Bradley did not mention UB40 (though ample space was afforded to other exclusively black British reggae bands such as Aswad, Black Slate, Matumbi, and Steel Pulse). One of the "choice quotes" used on the back cover to endorse the book was a review from *Mojo* magazine that declared: "And if UB40 get a mention, I missed it. Isn't that recommendation enough for you?" See Lloyd Bradley, *Bass Culture: When Reggae Was King* (London: Viking, 2000), back cover.

24 Lord Creator is one example. In the copyright-free era of Jamaican music, musicians such as Kentrick Patrick (a.k.a. Lord Creator) made a paltry ten pounds per song from Jamaican producers and received no royalties, even in the case of tracks that became significant hits, such as his "Kingston Town." By the early 1990s, Patrick was in a very poor way. Suffering in hospital from a stroke and not knowing how he was going to pay for his medical bills, he was saved by UB40's version of "Kingston Town" (a single that sold 581,000 units in France alone). As Patrick himself attested, "I have five and half acres of land and live in a big mansion and can buy anything I want. I'm thankful." Lord Creator, as quoted in Alan Brown and Marina Warsama, "*I Love Jamaica*" (London: BBC Television, 2002). See also Claude Mills, "Lord Creator has a passion for ballads," *Sunday Gleaner* (Jamaica), April 12, 1998, E3.

25 Ranking Miss P and Don Letts, as quoted in Brown and Warsama, "*I Love Jamaica.*"

26 "An era dies with Isaacs," *Gleaner* (Jamaica), November 14, 2010. See also UB40, *Labour of Love,* DEP International DEP 5, 1983; *Labour of Love II,* DEP International DEPCD 14, 1989; *Labour of Love III,* DEP International DEP CD 18/Virgin 7243 8 46469 29, 1998; and *Labour of Love IV,* Virgin CDV3072, 2010.

27 UB40, *The Fathers of Reggae,* DEP International DEPCD20/Virgin 7243 8 12675 2 3, 2002.

28 Lloyd Bradley has since been more generous towards UB40 and had high praise for the rerelease of the band's debut album *Signing Off*: "But pride of place must go to 12 minutes of Madam Medusa, the witty, wickedly perceptive verbal caricature of Margaret Thatcher and her rise to power, which issues a stark warning of what she might be capable of. It was the sharpest summing up of the Iron Lady outside of the satirical puppet show of the times." Similarly, *Mojo* magazine's four-star review of the rerelease struck a more charitable tone: "[*Signing Off*] is flinty, political and Britain-focused reggae." Likewise, *Record Collector* magazine said of the album that it "remains one of the most articulate and important political statements in British popular music." See Lloyd Bradley, "30th anniversary edition of the group's great debut album," *BBC Review,* November 9, 2010; Ian Harrison, "Review of UB40, *Signing Off*: Collector's edition," *Mojo,* November 2010, 121; Terry Staunton, "Thirtieth anniversary edition of a conscientious classic: UB40, *Signing Off,*" *Record Collector,* December 2010, 90; and James Brown, "*Signing Off* and the Press," UB40 website, November 6, 2010.

29 A pint glass was broken on his face. See interview, Ali Campbell.

30 Interview, Michael Virtue, Coventry, UK, November 8, 2010.

304 *Notes to pages 193–96*

31 Ibid.

32 The remaining twelve were made up mostly of original, politically conscious material. There was the band's blanket condemnation of twenty-first-century warfare on *Who You Fighting For?* (2005), the warning about HIV/AIDS on *Cover Up* (2001), and an appeal to young Jamaican gunmen to drop their weapons on *Guns in the Ghetto* (1997). See UB40, *Who You Fighting For?,* DEP International DEP CD 23, 2005; *Cover Up,* DEP International DEPDJ56, 2002; and *Guns in the Ghetto,* DEP International DEPCD16/Virgin 7243 8 44402 2 0, 1997.

33 Many academics in the field of hip hop scholarship, as stated earlier, are now considering a liberated notion of whiteness, one that extends beyond its usual linkages with domination and privilege. Henry Giroux and Todd Fraley are among these scholars. They are, however, at odds in one respect. Giroux sees the evolution of the construction of whiteness "as part of a broader project of cultural, social, and political citizenship," whereas Fraley warns that some of the strategies that white MCs employ "continue to essentialize and partition racial identities." See Henry Giroux, "Rewriting the Discourse of Racial Identity: Towards a Pedagogy and Politics of Whiteness," *Harvard Education Review* 67 (1997): 285–320; and Todd Fraley, "I Got a Natural Skill," 49. For other discussions on the intersections between race and identity, culture and politics, see Murray Forman, "Represent: Race, Space and Place in Rap Music," *Popular Music* 19, 1 (2000): 65–90; Ronald L. Jackson, *Scripting the Black Masculine Body: Identity, Discourse, and Racial Politics in Popular Media* (Albany: State University of New York Press, 2006); Perkins, "The Rap Attack," 1–45; Tricia Rose, *Black Noise: Rap Music and Black Culture in Contemporary America* (London: Wesleyan University Press, 1994); and Robyn Wiegman, *American Anatomies: Theorizing Race and Gender* (Durham, NC: Duke University Press, 1995). Bakari Kitwana called this "the new politics of race": see *Why White Kids Love Hip Hop: Wankstas, Wiggers, Wannabes, and the New Realities of Race in America* (New York: Basic Civitas Books, 2005).

34 Jeff Chang, "Overpowered by funk," *San Francisco Bay Guardian,* January 1, 2003. For the most compelling of the various Clash biographies, see Pat Gilbert, *Passion Is a Fashion: The Real Story of the Clash* (London: Aurum Press, 2004); and Chris Saleqicz, *Redemption Song: The Ballad of Joe Strummer* (New York: Faber and Faber, 2007).

35 See also Stephen Duncombe and Maxwell Tremblay, eds., *White Riot: Punk Rock and the Politics of Race* (London: Verso, 2011), 155.

36 For further discussion on Knibb's role in the emancipation movement, see Catherine Hall, *Civilising Subjects: Colony and Metropole in the English Imagination, 1830–1867* (Chicago: University of Chicago Press, 2002).

37 Wiegman, *American Anatomies,* 8.

38 Interview, Fergus Hambleton, Toronto, July 10, 2010.

39 James Ledbetter, "Imitation of Life," in *Gender, Race and Class in Media,* ed. Gail Dines and Jean M. Humez (Thousand Oaks, CA: Sage Publications, 1995), 541.

40 Interview, Isax InJah, Toronto, January 19, 2011.

41 Neil Bissoondath, *Selling Illusions: The Cult of Multiculturalism in Canada* (Toronto: Penguin, 2002), 170.

Notes to pages 196–206 305

42 Chris Dafoe, "UB40 redeems pop reggae," *Globe and Mail,* August 16, 1988, C11.
43 UB40 had no idea "Red Red Wine" was a Neil Diamond song. They believed the song was written by reggae artist Tony Tribe until Diamond's legal counsel got in touch with the band's management.
44 Liam Lacey, "Watered-down reggae from popular UB40," *Globe and Mail,* March 13, 1985, M7.
45 James Marck, "Sattalites don't ignite," *NOW,* June 25–July 1, 1987, 29.
46 James Marck, "Ward shows white stuff," *NOW,* July 2, 1987, 27, 29.
47 Christopher Jones, "Spence above crowd," *NOW,* January 5–11, 1989, 31.
48 Kim Hughes, "Penguins' island groove," *NOW,* April 7–13, 1988, 21.
49 Helen Lee, "Syren Sunday diverts burger bunch," *NOW,* August 4, 1988, 23.
50 Interview, Rupert "Ojiji" Harvey, Toronto, September 6, 2010.
51 Interview, Adrian Miller, Toronto, February 6, 2011.
52 Ibid.
53 Nicholas Jennings, "You want dancehall? Sattalites got it," *Eye* (Toronto), October 8, 1992, 15.
54 Interview, David Kingston, Toronto, September 1, 2010.
55 Interview, Sam Weller, Toronto, July 29 and August 5, 2010.
56 Interview, Errol Nazareth, Toronto, January 6, 2011.
57 Interview, Nicholas Jennings.
58 Interview, Isax InJah.
59 Interview, David Kingston.
60 Interview, Patti Habib, Toronto, February 28, 2011.
61 Interview, Bruce McGillivray, Toronto, August 19, 2011.
62 Interview, Nicholas Jennings.
63 Interview, Jeffrey Holdip, Toronto, January 20, 2011.
64 Interview, David Matthews, Brampton, ON, February 17, 2011.
65 Interview, Denise Jones, Toronto, February 8, 2011.
66 Interview, Leo Cripps, Calgary, January 9, 2011.
67 Interview, Mike Smith, Brampton, ON, July 15, 2010.
68 Interview, Willi Williams, Pickering, ON, February 19, 2011.
69 Interview, Ranford Williams, Toronto, January 20, 2011.
70 Interview, Peter Holung, Newmarket, ON, February 3, 2011.
71 Interview, Sebastian Cook, Toronto, February 11, 2011.
72 Interview, Mark Matthews, Toronto, January 12, 2011.
73 Interview, JuLion King, Toronto, January 28, 2011.
74 Interview, Paul Corby, Toronto, January 26, 2011.
75 Interview, Adrian Miller.
76 Interview, Dalton Higgins, Toronto, February 13, 2011.
77 Interview, David Fowler, Toronto, September 22, 2010.
78 Interview, Mark Matthews.
79 Kevin Howes, liner notes, various artists, *Jamaica to Toronto: Soul Funk and Reggae, 1967–1974,* Light in the Attic LITA019, 2006.
80 Interview, Carrie Mullings, North York, ON, February 7, 2011.

306   *Notes to pages 206–11*

81 In his time, Karl managed Hopeton Lewis, the Sheiks, the Fabulous Flames with Glen Ricketts, the Cougars with Jay Douglas, Ibadan, and Culture Shock (with Whitey Don and Friendly Man a.k.a Friendlyness). See interview, Carrie Mullings.

82 Interview, Errol Nazareth.

83 Neville Francis, as quoted in Jamie Kastner, "The Grand Ambassadors of Reggae Music in Canada: The Sattalites," *Canadian Musician* 18, 3 (1996): 45.

84 One need only witness a Canadian folk or jazz festival during the summer months, when workshop stages put divergent artists on stage together at the same time. The musicians, unrehearsed, have to play together. In many cases, the artists do not even share the same language; they speak through music alone. I have had the great privilege of being in such circumstances dozens of times across Canada and the United Kingdom.

85 Interview, David Fowler.

86 Interview, Jeffrey Holdip.

87 Interview, Natasha Emery.

88 Interview, Isax InJah.

Chapter 7: In Search of the Canadian Sound

1 In his impressive work in the field of aural history, social historian Mark Smith brings to light the importance of keynote sounds – represented and actual sounds that help shape people's understanding of themselves and the society in which they live. See Mark Smith, "Echoes in Print: Method and Causation in Aural History," *Journal of the Historical Society* 2, 3–4 (2002): 318; and Barbara Lorenzkowski, *Sounds of Ethnicity: Listening to German North America, 1850–1914* (Winnipeg: University of Manitoba Press, 2010), 7.

2 See Chalawa, featuring Stranger Cole, the Callander Sisters, Johnny Osbourne, and Collie Smith, *Capture Land,* Green Weenie, 1978; and Chalawa, *Exodus Dub,* Micron Music Limited MICCAN-0008, 1977.

3 Dave Tulloch, "If You Didn't See Them ... You Missed a Great Show," *The Spectrum: Making Minorities Visible* (Ottawa), May 16, 1987.

4 Adrian Miller, in Gary McGroarty, dir., *Rise Up: Canadian Pop Music in the 1980s* (Toronto: EMI Music Canada, 2009).

5 Quoted in Greg Quill, "Sattalites on the rise in the reggae scene," *Toronto Star,* May 15, 1987, D10.

6 The 20th Century Rebels enjoyed a lot of airplay with their track "Running from the F.B.I.," Messenjah with "Jam Session," and the Sattalites with "Gimme Some Kinda Sign" and "Wild."

7 This is discounting Sibbles' 1982 A&M release *Evidence,* which was not, even according to the man himself, strictly a reggae album. Dave Tollington at WEA was a huge reggae fan and was responsible for signing Messenjah. See interview, Nicholas Jennings, Toronto, January 17, 2011.

8 Interview, Mark Matthews, Toronto, January 12, 2011.

9 Interview, Willi Williams, Pickering, ON, February 19, 2011.

10 Interview, David Kingston, Toronto, September 1, 2010.

Notes to pages 211–18   307

11 Interview, JuLion King, Toronto, January 28, 2011.
12 Interview, Carrie Mullings, North York, ON, February 7, 2011.
13 Interview, Peter Holung, Newmarket, ON, February 3, 2011.
14 Interview, Paul Corby, Toronto, January 26, 2011.
15 Interview, Ranford Williams, Toronto, January 20, 2011.
16 Interview, Denise Jones, Toronto, February 8, 2011.
17 Interview, Mike Smith, Brampton, ON, July 15, 2010.
18 Interview, Carrie Mullings.
19 Interview, David Kingston.
20 Interview, Phil Vassell, Brampton, ON, December 8, 2010.
21 Interview, Dalton Higgins, Toronto, February 13, 2011.
22 Interview, Jeffrey Holdip, Toronto, January 20, 2011.
23 Interview, Natasha Emery, Toronto, December 29, 2010.
24 Interview, Paul Corby.
25 Interview, JuLion King.
26 Interview, Klive Walker, Pickering, ON, September 9, 2010.
27 Interview, Rupert "Ojiji" Harvey, Toronto, September 6, 2010.
28 Interview, Isax InJah, Toronto, January 19, 2011.
29 For further discussion, see Klive Walker, *Dubwise: Reasoning from the Reggae Underground* (Toronto: Insomniac Press, 2005).
30 Interview, Adrian Miller, Toronto, February 6, 2011.
31 Interview, Dalton Higgins.
32 Interview, Paul Corby.
33 Interview, Mike Smith.
34 Interview, Phil Vassell.
35 Truths and Rights, "Acid Rain"/"Live Up," Bucktu BT-45–1001, 1980; see Walker, *Dubwise*, 170–71.
36 Truths and Rights, "Metro's No. 1 Problem," written by Vance Tynes and Terrence "Chico" Paul, Rhythm Discs RD-500, 1981.
37 Interview, Rupert "Ojiji" Harvey.
38 Ibid.
39 Interview, Brian Robertson, Toronto, September 23, 2011.
40 Messenjah, "Jam Session," *Jam Session,* WEA 25–04551, 1984.
41 On Lillian Allen's second album, the dub poet chose to employ not only diasporic musicians such as bassist Terry Lewis and hand drummer Quammie Williams but also Parachute Club members Billy Bryans, Lauri Conger, and Dave Gray. Lillian Allen, *Conditions Critical,* Redwood Records RR8802, 1987; see Walker, *Dubwise,* 24–25.
42 Lillian Allen, *Revolutionary Tea Party,* Verse to Vinyl VV101, 1986.
43 Walker articulated the approach that forward-thinking reggae historian and DJ Dermott Hussey undertook: "Dermott said, 'Look, if jazz people use reggae, if rock people use reggae, it's a compliment to us, and what it shows is that the music is not going to get lost, it's not going to get co-opted, but it's going to become part of the language of music internationally, and this is a good thing.' And that was his lesson to me. That's all I needed." See interview, Klive Walker.
44 Interview, Ranford Williams.

308 *Notes to pages 218–27*

45 Interview, Jeffrey Holdip.
46 Interview, Sunray Grennan, Toronto, July 8, 2010.
47 Interview, Jeffrey Holdip.
48 Interview, Rupert "Ojiji" Harvey.
49 See ibid. Apart from Reggae Sunsplash, Messenjah also played the National Stadium in Kingston.
50 Interview, Bruce McGillivray, Toronto, August 19, 2011.
51 Interview, Fergus Hambleton.
52 Interview, Natasha Emery.
53 Gerald Reid, "Sattalites gives performances in local debut," *Weekend Star: The Entertainment Paper* (Kingston), May 29, 1987.
54 John Keating, "Rich Reggae/Pop Fare," *Daily Gleaner* (Jamaica), July 4, 1985, 6.
55 Diskreet, review of *Sattalites, Share*, June 20, 1985, 13.
56 Ibid.
57 Reid, "Sattalites Gives Performances in Local Debut."
58 Tulloch, "If You Didn't See Them ... You Missed a Great Show."
59 Interview, Rupert "Ojiji" Harvey.
60 Interview, Bruce McGillivray.
61 Ibid.
62 David Fowler, as quoted in Jamie Kastner, "The Grand Ambassadors of Reggae Music in Canada: The Sattalites," *Canadian Musician* 18, 3 (1996): 45.
63 Interview, Sam Weller, Toronto, July 29 and August 5, 2010.
64 Interview, Isax InJah.
65 Interview, JuLion King.
66 Interview, Denise Jones.
67 Interview, Paul Corby.
68 Ibid.
69 Liam Lacey, "Rare partnership key to Sattalites' success," *Globe and Mail*, August 17, 1985, 6.
70 Fergus Hambleton, as quoted ibid.
71 Interview, David Kingston.
72 Interview, Sebastian Cook, Toronto, February 11, 2011.
73 Interview, Mark Matthews.
74 Interview, Errol Nazareth, Toronto, January 6, 2011.
75 Sibbles had met Hambleton at a jam session with Bruce Cockburn. Hambleton had been signed to Capitol Records in the early 1970s and was later a member of the new wave band the Basics before cofounding the Sattalites with Bennett. See Lacey, "Rare partnership key to Sattalites' success"; and Liam Lacey, "American band more of brand x," *Globe and Mail*, November 21, 1983, 21.
76 Interview, Fergus Hambleton.
77 Ibid.
78 Tulloch, "If You Didn't See Them."
79 Neville Francis, as quoted in Sattalites, *Sattalites: Ten Years On* (Toronto: self-published, 1991), 4.
80 Interview, Wayne Hanson, Toronto, December 30, 2010.

81 Kastner, "The Grand Ambassadors," 46.

82 Interview, Bruce McGillivray.

83 Lacey, "American band more of brand x," 21.

84 Greg Quill, "Big reggae hullabaloo launches debut album," *Toronto Star,* May 14, 1985, D12.

85 Jo Jo Bennett, as quoted in Sattalites, *Sattalites,* 6.

86 Jo Jo Bennett, as quoted in Reid, "Sattalites gives performances in local debut."

87 Greg Hambleton also owned the publishing company Peer Music Canada, which handled the Sattalites' material.

88 Nicholas Jennings, "Dance Tunes for Idealists," *Maclean's,* August 26, 1985.

89 Liam Lacey, review of *Sattalites, Globe and Mail,* June 20, 1985, E5.

90 James Marck, "Sattalites' Strength," *NOW Magazine,* July 25–31, 1985.

91 Liam Lacey, "From sex, drugs and rock 'n' roll to feeding the world," *Globe and Mail,* December 28, 1985, D9.

92 Bob Thompson, "Forum swings to sounds of soul: Reggae turns on the heat," *Toronto Sun,* June 10, 1987, 69.

93 "Sattalites beam down a beauty," *Globe and Mail,* April 9, 1987.

94 Quill, "Sattalites on the rise in the reggae scene," D10.

95 "Top 40 Albums for June 1987," *National Campus Report,* June 1987.

96 Another Juno for the Sattalites followed in 1996, for the band's *Now and Forever* album: Elizabeth Renzetti, "You oughta know: Morissette sweeps Junos," *Globe and Mail,* March 11, 1996; and Peter Howell, "Morissette tweaks Twain again," *Toronto Star,* March 11, 1996.

97 Christopher Jones, "Satisfying Sattalites," *NOW Magazine,* November 23–29, 1989, 27.

98 Betsy Powell, "Reggae band fights for survival," *Toronto Star,* April 10, 1996.

99 Messenjah, "Could It Be I'm Falling in Love," *Rock and Sway,* Kick Up KUCD-001, 1990.

100 "Grammy board axes polka category to stay 'relevant and responsive,'" *CBC News,* June 4, 2009.

101 Davina Hamilton, "Is reggae dying a slow death?," *Voice-Online,* October 1, 2010.

102 David Rodigan, as quoted ibid.

103 Soloman, as quoted ibid.

104 Interview, David Kingston.

105 Interview, Jesse King, Toronto, February 15, 2011.

106 Interview, Tomaz Jardim, Toronto, August 21, 2010.

107 Ibid.

108 Interview, JuLion King.

109 David Young explores the dearth of francophones, blacks, and Indigenous people at the Juno Awards, a ceremony designed to celebrate excellence in the Canadian recording industry, in "Ethno-racial Minorities and the Juno Awards," *Canadian Journal of Sociology* 31, 2 (2006): 183–210. He targets the Canadian Academy of Recording Arts and Sciences and its official policies and promotional campaigns, which have, he argues, strategically reduced the representation of minorities while securing anglophone cultural hegemony. While Young's argument may seem overly conspiratorial, having been nominated twice for a Juno in a "black music" category, I can attest to

310 *Notes to pages 233–40*

the fact that the presentations of the Junos to the award winners in these categories are seldom televised, thus lessening the exposure of nondominant genres to the largest audience.

110 Peter Goddard, "Olivia makes a play for T.O. reggae," *Toronto Star,* January 12, 1980, F1.

111 Fergus Hambleton, as quoted in Lacey, "Rare partnership key to Sattalites' success," 6.

112 Ibid.

113 Walker, *Dubwise,* 162.

114 WEA rereleased Messenjah's *Rock You High* in 1983 (the band had released it independently the year before) and *Jam Session* in 1984. The Sattalites' third album, *Miracles,* was released on WEA's Risqué Disque label in 1989, while their fourth effort, *All Over the World,* came out on Intrepid/Capitol in 1992.

115 Goddard, "Olivia makes a play for T.O. reggae."

116 Frances Henry, *The Caribbean Diaspora in Toronto: Learning to Live with Racism* (Toronto: University of Toronto Press, 1994).

117 Interview, Carrie Mullings.

118 Interview, Sebastian Cook.

119 I crawled out of the concert hall one night after gunshots rang out on the second level of the Masonic Temple, just as Frankie Paul was about to take the stage.

120 Interview, Adrian Miller.

121 Interview, Dalton Higgins.

122 Interview, Nicholas Jennings.

123 For works that deal with this very Canadian theme, see Jonathan F. Vance, *A History of Canadian Culture* (Don Mills, ON: Oxford University Press, 2009); Mary Vipond, *The Mass Media in Canada* (Toronto: James Lorimer, 1989); and Maria Tippett, *Making Culture: English-Canadian Institutions and the Arts before the Massey Commission,* 3rd ed. (Toronto: University of Toronto Press, 1990).

124 Interview, Phil Vassell.

Chapter 8: A Strange Land

1 Norman Otis Richmond, "Reggae: The heartbeat goes on," *Globe and Mail,* September 21, 1983, 17.

2 Alan Niester, "Reggae's sun about to set," *Globe and Mail,* April 4, 1985, E4.

3 Stephen Duncombe and Maxwell Tremblay, eds., *White Riot: Punk Rock and the Politics of Race* (London: Verso, 2011), 217.

4 Interview, Willi Williams, Pickering, ON, February 19, 2011.

5 See Peter Goddard, "Olivia makes a play for T.O. reggae," *Toronto Star,* January 12, 1980, F1.

6 See Dick Hebdige, *Subculture: The Meaning of Style* (London: Methuen, 1979); and Simon Jones, *Black Culture, White Youth: The Reggae Tradition from JA to UK* (Basingstoke, UK: Macmillan, 1988).

7 The Specials, "Ghost Town," 2 Tone Records CHS TT 1217, 1981. See also Jones, *Black Culture, White Youth,* 110.

8 For further discussion, see Dick Hebdige, *Cut 'n' Mix: Culture, Identity and Caribbean Music* (London: Comedia, Methuen, 1987), 96.

9 Chips Richards, as quoted in Sebastian Clarke, *Jah Music: The Evolution of the Popular Jamaican Song* (London: Heinemann Educational Books, 1980), 151.

10 Interview, Rupert "Ojiji" Harvey, Toronto, September 6, 2010.

11 Interview, Bruce McGillivray, Toronto, August 19, 2011.

12 Colin Larkin, ed., *The Guinness Who's Who of Reggae* (London: Guinness Publishing, 1994), 256.

13 Snow, *Informer,* East/West/Warner, 1994.

14 Big Sugar, "Turn the Lights On," A&M AMCD032299, 1999.

15 Witness the works of Michie Mee, Dream Warriors, and Maestro Fresh Wes. See Klive Walker, *Dubwise: Reasoning from the Reggae Underground* (Toronto: Insomniac Press, 2005), 174–75.

16 Ibid., 173.

17 Bedouin Soundclash, "When the Night Feels My Song," B-Unique Records, BEDOUIN1, 2004.

18 Bedouin Soundclash, "Chart History," *Billboard.com.*

19 Interview, Kevin Howe, Vancouver, June 12, 2017.

20 Tim Perlich, "Jamaica to Toronto: Lost stars of the city's vibrant 60s R&B scene finally get their chance to shine," *NOW,* July 13, 2006, cover story.

21 July 15, 2006. I had the privilege of serving as the onstage musical director for the event.

22 Interview, Jay Douglas, Toronto, June 7, 2017.

23 Billboard Staff, "Charli XCX, Tove Lo, and other hit artists made 2014 an international year for pop," *Billboard.com,* December 14, 2014. Curiously, "Rude" only reached number six on the Canadian charts.

24 See The Insider, "Remember the BamBoo? Exploring Toronto's reggae roots," *Globe and Mail,* August 1, 2014; and Deana Sumanac, "Magic! tops Billboard chart with Rude, exposing Canada's reggae roots," *The National,* CBC, August 1, 2014.

25 Ibid.

26 See Dan Taekema, "Toronto's role in reggae: Bob Marley, Haile Selassie and the Lion of Judah have found a new wall of fame in Toronto," *Toronto Star,* September 19, 2015; and Shereita Grizzle, "Canada recognizes reggae music with huge mural," *Gleaner* (Jamaica), September 24, 2015.

27 Interview, Carrie Mullings, North York, ON, February 7, 2011.

28 Ibid.

29 Ibid.

30 Interview, Jay Douglas.

31 The Sattalites, "Understanding," *Live via Sattalites,* Axe Records, AXS 527, 1987.

Bibliography

Interviews

Jamaican Canadians
Jo Jo Bennett, Toronto, October 19 and November 23, 2010.
Paul Bennett, Toronto, August 17, 2010.
Carol Brown, Bolton, ON, January 30, 2011.
Leo Cripps, Calgary, January 9, 2011.
Karen Cyrus, North York, ON, February 14, 2011.
Jay Douglas, Toronto, June 7, 2017.
Sunray Grennan, Toronto, July 8, 2010.
Wayne Hanson, Toronto, December 30, 2010.
Carl Harvey, North York, ON, November 25, 2010.
Rupert "Ojiji" Harvey, Toronto, September 6, 2010.
Earle Heedram (a.k.a. the Mighty Pope), Richmond Hill, ON, December 13, 2010.
Peter Holung, Newmarket, ON, February 3, 2011.
Denise Jones, Toronto, February 8, 2011.
JuLion King, Toronto, January 28, 2011.
Adrian Miller, Toronto, February 6, 2011.
Leroy Sibbles, Kingston, Jamaica, March 1, 2011.
Mike Smith, Brampton, ON, July 15, 2010.
Marcia Vassell, Brampton, ON, February 17, 2011.
Phil Vassell, Brampton, ON, December 8, 2010.
Klive Walker, Pickering, ON, September 9, 2010.
Ranford Williams, Toronto, January 20, 2011.
Willi Williams, Pickering, ON, February 19, 2011.

Non-Jamaican Canadians
Andru Branch, Halifax, August 23, 2010.
Todd Britton, Guelph, ON, January 8, 2011.
Sebastian Cook, Toronto, February 11, 2011.
Paul Corby, Toronto, January 26, 2011.

Natasha Emery, Toronto, December 29, 2010.
David Fowler, Toronto, September 22, 2010.
Patti Habib, Toronto, February 28, 2011.
Fergus Hambleton, Toronto, July 10, 2010.
Jeffrey Holdip, Toronto, January 20, 2011.
Kevin Howes, Vancouver, June 12, 2017.
Isax InJah, Scarborough, ON, January 19, 2011.
Tomaz Jardim, Toronto, August 21 and November 24, 2010.
Nicholas Jennings, Toronto, January 17, 2011.
Perry Joseph, Orangeville, ON, June 9, 2017.
Jesse King, Toronto, February 15, 2011.
David Kingston, Toronto, September 1, 2010.
Greg Lawson, Toronto, February 7, 2011.
Mark Matthews, Toronto, January 12, 2011.
Bruce McGillivray, Toronto, August 19, 2011.
Errol Nazareth, Toronto, January 6, 2011.
Brian Robertson, Toronto, September 23, 2011.
Sam Weller, Toronto, July 29 and August 5, 2010.

First-Generation Canadians of Jamaican Heritage
Dalton Higgins, Toronto, February 13, 2011.
David Matthews, Brampton, ON, February 17, 2011.
Carrie Mullings, North York, ON, February 7, 2011.

Other
Ali Campbell: Toronto, June 21, 1999; Cleveland, OH, April 8, 2006; Montreal, April 10, 2006; Toronto, April 11, 2006; Toronto, August 31, 2016.
Brinsley Forde: Tenerife, June 18, 2005; Coventry, UK, November 8, 2010.
Ernest Ranglin: Tower Isle, Jamaica, May 1, 2006; Calgary, July 23, 2011.
David Swarbrick: Coventry, UK, November 8–11, 2010.
Michael Virtue: Toronto, June 21, 1999; Coventry, UK, November 8, 2010; Cleveland, OH, April 8, 2006; Montreal, April 10, 2006; Toronto, April 11, 2006; Toronto, August 31, 2016.
Terrence "Astro" Wilson: Toronto, August 31, 2016.

Discography

10CC. "Dreadlock Holiday." *Bloody Tourists*. Mercury 9102 503, 1978, LP.
20th Century Rebels. "Running from the F.B.I." *Rebelution*. Rebelution REB001, 1983, EP.
Abyssinians. "Forward on to Zion"/"Satta A Massagana." Klik KL 631, 1977, 7 inch.
Aitken, Laurel. "Boogie in My Bones"/"Little Sheila." Starlite [UK], ST.45 011, 1960, 7 inch.
Allen, Lillian. *Conditions Critical*. Redwood Records RR8802, 1987, LP.
–. *Freedom and Dance*. Verse to Vinyl VVI09, 1998, CD.

314   *Bibliography*

–. *Let the Heart See*. Verse to Vinyl 1987, LP.

–. *Nothing but a Hero*. 1992. Verse to Vinyl WRPM08, 1992, LP.

–. *Revolutionary Tea Party*. Verse to Vinyl VV101, 1986, LP.

Aswad. "Concrete Slaveship." *Aswad*. Island Records ILPS 9399, 1976, LP.

–. "Cool Runnings Inna W11 Area." *Aswad: The BBC Sessions*. Strange Fruit SFRCD 002, 1997, CD.

Beatles, The. "Got to Get You into My Life." Capitol Records 4274, 1976, 7 inch.

Bedouin Soundclash. "When the Night Feels My Song." B-Unique Records, BEDOUIN1, 2004, CD single.

Belafonte, Harry. *Belafonte Sings of the Caribbean*. RCA Victor LPM1505, 1957, LP.

–. *Calypso*. RCA Victor LPM-1248, 1956, LP.

–. "Jamaica Farewell." RCA Victor 47-6663, 1956, 7 inch.

Bennett, Jo Jo, and Mudie's All Stars. "Leaving Rome." Moodisc Records International HM-148, 1969, 7 inch.

Bennett, Louise. *Children's Jamaican Songs and Games*. Folkways Records FW07250/ FC 7250, 1957, LP/CD.

Big Sugar. "Turn the Lights On." A&M AMCD032299, 1999, CD.

Black Uhuru. *Red*. Island Records ILPS 9625, 1981, LP.

Blackwood, Errol. *Chant, Chant*. Blade CCR-9240, 1987, LP.

Bobby and the Midnites (a.k.a. Bob Weir). *Bobby and the Midnites*. Arista 204.175, 1981, LP.

Boney M. "Rivers of Babylon"/"Brown Girl in the Ring." Hansa Records/Sire Records/ Atlantic Records, 1978, 7 inch.

Brown, Dennis. "Promised Land." Simba SM003, 1979, 12 inch.

Brown, Leroy. *Rent a Tile*. Dakarai, 2004, CD.

Burning Spear. *Burning Spear Live*. Island Records/Mango B000003QH8, 1990 [1977], LP.

–. "Marcus Garvey." Capo Records CA-070, 1974, 7 inch.

Bush, Kate. "Kite." *The Kick Inside*. EMI America SW17003, 1978, LP.

Caiola, Al. *Solid Gold Guitar*. United Artists Records ULP 1003, 1962, LP.

Chalawa. *Chalawa Meets Chapter XII*. EMI Music Netherlands 5C 062-23830, 1979, LP.

–. *Exodus Dub*. Micron Music Limited MICCAN-0008, 1977, LP.

–. *Hop, Skip and Jump*. Generation GEN 3009, 1979, LP.

Chalawa, featuring Stranger Cole, the Callander Sisters, Johnny Osbourne, and Collie Smith. *Capture Land*. Green Weenie 1978, LP.

Church, Jarvis. "Run for Your Life." BMG USA 48342, 2002, 12 inch.

Clapton, Eric. "I Shot the Sheriff." *461 Ocean Boulevard*. RSO 2394 138, 1974, LP.

Clash, The. *Black Market Clash*. Epic WPE38540, 1980, LP.

–. *London Calling*. Epic E2 36328, 1979, LP.

–. "London's Burning." *The Clash*. CBS S CBS 82000, 1977, LP.

–. *Sandinista!* Epic E 37037, 1980, LP.

–. "White Man in Hammersmith Palais." CBS S CBS 6383, 1978, 7 inch.

–. "White Riot." CBS S CBS 5058, 1977, 7 inch.

Cockburn, Bruce. *Dancing in the Dragon's Jaws*. True North Records TN37, 1979, LP.

Collins, Dave and Ansell. *Dave and Ansil Collins in Toronto*. G-Clef CLEF-0011, 1974, LP.

Collymore, Sonia. *WYSIWYG (What You See Is What You Get)*. XES/Music Nuff Entertainment/IndiePool 2005, CD.

–. *You Won't See Me Cry*. Fiwi/XES 2003, CD.

Crack of Dawn. *Crack of Dawn*. Columbia/CBS ES-90336, 1976, LP.

Davis, Carlene. "It Must Be Love." Generation GGG 007, 1983, 12 inch.

Dekker, Desmond. "Israelites." Green Light GLS 411, 1969, 7 inch.

Eagles, The. *Hotel California*. Asylum Records AS13084, 1976, LP.

Earth, Roots and Water. *Innocent Youths*. Light in the Attic 2008, CD.

Ellis, Noel. *Rocking Universally*. Light in the Attic 2006, CD.

English Beat, The. *I Just Can't Stop It*. Go-Feet Records BEAT 1, BEAT 001, 1980, LP.

Generation X. *Generation X*. Chrysalis PV 41169, 1978, LP.

Harriott, Derrick, with Audley Williams and Combo. "John Tom." *Dip and Fall Back: Dr. Kinsey to Haile Selassie, Classic Jamaican Mento*. WIRL Records, 1965/Trojan Records, 2005, CD.

Harriott, Joe. *The Joe Harriott Story*. Proper Properbox160, 2011, 4 CDs. Liner notes by Joop Visser.

Heptones, The. "Book of Rules." *Book of Rules*. HJ 112/Island Records ILPS 9297, 1973, LP.

–. *Night Food*. Island Records ILPS 9381, 1976, LP.

Irie, Tippa. "Complain Neighbour." UK Bubblers TIPPA T 2, 1985, 12 inch.

Ishan People. *Ishan People*. GRT 9230–1071, 1977, LP.

–. *Roots*. GRT 9230–1064, 1976, LP.

Jackson, R. Zee. *Seat Up*. Rio RIO-1006, 1980, LP.

Jackson, R. Zee, and Johnny Osbourne. "Brooklyn Special / Zee In De Saddle / Rock Yu Punky Reggae." Culture International BZ.SP-IC0001, 1980, 12 inch.

Johnson, Linton Kwesi. *Independant Intavenshan: The Island Anthology*. Island Records 524575–2, 1998, CD. Liner notes by Tom Terrell.

Joseph, Clifton. Dub Poet at large with the Livestock Band. *Oral/Trans/Missions*. Blue Moon BM 129, 1990, LP.

Lazo. *Satisfaction Guaranteed*. Spynn CCR-9999, 1987, LP.

Led Zeppelin. "D'yer Mak'er." *Houses of the Holy*. Atlantic SD 7255, 1973, LP.

Lewis, Hopeton. *Take It Easy: Rocksteady with Hopeton Lewis*. Island UK ILP 957, 1967, LP.

Marley, Bob, and the Wailers. "Blackman Redemption." *Confrontation*. Tuff Gong/Island Records, 422–846 207–1, 1983, LP.

–. *The Complete Bob Marley and the Wailers, 1967 to 1972 Soul Rebels*. Fiftyfive Records FF 1389–2, 1998.

–. *Exodus*. Island 9123 021, 1977, LP.

–. "Jamming"/"Punky Reggae Party." Island Records 109 072, 1977, 7 inch.

–. *Natty Dread*. Tuff Gong 422–846 204–1, 1974, LP.

–. "No Woman, No Cry." *Live!* Tuff Gong/Island Records, 1975.

Bibliography

–. "One Love/People Get Ready"/"So Much Trouble in the World"/"Keep on Moving." Tuff Gong 12 TGX 1, 1984 [1977], 12 inch.

–. "Redemption Song." Island Records WIP 6653, 1980, 7 inch.

–. "Trench Town Rock." Tuff Gong, 1970, 7 inch.

Matumbi. "Nothing To Do With You." *Point of View.* EMI RDC 2001, 1979, LP.

McGhie, Wayne, and the Sounds of Joy. *Dirty Funk.* Light in the Attic 2004, CD.

McLean, Nana. *Dream of Life.* G Clef GCLP-101, 1979, LP.

–. *Nana McLean.* Penthouse, 1997, CD.

Melodians, The. "By the Rivers of Babylon." Summit/Trojan SUM-6508, 1970, 7 inch.

Messenjah. *Cool Operator.* Version VLP-001, 1987, LP.

–. "Jam Session." *Jam Session.* WEA 25–04551, 1984, LP.

–. *Rock and Sway.* Kick Up KUCD-001, 1990, CD.

–. *Rock You High.* WEA 25–02021, 1983 [1982], LP.

Mighty Diamonds, The. "Pass the Kouchie." Island Records 12WIP 6838, 1982, 12 inch.

Miller, Adrian. *Empty Promises.* Bridge BR-1, 1987, LP.

Mittoo, Jackie. *Let's Put It All Together.* United Artists, 1975, LP.

–. *Reggae Magic.* Canadian Talent Library 477–5164, 1972, LP.

–. *Wishbone.* Summus Records SUS 50,002, 1971/Light in the Attic Records LITA021, 2006, CD. Liner notes by Kevin Howes.

Mittoo, Jackie, and Sound Dimension. "Full Up." Studio One, 1968, 7 inch.

–. "Real Rock." Studio One, 1967, 7 inch.

Morris, Eric "Monty." "Penny Reel." *Intensified: Original Ska, 1962–66.* Mango Records, 1979 [1964].

Musical Youth. "Pass the Dutchie." MCA Records Canada MCA-13961, 1982, 12 inch.

Nash, Johnny. *Hold Me Tight.* JAD JS-1207, 1968, LP.

–. "I Can See Clearly Now"/"Stir It Up." Epic 15–2329, 1972, 7 inch.

–. *Tears on My Pillow.* CBS S 69148, 1975.

Oasis. *Standing on the Shoulder of Giants.* Big Brother RKIDCD 002, 2000, CD.

Ojiji. *The Shadow.* Ultra Records URN2101, 1979, LP.

Osbourne, Johnny, and the Sensations, with Boris Gardiner and the Love People. *Come Back Darling.* Trojan Records TTL-29, 1970, LP.

Pablo, Augustus. *King Tubby Meets Rockers Uptown.* Shanachie SH 1007, 1987, LP.

Sattalites, The. *All Over the World.* Intrepid Records, 1992, CD.

–. *Live via Sattalites.* Axe Records AXS 527, 1987, LP.

–. *Miracles.* Risqué Disque/WEA CD-56996, 1989, CD.

–. *Now and Forever.* Childsplay/Sattalite Productions, 1996, CD.

–. *Reggaefication.* Solid Gold Records, 2003, CD.

–. *Sattalites.* Axe Records AXS 525, 1985, LP.

–. *Singles and Remixes.* Sattalite Productions, 1996, CD.

Sibbles, Leroy. *Evidence.* A&M SP-9075, 1982, LP.

–. *Now.* Micron MICCAN-0031/Generation GEN-3012, 1979, LP.

–. *On Top.* Micron MICCAN-0052, 1983, LP.

Simon, Paul. "Mother and Child Reunion." Columbia 4–45547, 1972, 7 inch.

Slits. The. *Cut.* Island Records 200 874–320, 1979, LP.

–. "Man Next Door." Y Records/Rough Trade Y 4, RT 044 UK, 1980, 7 inch.

Small, Millie. "My Boy Lollipop"/"Something's Gotta Be Done." Island/Fontana/ Smash, 1964, 7 inch.

Small Faces. *Small Faces.* Immediate IMLP 008, 1967, LP.

Smith, Ernie, and the Roots Revival. "Don't Down Me Now"/"To Behold Jah." Generation GGG 003, 1979, 12 inch.

–. "Duppy or a Gunman." Various artists, *Original Wild Flower Reggae Hits.* Federal/ Wildflower LP 367, 1974, LP.

–. *To Behold Jah.* Generation GEN-3011, 1979, LP.

Specials, The. "Ghost Town." 2 Tone Records CHS TT 1217, 1981, 12 inch.

–. *The Specials.* 2 Tone Records CDL 1265, 1979, LP.

Spencer Davis Group, The. "Keep on Running." Fontana TF 632, 267514 TF, 1965, 7 inch.

Steely Dan. "Haitian Divorce." ABC Records ABC 4152, 1976, 7 inch.

Snow. *Informer.* EastWest Records America 7567-98436-7, 1994, 7 inch.

–. *Two Hands Clapping.* Virgin/EMI, 2003, CD.

Third World. "96° in the Shade." *96° in the Shade.* London Island Records, 1977.

Truths and Rights. "Acid Rain"/"Live Up." Bucktu BT-45–1001, 1980, 7 inch.

–. "Metro's No. 1 Problem." Rhythm Discs RD-500, 1981, 12 inch.

UB40. *Cover Up.* DEP International DEPDJ56, 2002.

–. *The Fathers of Reggae.* DEP International DEPCD20/Virgin 7243 8 12675 2 3, 2002, CD.

–. *Guns in the Ghetto.* DEP International DEPCD16/Virgin 7243 8 44402 2 0, 1997.

–. *Labour of Love.* DEP International DEP 5, 1983, LP.

–. *Labour of Love II.* DEP International DEPCD 14, 1989, CD.

–. *Labour of Love III.* DEP International DEPCD 18/Virgin 7243 8 46469 2 9, 1998, CD.

–. *Labour of Love IV.* Virgin CDV3072, 2010.

–. "Red Red Wine." DEP International DEP 7, 1983, 7 inch.

–. *Signing Off.* Graduate Records GRAD LP2, 1980, LP.

–. *Who You Fighting For?* DEP International DEP CD 23, 2005.

Various artists. *Alpha Boys' School: Music in Education.* Trojan Records 06076–80550–2, 2006. Liner notes by Mark Williams.

Various artists. *Drums of Defiance: Maroon Music from the Earliest Free Black Communities of Jamaica.* Smithsonian/Folkways Recordings SF 40412, 1992, CD. Liner notes by Kenneth Bilby.

Various artists. *Jamaica to Toronto: Soul Funk and Reggae, 1967–1974.* Light in the Attic LITA019, 2006, CD. Liner notes by Kevin Howes.

Various artists. *QSW: The Rebel Zone.* Columbia CK 80698, 2001. Liner notes by Nicholas Jennings.

Various artists. *Real Roots Reggae: A Canadian Story.* Canadianreggaeworld.com, 2007, CD.

Various artists. *Rockers.* Original soundtrack from the film. Island ILPS 9587, 1979, LP.

Various artists. *Summer Records Anthology, 1974–1988.* Light in the Attic LITA029, CD. Liner notes by Kevin Howes.

318   *Bibliography*

Various artists. *Take Me to Jamaica: The Story of Jamaican Mento.* Pressure Sounds PSCD 51, 2006, CD. Liner notes by Noel Hawkes.

Wailers, The. "What's New Pussycat." Island Records WI-254, 1965, 7 inch.

Wailing Wailers, The. *The Wailing Wailers.* Studio One SOCD 1001, 1996 [1965], CD.

Williams, Willie. "Armagideon Time." Studio One SO 0099, 1978, 7 inch.

Wilson, Delroy. "Better Must Come." Jackpot JP 763, 1971, 7 inch.

Yellowman. "Zungguzungguguzungguzeng." *Yellowman Most Wanted.* Greensleeves, 2007 [1982–87], 12-inch mix.

Other Sources

Adams, Charles Dennis. *Flowering Plants of Jamaica.* Mona, Jamaica: University of the West Indies, 1972.

Alexander, A.L., ed. *Poems That Touch the Heart.* New York: Doubleday, 1956 [1941].

Alleyne, Mike. "Resistance and Subversion in Caribbean Popular Music." *The Griot* 16, 1 (1997): 58–64.

–. "White Reggae: Cultural Dilution in the Record Industry." *Popular Music and Society* 24, 1 (2000): 19–20.

Appadurai, Arjun. *Modernity at Large: The Cultural Dimensions of Globalization.* Minneapolis: University of Minnesota Press, 1996.

Applied History Research Group. *The Peopling of Canada, 1946–1976* [online tutorial]. Calgary: Applied History Research Group, 1997.

Armstrong, Bromley, and Sheldon Taylor. *Bromley: Tireless Fighter for Just Causes.* Pickering, ON: Vitabu Publishing, 2000.

Arnander, Primrose. "Jekyll Family History." In *Gertrude Jekyll: Essays on the Life of a Working Amateur,* edited by Michael Tooley and Primrose Arnander, 7–20. Durham, NC: Michaelmas Books, 1995.

Avery, Donald H. *Reluctant Host: Canada's Response to Immigrant Workers, 1896–1994.* Toronto: McClelland and Stewart, 1995.

Badets, Jane, Jennifer Chard, and Andrea Levett. *Ethnic Diversity Survey: Portrait of a Multicultural Society.* Ottawa: Statistics Canada/Canadian Heritage, 89–593-XIE, 2003.

Bailey, Peter. "Conspiracies of Meaning: Music-Hall and the Knowingness of Popular Culture." *Past and Present* 144 (1994): 138–70.

Baker, Houston A., Jr. *Blues, Ideology, and Afro-American Literature: A Vernacular Theory.* Chicago: University of Chicago Press, 1984.

Ballatyne, Tony. "Mr. Peal's Archive: Mobility and Exchange in Histories of Empire." In *Archive Stories: Facts, Fictions, and the Writing of History,* edited by Antoinette Burton, 87–110. Durham, NC: Duke University Press, 2005.

Baraka, Amiri. *Blues People.* New York: Morrow Quill, 1963.

Baring-Gould, Sabine, and H. Fleetwood Sheppard. *Songs of the West: Folk Songs of Devon and Cornwall Collected from the Mouths of the People.* 4 vols. London: Patey and Willis, 1889–91/Methuen, 1895.

Barrow, Steve, and Peter Dalton. *Reggae: The Rough Guide*. London: Rough Guides, 1997.

Barth, Frederick. Introduction. *Ethnic Groups and Boundaries: The Social Organization of Cultural Difference*. Boston: Little, Brown, 1969.

Barthes, Roland. *Mythologies*. Paris: Editions de Seuil, 1957.

Basch, Linda, Nina Glick Schiller, and Christina Szanton Blanc. *Nations Unbound: Transnational Projects, Postcolonial Predicaments, and Deterritorialized Nation-States*. Luxembourg: Gordon and Breach, 1994.

Bashi, Vilna. "Globalized Anti-blackness: Transnationalizing Western Immigration Law, Policy, and Practice." *Ethnic and Racial Studies* 27, 4 (2004): 584–606.

–. "Neither Ignorance nor Bliss: Race, Racism, and the West Indian Immigrant Experience." In *Race, Migration, Transnationalism, and Race in a Changing New York,* edited by Hector R. Cordero-Guzman, Ramon Grosfoguel, and Robert Smith, 212–38. Philadelphia: Temple University Press, 2001.

–. "Racial Categories Matter Because Racial Hierarchies Matter: A Commentary." *Ethnic and Racial Studies* 21, 5 (1998): 959–68.

Baxter, Ivy. *The Arts of an Island: The Development of the Culture and of the Folk and Creative Arts in Jamaica, 1494–1962 (Independence)*. Metuchen, NJ: Scarecrow Press, 1970.

Bearman, Stuart. "Rastaman Variations: Jason Wilson and Tabarruk." *Eye Magazine,* May 21, 1998.

Beckford, George, and Michael Witter. *Small Garden, Bitter Weed: The Political Economy of Struggle and Change in Jamaica*. London: Maroon Publishing House, 1980.

Beckwith, Martha. "The English Ballad in Jamaica: A Note upon the Origin of the Ballad Form." *Publications of the Modern Language Association of America* 39 (1924): 455–83.

–. *Jamaica Folk-Lore*. New York: American Folk-Lore Society, 1928.

Benjamin, Akua. "The Social and Legal Banishment of Anti-racism: A Black Perspective." In *Crimes of Colour: Racialization and the Criminal Justice System in Canada,* edited by Wendy Chan and Kiran Mirchandani, 177–90. Peterborough, ON: Broadview Press, 2002.

Bennett, Louise. *Aunty Roachy Seh,* edited by Mervyn Morris. Kingston, Jamaica: Sangster's, [1944] 1993.

–. *Jamaica Labrish: Jamaica Dialect Poems*. Kingston, Jamaica: Sangster's, 1966.

–. "Me and Annancy." In Jekyll, *Jamaican Song and Story,* ix–xi.

Bennett, Milton J. *Basic Concepts of Intercultural Communication*. Boston: Intercultural Press, 1998.

Bilby, Kenneth. "The Caribbean as a Musical Region." In *Caribbean Contours,* edited by Sidney W. Mintz and Sally Price, 181–218. Baltimore, MD: Johns Hopkins University Press, 1985.

–. "Gumbay, Myal, and the Great House: New Evidence on the Religious Background of Jonkonnu in Jamaica." *ACIJ Research Review* 4 (1999): 47–70.

–. "Kromanti Dance of the Windward Maroons of Jamaica." *Nieuwe West-Indische Gids* 55, 1–2 (1981): 52–101.

320 *Bibliography*

Bissoondath, Neil. *Selling Illusions: The Cult of Multiculturalism.* Toronto: Penguin Group, 1994.

Bohlman, Philip V. "On the Unremarkable in Music." *19th-Century Music* 16, 2 (1991): 214.

Bold, Valentina. "'Nouther Right Spelled nor Right Setten Down': Scott, Child and the Hogg Family Ballads." In Cowan, *The Ballad in Scottish History,* 116–41.

Bonner, James C. *Georgia's Last Frontier: The Development of Carroll County.* Athens: University of Georgia Press, 1971.

Boothroyd, Ted. "Album Review: *The Peacemaker's Chauffeur.*" *Beat* (Los Angeles) 28, 1 (2009): 51–52.

Bootles, Nannie. *When the Doodle Was the Most Wonderful Doodle in the World: And Makes the Bestest Music in the Whole Wide World,* a reggae memoir. Stouffville, ON: publication pending, 2010.

Bradley, Lloyd. *Bass Culture: When Reggae Was King.* London: Viking, 2000.

–. *Reggae on CD.* London: Kylie Cathy, 1996.

Brand, Dionne. *No Burden to Carry: Narratives of Black Working Women in Ontario, 1920s–1950s.* Toronto: University of Toronto Press, 1989.

Brandel, Rose. *The Music of Central Africa.* The Hague: Martinus Nijhoff, 1962.

Brathwaite, Edward. *The Development of Creole Society in Jamaica, 1770–1820.* Oxford: Oxford University Press, 1971.

"Brief Presented to the Prime Minister, the Minister of Citizenship and Immigration, and Members of the Government of Canada by the Negro Citizenship Association." Ontario Labour Committee Papers, vol. 19, April 27, 1954. Library and Archives Canada.

Broadwood, Lucy E. "English Airs and Motifs in Jamaica." In Jekyll, *Jamaican Song and Story,* 285–88.

Broadwood, Lucy E., and J.A. Fuller Maitland. *English County Songs.* London: Leadenhall Press, 1893.

Brodber, Erna. "Reggae as Black Space." Opening plenary delivered at the Global Reggae Conference, University of the West Indies, Mona, Jamaica, February 18, 2008.

Brodber, Erna, and J. Edward Greene. *Reggae and Cultural Identity in Jamaica.* Mona, Jamaica: Institute of Social and Economic Research, University of the West Indies, 1988.

Brown, Alan, and Marina Warsama. *"I Love Jamaica."* London: BBC Television, 2002.

Brubaker, Rogers. "Ethnicity without Groups." *Archives européennes de sociologie* 43, 2 (2002): 167–68.

Burnet, Jean, and Howard Palmer. *"Coming Canadians": An Introduction to a History of Canada's Peoples.* Toronto: McClelland and Stewart, 1988.

Burns, Robert. *The Works of Robert Burns.* Ware, UK: Wordsworth Editions, 1994.

Calliste, Agnes. "Race, Gender and Canadian Immigration Policy: Blacks from the Caribbean, 1900–1932." *Journal of Canadian Studies* 28, 4 (1993–94): 131–48.

Calliste, Agnes, and George Dei. *Anti-racist Feminism, Critical Race and Gender Studies.* Halifax: Fernwood, 2000.

Carby, Hazel V. *Cultures in Babylon: Black Britain and African America.* London: Verso, 1999.

CARICOM Capacity Development Programme. *2000 Round of Population and Housing Census Project: National Census Report, Jamaica.* Greater Georgetown, Guyana: Regional Statistics Sub-Programme Information and Communication Technologies Caribbean Community, 2000.

CBC Television. "The Grateful Dread: Jason Wilson." *The National,* with Peter Mansbridge, August 19, 2004.

Central Intelligence Agency. "Jamaica." In *The World Factbook.* Washington, DC: CIA, 2013–14.

Chang, Kevin O'Brien, and Wayne Chen. *Reggae Routes: The Story of Jamaican Music.* Philadelphia: Temple University Press, 1998.

Chartier, Roger. *Cultural History: Between Practices and Representations.* Ithaca, NY: Cornell University Press, 1988.

Chevannes, Barry. *Rastafari: Roots and Ideology.* Syracuse: Syracuse University Press, 1995.

Child, Francis James. *The English and Scottish Popular Ballads.* New York: Dover Publications 1965 [1904].

Citizen K. "The Heptones: Book of Rules." *Just a Song: Thoughts on Songs and Song-writers,* blog, April 28, 2009, http://justasong2.blogspot.com/2009/04/heptones -book-of-rules.html.

Clarke, Sebastian. *Jah Music: The Evolution of the Popular Jamaican Song.* London: Heinemann Educational Books, 1980.

Clerk, Astley. *The Music and Musical Instruments of Jamaica: A Lecture Delivered at: Edmondson Hall (Wesley Guild), 19 November, 1913; and Jamaica Institute (Kingston Athenaeum), 15 December, 1913.* Kingston, Jamaica: self-published, 1914. 28 pages.

Cobham, Rhonda. "Jekyll and Claude: The Erotics of Patronage in Claude McKay's *Banana Bottom.*" In *Queer Diasporas,* edited by Cindy Patton and Benigno Sánchez-Eppler, 55–78. Durham, NC: Duke University Press, 2000.

Code, Merl. "Black History Month Presentation." Presentation delivered at Christ Church Episcopal School, Greenville, SC, February 15, 2011.

Collier, James Lincoln. *The Making of Jazz: A Comprehensive History.* New York: Dell, 1978.

Constant, Denis. *Aux sources du reggae: Musique, société et politique en Jamaïque.* Roquevaire, France: Parenthèses, 1982.

Conville, Vincent G. "The Jamaican Canadian Association in a Multiracial and Multi-cultural Society: Four Decades of Service." PhD diss., University of Toronto, 2004.

Conway, Dennis, and Robert B. Potter. "Caribbean Transnational Return Migrants as Agents of Change." *Geography Compass* 1, 1 (2007): 25–45.

Conzen, Kathleen Neils, David A. Gerber, Ewa Morawska, George E. Pozzetta, and Rudolph J. Vecoli. "The Invention of Ethnicity: A Perspective from the U.S.A." *Journal of American Ethnic History* 12, 1 (1992): 3–40.

Cook, Richard, and Brian Morton. *The Penguin Guide to Jazz Recordings.* 9th ed. London: Penguin Books, 2008.

322 *Bibliography*

Cooper, Carolyn. *Noises in the Blood: Orality, Gender and the "Vulgar" Body of Jamaican Culture*. Kingston, Jamaica: Macmillan Caribbean, 1993.

–. *Sound Clash: Jamaican Dancehall Culture at Large*. New York: Palgrave McMillan, 2004.

Cooper, Wayne F. *Claude McKay: Rebel Sojourner in the Harlem Renaissance – A Biography*. Baton Rouge: Louisiana State University Press, 1987.

Cornell, Saul. "Splitting the Difference: Textualism, Contextualism, and Post-Modern History." *American Studies* 36, 1 (1995): 57–80.

Cowan, Edward J., ed. Cowan, *The Ballad in Scottish History*. Phantassie, UK: Tuckwell Press, 2000.

–. "Hunting of the Ballad." In Cowan, *The Ballad in Scottish History*, 1–18.

Creates, Marlene. *Places of Presence: Newfoundland Kin and Ancestral Land, Newfoundland, 1989–1991*. St. John's, NL: Killick Press, 1997.

Creighton, Donald G. *The Commercial Empire of the St. Lawrence, 1760–1850*. Toronto: Ryerson Press/Carnegie Endowment for International Peace, Division of Economics and History, 1937.

Cresswell, Tim. *Place: A Short Introduction*. Malden, MA: Blackwell, 2004.

Cruikshank, Julie. *Do Glaciers Listen? Local Knowledge, Colonial Encounters, and Social Imagination*. Vancouver: UBC Press, 2005.

Cundall, Frank. "Folk-Lore of the Negroes of Jamaica." *Folklore* 15–16 (1904–5): vol. 15: 87–94, 206–14, 450–56; 16: 68–77.

Dahlie, Jorgen, and Tissa Fernando, eds. *Ethnicity, Power and Politics in Canada*. Toronto: Methuen, 1981.

Davis, Stephen. *Bob Marley*. London: Plexus, 1993 [1985].

Davis, Stephen, and Peter Simon. *Reggae Bloodlines: In Search of the Music and Culture of Jamaica*. New York: Da Capo Press, 1992 [1977].

–, eds. *Reggae International*. New York: Rogner and Bernhard, 1982.

Dawes, Kwame. *Bob Marley: Lyrical Genius*. London: Sanctuary, 2002.

–. *Natural Mysticism: Towards a New Reggae Aesthetic in Caribbean Writing*. Leeds, UK: Peepal Tree, 1999.

de Certeau, Michel. *The Practice of Everyday Life*. Berkeley: University of California Press, 1984.

De Koningh, Michael, and Laurence Cane Honeysett. *Young, Gifted and Black: The Story of Trojan Records*. London: Sanctuary Publishing, 2003.

De Neve, Geert, and Henrike Donner, eds. *The Meaning of the Local: Politics of Place in Urban India*. London: Routledge, 2006.

Derrida, Jacques. *Of Grammatology*. Translated by Gayatri Chakravorty Spivak. Baltimore, MD: Johns Hopkins University Press, 1976.

DeVeaux, Scott. *The Birth of Bebop: A Social and Musical History*. Berkeley: University of California Press, 1997.

Duany, Jorge. "Beyond the Safety Valve: Recent Trends in Caribbean Migration." *Social and Economic Studies* 43, 1 (1994): 95–122.

Duffin, Charles. "Fixing Tradition: Making History from Ballad Texts." In Cowan, *The Ballad in Scottish History*, 19–35.

Duncombe, Stephen, and Maxwell Tremblay, eds. *White Riot: Punk Rock and the Politics of Race.* London: Verso, 2011.

Eaton, George E. "Jamaicans." In *Encyclopedia of Canada's Peoples,* edited by Paul R. Magocsi. Toronto: University of Toronto Press, 1999.

Eldridge, Colin C. *The Imperial Experience: From Carlyle to Forster.* London: Macmillan Press, 1996.

Epp, Marlene, Franca Iacovetta, and Frances Swyripa, eds. *Sisters or Strangers? Immigrant, Ethnic, and Racialized Women in Canadian History.* Toronto: University of Toronto Press, 2004.

Escobar, Arturo. "Culture Sits in Places: Reflections on Globalism and Subaltern Strategies of Localization." *Political Geography* 20 (2001): 139–74.

Evans, Amy. *Race Relations Bibliography.* Compiled for the Urban Alliance Centre on Race Relations. Toronto: Urban Alliance on Race Relations, 1985.

Evans, David. "Introduction." *American Music* 14, 4 (1996): 397–401.

Flynn, Karen C. "Experience and Identity: Black Immigrant Nurses to Canada, 1950–1980." In Epp, Iacovetta, and Swyripa, *Sisters or Strangers?,* 381–98.

–. "Race, Class, and Gender: Black Nurses in Ontario, 1950–1980." PhD diss., York University, 2004.

Forman, Murray. "Represent: Race, Space and Place in Rap Music." *Popular Music* 19, 1 (2000): 65–90.

Fraley, Todd. "I Got a Natural Skill ... : Hip-Hop, Authenticity, and Whiteness." *Howard Journal of Communications* 20 (2009): 37–54.

Frazier, Edward Franklin. *The Negro Family in the United States.* Rev. and abr. Chicago: University of Chicago Press, 1966 [1948].

French, Neil, dir. Maggie Smith reciting a "A Bag of Tools," advertisement for the Union Bank of Switzerland, 1998.

Freyburg, Annabel. "Edward and Julia Jekyll and Their Family." In *Gertrude Jekyll: Essays on the Life of a Working Amateur,* edited by Michael Tooley and Primrose Arnander, 21–42. Durham, NC: Michaelmas Books, 1995.

Frith, Simon. "Music and Identity." In *Questions of Cultural Identity,* edited by Stuart Hall and Paul du Gay, 108–50. London: Sage Publications, 1996.

Gammon, Vic. "Folk Song Collecting in Sussex and Surrey: 1843–1914." *History Workshop Journal* 10 (1980): 61–89.

Gans, David. *Conversations with the Dead: The Grateful Dead Interview Book.* Cambridge, MA: Da Capo Press, 2002.

Gates, Henry Louis, Jr. *The Signifying Monkey: A Theory of Afro-American Literary Criticism.* New York: Oxford University Press, 1988.

Geertz, Clifford. *The Interpretation of Cultures: Selected Essays.* New York: Basic Books, 1973.

–. *Local Knowledge: Further Essays in Interpretive Anthropology.* New York: Basic Books, 1983.

Gibson, Chris, and John Connell. *Music and Tourism: On the Road Again.* Tonawanda, NY: Channel View Publications, 2005.

324 *Bibliography*

Gilbert, Pat. *Passion Is a Fashion: The Real Story of the Clash.* London: Aurum Press, 2004.

Gilkes, Alwyn D. "Among Thistles and Thorns: West Indian Diaspora Immigrants in New York City and Toronto." PhD diss., City University of New York, 2005.

Gilroy, Paul. *The Black Atlantic: Modernity and Double Consciousness.* Cambridge, MA: Harvard University Press, 1994.

–. *There Ain't No Black in the Union Jack: The Cultural Politics of Race and Nation.* Chicago: University of Chicago Press, 1987.

Giovannetti, Jorge L. "Popular Music and Culture in Puerto Rico: Jamaican and Rap Music as Cross-Cultural Symbols." In *Musical Migrations: Transnationalism and Cultural Hybridity in Latino America,* edited by Frances R. Aparicio and Candida F. Jáquez, 81–98. New York: Palgrave, 2003.

Giroux, Henry. "Rewriting the Discourse of Racial Identity: Towards a Pedagogy and Politics of Whiteness." *Harvard Education Review* 67 (1997): 285–320.

Glick, Carl, ed. *A Treasury of Masonic Thought.* London: Robert Hale, 2003 [1950].

Goddard, Peter. "Nightbeat." *Performance: Canada's Leading Theatre Magazine,* May 6–12, 1985.

Goldman, Vivien. *The Book of Exodus: The Making and Meaning of Bob Marley and the Wailers' Album of the Century.* New York: Three Rivers Press, 2006.

–. "Interview, Bob Marley." *Sounds* (London), September 3, 1977.

Gomme, Alice B. *The Traditional Games of England, Scotland and Ireland: With Tunes, Singing Rhymes and Methods of Playing according to the Variants Extant and Recorded in Different Parts of the Kingdom.* London: Nutt, 1894.

Goode, Coleridge, and Roger Cotterrell. *Bass Lines: A Life in Jazz.* London: Northway Books, 2002.

Gooden, Amoaba. "Community Organizing by African Caribbean People in Toronto, Ontario." *Journal of Black Studies* 38, 3 (2008): 413–26.

Gooden, Lou. *Reggae Heritage: Jamaica's Culture and Politics.* Kingston, Jamaica: Olivier Printery, 2003.

Goodison, Lorna. *From Harvey River: A Memoir of My Mother and Her Island.* New York: HarperCollins, 2007.

Goodyear, Ian. "Rock Against Racism: Multiculturalism and Political Mobilization, 1976–81." *Immigrants and Minorities* 22, 1 (2003): 44–62.

Gordillo, Gaston R. *Landscapes of Devils: Tension of Place and Memory in the Argentinean Chaco.* Durham, NC: Duke University Press, 2004.

Gordon, Alan. *Making Public Pasts: The Contested Terrain of Montreal's Public Memories, 1891–1930.* Montreal: McGill-Queen's University Press, 2001.

Gosciak, Josh. "Between Diaspora and Internationalism: Claude McKay and the Making of a Black Public Intellectual." PhD diss., City University of New York, 2002.

Gosse, Van. *Rethinking the New Left: An Interpretive History.* New York: Palgrave, 2005.

Grant, Colin. *The Natural Mystics: Marley, Tosh and Wailer.* London: Random House, 2011.

–. *Negro with a Hat: The Rise and Fall of Marcus Garvey.* London: Vintage Books, 2009.

Greene, Jo-Ann. Review of "Book of Rules." *Allmusic.com,* 2011.

Gurtman, Scott. "The Influence of Bob Marley's Absent, White Father." Essay for Rhetoric of Reggae Music, University of Vermont, Burlington, 2002.

Gyokeres, Nancy. "Jackson Fights the Reggae Cause." *Music Scene,* January-February 1984.

Hall, Catherine. *Civilising Subjects: Colony and Metropole in the English Imagination, 1830–1867.* Chicago: University of Chicago Press, 2002.

Hall, Stuart. "Introduction: Who Needs 'Identity'?" In *Questions of Cultural Identity,* edited by Stuart Hall and Paul du Gay, 1–17. London: Sage, 1996.

Harris, Joel Chandler, Brigadier General Clement A. Evans, and W.J. Northen. *Memoirs of Georgia: Historical and Biographical Containing Historical Accounts of the State's Civil, Military, Industrial and Professional Interests, and Personal Sketches of Many of Its People.* Georgia: Southern Historical Association, 1895.

Harvie, Christopher. "Ballads of a Nation." *History Today* 49, 9 (1999): 10–16.

Harzig, Christiane. "'The Movement of 100 Girls': 1950s Canadian Immigration Policy and the Market for Domestic Labour." *Zeitschrift Für Kanada-Studien* 19, 2 (1999): 131–46.

Hawkins, Freda. *Canada and Immigration: Public Policy and Public Concern.* Montreal: McGill-Queen's University Press, 1972.

Hayden, Dolores. *The Power of Place: Urban Landscapes as Public History.* Cambridge, MA: MIT Press, 1995.

Haynes, W.F. "Pastoral Reflections," St. Simons Island, GA. In *Lifeline: Sharing God's Love,* May 22, 2011.

Heathcott, Joseph. "Urban Spaces and Working-Class Expressions across the Black Atlantic: Tracing the Routes of Ska." *Radical History Review* 87 (Fall 2003): 183–206.

Hebdige, Dick. *Cut 'n' Mix: Culture, Identity and Caribbean Music.* London: Comedia, Methuen, 1987.

–. *Subculture: The Meaning of Style.* London: Methuen, 1979.

Henderson, Stuart. *Making the Scene: Yorkville and Hip Toronto in the 1960s.* Toronto: University of Toronto Press, 2011.

Henry, Frances. *The Caribbean Diaspora in Toronto: Learning to Live with Racism.* Toronto: University of Toronto Press, 1994.

–. *The Dynamics of Racism in Toronto: Research Report.* Ottawa: Group Understanding and Human Rights Program, Department of the Secretary of State, 1978.

Herskovits, Melville J. *The Myth of the Negro Past.* New York: Harper and Brothers, 1941.

Hickling-Hudson, Anne. "Postcolonialsim, Hybridity and Transferability: The Contribution of Pamela O'Gorman to Music Education in the Caribbean." *Caribbean Journal of Education* 1–2 (2000): 36–55.

High, Steven. "Placing the Displaced Worker: Narrating Place in Deindustrializing Sturgeon Falls, Ontario." In Opp and Walsh, *Placing Memory and Remembering Place in Canada,* 159–86.

High, Steven, and David W. Lewis. *Corporate Wasteland: The Landscape and Memory of Deindustrialization.* Toronto: Between the Lines, 2007.

Bibliography

Hill, Donna, ed. *A Black Man's Toronto: The Reminiscences of Harry Gairey*. Toronto: Multicultural History Society of Ontario, 1981.

Himmelfarb, Gertrude. "Telling It as You Like It: Post-Modernist History and the Flight from Fact." *Times Literary Supplement*, October 16, 1992.

Hodd, Jack Lorne, and R.L. Sharpe. *A Bag of Tools: For Voice and Piano*. Leslie Vocal Series no. 7068. Oakville, ON: Leslie Music Supply, 1988.

Hodge, Jennifer, and Roger McTair, dirs. *Home Feeling: Struggle for a Community*. Toronto: National Film Board of Canada, 1983.

Hoelscher, Steven, and Derek H. Alderman. "Memory and Place: Geographies of a Critical Relationship." *Social and Cultural Geography* 5, 3 (2004): 347–55.

Hogden, Margaret T. *The Doctrine of Survivals*. London: Allenson, 1936.

Hunt, Ken. "Review: Wilson & Swarbrick, *Lion Rampant*." *fRoots*, April 2014.

Huttenback, Robert A. "The British Empire as a 'White Man's Country': Racial Attitudes and Immigration Legislation in the Colonies of White Settlement." *Journal of British Studies* 13, 1 (1973): 108–37.

–. *Racism and Empire: White Settlers and Colored Immigrants in the British Self-Governing Colonies, 1830–1910*. Ithaca, NY: Cornell University Press, 1976.

Huyssen, Andreas. *Present Pasts: Urban Palimpsests and the Politics of Memory*. Palo Alto, CA: Stanford University Press, 2003.

Iacovetta, Franca. *Gatekeepers: Reshaping Immigrant Lives in Cold War Canada*. Toronto: Between the Lines, 2006.

Irwin, Colin. "Rebel Music: Dave Swarbrick, Jason Wilson and David Francey." *Penguin Eggs*, Summer 2009, 22–24.

Jackson, Ronald L. *Scripting the Black Masculine Body: Identity, Discourse, and Racial Politics in Popular Media*. Albany: State University of New York Press, 2006.

Jahn, Brian, and Tom Weber. *Reggae Island: Jamaican Music in the Digital Age*. New York: Da Capo, 1998.

Jakubowski, Lisa M. *Immigration and the Legalization of Racism*. Black Point, NS: Fernwood Publishing, 1997.

Jay, Paul. "Hybridity, Identity and Cultural Commerce in Claude McKay's Banana Bottom." *Callaloo* 22, 1 (1999): 176–94.

Jekyll, Gertrude. *Old English Household Life: Some Account of Cottage Objects and Country Folk*. British Heritage Series. London: B.T. Batsford, 1939.

–. *Old West Surrey: Some Notes and Memories*. London: Longmans, Green, 1904.

Jekyll, Walter, ed. *Jamaican Song and Story: Annancy Stories, Digging Sings, Ring Tunes, and Dancing Tunes*. With an introduction by Alice Werner. London: David Nutt/Folk-Lore Society, 1907; repr., Mineola, NY: Dover, 2005 [1966].

Jennings, Nicholas. "Album Review: *The Peacemaker's Chauffeur*." *Inside E Canada* 7, 6 (2008): 108.

–. "Dance Tunes for Idealists." *Maclean's*, August 26, 1985.

Jensen, Peta Gay. *The Last Colonials: The Story of Two European Families in Jamaica*. London: Radcliffe Press, 2005.

Jones, Arthur M. *Studies in African Music*. Oxford: Oxford University Press, 1959.

Jones, Simon. *Black Culture, White Youth: The Reggae Tradition from JA to UK*. Basingstoke, UK: Macmillan, 1988.

Jones, Terry-Ann. "Comparative Diasporas: Jamaicans in South Florida and Toronto." PhD diss., University of Miami, 2005.

Kastner, Jamie. "The Grand Ambassadors of Reggae Music in Canada: The Sattalites." *Canadian Musician* 18, 3 (1996): 45.

Katz, David. *Solid Foundation: An Oral History of Reggae.* New York: Bloomsbury, 2003.

Kelley, Ninette, and Michael Trebilcock. *The Making of the Mosaic: A History of Canadian Immigration Policy.* Toronto: University of Toronto Press, 1998.

Kerrigan, Catherine. "Reclaiming History: The Ballad as a Women's Tradition." *Etudes Ecossaises* 1 (1991): 343–50.

Kidson, Frank. *Traditional Tunes: A Collection of Ballad Airs.* Wakefield, UK: S.R. Publishers, 1970.

Kiernan, Peter. "Walter Jekyll and His Jamaica Garden." Slide show lecture delivered at the Garden History Society, Winter Lectures, the Gallery, London, February 2, 2005.

Kitwana, Bakari. *Why White Kids Love Hip Hop: Wankstas, Wiggers, Wannabes, and the New Realities of Race in America.* New York: Basic Civitas Books, 2005.

Knowles, Valerie. *Strangers at Our Gates: Canadian Immigration and Immigration Policy, 1540–2006.* Toronto: Dundurn Press, 2007.

Laade, Wolfgang. *Die Situation von Musikleben und Musikforschung in den Laendern Afrikas und Asiens und die neuen Aufgaben der Musikethnologie.* Tutzing, Germany: Hans Schneider, 1969.

Lamperti, Giovanni Battista. *The Art of Singing: According to Ancient Tradition and Personal Experience – Technical Rules and Advice to Pupils and Artists.* Translated by Walter Jekyll. London: G. Ricordi, 1884.

Larkin, Colin, ed. *The Guinness Who's Who of Reggae.* London: Guinness Publishing, 1994.

–. *The Virgin Encyclopedia of Reggae.* London: Virgin Books, 1998.

Ledbetter, James. "Imitation of Life." In *Gender, Race and Class in Media,* edited by G. Dines and J. Humez, 540–44. Thousand Oaks, CA: Sage Publications, 1995.

Levi, Darrell E. *Michael Manley: The Making of a Leader.* Athens: University of Georgia Press, 1990.

Lewin, Olive. "Jamaican Folk Music." *Caribbean Quarterly* 14 (1968): 49–56.

–. *Rock It Come Over: The Folk Music of Jamaica.* Mona, Jamaica: University of the West Indies Press, 2000.

Lindsay, Colin. *Profiles of Ethnic Communities in Canada: The Jamaican Community in Canada, 12.* Ottawa: Statistics Canada, 89–621-XIE, 2007.

Lipsitz, George. *Dangerous Crossroads: Popular Music, Postmodernism and the Poetics of Place.* New York: Verso, 1994.

Lorenzkowski, Barbara. *Sounds of Ethnicity: Listening to German North America, 1850–1914.* Winnipeg: University of Manitoba Press, 2010.

Macdonald, Kevin, dir. *Marley.* New York: Magnolia Pictures/Universal Pictures, 2012.

Mackenzie, Ian. "Early Movements of Domestics from the Caribbean and Canadian Immigration Policy." *Alternate Routes: A Journal of Critical Social Research* 8 (1988): 124–43.

328   *Bibliography*

Magocsi, Paul R, ed. *Encyclopedia of Canada's Peoples.* Toronto: University of Toronto Press, 1999.

Marre, Jeremy, dir. *Bob Marley and the Wailers: Catch a Fire.* Classic Albums. Los Angeles: Image Entertainment, 1999.

–, dir. *Reggae Britannia.* London: BBC Four, 2011.

–. "Reggae Britannia." *BBC Music Blog,* February 7, 2011. https://www.bbc.co.uk/blogs/bbcmusic/2011/02/reggae_britannia.html.

Marshall, Dawn I. "A History of West Indian Migrations: Overseas Opportunities and 'Safety-Valve' Policies." In *The Caribbean Exodus,* edited by Barry B. Levine, 15–31. New York: Praeger, 1987.

Mason, Laura. *Singing the French Revolution: Popular Culture and Politics, 1787–1799.* Ithaca, NY: Cornell University Press, 1996.

Masouri, Jon. *Wailing Blues: The Story of Bob Marley's Wailers.* London: Omnibus Press, 2009.

McAllister, Kirsten Emiko. "Archive and Myth: The Changing Memoryscape of Japanese Canadian Internment Camps." In Opp and Walsh, *Placing Memory and Remembering Place in Canada,* 215–46.

McCarthy, Len J. "The Significance of Corporeal Factors and Choreographic Rhythms in Jamaican Popular Music between 1957–1981 (Ska, Rocksteady, Reggae), with an Historical and Critical Survey of all Relevant Literature Dealing with Jamaican Folk, Religious and Popular Musics and Dance." PhD diss., York University, 2007.

McCuaig, Keith. "Jamaican Canadian Music in Toronto in the 1970s and 1980s: A Preliminary History." Master's thesis, Carleton University, 2012.

McGroarty, Gary, dir. *Rise Up: Canadian Pop Music in the 1980s.* Toronto: EMI Music Canada, 2009.

–, dir. *This Beat Goes On: Canadian Pop Music in the 1970s.* Toronto: EMI Music Canada, 2009.

McKay, Claude. *Banana Bottom.* New York: Harper and Row, 1933; repr., London: Serpent's Tail, 2005.

–. *A Long Way from Home.* New York: Arno Press/New York Times, 1969.

–. *My Green Hills of Jamaica.* Kingston, Jamaica: Heinemann Educational Books, 1979.

McKay, Ian. *Quest of the Folk: Antimodernism and Cultural Selection in Twentieth-Century Nova Scotia.* Montreal: McGill-Queen's University Press, 1994.

Milan, Anne, and Kelly Tran. "Blacks in Canada: A Long History." *Canadian Social Trends* 72 (Spring 2004): 2–7.

Milner, Lord Alfred. "Address to the Municipal Congress, Johannesburg," May 18, 1903. In *The Milner Papers: South Africa.* Vol. 2, *1899–1905,* edited by C. Headlam, 467. London: Cassell, 1933.

Mintz, Sydney W., and Richard Price. *The Birth of African-American Culture: An Anthropological Perspective.* Boston: Beacon Press, 1992.

Mintz, Sidney W., and Sally Price, eds. *Caribbean Contours.* Baltimore, MD: Johns Hopkins University Press, 1985.

Moffat, Alfred, and Frank Kidson. *Children's Songs of Long Ago.* London: Augener, 1905.

Monk, Janice. "Race and Restrictive Immigration: A Review Article." *Journal of Historical Geography* 4, 2 (1978): 192–96.

Moore, Don. *Don Moore: An Autobiography.* Toronto: Williams-Wallace, 1985.

Morrison, James Dalton, ed. *Masterpieces of Religious Verse.* New York: Harper and Brothers Publishers, 1948.

Moskowitz, David. *Caribbean Popular Music: An Encyclopedia of Reggae, Mento, Ska, Rock Steady and Dancehall.* Westport, CT: Greenwood Press, 2006.

Muraldo, Caroline. "The Caribbean Quadrille," 2007. https://www.muraldodc.com.

Murray, Tom, ed. *Folk Songs of Jamaica.* Oxford: Oxford University Press, 1951.

Myers, Charles Samuel. "Traces of African Melody in Jamaica." In Jekyll, *Jamaican Song and Story,* 278–84.

Neatby, Hilda B. "The New Century." In *The Canadians 1867–1967,* edited by J.M.S. Careless and R.C. Brown, 137–71. Toronto: Macmillan, 1968.

Neely, Daniel Tannehill. "Long Time Gal! *Mento* Is Back!" *The Beat* 20, 6 (2001): 38–42.

–. "'Mento, Jamaica's Original Music': Development, Tourism and the Nationalist Frame." PhD diss., New York University, 2008.

Nettleford, Rex M. "Jamaican Song and Story and the Theatre." In Jekyll, *Jamaican Song and Story,* xiii–xv.

–. *Mirror Mirror: Identity, Race and Protest in Jamaica.* Kingston, Jamaica: LMH, 1998 [1970].

Nguyen, Paul, dir. "Lost in the Struggle." *The Fifth Estate.* Toronto: CBC, 2006.

Nketia, J.H. Kwabena. *African Music in Ghana.* Evanston, IL: Northwestern University Press, 1963.

–. *The Music of Africa.* New York: W.W. Norton, 1974.

North, Marianne. *Recollections of a Happy Life: Being the Autobiography of Marianne North.* Edited by her sister, Mrs. John Addington Symonds. Charlottesville: University Press of Virginia, 1993 [1894].

North, Michael. *The Dialect of Modernism: Race, Language and Twentieth-Century Literature.* New York: Oxford University Press, 1994.

O Maolain, Ciaran. *The Radical Right: A World Directory.* Burnt Mill, UK: Longman, 1987.

O'Brien, Richard, and Patti Habib. *The Bamboo Cooks: Recipes from the Legendary Nightclub.* Toronto: Random House, 1997.

Ojo, Adebayo. *Bob Marley: Songs of African Redemption.* Lagos: Malthouse Press, 2000.

Oliver, Paul. "That Certain Feeling: Blues and Jazz ... in 1890?" *Popular Music* 10, 1 (1991): 11–20.

Opp, James, and John C. Walsh. *Placing Memory and Remembering Place in Canada.* Vancouver: UBC Press, 2010.

Osborne, Brian. "From Patriotic Pines to Diasporic Geese: Emplacing Culture, Setting Our Sights, Locating Identity in a Transnational Canada." *Canadian Journal of Communication* 31, 1 (2006): 147–75.

Packer, Boyd K. "The Unwritten Order of Things." Delivered at Brigham Young University on October 15, 1996. In Church of Jesus Christ of Latter-Day Saints,

330 *Bibliography*

Principles of Leadership: Teacher Manual, 111. Salt Lake City, UT: Church of Jesus Christ of Latter-Day Saints, 2001.

Palmer, Bryan D. *Descent into Discourse: The Reification of Language and the Writing of Social History.* Philadelphia: Temple University Press, 1990.

Panish, Jon. *The Color of Jazz: Race and Representation in Postwar American Culture.* Jackson: University Press of Mississippi, 1997.

Patterson, Orlando. *The Sociology of Slavery: An Analysis of the Origins, Development and Structure of Negro Slave Society in Jamaica.* Cranbury, NJ: Associated University Presses, 1969.

Perkins, William E. "The Rap Attack: An Introduction." In *Droppin' Science: Critical Essays on Rap Music and Hip Hop Culture,* edited by William E. Perkins, 1–45. Philadelphia: Temple University Press, 1996.

Perks, Robert, and Alistair Thomson, eds. *The Oral History Reader.* Abingdon-on-Thames, UK: Routledge, 2006.

Pichler, Michalis. "Statements on Appropriation." *UbuWeb Papers,* 2009. http://www.ubu.com/papers/pichler_appropriation.html.

Plaza, Dwaine. "The Construction of a Segmented Hybrid Identity among One-and-a-Half-Generation and Second-Generation Indo-Caribbean and African Caribbean Canadians." *Identity* 6, 3 (2006): 207–29.

Portelli, Alessandro. *The Death of Luigi Trastulli, and Other Stories: Form and Meaning in Oral History.* Albany: State University of New York Press, 1990.

–. "Oral History as a Genre." In *Narrative and Genre,* edited by Mary Chamberlain and Paul Thompson, 23–45. London: Routledge, 1998.

–. *They Say in Harlan County: An Oral History.* New York: Oxford University Press, 2011.

Potash, Chris, ed. *Reggae, Rasta, Revolution: Jamaican Music from Ska to Dub.* New York: Schirmer Books, 1997.

Prazniak, Roxann, and Arif Dirlik, eds. *Places and Politics in an Age of Globalization,* Lanham, MD: Rowman and Littlefield, 2001.

Price, Richard. *The Convict and the Colonial.* Boston: Beacon Press, 1998.

Rachel, Daniel. *Walls Come Tumbling Down: The Music and Politics of Rock Against Racism, 2 Tone and Red Wedge.* London: Picador, 2016.

Ramcharan, Subhas. "The Adaptation of West Indians in Canada." PhD diss., York University, 1974.

Ramsey, Guthrie P. *Race Music: Black Cultures from Bebop to Hip-Hop.* Berkeley: University of California Press, 2003.

Rath, Richard Cullen. "African Music in Seventeenth-Century Jamaica: Cultural Transit and Transition." *William and Mary Quarterly,* third series, 50, 4 (1993): 700–26.

Ratnapalan, Laavanyan. "E.B. Tylor and the Problem of Primitive Culture." *History and Anthropology* 19, 2 (2008): 131–42.

Rinaldo, Sandie. "Bob Marley at Maple Leaf Gardens." *Canada AM,* CTV, June 9, 1978.

Reckford, Verena. "Rastafarian Music: An Introductory Study." *Jamaica Journal* 11, 1–2 (1977): 3–13.

Richmond, Norman Otis. "Bathurst St. Has Always Been Part of Black Life in T.O." *Share* (Toronto), October 14, 2009.

Roberts, Helen. "Possible Survivals of African Songs in Jamaica." *Musical Quarterly* 12, 3 (1926): 340–58.

–. "Some Drum and Drum Rhythms of Jamaica." *Natural History* 24 (1924): 241–51.

–. "A Study of Folk Song Variants Based on Field Work in Jamaica." *Journal of American Folk-Lore* 38, 148 (1925): 149–216.

Robertson, Alan. *Joe Harriott: Fire in His Soul*. London: Northway Publications, 2012.

Rodney, Winston (a.k.a. Burning Spear). "Wisdom to Do What Is Right." *Burning Spear Blog,* August 23, 2009.

Rohlehr, Gordon. "Some Problems of Assessment: A Look at New Expressions in the Art of the Contemporary Caribbean." *Caribbean Quarterly* 17, 3–4 (1971): 92–113.

Rommen, Timothy. "Protestant Vibrations? Reggae, Rastafari, and Conscious Evangelicals." *Popular Music* 25, 2 (2006): 235–63.

Rose, Euclid A. *Dependency and Socialism in the Modern Caribbean: Superpower Intervention in Guyana, Jamaica and Grenada, 1970–1985*. Boston: Lexington Books, 2002.

Rose, Tricia. *Black Noise: Rap Music and Black Culture in Contemporary America*. London: Wesleyan University Press, 1994.

Roszak, Theodore. *The Making of a Counterculture*. Garden City, NY: Doubleday Anchor, 1969.

Rouse, Marylin. *Jamaican Folk Music: A Synthesis of Many Cultures*. Lewiston, NY: Edwin Mellen Press, 2000.

Royal Botanic Gardens, Kew. *Marianne North at Kew Gardens*. Exeter: Webb and Bower/Royal Botanic Gardens, Kew, 1990.

Ryman, Cheryl. "Astley Clerk 1868–1944: Patriot and Cultural Pioneer." *Jamaica Journal* 18, 4 (1985–86): 17–26.

Saleqicz, Chris. *Redemption Song: The Ballad of Joe Strummer*. New York: Faber and Faber, 2007.

Sattalites. *Sattalites: Ten Years On*. Toronto: self-published, 1991.

Satzewich, Vic. "Racism and Canadian Immigration Policy: The Government's View of Caribbean Migration, 1962–1966." *Canadian Ethnic Studies* 21, 1 (1989): 77–97.

Saul, Scott. *Freedom Is, Freedom Ain't: Jazz and the Making of the Sixties*. Cambridge, MA: Harvard University Press, 2003.

Saunders, Mahogany. "Where Jamaicans Live." *Jamaicans.com: Out of Many One People Online,* August 1, 2003. https://www.jamaicans.com.

Schwartz, Joan. M. "Constituting Places of Presence: Landscape, Identity and the Geographical Imagination." In Creates, *Places of Presence*, 1–18.

Seenath, Harriet, Navin Joneja, and Antoni Shelton. *Race and the Canadian Justice System: An Annotated Bibliography*. Toronto: Urban Alliance on Race Relations, 1995.

Sharpe, R.L. "Bag of Tools." *Best Loved Poems of the American People,* edited by Hazel Felleman, 99. New York: Doubleday, 1936.

–. "The Illusion of Time." *The Theosophical Path* 39, 3 (1931): 222–24.

Shea, Kevin. "Big Shinny Tunes: Jason Wilson." *Legends Magazine,* Fall 2003.

Sher, Julian. *White Hoods: Canada's Ku Klux Klan*. Vancouver: New Star Books, 1983.

Bibliography

Sheridan, Maureen. *Bob Marley: Soul Rebel – The Stories Behind Every Song, 1962–1981.* Cambridge, MA: Da Capo Press, 1999.

Sherlock, Philip. "The Living Roots." In Jekyll, *Jamaican Song and Story,* v-viii.

Sloane, Hans. *Voyage to the Islands Madera, Barbados, Nieves, S. Christophers and Jamaica* ... 2 vols. London: B.M. for the author. 1707.

Small, Christopher. *Music of the Common Tongue: Survival and Celebration in Afro-American Music, 1927–2011.* London: J. Calder/New York: Riverrun Press 1987.

Smith, Mark. "Echoes in Print: Method and Causation in Aural History." *Journal of the Historical Society* 2, 3–4 (2002): 317–36.

Social Planning Council of Metropolitan Toronto and Urban Alliance on Race Relations. *Law Enforcement and Race Relations.* Urban Seminar Series 4. Toronto: Social Planning Council of Metropolitan Toronto, 1976.

Statistics Canada. *Ethnic Diversity Survey 2002.* Ottawa: Statistics Canada/Canadian Heritage, 89M0019XCB, 2003.

Stephens, Gregory. *On Racial Frontiers: The New Culture of Frederick Douglass, Ralph Ellison, and Bob Marley.* Cambridge: Cambridge University Press, 1999.

Stephens, Michelle A. "Re-imagining the Shape and Borders of Black Political Space." *Radical History Review* 87 (Fall 2003): 169–82.

Stokoe, John, and Samuel Reay. *Songs and Ballads of Northern England.* Collected and edited by John Stokoe; harmonized and arranged for pianoforte by Samuel Reay. Darby, PA: Norwood Editions, 1973 [1892].

Stolzoff, Norman. *Wake the Town and Tell the People: Dancehall Culture in Jamaica.* Durham, NC: Duke University Press, 2000.

Storti, Craig. *Cross-Cultural Dialogues.* Boston: Intercultural Press, 1994.

Stranger-Ross, Jordan. *Staying Italian: Urban Change and Ethnic Life in Postwar Toronto and Philadelphia.* Chicago: University of Chicago Press, 2009.

Suppanz, Mark. "Review: Jason Wilson, *Perennials.*" *Big Takeover* 79 (2016): 37.

Swyripa, Frances. "Edmonton's Jasper Avenue: Public Ritual, Heritage, and Memory on Main Street." In Opp and Walsh, *Placing Memory and Remembering Place in Canada,* 81–106.

Tafari, I. Jabulani. "Jackie Mittoo." *Reggae Report* 6 (1988): 8–9.

Taussig, Michael. *Mimesis and Alterity.* New York: Routledge, 1993.

Tattrie, Jon. *Redemption Songs: How Bob Marley's Nova Scotia Song Lights the Way Past Racism.* Lawrencetown Beach, NS: Pottersfield Press, 2017.

Taylor, Kenneth Wayne. "Racism in Canadian Immigration Policy." *Canadian Ethnic Studies* 23, 1 (1991): 1–20.

Taylor, Timothy D. *Global Pop: World Music, World Markets.* New York: Routledge, 1997.

Thomas, Deborah. *Modern Blackness: Nationalism, Globilization and the Politics of Culture in Jamaica.* Durham, NC: Duke University Press, 2004.

Thomas-Hope, Elizabeth. *Migration Situation Analysis, Policy and Program Needs for Jamaica.* Kingston: Planning Institute of Jamaica, PIOJ, and UNFPA, 2004.

Thompson, Dave. *Wheels Out of Gear: 2-Tone, the Specials and a World in Flame.* London: Soundcheck Books, 2004.

Tippett, Maria. *Making Culture: English-Canadian Institutions and the Arts before the Massey Commission.* 3rd ed. Toronto: University of Toronto Press, 1990.

Toronto. *City of Toronto Priority Neighbourhoods: Overview of Demographics and Community Services, Jane-Finch – #2.* Toronto: City of Toronto Social Development, Finance and Administration Division, 2006.

Tuber, Keith. "Reggae's Carlene Davis Sends a Message from Jamaica." *Orange Coast Magazine* (January 1983): 88–90.

Tulloch, Dave. "If You Didn't See Them ... You Missed a Great Show." *Spectrum: Making Minorities Visible* (Ottawa), May 16, 1987.

Turkel, William. *The Archive of Place: Unearthing the Pasts of the Chilcotin Plateau.* Vancouver: UBC Press, 2007.

Tylor, Edward B. *Researches into the Early History of Mankind and the Development of Civilization.* London: John Murray, 1865.

–. "Wild Men and Beast Children." *Anthropological Review* 1 (1863): 21–32.

Urry, John. *The Tourist Gaze.* 2nd ed. London: Sage, 2002.

US Department of State. *July–December, 2010 International Religious Freedom Report: Jamaica.* Washington, DC: Bureau of Democracy, Human Rights, and Labor, 2011.

Van Biema, David. "The Legacy of Abraham." *Time,* September 30, 2002.

Van Pelt, Carter. Interview with Leroy Sibbles, c. 2010. https://leroysibbles.com.

Vance, Jonathan F. *A History of Canadian Culture.* Don Mills, ON: Oxford University Press, 2009.

Vipond, Mary. *The Mass Media in Canada.* Toronto: James Lorimer, 1989.

Von Eschen, Penny. *Race against Empire: Black Americans and Anticolonialism, 1937–1957.* Ithaca, NY: Cornell University Press, 1997.

Wade, Nicholas. *A Troublesome Inheritance: Genes, Race and Human History.* New York: Penguin Books, 2014.

Wald, Elijah. *Escaping the Delta: Robert Johnson and the Invention of the Blues.* New York: Amistad, 2004.

Walker, David. "DVD Review: *Rockers.*" *DVD Talk,* June 21, 2005. https://www.dvdtalk.com/reviews/17242/rockers-25th-anniversary-edition/.

Walker, James W. St. G. *"Race," Rights and the Law in the Supreme Court of Canada: Historical Case Studies.* Toronto and Waterloo: Osgoode Society for Canadian Legal History/Wilfrid Laurier University Press, 1997.

Walker, Klive. *Dubwise: Reasoning from the Reggae Underground.* Toronto: Insomniac Press, 2005.

Walker, Martin. *The National Front.* Glasgow: Fontana Collins, 1978.

Watts, Steven. "The Idiocy of American Studies: Post-Structuralism, Language, and Politics in the Age of Self-Fulfillment." *American Quarterly* 43 (1991): 625–60.

Werner, Alice. Introduction to Jekyll, *Jamaican Song and Story,* xxiii–lii.

White, Garth (a.k.a. Razac Blacka). "Master Drummer." *Jamaica Journal* 11, 1–2 (1977): 16–17.

–. "Rudie, Oh Rudie!" *Caribbean Quarterly* 13, 3 (1967): 39–44.

–. "Traditional Music Practice in Jamaica and Its Influence on the Birth of Modern Jamaican Music." *African Caribbean Institute of Jamaica Newsletter* 7 (1982): 70.

White, Newman I. *American Negro Folk-Songs*. Hatboro, PA: Folklore Associates, 1965 [1928].

White, Timothy. *Catch a Fire: The Life of Bob Marley*. New York: Henry Holt, 1998.

Whitney, Malika Lee, and Dermott Hussey. *Bob Marley: Reggae King of the World*. Kingston, Jamaica: Kingston Publishers, 1984.

Whitzman, Carolyn. *Suburb, Slum, Urban Village: Transformations in Toronto's Parkdale Neighbourhood, 1875–2002*. Vancouver: UBC Press, 2009.

Whylie, Marjorie. *Mento: The What and the How*. Kingston, Jamaica: Whylie Communications, 2000.

Widgery, David. *Beating Time*. London: Pluto, 1986.

Wiegman, Robyn. *American Anatomies: Theorizing Race and Gender*. Durham, NC: Duke University Press, 1995.

Williams, Ursula Vaughan. *R.V.W: A Biography of Ralph Vaughan Williams*. London: Oxford University Press, 1965.

Wilson, John Jason Collins. "Ernest Ranglin: Reggae Pioneer." *Word Magazine*, December 2005.

–. "The Fast Bowling Ernest Ranglin." *Word Magazine*, Caribana edition, July 2006.

–. "UB40's Got Plenty More." *Word Magazine*, April 2006, 18.

Winks, Robin W. *The Blacks in Canada: A History*. Montreal: McGill-Queen's University Press, 1971.

Witmer, Robert. "'Local' and 'Foreign': The Popular Music Culture of Kingston, Jamaica, before Ska, Rock Steady, and Reggae." *Latin American Music Review* 8, 1 (1987): 1–25.

Young, David. "Ethno-racial Minorities and the Juno Awards." *Canadian Journal of Sociology* 31, 2 (2006): 183–210.

Young, Robert J.C. *Colonial Desire: Hybridity in Theory, Culture and Race*. London: Routledge, 1995.

Young, Terence, dir. *Dr. No*. Produced by Harry Saltzman and Albert R. Broccoli. London: EoN Productions/United Artists, 1962.

Index

Note: "(i)" after a page number indicates an illustration.

10CC, 57
20th Century Rebels, 13, 117, 119, 133, 154, 208, 210, 213, 216, 229, 286*n*77
2Tone (record label), 157

A&M (record label), 123
the Abyssinians, 50, 197, 300*n*15
the Aces, 300*n*15
Aitken, Laurel, 157, 237
Alexander, A.L., 129
Alexander, Donnell, 300*n*4
Alexander, Monty, 15
Allen, Lillian, 13, 46, 133, 208, 216, 217, 287*n*100, 307*n*41
Alleyne, Mike, 302*nn*16–17
Alpha Boys' School, 44, 49–52, 55, 157, 225, 256*n*2, 269*n*34; Alpha Boys' Band, 50, 52, 77, 269*n*32
Ammoye, 245
Ancient Mystic Order of Ethiopia, 47
Anderson, Al, 56
Andy, Bob, 58, 137, 193, 300*n*15
Andy, Horace, 147
Annancy the Spider, 25, 33, 38, 41, 99
anticolonial, 27, 45, 48, 70, 204. *See also* colonial
apartheid, 64, 86, 202
Armstrong, Eric Vernon "Tiger" Jr., a.k.a. Lord Power, 107, 285*n*48

Astro, 10
Aswad, 10, 12, 51, 58, 140, 147, 153, 157, 165, 191, 218, 229, 241, 251*n*11, 284*n*22, 288*n*132, 294*n*203, 302*n*17, 303*n*23
Axe Records (record label), 228, 229

Babylon by Bus (recording), 149
Bacharach, Burt, 56
Bachman Turner Overdrive, 56
Bad Manners, 118, 146, 157
"Bag of Tools," 129, 136, 290*n*157, 291*n*163
Bailey, Peter, 125
Bakara, Amiri, 254*n*38
Bamboo Club. *See* Toronto music venues
Banas, Carl, 286*n*72
Baptiste, 22
Barker, Newton "Dizzy," 105
Barth, Frederick, 283*n*11
Barthes, Roland, 297*n*81
the Basics, 308*n*75
Basso, Guido, 111
Batten, Jack, 106
Battisti, Lucio, 120
Baxter, Ivy, 52
the Beat (a.k.a. the English Beat), 58, 118, 146, 157, 159–60
the Beatles, 51, 56, 105, 192, 228
Beckford, Stanley, 37

336 *Index*

Beckford, Theophilus, 50, 300*n*15

Beckwith, Martha, 34, 35, 263*n*72

Beddoes, Dick, 103

Bedouin Soundclash, 243

Belafonte, Harry, 61, 293*n*177; *Calypso,* 273*n*6

Bennett, Headley (a.k.a Deadly Headley), 51, 254*n*41

Bennett, Jo Jo, 51–52, 69, 77–78, 105, 180(i), 220, 225–28, 245, 248, 256*n*2, 270*n*48, 308*n*75

Bennett, Louise (a.k.a. Miss Lou), 44–46, 85, 220, 263*n*72, 268*n*9

Bennett, Paul, 80, 87

Bennett, Willie P., 134

bhangra music, 121, 255*n*42

Big Sugar, 242, 293*n*180

Bilby, Kenneth, 23

Billboard, 114, 243

bilyj holos music, 121

Bissoondath, Neil, 8, 103, 195

Black Market Clash (album), 150, 154

Black Sabbath, 163

Black Slate, 147, 303*n*23

Black Uhuru, 115, 288*n*132

Blackwell, Chris, 20, 57, 234

Bloodfire, 164, 213

the Blues Busters, 78, 109

blues music, 254*n*38

Bob and Marcia, 58

Bob and Wisdom, 243

Bob Marley and the Wailers, 15, 56, 61, 96, 114, 151, 162, 194, 238, 300*n*15

Bobby and the Midnites, 131

the Bodysnatchers (a.k.a. the Belle Stars), 118, 146

Bonconganistas, 133, 183(i)

Boney M., 51

"Book of Rules," 110, 127, 129–31, 134, 292*n*169

Booker, Cedella, 190–91

Boone, Pat, 53

Boothe, Ken, 128, 151, 165, 193, 241, 300*n*15

Bovell, Dennis, 296*n*42

Boyd, Liona, 124

Boyle, Ernest, 261*n*42

Brabazon, Hercules, 28

Bradley, Lloyd, 303*n*23, 303*n*28

Bradshaw, Sonny, 51

Branch, Andru, 117–18, 141, 165, 186(i), 214, 295*n*15

Brathwaite, Edward Kamau, 23, 46, 258*n*15, 258*n*18

Britton, Todd, 159, 164

Brixton Riot, 152

Broadwood, Lucy, 32, 34, 35, 38–40

Brodber, Erna, 16

Brown, Carol, 47, 94, 238

Brown, Dennis, 58, 168, 288*n*132

Brown, James, 53, 105

Brown, Jerry, 112

Brown, Leroy, 110

Bryan, Karl "King Cannonball," 51, 270*n*44

Bryans, Billy, 293*n*180, 307*n*41

Bundrick, John "Rabbit," 56

Burning Spear, 13, 50, 58, 115, 197, 253*n*28

Burrill, William, 121

Bush, Kate, 57

Bustamante, William Alexander Clarke, 70

Butcher, Chris, 238

Byron Lee and the Dragonaires, 55, 77, 78, 109. *See also* Lee, Byron

Cable, Howard, 111

Calgary ReggaeFest, 80, 202

calypso, 53, 104, 105, 109, 288*n*121

Cameron, Kim, 115–16, 287*n*97

Campbell, Ali, 10, 192, 193, 196

Campbell, Frankie, 300*n*15

Campbell, Granville, 31

Campbell, Ian, 192

Campbell, Mikey (a.k.a. Mikey Dread), 150

Canadian Black Music Awards, 121

Canadian National Exhibition, 80

Canadian Talent Library, 111
Capture Land (album), 209
Cargnelli, Walter (constable), 82
Caribana festival (Toronto), 108, 109
Carnival (Trinidad), 37, 108, 109
Cash, Johnny, 53–54
Castro, Fidel, 71, 277n60
Chalawa, 108, 116, 179(i), 287n100
Chang, Jeff, 194
Chen, Wayne, 300n15
Child, Frances James, 39
Chin, Ivan, 37
Chung, Mikey, 238
Cimarons, 148
Cinema Lumiere, 109
Citizen K., 131
civil rights movement, 86
Clapton, Eric, 57, 110, 150, 153
Clarendon, Jamaica, 76
Clarke, Sebastian, 297n81
the Clash, 48, 79, 118, 150–51, 152–53, 154, 156, 159, 160, 194, 224, 284n22, 296n52
Clayton-Thomas, David, 112
Cleary, Jay, 238
Clerk, Astley, 19–20, 30–32, 41, 256n2
Cliff, Jimmy, 15, 86, 96, 109, 163, 165, 172, 300n15
Cline, Patsy, 53
Cobham, Rhonda, 262n55
Cockburn, Bruce, 114–15, 123, 124, 148, 287n89, 308n75
Cole, Stranger, 107, 110, 179(i), 209, 215, 236, 237, 238
Coleman, Ornette, 51
Colle, Josh, 245
Collins, Ansell, 110, 241
Collins, Dave, 110, 241
colonial, 21, 22, 26, 29, 34, 35, 43, 142, 143, 190. *See also* anticolonial
Conger, Lauri, 307n41
Contrast (magazine), 108, 234
Cook, Sebastian, 149, 168, 203, 225, 235
Cooper, Wayne F., 262n55

Corby, Paul, 164, 170, 172, 178(i), 198, 204, 212, 214, 215, 223
Cornelius, Eddie, 230
Cornell, Saul, 290n151
Costello, Elvis, 153
the Cougars, 105, 108, 109, 243, 284n41, 306n81
country and western music, 43, 53–54, 59
Creary, Anthony "Benbow," 114, 209
Creates, Marlene, 282n3
Creighton, Donald, 282n4
Cripps, Leo, 80, 89, 90, 93, 202, 274n24
CRTC, 9, 233, 245
Culture, 197, 236
Culture Shock, 126, 133, 213, 220, 306n81
Cundall, Frank, 263n83

Dafoe, Chris, 196
the Damned, 152
dancehall (musical style), 24, 38, 137, 218, 230, 231, 255n42
Dancing in the Dragon's Jaws (album), 114
David, Hal, 56
Davies, Omar, 300n15
Davis, Carlene, 14, 116–17, 148, 162, 179(i), 215, 237, 287n100
Dean, Raffa, 166
Dee, Willie, 285n54
DeHaney, Carl, 111
Dekker, Desmond, 51, 109, 131, 145, 148, 157, 241, 300n15
Delgado, Ruben, 52
Delpratt, Lloyd, 110, 243
Derrida, Jacques, 127, 290nn151–52
Desmond, Viola, 62, 273n12
Diamond, Neil, 305n43
diaspora, 5, 9, 16, 73, 90, 128, 149, 215, 243
the Dilliters, 287n100
Dixon, Irene, 26
Dixon, Lorna, 287n100
DJ Shadow, 300n4
Dodd, Coxsone, 56, 110

338 *Index*

Domino, Fats, 53
Don, Whitey, 213, 306n81
Donaldson, Eric, 300n15
Donaldson, Gordon, 65–66
Double Barrel, 110
Douglas, Jay (a.k.a. Clive Barry), 53, 65, 77, 94, 105, 234, 236, 244, 246, 274n23, 306n81
Doumerc, Eric, 130
Dr. Feelgood, 152
Dragonaires. *See* Byron Lee and the Dragonaires
Dream Band, 214
Dream Factory, 293n183
Dream Warriors, 311n15
Drummond, Don, 50, 300n15
dub, 24, 44, 46, 141–42, 156, 159, 209, 217, 218, 220
Dugiol, Louise, 49
Dunbar, Sly, 50, 238, 300n15
Duncomb, Stephen, 239
Dunkley, Archibald, 47
Dylan, Bob, 233

the Eagles, 57
Earth, Roots and Water, 112, 211, 243, 286n77, 287n100
Edwards, Wilfred "Jackie," 57, 148, 237
Eldridge, Colin C., 29
Ellis, Alton, 165, 193, 237, 286n77, 300n15
Ellis, Hortense, 166
Ellis, Noel, 112, 238, 243, 286n77
Emergency Measures Act, 71
Emery, Natasha, 155, 167, 171, 184(i), 207, 213, 219
Ethiopian World Federation, 47
Evans, Bill, 15
Evidence (album), 123, 124, 136, 234
Exodus (album), 57, 61, 163, 209, 273n4
Exodus Dub (album), 209
Expo 67, 108, 167

Fab Five, 126, 300n15
Fabulous Flames, 306n81
Fairclough, Ellen, 275n33

Fame, Georgie, 51
Family Dog, 167
Felleman, Hazel, 129
Finkelstein, Bernie, 114
the Folkes Brothers, 300n15
Forbes, John, 209
Forde, Brindsley, 10, 191, 302n17, 302n19
Foucault, Michel, 290n151
Fowler, David, 164, 167, 205, 207, 219, 222, 299n120
Fraley, Todd, 304n33
Francis, Neville, 205, 226
Fraser, Dean, 300n15
Fredlocks Asher and the Ultra Flex Crew, 213
Freedman, Adele, 108, 116, 120
Friendlyness, 186(i), 213, 238, 306n81
Fudge Brothers, 287n100
Fujahtive, 126, 133, 185(i)
Funk Brothers, 110

Gainsbourg, Serge, 233
Gairey, Harry, 104–5
Gamble, Eric, 142
Gardiner, Boris, 300n15
Garrick, Michael, 182(i)
Garvey, Marcus, 3, 4, 21, 48, 50
Gaynair, Bobby, 105
Geertz, Clifford, 250n9
Generation X, 296n42
Gibbs, Joe, 104
Gilkes, Alwyn, 277nn72–73
Gilroy, Paul, 297n59
Giroux, Henry, 304n33
the Gladiators, 120
Goddard, Peter, 112, 121, 128, 133, 240
Goldman, Vivien, 36, 100–1, 150, 271n55, 284n22, 297n67
Goldsmith, Jon, 123
Goode, Coleridge, 270n41
Goodison, Yaughn "Bunny," 300n15
Gopthal, Lee, 234
Gordillo, Gaston, 282n5
Gordon, George William, 20
Gordon, Rosco, 50–51, 53, 271n54

Gordon, Vin, 51
Gosciak, Josh, 265*n*88
Grange-Walker, Olivia, 108, 112
the Grateful Dead, 131
Gray, Dave, 307*n*41
Gray, Owen, 57, 237
Green, Lorne, 79
Green Bay Massacre, 71
Grennan, Sunray, 74, 85, 87, 90, 92, 102, 218, 238, 272*n*84, 278*n*79
Grennan, Winston, 218, 272*n*84
Griffiths, Marcia, 124, 136, 163
GRT (record label), 112, 234

Habib, Patti, 133, 200
Hambleton, Fergus, 37, 131, 142, 143, 163, 166–67, 180(i), 194, 198, 210, 214, 219, 220, 224, 225–26, 228, 233, 238, 295*n*5, 308*n*75
Hambleton, Greg, 309*n*87
Hammond, Beres, 238
Hanson, Wayne, 80, 88, 93, 101, 169, 171, 184(i), 213, 226–27, 280*n*137
The Harder They Come (film), 10, 15, 109, 130, 152, 165, 285*n*66
Harlem Dance Theatre, 76
Harlem Renaissance, 3
Harriott, Joe, 15, 51, 54, 270*n*41
Harris, Walter, 64
Hart, Lisa, 134
Harvey, Carl, 76, 80, 175(i), 177(i)
Harvey, Richard, 278*n*88
Harvey, Rupert "Ojiji," 46, 76, 80, 84, 87, 92–93, 99, 175(i), 181(i), 214–15, 217–19, 221, 241
Harzig, Christiane, 274*n*22
Hayles, Adrian, 245
Heathcott, Joseph, 271*n*68
Hebdige, Dick, 145, 297*n*81
Heedram, Earle "Mighty Pope," 24, 26, 54, 55, 76, 79, 80, 87, 89, 92, 105, 108, 173(i), 243, 256*n*2, 259*n*32
Henderson, Stuart, 250*n*5
Hendrix, Jimi, 51
Henry, Frances, 234

Henzell, Perry, 285*n*66
the Heptones, 110, 121, 122, 130, 131, 134, 136, 292*n*169
Hibbert, Anthony Bassie, 238
Hibbert, Joseph, 47
Hibbert, Lennie, 50
Hibbert, Toots, 54, 193
Higgins, Dalton, 204, 213, 215, 235, 236
Hill, James, 106, 113, 155
hip hop, 189, 211, 224, 239, 242–43, 300*n*4
the Hitch-Hikers, 105, 108, 243
Hodd, Jack Lorne, 291*n*163
Hodge, Jennifer, 122
Holdip, Jeffrey, 37–38, 144, 149, 159, 165, 169, 201, 207, 213, 218, 299*n*112
Holt, John, 193, 241, 296*n*42
Holung, Peter, 35, 26, 56, 75, 81, 90, 203, 211–12, 271*n*75
Home Feeling: Struggle for a Community (film), 123
Homefry, Snappy, 238
Hopping Penguins, 197
Howell, Leonard P., 47
Howes, Kevin (a.k.a. Sipreano), 104, 243
the Human Rights, 238
Hunt, James, 262*n*51
Hussey, Dermott, 307*n*43
Hyde, Paul, 113

Iacovetta, Franca, 283*n*9
Ibadan, 214, 306*n*81
Idol, Billy, 296*n*42
immigration policy, Canada, 4, 11, 60–69, 76, 92, 203
Inglis, William (constable), 82
InJah, Isax (a.k.a. Richard Howse), 166, 171–72, 188(i), 195, 198–200, 207, 222
Inner Circle, 131
interviews, author's approach to, 252*n*24
Irie, Tippa, 284*n*29
Isaacs, Gregory, 38, 130, 147, 193, 224
Isaacs, Joe, 110
Ishan People, 51, 112, 114, 234, 287*n*100
Island Records (record label), 234

340 *Index*

ital. *See* reggae: authenticity in
Iwata, 166

Jackson, R. Zee, 155, 226
Jagger, Mick, 233
Jah Punk, 154
the Jam, 152
Jam Session (song), 217, 234
Jamaica Military Band, 52, 269*n*32
Jamaican Canadian Association, 73,
    277*n*75, 278*n*77
Jamaican Constabulary Band, 269*n*32
Jamaican music: Afro-European influ-
    ences on, 18, 19, 20, 21–22, 23, 25, 26–
    27, 33, 35, 58; folk, 5, 11, 14, 18–19, 21,
    25–26, 28, 31, 37, 38, 40–41, 45–46, 48,
    99, 263*n*61; popular, 6, 20, 25, 38, 43,
    48, 50, 52, 57, 86, 87, 127, 130, 142, 159,
    218, 224, 237, 247; traditional, 19, 20,
    35. *See also* reggae
Jamaican Regiment Band, 269*n*32
James, Tony, 296*n*42
Jamfest '85 (Jamaica), 124
Jardim, Tomaz, 32, 144, 148–49, 160,
    169, 232, 256*n*2, 295*n*16, 296*n*36
jazz, 15, 43, 51, 53, 54, 59, 90, 106, 111, 127,
    133, 141, 166, 171, 200, 206, 211, 254*n*38
Jekyll, Edward, 263*n*73
Jekyll, Gertrude, 259*n*30, 261*n*46
Jekyll, Julia, 261*n*44, 263*n*73
Jekyll, Walter, 19–20, 21, 25, 27–35, 38–
    41, 43, 45, 46, 49, 164, 256*n*2, 256*n*5,
    259*n*28, 259*n*30, 259*n*33, 259*n*35,
    260*nn*38–40, 261*n*42, 261*n*44,
    261*nn*46–47, 262*nn*54–55, 263*n*73,
    265*nn*88–89, 267*n*134
Jennings, Nicholas, 143, 153–54, 156, 199,
    200, 228, 236
Jericho, 143, 295*n*15
Jerry Jerome and the Cardells, 104
Joe Gibbs Record Store, 104, 113
John, Elton, 148
Johnson, Albert, 82, 217
Johnson, Bruce, 141
Johnson, Gordie, 293*n*180

Johnson, Harry (a.k.a. Harry J),
    292*n*169, 292*n*175
Johnson, Jerry, 130–31
Johnson, Linton Kwesi, 46, 160
Jo-Jo and the Fugitives, 108, 226, 243
Jolly Boys, 37, 218
Jones, Christopher, 197
Jones, Denise, 71, 76, 86, 91, 93, 201–2,
    212, 223
Jones, Grace, 233
Jones, Hedley ("Deadly Hedley"), 107
Jones, Mick, 151
Jones, Simon, 157, 297*n*81, 298*n*84
Jordan, Louis, 53
Joseph, Clifton, 46
Joseph, Perry, 165
Juno Awards, 121, 142, 229, 232, 245,
    309*n*109
Justin Hinds and the Dominoes, 300*n*15

Kafinal, 245
Kane Middle School, 82
Kardinal Offishall, 243
Kartel, Vybz, 218
Katrina and the Waves, 230
Keane, Shake, 270*n*41
Ken and the Blues Busters, 78
Kenny, Enda, 291*n*162
Khouri, Ken, 37
King, Alex, 209
King, Jesse (a.k.a. Dubmatix), 141, 159,
    232
King, JuLion, 71, 76, 86, 91, 93, 174(i),
    201–2, 212, 223
King Crimson, 163
King Selah, 238
King Tubby Meets the Rockers Uptown
    (album), 142
Kingston, David, 50, 102, 108, 143, 198,
    200, 211, 213, 224, 231
Kinsey, Donald, 56
Kitwana, Bakari, 304*n*33
Knibb, Lloyd, 50
Knibb, Williams, 194
Koffman, Moe, 111

Kraglund, John, 103
Ku Klux Klan, 153
Kwame, 166

L'Étranger, 154
Labour of Love (album), 119
Lacey, Liam, 124, 196, 223, 229
Lamperti, Francesco, 263*n*73
Laws, Dudley, 154
Lawson, Greg, 142, 156, 170, 172
Led Zeppelin, 57, 168
Lee, Bunny, 57
Lee, Byron, 52, 77, 78, 270*n*48, 285*n*63.
   See also Byron Lee and the
   Dragonaires
Lee, Helen, 197
Leejahn, 213
Let's Put It All Together (recording), 111
Letts, Don, 148, 150, 192
Levi, Exco, 245
Lewin, Olive, 40
Lewis, Hopeton, 14, 306*n*81
Lewis, Terry, 307*n*41
Light in the Attic (record label), 243
Limbo Springs, 115
Lipsitz, George, 15
Littler, William, 118
Llewellyn, Barry, 130, 292*n*169, 292*n*175
London venues: A-Train, 6; The 59, 6;
   Flamingo, 6; The Roxy, 150; Ska Bar,
   145, 153; Sunset Club, 6
Lord Tanamo, 37, 104, 110, 236, 237
Lorenzkowski, Barbara, 251*n*16,
   283*n*9
Lovejoy, Sid, 106
Lovejoy Records and Productions
   (record label), 106
Lowe, Garry, 242, 293*n*180
Lucey, Clarence, 105
Lyn, Kermit, 105
Lyn, Kingsley, 105
Lyn, Robbie, 238, 254*n*41

Macaulay, Zachary, 20
Mad Professor, 218

Madness, 118, 157
Maestro Fresh Wes, 311*n*15
Magic!, 244
Malinowski, Jay, 243
Mama Africa (album), 149
Mandeville, 143
Manley, Michael, 70–72, 147, 276*n*57
Manley, Norman Washington, 70
Mansbridge, Peter, 8
Marchand, Jean, 68
Marley, Bob, 2, 4, 12, 14, 15, 46, 51, 56–
   58, 61, 71, 78, 86, 96, 107, 114, 119, 120,
   123, 140, 146, 148–51, 155, 160–65, 171,
   172, 189–92, 204, 230, 239, 245, 250*n*4,
   268*n*9, 296*n*36, 299*n*108, 302*n*16,
   302*n*19. *See also* Bob Marley and the
   Wailers
Marley, Norval Sinclair, 190–91
Marley, Rita, 124, 163
Marley, Robert Nesta, 168, 190
Marley, Ziggy, 124, 230
Marsh, Hugh, 123
Martin, Ivanhoe "Rhyging," 109
Martin, Lionel Augustus (a.k.a. Saxa),
   157
Martin, Robert, 109, 160
Marvin, Junior, 56
Massey Hall, 120, 160, 238, 239, 246
Matthews, David, 201
Matthews, Mark (a.k.a. Prince Blanco),
   143, 147, 158, 203, 205, 210, 225
Matumbi, 58, 147, 153, 241, 284*n*29,
   296*n*42, 303*n*23
Maxi Priest, 241, 294*n*203
Mayfield, Curtis, 58
MC Collizhun, 243
MC Serch, 300*n*4
McCarthy, Len J., 302*n*16
McCartney, Paul, 148
McConnell, Rob, 111
McCook, Tommy, 50, 270*n*48, 285*n*49
McGhie, Wayne, 110, 141, 243, 244
McGillivray, Bruce, 142, 220, 219, 221–
   22, 238, 242, 295*n*5
McGrath, Paul, 118, 167

McGregor, Freddie, 236

McKay, Claude, 26, 27, 28, 29, 31, 33, 57, 85, 260*n*38, 265*nn*87–88

McLauchlan, Murray, 123

McTair, Roger, 123

Mee, Michie, 311*n*15

the Melodians, 11, 61, 109, 300*n*15

Mendelssohn, Felix, 263*n*73

mento, 6, 11, 18, 24, 33, 35–38, 43–45, 54, 59, 61, 78, 100, 218, 221, 265*n*87, 266*n*111, 266*n*113, 268*n*9, 273*n*6

Messenjah, 13, 46, 76, 80, 108, 116, 124, 133, 137, 181(i), 197, 208, 210, 213–14, 216–19, 221, 229, 306*n*7, 310*n*114

Mighty Diamonds, 193, 209, 254*n*41

Mighty Mystics, 287*n*100

Mighty Pope. *See* Heedram, Earle "Mighty Pope"

military brass band, 49–50, 52, 59

Miller, Adrian, 79, 82, 88, 89, 93, 130, 136, 146, 147, 154–55, 182(i), 197–98, 204, 210, 215, 217, 234, 235–36, 286*n*77

Miller, Jacob, 130, 218

Miller, Herbie, 281*n*161

Miller, Mark, 136

Milner, Lord Alfred, 30

Mintz, Sidney W., 258*n*18

Miracles (album), 229, 234

Misty in Roots, 148

Mittoo, Jackie, 4, 78, 79, 104, 109–12, 116, 121, 141, 176(i), 177(i), 205, 215, 236, 237, 243, 244, 254*n*41, 286*n*70, 286*n*72, 287*n*100

mods, 118, 146, 151, 159

Mohjah, 293*n*180

Mojo (magazine), 303*n*23, 303*n*28

Monica's Hairdressing, Cosmetics and Records, 104, 106, 117

Monro, Matt, 105

Moonfood, 142

Moore, Dizzy, 50

Moore, Don, 64

Moore, Joseph G., 263*n*71

Morris, Eric "Monty," 55, 218

Morrison, James Dalton, 129

Moses, Kathryn, 123

Motta, Stanley, 37

Mountain Edge, 214

Mowatt, Judy, 163

Moxley, Jim, 105

Mozart, Wolfgang Amadeus, 33

MTV, 16

MuchMusic, 108, 234

Mullings, Carrie, 205–6, 211, 212, 235, 245

Mullings, Karl, 108, 177(i), 284*n*41, 306*n*81

Mullings, Tanya, 187(i), 205–6

Mullins, George, 259*n*33

multiculturalism, 8–9, 12, 17, 74, 82, 97, 103, 113, 140, 231, 248

Muraldo, Caroline, 20

Murvin, Junior, 130, 150

Musical Youth, 15, 254*n*41, 288*n*132

Mutabaruka, 46

Myers, Charles Samuel, 35

Nash, Johnny, 54, 58, 110

Nathan Philips Square, 238

National Front (UK), 152–53

Natty Dread (album), 164

Nazareth, Errol, 143, 159, 199, 206, 225

Neatby, Hilda, 140

Neely, Daniel, 35, 256*n*5, 265*n*96

Nefarius, 243

Negro Citizenship Committee/Council, 64, 105

Negro Library (Toronto), 103

Nester, Alan, 239

Nettleford, Rex, 20, 33, 85, 263*n*72, 279*n*115

New Musical Express, 146

Niester, Alan, 122, 239

North, Marianne, 27

North, Michael, 265*n*88

Notting Hill Carnival, 251*n*11

Nyabinghi, 258*n*24

O. Travis, 108, 287*n*100

Oasis, 291*n*163

Obrebski, Josef, 263*n*71
Obrebski, Tamara, 263*n*71
O'Brien, Richard, 133, 293*n*183
O'Hara, Catherine, 133, 293*n*183
O'Hara, Marcus, 293*n*183
O'Hara, Mary Margaret, 134, 293*n*183
On Top (album), 136
one drop (reggae beat), 24, 85, 135, 160, 164–65, 218, 232
Opel, Jackie, 57, 77
Opp, James, 282*n*6
Ørsted Pedersen, Niels-Henning, 254*n*40
Osbourne, Johnny, 51, 110, 112, 155, 209, 237, 243
O'Toole, Lawrence, 110
Ouzounian, Richard, 285*n*66

Pablo, Augustus, 38, 209
Paget, Hugh, 256*n*4
Palmer, Robert, 148
Pan-Am Dance, 134
Papa Levy, 238
the Parachute Club, 124, 293*n*177
Parker, Ken, 78
patois, Jamaican, 24, 27, 31, 45, 55, 126, 143, 160, 209, 242
Patrick, Kentrick (a.k.a. Lord Creator), 303*n*24
Patterson, Orlando, 23, 258*n*15, 258*n*18
Paul, Everton "Pablo," 105, 141, 284*n*41
Paul, Frankie, 310*n*119
Payne, Bill, 107
the Payolas, 113
Peabody's Clef Records and Music, 106
Penn, Dawn, 165
People's National Party (Jamaica), 44, 70
Perkins, Wayne, 56
Perkins, William, 300*n*4
Perry, Lee "Scratch," 78, 107, 148, 150, 151, 209, 238
Peterson, Colleen, 123
Phoenix Concert Theatre, 238

Pickles, Dill, 118
Pitters, Bernie, 166, 238, 245
Pocomania, 22, 24, 36
the Police, 118, 224
population statistics: blacks in Canada, 275*n*30, 276*n*43; in Jamaica (1962), 190, 300*n*5; Jamaicans in Toronto, 276*n*50, 276*n*55, 294*n*197
Powell, Enoch, 152–53
prejudice, 19, 29–30, 34, 64, 66, 81, 160, 218, 278*n*79. *See also* racism
Presley, Elvis, 53, 192
Price, Richard, 258*n*18
Pride, Charlie, 54
Prince, Roland, 105
Prince Buster, 15, 55, 57, 145, 157
Prince Jammy, 237
protest music, 145, 156
punk, 4, 12, 48, 104, 115, 122, 132, 134, 140, 143, 145, 146, 224. *See also* reggae: punk and
Pyne, Patsy, 67, 275*n*38

quadrille, 21, 24, 35–37, 59
Queen, 192

R&B, 36, 50, 52–3, 108, 158, 166, 211, 231, 233
race, attitudes toward in Canada, 11, 30, 60–68, 73–74, 82, 83, 104, 189, 207
race relations, 65, 82, 152
racial unity, 5, 54, 143, 154, 203, 228
racism, 4, 29, 33, 62, 65, 80, 82, 83, 92, 98–99, 152, 190, 196, 204, 278*n*80. *See also* prejudice
Radio Jamaica and Rediffusion (RJR), 52
radio stations: CFNY, 107, 118, 119, 210, 228; CHIN, 107; CHWO, 107; CIUT, 119; CJMR, 107; CKFM, 286*n*72; CKLN, 108, 118, 119; Q107, 147, 210; WUFO, 107
RaLion, 238, 245
Ramsey, Guthrie, 254*n*38
Ranglin, Ernest, 10, 15, 57, 265*n*112

344 *Index*

Ranking Miss P, 192
rap music, 55, 224, 239, 242–43
Rascalz, 243
Rasta/Rastafarian (individual), 4, 14, 15, 16, 24, 45, 47, 99, 128, 132, 134, 144, 148, 151, 161, 167, 169–72, 191, 195–96
Rasta/Rastafarianism/Rastafari (religion), 12, 13, 47–48, 55, 140, 156, 161–63, 167, 169–72, 189, 191, 194, 200, 216, 300*n*15; misconceptions of, 161–62
RCA (record label), 26
Rebel Music (newsletter), 153–54
Record Collector (magazine), 303*n*28
Redding, Otis, 54
reggae: authenticity in, 13, 15–16, 48, 119, 125–28, 138, 189, 191, 194, 197–99, 209, 210, 213, 216, 220, 231, 247; cultural appropriation in, 138, 194–96, 198, 231; non-Jamaicans' attraction to, 7, 12, 84, 101, 109, 116, 141, 164–65, 189, 246; punk and, 148, 150–60, 172, 194, 202, 239; rock and, 57, 108, 116, 153, 155, 158, 166, 220, 223, 243; spirituality in, 168–69, 248; "Top 100" songs, 300*n*15
reggae, Canadian: golden age of, 9, 10, 14, 17, 96, 104, 132, 133, 140, 201, 208, 230, 233, 239, 242, 245; reception in Jamaica of, 218–20. *See also* Reggae Canadiana
Reggae Canadiana, 70, 112, 128, 140, 145, 183(i), 225, 229, 247. *See also* reggae, Canadian: golden age of
Reggae Cowboys, 214
Reggae Magic (album), 111
Reggae on the River festival, 228–29
Reggae Showcase (radio show), 108
Reggae Sunsplash (Jamaica), 122, 218, 219, 229, 289*n*148
Reggae Sunsplash (Toronto), 239
Reid, Duke, 53
Reid, Gerald, 220
Revelation, 213
Revolutionary Tea Party (album), 217
Richards, Chips, 241

Richards, Keith, 148
Richmond, Norman Otis, 103
Ricketts, Glen, 306*n*81
Rinaldo, Sandie, 161–62
Ripoll, Justina, 49
Risqué Disque (record label), 210, 229
Roberts, Helen, 34–35, 263*n*72
Robertson, Brian, 119, 146, 156, 217
Robinson, Bruce "Preacher," 188(i), 230
Robinson, Tom, 153
Robinson, William, 261*n*46
rock, 15, 43, 56, 103, 118, 133, 160, 163, 165, 211, 221, 222, 226; lovers rock, 212–13, 230, 293*n*185; pop rock, 192. *See also* reggae: rock and
Rock Against Racism, 143, 153–54, 200–1, 240, 296*n*57, 297*n*59
rock and roll. *See* rock
Rockers (film), 130, 292*nn*167–68
rocksteady, 6, 11, 14, 15, 18, 24, 35, 43, 45, 50, 57, 58, 90, 98, 104, 105, 108, 134, 156, 218, 247
Rodigan, David, 231
Rodriguez, Rico, 51, 157
the Rolling Stones, 51, 147
Romeo, Max, 193
Rose, Rap, 113
Roseau, Bobby, 105, 284*n*41
rub-a-dub dancing, 101, 134, 137
rude boy(s), 4, 53, 55–56, 145–46, 191, 240
Rusea, Martin, 259*n*33
Ryan, Jan, 285*n*66

Sandinista! (album), 150
Satchmo, Pluggy, 110
Sattalite Music School, 225–26, 230
the Sattalites, 10, 13, 20, 37, 77, 108, 116, 126, 131, 133, 137, 142, 163, 164, 167, 180(i), 188(i), 197, 198, 200, 206, 208, 210, 213, 216, 219–30, 233–34, 238, 241–42, 244, 247, 308*n*75, 309*n*87, 309*n*96, 310*n*114
Satzewich, Vic, 275*n*39

Schwartz, Joan M., 282*n*4
sea shanties, 18, 35, 56
Seaga, Edward, 71, 277*n*59
Seaman, Phil, 270*n*41
Sebastian, Tom "the Great," 53
Segarini, Bob, 134
Segato, Lorraine, 293*n*180. *See also* Parachute Club
Selassie, Haile, 13, 47–48, 163, 171, 189, 245, 276*n*57
the Selecter, 118, 146, 157
Sham 69, 153
Share (magazine), 220, 234
Sharpe, Robert Lee, 128–31, 134, 136, 290*nn*156–57, 291*n*161
Shatner, William, 79
Shearer, Hugh, 71
the Sheiks, 51, 77, 105, 108, 110, 205, 243, 306*n*81
Shep and the Limelites, 77
Shepherd, Elaine, 245
Sherlock, Philip, 33, 263*n*72
Shervington, Pluto, 131
Sibbles, Leroy, 4, 9, 13, 17, 70, 79, 108, 110, 112, 113, 116, 118, 121–24, 130–31, 134–38, 142, 153, 176(i), 193, 209, 214, 215, 221, 222, 225–26, 233, 234, 236, 237, 245, 254*n*41, 287*n*93, 287*n*100, 288*n*132, 292*n*169, 293*n*177, 293*n*186, 306*n*7, 308*n*75
Siberry, Jane, 124
Signing Off (album), 193
Silvera, Larry, 114
Simon, Paul, 57, 107, 218, 272*n*84
Simonon, Paul, 151, 251*n*11, 296*n*52
Simpson, George Eaton, 263*n*71
Sinclair, Eon, 243
ska music, 4, 6, 11, 12, 14, 15, 18, 24, 34, 36, 38, 43, 45, 50–58, 69, 77, 87, 98, 99, 100, 102, 104–9, 118, 126, 137, 145, 146, 151, 156, 157, 158, 160, 165, 197, 202, 203, 207, 218, 225, 227, 232, 238, 240, 247, 266*n*112, 271*n*54, 271*nn*67–68
the Skatalites, 50, 54, 55, 110, 157
skinheads, 146

slavery, 3, 14, 16, 20, 21–24, 28, 33, 36–37, 40, 151
the Slickers, 109
Slim and Slam, 37, 52
the Slits, 296*n*42
Sloane, Hans, 22
Sly and Robbie, 124, 136, 193, 228, 233
Small, Millie, 55, 241, 300*n*15
Small, Robin "Bongo Jerry," 46
Small Faces, 270*n*42
Smith, Ernie, 49, 54, 71, 108, 110, 116–17, 178(i)
Smith, Mark, 306*n*1
Smith, Mike, 47, 74, 76, 79, 82, 83, 92, 94, 100, 102, 103, 175(i), 185(i), 202, 212, 216, 274*n*24
Smythe, Pat, 270*n*41
Snow (a.k.a. Darrin O'Brien), 242
Solar Sounds, 104
Soloman, 231
Soul Vendors, 110
Souljah Fyah, 214
Sound Dimension, 110, 254*n*41
Sounding a Mosaic (album), 243
the Specials, 51, 58, 118, 146, 157, 159–60, 238, 240
Spence, Lloyd, 105
Spencer, Eddie, 110, 243
Spencer, Herbert, 29
Spencer, Neil, 156
Spencer Davis Group, 148
the Spinners, 230
St. George, Michael, 46
St. Juste, Francois, 300*n*15
Stanford, Charles Villiers, 263*n*73
Steckles, Gary, 289*n*148
Steel Pulse, 12, 58, 140, 146, 147, 153, 157, 165, 229, 241, 284*n*22, 294*n*203, 302*n*17, 303*n*23
Steely Dan, 57, 164
Sterling, Lester, 50
Stevenson, Robert Louis, 263*n*73
Stiff Little Fingers, 153
strathspey, 35, 36, 38, 56
Strummer, Joe, 151, 194, 251*n*11

346　*Index*

Studio One, 110, 168, 222, 231
Sullivan, Matt, 243
Summer Records (record label), 112
Sunforce, 126, 133, 182(i), 220, 229
Sutherland, Donald, 79
Swarbrick, David, 11
Syren, 197

Tabarruk, 133, 214, 234, 252*n*24
Tafari, I. Jabulani, 111
Taitt, Lynn, 177(i)
Taylor, K. Wayne, 275*n*39
Taylor, Mike, 295*n*15
Thatcher, Margaret, 303*n*28
Theo's Record Shop, 104
Third World, 58, 115, 302*n*17
Third World Books and Crafts, 103
Thomas, Deborah, 257*n*9
Thompson, Dave, 302*n*21, 303*n*22
Thornton, Eddie "Tan Tan," 51
Tollington, Dave, 306*n*7
Tom Robinson Band, 153
Tomkin, Dmitri, 56
Toots and the Maytals, 76, 96, 109, 119, 196, 218, 300*n*15
Toronto music venues: Bamboo Club, 6, 97, 114, 126, 132–36, 138, 183(i), 200, 227, 228, 229, 233, 235, 282*n*7, 293*n*180, 293*n*183, 293*n*186; Bermuda Tavern, 104; Brunswick House, 120; Calypso Club, 104, 285*n*48; Carib Restaurant and Tavern, 104; Caribbean Club (a.k.a. the Carib), 104, 114; Chelsea International Show Lounge and Disco, 115; Club Jamaica, 6, 77, 105, 108; Club Trinidad, 104; Club Tropics, 104; Danforth Music Hall, 238; Dr. Livingston's, 116; El Mocambo (a.k.a. the Elmo), 115, 133, 134; Harbourfront Centre, 114, 116, 183(i), 229, 236, 244, 246; the Horseshoe, 115, 132, 133, 233, 287*n*93; Isabella Hotel, 227; Kingswood Music Theatre, 120, 196; Larry's Hideaway, 134; Latin Quarter Club,

104; Le Coq d'Or, 104; Maple Leaf Gardens, 109, 114, 115, 149, 161, 246; Masonic Temple (a.k.a. the Concert Hall), 120, 137, 158; Massey Hall, 120, 160, 238, 239, 246; Ontario Place Forum, 116, 188(i), 229, 246; Palais Royale, 117–18; the Rivoli, 132, 134; Soul Palace, 104; Thymeless Reggae Bar, 3; Tiger's Coconut Grove, 107; West Indian Federation Club, 6
Toronto neighbourhoods: Black Bottom, 6, 69, 75, 96, 103, 106, 107; Don Mills and Sheppard, 75, 81; Eglinton West, 6, 65, 69, 74, 96, 102, 104, 106, 107, 208, 226, 236, 245; Greektown, 87; Jane-Finch Corridor, 6, 9, 69, 96, 102, 106, 121, 123, 138, 208, 236; Keelsdale, 82; Kensington Market, 96, 107; Lawrence Heights (a.k.a. the Jungle), 69; Little Jamaica, 6, 96, 245; Oakwood, 75, 76, 84, 165, 236, 245, 236; Queen Street West, 6, 96, 115, 117, 124, 132–34, 145, 242, 244, 246; St. Lawrence Market, 153; Regent Park, 208, 216
Tosh, Peter, 128, 148–49, 155, 163, 171
Townshend, Pete, 148
Treasure Isle (record label), 57
Tremblay, Maxwell, 239
Tréson, 238
Tribe, Tony, 305*n*43
Trojan Records (record label), 58, 234, 241, 269*n*34
Tropical Energy Experience, 287*n*100
Tropical Gift and Record Store, 106
Trudeau, Pierre, 71, 72, 92, 147
Truths and Rights, 13, 116, 117, 119, 133, 154, 169, 170, 179(i), 213, 216
Tulloch, Dave, 210, 221
Tutu, Bishop Desmond, 293*n*177
two-tone movement, 12, 51, 118, 140, 143, 146, 155, 157–59, 172, 201, 220, 238
Tyler, Gary, 193
Tylor, Edward B., 265*n*91

UB40, 10, 12, 15, 20, 58, 119–20, 123, 140, 146, 157, 158, 165, 192–94, 196, 220–30, 238, 241, 247, 249, 294n203, 298n82, 302n21, 303nn22–24, 303n28, 304n32, 305n43
UNESCO, 84
United Negro Improvement Association, 3
University of West Indies, 16
University of Windsor, 76
Urban Alliance on Race Relations, 82
U-Roy, 300n15

"V," 293n180
Vassell, Marcia, 74, 80, 84, 86, 92, 94
Vassell, Phil, 75, 85, 86, 90, 100, 103, 106, 114, 134, 213, 216, 236, 289n134
Vaughan Williams, Ralph, 263n78
Virtue, Michael, 10
Virtue, Sid, 275n34
von Maltzahn, Millicent, 261n44

Wade, Nicholas, 300n2
Wailer, Bunny, 190, 218
the Wailers, 300n15
Waite, Frederick, 254n41
Wakenius, Ulf, 254n40
Walker, David, 292n168
Walker, Klive, 46, 54, 79, 81, 90, 114, 146, 148, 149, 162, 214, 218, 234, 243, 252n18, 252n21, 268n4, 281n161, 297n78, 307n43
Walker, Noel, 106, 112, 238, 243
Wallace, Leroy "Horsemouth," 50
Walsh, John, 282n6
Walters, Basil, 300n15
Wayne McGhie and the Sounds of Joy (album), 243–44
WEA (record label), 210, 229

Weir, Bob, 131
Weller, Sam, 141, 165, 198, 222, 238
Werner, Alice, 35, 266n98
West India Regiment Band, 269n32
West Indian Carnival (London), 152
West Indies Federation Club (WIF), 104–5, 206
White, Newman, 254n38
Wilkins, Terry, 293n180
Williams, Bob, 110
Williams, Hank, 53, 54
Williams, Mark, 269n34
Williams, Quammie, 307n41
Williams, Ralph Vaughan, 34
Williams, Ranford (Rannie) "Bop," 41, 54, 78, 88, 91, 94–95, 107, 203, 212, 218, 238, 270n48, 285n49
Williams, Oswald, 258n24
Williams, Willi, 48, 79, 88, 91, 110, 112, 154, 156, 202, 210–11, 233, 239
Wilson, Delroy, 151, 237, 276n57
Wilson, Jason, xi–xiii, 295n15
Wintraub, Harold, 285n48
Wisdom, Jimmy, 110
Wishbone (album), 104, 111, 244
Wood, Ron, 147

Ximenes, Josephina, 49

Yahwedeh, 107
Yard, 54, 92, 104, 127, 209, 213, 214, 242. *See also* Jamaican music
Yellowman, 124
Yes, 163
Young, David, 309n109
Young, Robert, 265n91
Young Lions, 154

Zeb, Drummie, 231